J. Pine pinx! I.F.E. Prudhomme Sc.

REV. ELIJAH HEDDING, D.D.

LATE

Sen. Bishop of the Methodist Episcopal Church

LIFE AND TIMES

OF

REV. ELIJAH HEDDING, D. D.,

LATE SENIOR BISHOP OF THE METHODIST EPISCOPAL CHURCH.

BY REV. D. W. CLARK, D. D.

WITH AN INTRODUCTION,

BY REV. BISHOP E. S. JANES.

New-York:
PUBLISHED BY CARLTON & PHILLIPS,
200 MULBERRY-STREET.
1855.

PREFACE.

When the preparation of the biography comprised in the following pages was committed to the author, it was his purpose to make it strictly personal, and to comprise it, if possible, in a duodecimo volume of some four hundred pages. But when he entered upon the work, he found the history of Bishop Hedding so intertwined and blended with the early history of the Church in New-England, and, at a later day, with the history of the whole Church, that the full development of his character and services could not well be made without keeping in view the concurrent aspects of the great Methodistic reformation in this country. The carrying out of this idea involved a vast amount of extra labour. It has also enlarged, but, he trusts, likewise enriched the volume. The title was conformed to this idea;—hence, "The Life and Times of Hedding."

The material for this work has been drawn from various sources. Much of the personal statistics was derived from the manuscript journal of the bishop; other portions of the material from manuscripts written by Rev. Moses L. Scudder and Rev. L. M. Vincent—both of whom wrote for him when he became disablod; and still other portions were drawn from manuscript notes and sketches taken during the last year of the bishop's life, by Rev. William H. Ferris, and by the author. There was also a large accumulation of papers and letters, all of which were carefully examined and laid under contribution. The author must also acknowledge his indebtedness to Rev. Dr. C. Elliott for the use of complete files of "The Wesleyan Repository," "The Mutual Rights," "The Itinerant," "The Zion's Herald," "The Christian Advocate and Journal," and "Zion's Watchman." In addition, he has gathered material from the bound volumes of "The Minutes of the Conferences," the bound volumes of "The Methodist Magazine," "Asbury's Journals," "Lee's Methodism," Stevens's "Memorials of Methodism," Bangs's "History of the Methodist Episcopal Church," and various other works. The material gathered from these various sources the author has endeavoured to blend into a new and homogeneous production; not a mere bald, historical detail—but history illustrated by incident, and illustrating philosophy.

On some portions of the work the author has bestowed more critical and extended attention, because of the important principles involved; and especially because Bishop Hedding desired that his memory should be vindicated by a full and truthful report of his administration

The place of publication being distant from the author, he was compelled to read the proof-sheets without being able to verify the statistics by comparison with the copy. Still he trusts that no important error has escaped correction.

With the humble desire that it may, in some degree, worthily perpetuate the memory of a great and good man to coming ages, and thus prove a blessing to the Church of Christ and to the world, the volume is now sent forth.

THE AUTHOR.

CONTENTS.

CHAPTER I.

FROM HIS BIRTH TO HIS CONVERSION.

CHAPTER II.

COMMENCES HIS ITINERANT CAREER.

CHAPTER III.

LABOURS ON FLETCHER, BRIDGEWATER, AND HANOVER CIRCUITS.

CHAPTER IV.

MR. HEDDING UPON BARRE AND VERSHIRE CIRCUITS.

CHAPTER V.

MR. HEDDING ON NEW-HAMPSHIRE DISTRICT.

CHAPTER VI.

MR. HEDDING ON NEW-LONDON DISTRICT.

CHAPTER VII.

LABOURS IN BOSTON, NANTUCKET, AND LYNN STATIONS.

CHAPTER VIII.

LABOURS IN BOSTON, PORTLAND, LYNN, AND NEW-LONDON.

CHAPTER IX.

MR. HEDDING ON BOSTON DISTRICT AND IN BOSTON—FROM 1821 TO 1824.

CHAPTER X.

GENERAL CONFERENCE OF 1824, AND MR. HEDDING'S ELECTION TO THE EPISCOPACY.

CHAPTER XI.

FIRST QUADRENNIAL OF EPISCOPAL LABOUR.

CHAPTER XII.

SECOND QUADRENNIAL OF EPISCOPAL LABOURS.

CHAPTER XIII.

SECOND QUADRENNIAL OF EPISCOPAL LABOURS—CONCLUDED.

CHAPTER XIV.

THIRD QUADRENNIAL OF EPISCOPAL LABOURS.

CHAPTER XV.

FOURTH QUADRENNIAL OF EPISCOPAL LABOURS.

CHAPTER XVI.

BISHOP HEDDING AND THE ABOLITION CONTROVERSY.

CHAPTER XVII.

THE GENERAL CONFERENCE OF 1840, AND THE FIFTH QUADRENNIAL OF EPISCOPAL LABOUR.

CHAPTER XVIII.

SIXTH QUADRENNIAL OF EPISCOPAL LABOUR.

CHAPTER XIX.

SEVENTH QUADRENNIAL OF EPISCOPAL LABOUR.

CHAPTER XX.

LAST HOURS OF BISHOP HEDDING.

CHAPTER XXI.

ESTIMATE OF THE CHARACTER AND SERVICES OF BISHOP HEDDING.

INTRODUCTION.

The truthful biography of eminent Christian ministers whom death has removed, so far replaces those golden candlesticks that by reflection, at least, they continue to mingle their holy radiance with the effulgence of that Church which is "the light of the world." By its office, therefore, such being dead, yet speak,—being absent in body, they are retained with us in spirit,—though entered into rest, they are made to reënact before us the blessed activities and glorious triumphs of their probationary state. Its office is, therefore, most interesting and important. It increases the moral wealth of the Church, by wresting those bright examples of Christian excellence from the oblivious power of death, and constellating them, with all their heavenly lustre and winning loveliness, before the world. It augments the spiritual strength of the Church, by showing the timid and fearful, among her struggling hosts, how others of like passions, encompassed with the same infirmities, and conflicting with the same "principalities and powers," have overcome by grace, and by faith have even triumphed over the "last enemy;" thus demonstrating to them the possibility of their becoming more than conquerors through "Him that has loved them," and animating them to continue the "good fight."

It has edified the ministry of the Church, by placing before them, for their imitation and encouragement, examples of ministerial excellence, of pastoral fidelity, of cheerful sacrifice, of patient toil, of many sufferings, of holy living, and of happy dying. The biographical notices of the apostles, and of their contemporary labourers, furnished by the New Testament Scriptures, are full of holy inspirings. The heroic devotion of St. Paul has exerted a powerful influence upon the ministers of Jesus Christ in all ages. So also with the eminent servants of Christ in later times. Who has ever contemplated the intrepid spirit and valiant conduct of Martin Luther, when he braved the fury of an enraged and unscrupulous priesthood, the wrath of crowned heads, and the thunders of the Vatican, that he might vindicate the truth of God, and reform a corrupt Church,—and not felt a holy heroism stirring within him, inspiring him with something of the same moral grandeur of character? And who, through their memoirs, has made himself acquainted with the spirit, the lives, and labours of the Wesleys,—their enlightened and fervent piety, their crucifixion to the world, their oneness of purpose, their ardent and inextinguishable zeal, their able and eloquent ministry, and their stupendous and glorious achievements,—without having his whole soul moved with a desire to imitate their piety, their devotion, and their zeal? Who has ever reflected upon the missionary services and martyr sacrifices of a Brainerd, a Martyn, a Carey, and a Cox, without feeling a missionary fire kindling in his heart, burning in his very bones, and nerving his soul with the determination to have some agency in the great work of evangelizing the world? Or, who has ever brought home to his own heart the fragrant memory and reviewed the spiritual lives of such devout and holy men as John Fletcher, Edward Payson, and Wilbur Fisk, and not felt himself in a garden of spices, where all his senses were regaled, as it were, with celestial odours? The glorious illustrations of the purity and power of Christianity, exhumed by biography from the tomb of time, and held up before the Church, form a pillar of cloud by day, and of fire by night, to direct, enlighten, and encourage the Israel of God in their journeyings to the heavenly Canaan.

One of the elements of the interest, power, and usefulness of Christian biography is its variety. Human characters and experiences are almost endlessly diversified. Every man has his peculiarities. His physical peculiarities give him his identity of person; his mental and moral peculiarities his identity of character; and his peculiar exercises of mind and of body his identity of history. The faithful biographer daguerreotypes all these peculiarities, and exhibits each individual in the special characteristics of his person, his character, and his life. His powers, however, vastly transcend those of the artist. The pictures he draws are instinct with life, intelligence, and love. Does the sculptor "make the marble speak?" With his statue the biographer does more: it breathes and moves, it speaks and acts, it sacrifices and suffers, it illustrates great virtues and performs noble deeds.

Each biography, therefore, like the personage it represents, has not only its distinctive character, but its peculiar sphere of interest and influence.

Another element of its power is found in the law of assimilation. As the beautiful and sublime in nature awaken corresponding emotions and inspire corresponding sentiments, so the contemplation of the lovely, the useful, the great, the good in human character and conduct, inspires corresponding sympathies, kindles corresponding aspirations, and leads to corresponding activities in the great theatre of life. The student of Christian biography lives with the blessed dead—not in their life of glory, but in their life of grace,—that life which is by tho faith of the Son of God—a life of devotions and duties, of aims and conflicts, of services and sacrifices, and of trials and triumphs. Associating with them, he becomes like them; conversing with them, contemplating their character and life, he is changed into the same image; witnessing their continuous toil and patient endurance, he also becomes steadfast, unmovable, always abounding in the work of the Lord. This power of assimilation endows Christian biography with vast moral influence, and makes it a most precious means of grace. The lives of holy men are endowed with vital power; they not only point out and illustrate the way, but they draw the soul heavenward.

Its force is also found in its illustrations of religious truth. Abstract teachings have but little interest for the common mind. Indeed, for the most part, even informed and cultivated persons do not seek them for the pleasure they afford, but for edification. All minds appreciate apt illustrations, beautiful descriptions. Hence the charms of poetry and the attractions of a figurative style of composition. This is one of the things that makes the gospel the power of God unto salvation. It not only contains the glorious truth of Christianity, but gives us that truth illustrated and exemplified in the parables and life of Christ, and in the lives of his apostles. What Christ *did* is as instructive as what Christ *said*. His conduct and spirit, in the varying circumstances of his eventful life, are as edifying as his discourses. Indeed, the former beautifully illustrate and enforce the latter. The example of Jesus—the life that he lived—is, therefore, as instructive as the gracious words which proceeded out of his mouth. By multitudes the instructions furnished by the holy and useful life of the Saviour are more clearly perceived, more fully comprehended, and more forcibly felt than even the revelations and precepts that he uttered with his lips. The man who can hardly comprehend the abstract statement or demonstration of truth, will perhaps be the first to perceive it and to feel its power when, as a living embodiment, it stands before him. Christian biography possesses this useful attribute: it furnishes apt, plain, and affecting illustrations of all the experimental and practical truths of the gospel. As in mathematical text-books, each rule is accompanied with some problems worked out in order to show the student how the rule is to be applied; so religious biography furnishes examples under all the rules and principles of Christianity, clearly showing how its problems of penitence, and faith, and practical duty are to be solved. For instance, in the life of Bishop Hedding we have a most striking example of penitence, of powerful conversion, of strong faith in the midst of great trials and severe temptations, of pure-mindedness and holy living, of unyielding perseverance in great and long-continued labours in the cause of Christ, and, in the end, of holy triumph over the fear of death and the grave. No one can read his life without obtaining a clearer knowledge of the things that pertain to salvation—especially to the Christian faith and life—than they could possibly have gained from the most elaborate and able dissertations upon the abstract subjects. Religious biography sustains to didactic theology the same relation the atlas does to the geography. The one states and argues the subject; the other exhibits and illustrates it. To a large class of minds this illustration is almost indispensable, and there is no class that may not be benefited by it.

A well-written memoir of any eminently religious, laborious, or useful person, is, therefore, a work of great spiritual interest. It is another beacon-light upon the shores of time, pointing out the channel of safety and success to those who navigate its dangerous straits. It is another "still, small," but eloquent voice, pleading for Jesus and wooing souls to Christ. It is another problem of salvation to the uttermost, worked out and placed before us so that we may mark its successive stages, and be assisted in making our own calling and election sure. How invaluable, then, is such a work! How helpful to young disciples, and how strengthening to older believers! It is at once a practical confirmation of the truth of Christianity, and also a practical exhibition of its blessed fruits.

All these elements of usefulness appertain to the biographies of eminent private Christians. Their experience, their patience, their holy life, and their final triumph, exhibit the great beauty and blessedness of Christianity. As we read their lives, we almost insensibly imbibe their spirit—become inspired by like love, animated by the same faith, and stimulated by the same high and holy motives. As intimacies in life tend to produce similarity of character, so the biographies of the great and the good exert a transforming influence upon those who make them a subject of study and meditation. Their influence is silent, but powerful. It is like one of those currents flowing beneath the earth, whose course is traced only by the superior verdure of the earth above it. Thus the biographies of even private Christians often prove a source of blessing to the Church, wide-spread and long-continued.

But, as a general rule, the more prominent position the subject of the memoir occupied in the Church, the more fully he was set apart for spiritual services; and the more devoted his labours and signal his successes in the work of the Lord, the greater will be the interest that must be attached to such a work, and the wider will be the sphere of its influence and usefulness. Hence the memoirs of truly devoted and really eminent Christian ministers are transcendant in their power and usefulness. The experimental and practical godliness of such men, their trials and faith, their conflicts and victories, all exemplifying the economy of God, and showing the plan of salvation to be the same in its relations to all Christians, whether of the ministry or the laity, afford an instructive lesson. They signalize the power of divine grace by showing what attainments in holiness and usefulness were made by men who, after all, were men of like passions and like infirmities with us all.

The official experience and work of such men exhibit the further plenitude of grace in that they are made the savour of life unto those who were lost and perishing. The Christian ministry is a "high calling," "a weighty work." "To be messengers, watchmen, and stewards of the Lord, to teach and to premonish, to feed, and to provide for the Lord's family, to seek for Christ's sheep that are dispersed abroad, and for his children who are in the midst of this evil world, that they may be saved through Christ forever," is the highest vocation in which human powers can be employed.

> "'Tis not a cause of small import
> The pastor's care demands;
> But what might fill an angel's heart,
> And fill'd a Saviour's hands."

These are "the greater works" than those done by Christ, and which he declared should be accomplished by those who believed on him, after he had gone unto the Father. John xiv, 12. To the end that they might be qualified for such a work, the promise of being endued with the Holy Spirit from on high was made. The utter insufficiency of man —unaided by the Spirit of God—for such a work, is thus shown by our Saviour. What solemn and awful responsibilities centre in this calling! What momentous and eternal results depend upon it! To meet such responsibilities, and to encompass such results as are contemplated in the work of the ministry, call not only for the deepest piety and the purest faith, but for the constant exercise of a devoted and self-consuming zeal.

In his exalted station in the Church, the minister is exposed to two peculiar sources of trial. The expectations of the people are often extravagant; they look for superhuman perfection and power in their pastor; they forget that he is a man of like passions with themselves—that he is encompassed with infirmities—that he is subject to temptations and trials, and that, though a depositary of sacred treasure, after all he is but an earthen vessel. They often seem to expect to find in him a being exempt from the ordinary infirmities and imperfections of our nature; nay, their very feelings toward religion will, in a measure, be regulated by those inspired by the personal character and address of the minister of Christ. When the priests, who accompanied the Spaniards in their early invasion of Mexico, desired to baptize the children of the natives, "No!" said they; "he must be a wicked God who has such wicked servants!" Thus does the minister in a peculiar manner stand as the representative of Christ and his religion. The very truth he proclaims is to be weighed and tested, not merely in the light of his words, but also in the light of his character and life. For a minister to meet all these conditions—so to demean himself as to be of good report both in and out of the Church, and at the same time to retain the testimony that he pleases God—is an achievement wonderful as it is difficult. Its accomplishment attests the sufficiency of divine grace. To fill this sacred office without reproach while living, and to leave a memory fragrant with that which is pure and good after he has gone to his reward, is a manifestation of grace in the minister of Christ at once glorious in itself and cheering to the heart of every Christian.

Another source of trial to the Christian minister is the fact that he is subjected in a peculiar manner to the fiercest assaults of Satan. His ability to thwart the devices of the evil one and to do good, the important relation he sustains to the Church and truth of God, and his aggressive warfare against the usurped dominion of sin upon the earth, all make him a peculiar object of subtle hatred to the powers of darkness. The great adversary knows well that if a minister saves his own soul he will also save others; and, on the other hand, if he fall, he will carry others with him. He can neither be saved nor lost alone. If he pass over the "highway of holiness" to the celestial city, he will perform an office like that of the locomotive upon the railroad; he will draw along with and after him a train freighted with immortal spirits, redeemed and saved by the blood of Christ. If he becomes ensnared and perishes, it is as the noble vessel that founders at sea, engulfing a whole crew in the fathomless depths. If the spiritual Samson falls with his hands upon the pillars of the temple of God, multitudes share the awful destruction. Our wily foe is not ignorant of the wide-spread ruin consequent upon a minister's fall. The destruction of one minister, then, is more of an object to him than the overthrow of many others whose position and influence are less powerful; hence with double effort he endeavours to accomplish his end. Such is the condition of the minister: subjected to the common infirmities of our nature, he is still left to battle in the midst of sore trials, and to withstand the special assaults of Satan. Has he bravely withstood all these adverse evil influences, and nobly risen above them? It is because he was girded with the whole armour of God; because he was strengthened with might by his spirit in the inner man. Under all these circumstances, and in spite of these adverse influences, is he for a long series of years steadfast, immovable, always abounding in the work of the Lord—maintaining the good fight, keeping the faith, and finally finishing his course with joy? then have we an exemplification and a triumph of grace that may awaken our admiration, and fill our hearts with praise to God. There is, therefore, a peculiar interest and a special importance attached to the biographies of distinguished Christian ministers.

But if the subject of the memoir be a general superintendent or a bishop of the Church, the importance of the work is still increased. The higher the office one fills in an army—the more of public weal entrusted to him—the greater the difficulties in which he is involved, (though these add nothing to his personal merits,) the deeper is the interest felt in the manner in which he meets his responsibilities. Upon the same principle, the biography of one who had long and successfully filled the office of a bishop in the Methodist Episcopal Church, cannot be without additional and special interest. Few men, if any, whether in Church or state, have devolved upon them higher obligations, or are called to encounter greater difficulties in discharging their official duties. He has the care of all the Churches; he is "to oversee the temporal and spiritual interests of the Church." Such a supervision is a work of magnitude in any Church; but in the Methodist Episcopal Church, its itinerant economy makes its general superintendency not only a work of great magnitude, but also of great delicacy and difficulty. Let us indicate some of these.

In such an economy there must be an umpire, some one to "fix the appointments" of the preachers definitely and authoritatively. In the Methodist Episcopal Church this task is devolved upon her bishops. But they cannot do this by a merely arbitrary exercise of authority. It demands the most affectionate sympathy with both the Churches and the preachers, the most thorough and patient investigation of the condition of the Churches and the circumstances of the preachers, the most careful examination of the adaptation of ministers and appointments. All this must sometimes be done in a conference of two hundred or more ministers in a few days, besides presiding in the conference sessions. This can only be accomplished by the most intense and prayerful application. But after having heard kindly and patiently the representations of both preachers and people, and taken the best counsel the case admits, and arranged the plan of appointments with the utmost tenderness and care, the bishop often finds them unsatisfactory. Indeed, how could it be otherwise, unless he could work miracles? For instance, if half a dozen Churches ask for one man, the bishop can appoint him to only one of them, and the others must be disappointed; or if two or three ministers desire the same appointment, but one can have it, and the others will feel more or less afflicted. Or if a Church is divided,—one part wishing one minister, and the other part another,—it is plain that the wishes of both cannot be met; and yet the disappointed party not unfrequently blames the bishop. In many such cases, to avoid blame is utterly impracticable, because it would require him to meet at one and the same time the antagonistic wishes of both parties. It is almost impossible to conceive the delicacy and difficulty of the position held by the stationing power under such circumstances.

Again, in the representations made of claims and interests, the reasons urged are often as conflicting as the wishes expressed. For example, one Church must have a first-class minister this year, because the other Churches of the place are without ministers, and there is an opportunity to do great good and build up the Church; another must have a first-class minister, because the other Churches of the place have very able ministers, and are drawing away their people; one Church has had an unacceptable minister for the last year or two, and the congregation is so scattered, and the Church so prostrated, that they must have a man to raise them; another has had a man of talent for one or two years, and they have a large congregation, and now they must have a popular man to sustain them. One society wants to build a church this year, and must have a minister who has talent and influence to aid them; another society has just built a new church, and now must have an attractive minister to fill it. It is easy to see how these conflicting reasons could all be urged with candour and propriety, but it is not so easy to see how the bishop could be controlled by each of them; or if he were disposed to be, how each society could possibly be accommodated.

The reasons urged by the preachers in reference to their wishes are often equally antagonistic. For instance, one preacher has had a first-class appointment, and must have another like it, or be disgraced by taking an inferior one. Another has had poor appointments, and the time has come when he is entitled to better ones, to give him character, position, and usefulness. One preacher has travelled, laboured, and sacrificed many years, and in view of past services is entitled to consideration in his appointments. The people express a wish for a younger man, and he thinks he ought to have the better appointment in preference to the older brother, because his popularity has induced this petition from the people. Not unfrequently the young men who urge this motive soon lose a measure of their health, or in some way a degree of their effectiveness, and, consequently, their popularity with the people, and then turn to the bishop as their help in the time of affliction—not unfrequently falling back upon the plea of age and service as reasons why they should be favoured with short moves and comfortable appointments. Another preacher has just left a lucrative employment, and, in view of his financial sacrifices, claims special notice in his allotment. Another is poor, and must be relieved by his next appointment. Another has children to be educated, and facilities and means must be secured in arranging the work assigned to him in his next appointment. One man had a long distance to move in his last appointment, and ought not to be subjected to a similar. The family of another brother is sick, and he must, therefore, have an appointment contiguous to the one he is leaving. The health of one brother has partially failed, and he must have light work. Another brother has been over-tasked with a heavy appointment, and he must now have an easier one.

These are only specimens of the representations of Churches and ministers, which are made to the bishops and their council, and which are to be affectionately regarded and adjusted by them in stationing the preachers. Although it may be affirmed, without fear of successful contradiction, that there is no denomination in which there is so little irritation between Churches and pastors, and where so high a degree of satisfaction exists, as in the Methodist Episcopal Church; still it must be seen that our itinerant system cannot be carried on without some friction. Disappointments and afflictions will sometimes occur. The bishop, upon whom devolves the responsibility of fixing and changing these pastoral relations, cannot reasonably expect to escape censure. And further, he has no power to enforce his authority. If a preacher refuses to go to the appointment assigned to him, the bishop can inflict no penalty. The determination of the case is with the annual conference. His power, therefore, is only commensurate with the confidence of the Church in his integrity, wisdom, and carefulness.

It is, therefore, a question of deep interest, concerning one who has filled this office for a long series of years, How did he succeed in discharging all these delicate and difficult duties, and in meeting all these peculiar and weighty responsibilities? A biography that answers at length this inquiry must be a work of much general interest. The Life of Bishop Hedding therefore, being the biography of a deeply experienced and exemplary Christian, of a devoted and eminent minister, and of an able and successful bishop, not only embraces all these elements of interest of which we have heretofore spoken—such as, standing alone, would render it a most desirable and useful work; but combined as his history was with the early history of Methodism, and with the progress and development of the Church, during his long and successful ministry, the work must possess much additional interest. Accordingly, in this work we shall find the concurrent progress of the Church briefly delineated, embodying many incidents illustrative of the earlier history of the Methodistic movement in this country—the obstacles encountered by the early preachers, their modes of aggressive warfare, and the philosophy of their success—and also outline sketches of the character and career of some of the noble associates of Hedding in the great work of founding Methodism in the land.

It is to be regretted that Bishop Hedding did not keep a diary. The loss sustained by this omission is irreparable. To some extent, however, it has been remedied; and all the accessible material that could perfect his biography, or illustrate his character, has been carefully gleaned for this work. In 1847 the Rev. Moses L. Scudder was stationed in Poughkeepsie, then the residence of Bishop Hedding. He proposed that the bishop should relate to him the events of his life and he would write them down. The bishop was very reluctant to this; but upon being assured that after his death some one would attempt a biography of him, he assented to the proposition. His engagements and his ill health, however, hindered the progress of the work. In 1848 the General Conference, at its session in Pittsburgh, passed the following resolution, namely: "Resolved, That this General Conference do most earnestly and affectionately request our respected and venerated Bishop Hedding to prepare his biography for publication, including especially his observations and opinions in relation to Methodism."

The passage of this resolution induced the bishop more willingly to allow the record of the incidents of his life; and after the removal of Mr. Scudder to another pastoral charge, his successor, the Rev. L. M. Vincent, continued to write for him. But the bishop's official duties, together with his increasing infirmities, greatly embarrassed and delayed the prosecution of the work. Yet much was rescued from oblivion by these efforts. I desire especially to record the persevering and indefatigable exertions of Mr. Scudder in procuring materials for this work both while at Poughkeepsie and subsequently. By his agency most of such materials were secured and preserved. After the death of Bishop Hedding the following article was found in his will:—

"Whereas the General Conference of eighteen hundred and forty-eight were pleased to adopt the following resolution, viz.:—

"'Resolved, That this conference do most earnestly and affectionately request Bishop Hedding to prepare his biography for publication, including especially his observations and opinions in relation to Methodism;' and whereas I have done what I could, by the assistance of Rev. M. L. Scudder and other friends, but through my heavy labours while I had strength to labour, and through my protracted illness of more than a year, the papers will probably be left but in an imperfect state; now, I hereby appoint my beloved colleague, Bishop Janes, or, in case of his death, Bishop Waugh, to receive those papers, write the biography, or appoint some one else to write it, and to cause it to be published for the benefit of the Methodist Episcopal Church, of which the said Janes is one of the bishops."

Accordingly, his executors placed in my hands the papers referred to, in order that the provision of the will might be executed, and the desire of the Church gratified in the publication of the biography of one who had been so eminent both in the broad fields of her labour and in her highest councils.

After consulting with my colleagues, I appointed Rev. D. W. Clark, D. D., to write the biography. My official duties while the work has been passing through the press have not allowed me time to examine it critically; but my knowledge of Dr. Clark's abilities, and of the labour he has bestowed upon the work, enable me most confidently to commend it to the Christian public. In closing this introduction, it gives me great pleasure to insert the following notice, from the pen of Bishop Morris:—

"Having been favoured with the privilege of reading this work in MS., I take pleasure in commending it to the attention of readers generally, especially the lovers of Christian biography. Few individuals in the United States, if any, had a more extensive acquaintance, or enjoyed the confidence of more numerous personal friends than Bishop Hedding. No one was more worthy to be highly esteemed and loved for his work's sake. He was actively engaged in the gospel ministry fifty successive years. Others wrote more for posterity; but no man of modern times, I believe, has performed more pastoral labour, or done it better than he did. His term of active toil embraced the first half of the nineteenth century. When he first entered the itinerant service it was in 'the day of small things,' and there were enemies to confront and obstacles to overcome unknown to us of this generation; but he was favoured with grace according to his day and trial. The part he acted as a pioneer deserves a place on the pages of history. I scarcely know which to admire more, the strength with which he threshed mountain difficulties, or the well-balanced judgment with which that strength was directed. Apparently unconscious of possessing either, he trusted only in God for success, and gave to him all the glory. Whatever appears properly authenticated of such a character will not fail to interest the American people. His early history, conversion, and call to the ministry; his usefulness and well-earned popularity, suffering and patience, perils and escapes, toils and triumphs, will all be read with profit. Indeed, the entire process by which he rose from the obscurity of a country lad to the highest office in the largest Christian body in America, and the wisdom and firmness with which he filled it, will be examined with interest. The closing scene of the pious bishop's life will amply compensate for a second reading, and prepare the mind to enjoy the final summing up of his character and public service.

"To write the Life of Bishop Hedding involves no inconsiderable amount of responsibility; but the author, Rev. D. W. Clark, D. D., in my opinion, has proved himself equal to the trust confided to him. The work is not burdened with stale documents. Important events of the times, ecclesiastically, are interspersed, and honourable mention is made of the subject's early coadjutors; but not so as to break, or materially obscure, the chain of personal history. I trust that hundreds of thousands will realize what I enjoyed in the perusal of it—a rich mental repast and heartfelt pleasure."

E. S. JANES.

NEW-YORK, *June* 1, 1855.

LIFE AND TIMES

OF

REV. ELIJAH HEDDING, D.D.

Methodism, having its origin in 1728, with a few students in the University of Oxford, who were seeking a higher tone of piety, a greater simplicity and purity of manner, and a clearer realization of experimental and practical truth than was common in that age, has continued through the lapse of a century and a quarter to develop and move forward to the accomplishment of its mission. Its rise constitutes a signal epoch in the history of the world. In its progress it has developed new sources of power, and brought new forces into the field where Christianity is waging its conflict against the kingdom and power of darkness. Its ecclesiastical organization, like that of the apostolic Church, did not come forth plotted and devised in conclave by a few master minds, but was the offspring of a Providence which at once overruled the action of the wisest, and guided to results as unexpected as they were magnificent. In the abundance of their labours, and the zeal and self-sacrificing spirit, as well as oneness of purpose, with which those labours were carried on, the leading spirits in the "Methodistic company," as Isaac Taylor calls them, have not been surpassed since the apostolic age.

In this country Methodism dates its origin thirty-eight years later than in England; but its distinct organization, under the title of the "Methodist Episcopal Church," did not take place till 1784, when the growing interests of the work, combined with our political severance from the mother country, rendered such organization necessary. The last half of the eighteenth century may be regarded as the heroic age of Methodism in England; and the last quarter of the same century and the first quarter of the present may be regarded as its heroic age in this country. In those days there were giants in the land. They constituted the thundering legion—*legio tonans*—of Methodism. They went out "without scrip or purse;" they heeded no danger and shrunk from no labour; they forded streams, crossed mountains, traversed wildernesses, everywhere preaching the word of life, and striving "to spread Scriptural holiness over all these lands." Many of them were untaught in the schools of human learning; but they had been thoroughly, severely drilled in the school of Christ, and their theology was not merely theoretical, but actual. They were undisciplined in the logic of the schools; but they were also untrammelled by the conventionalities of art, and mighty in the logic of common sense. They had one work—one aim; and borne away by the inspiration of that mighty work, they moved with a momentum irresistible, and with a power that shook the moral universe. Nobly have they done their work! All succeeding ages will bear witness unto them. But they have ceased from their labours and gone to their reward.

Methodism in its organic state is the monument they have left behind them,—Methodism on both sides of the Atlantic, with its missionary stations in almost every part of the globe,—Methodism, with its distinctive characteristics and regulations, with its ample and widely-diffused literature, with its seminaries, colleges, and theological schools, with its nearly two million communicants and its eight million souls dependent upon its fifteen thousand ministers for spiritual instruction and guidance,—and, above all, Methodism, with its millions of garnered trophies in the kingdom of God, and its millions more still attesting that

"The holy to the holiest leads."

These are some of the grand results of the Wesleyan reformation, so far as it concerns organic Methodism.

But we must not forget that the whole Christian Church has felt the mighty impulse, and the spiritual vitality of sister denominations has been kindled anew; so that it is difficult to tell whether the grandest results of Methodism have been wrought without or within the pale of her organization.

In our own country Methodism has played no inconsiderable part in developing its civilization; and especially in producing that paramount Christian influence among the native population, which constitutes one of the leading elements of that civilization. Borne by the self-sacrificing itinerant, it has gone side by side with the hardy pioneer, illuminating his rude cabin with the light of salvation, and shedding around him the genial influences of the cross of Christ. And when the wild wilderness gave place to the cultivated field and bustling village, the church and the school-house, as well as the appliances of art and science to the purposes of life, attested that the noblest element of modern civilization, Christianity, had exerted an all-pervading influence in the transformation that had been wrought. Nor is it an inconsiderable agency that Methodism has had in Americanizing and Christianizing the millions of immigrants from the old world that have landed upon our shores. Brought under the genial influence of the same civil institutions, and under the transforming power of the same religious faith, they cease to be foreigners and become one with us—one with us in social condition and feeling, and one with us through the transforming power of a living faith.

It will be the object of the following pages to delineate the life and character of one of those heroic men, who, like the apostles of old, forgetful of ease or of worldly honour, devoted themselves to the great work of blessing and saving men. Born while yet the great struggle for our national independence was progressing, and while the vast expanse of a new and hitherto unbroken country was being overspread by a hardy and daring people, his character embodied in it those elements of strength and self-reliance which the spirit that animated the people and the stirring activity of the times were calculated to produce. Methodism, too, which before had been inchoate in this country, underwent its forming process contemporaneously, and under the action of the same agencies. Thus born and nurtured, he became fitted by experience and grace to take a leading part in the Methodistic movement on this side of the Atlantic. In planting Methodism in waste places and among the sparse and newly-settled population, few were more laborious or successful. In developing organic Methodism, perfecting its ecclesiastical organization, giving form and character to its jurisprudence, he stands perhaps unequalled, except by the sainted Asbury, in the Church. To him will Methodism ever be indebted, under God, for much that is noble in its organic existence and glorious in its eventful career. The works of such men survive them, and continue to operate with unspent power when the vanity of human ambition has long been humbled in the dust. Their history is no less an indispensable element of the world's history than that of statesmen and heroes. "If it has not to treat," as Mr. Southey has well observed, "of actions wherewith the world has rung from side to side, it appeals to the higher part of our nature, and may, perhaps, excite more salutary feelings, a worthier interest, and wiser meditations."

CHAPTER I.

FROM HIS BIRTH TO HIS CONVERSION.

Birth—Ancestry—Early Religious Instruction—Prayer in Childhood—A Mother's Influence—The Dutchess Circuit—Benjamin Abbot—Wonderful Displays of Divine Power—Grandmother and Mother converted—Exhorted by Abbot in Class-meeting—Removed to Vermont—Temptations to Infidelity—Deism—Atheism—Universalism—Mental Conflicts—A Critical Period—Narrow Escape—Spiritual Destitution of Starksborough—Advent of a Methodist Family—Meetings established—Young Hedding reads Sermons—Studies Methodist Theology—The Methodist Itinerancy—NOTE, A Picture of Aggressive Methodism—Vergennes Circuit—Joseph Mitchell—Wonderful Revival—A Mother in Israel—NOTE, Conversion of Mrs. Bushnell—Young Hedding powerfully awakened—His Resolve and Dedication—Sermon from Joseph Mitchell—Obtains Peace—Becomes a Probationer—Obtains the Witness of the Spirit—Triumph over Sin—State of his Mind and his Studies—A Striking Conversion—Point reached in the Narrative—School in which the Prospective Servant of Christ had been trained—Principal Agencies in his Conversion.

ELIJAH HEDDING was born in Dutchess County, New-York, June 7th, 1780. His grandfather many years before had settled in the section then called "The Nine Partners," and here his father resided at the time of his birth. The homestead was situated near the south-western corner of what is now the town of Pine Plains. His paternal ancestry were of English origin, and strongly marked with English peculiarities. Of his grandfather, who was a man of considerable prominence in the community, several amusing anecdotes are still handed down in the neighbourhood.

He was a "high liver," and his general character accorded much with the prevailing habits of the times and of the state of society around him.

Neither of the parents of Elijah was a professor of religion at the time of his birth; but his mother was the subject of deep religious convictions, and was evidently a woman of prayer. She took great pains to guard his moral character, and to instruct him in the truths and duties of the Christian religion. The elements of a religious education were so clearly imparted by even this unconverted mother, and so firmly grafted into his youthful mind, that, at the early age of four years, he was able to pray with a tolerable understanding of the nature and obligations of prayer. The habit of secret prayer thus formed in early childhood was maintained for several years, and until, through the influence of evil associates, he had in a measure thrown off the restraints of religion. So conscientious was he in the performance of this duty, that if he chanced to lie down at night without saying his evening prayer it disturbed his rest, and he could not compose himself to sleep till he had solemnly and earnestly repeated it. His mother had taught him to repeat that verse which stands prominently among the holiest recollections of early childhood in the minds of uncounted millions:—

"And now I lay me down to sleep,
I pray the Lord my soul to keep,
If I should die before I wake,
I pray the Lord my soul to take."

It is a striking evidence of the force and beauty of the impression made by this germing petition upon his infantile heart, that he continued to repeat it in later years; and even in his old age it formed the appropriate and beautiful close of the secret prayer breathed forth to his Maker each night before retiring to rest. So clear were his convictions of religious truth, and so powerful were the operations of the Spirit of God upon his heart in this early period of his history, that, had he been guarded from evil associations and surrounded by those who were themselves possessed of vital godliness, and instructed and encouraged by them in the great matters of religious experience and duty, it might perhaps have been said of him that from a child he had known the way of the Lord. But, as it was, religious truth was strongly intrenched in his understanding. When surrounded afterward by men of sceptical views on the subject of religion, and when powerfully assailed by their infidelity—so congenial to the impulses of our sin-polluted natures—the knowledge of the word and truth of God, acquired thus early, rose up like an invincible wall of defence around him. Often in later years he referred, with tender and grateful feelings, to those early instructions of his mother, as having exerted a powerful influence upon his whole character and life.

To the illustrious examples of a mother's influence in planting the germs of whatever is great and good in the virgin soil of the young heart, must be added that of the mother of Hedding. Another prominent agency in his actual conversion will appear; but these early instructions antedated all other influences, and were superior to them in the development of his character. Could that mother, prosecuting her Christian duty to her son, unappalled by the prevailing irreligion of the times and by the adverse influences around her, have had the coming future unveiled to her vision—could she have traced the career of her first-born, first as a holy man, and an able minister of the New Testament winning souls to Christ, then filling with honour the highest office in the Church of God, and finally, full of years and of services, closing his long and honoured career—the patriarch of the Church—his name crowned with immortal honour and his soul inspired with immortal hope, the discouragements she experienced and the obstacles she encountered—at which, no doubt, her faith was often staggered—would have shrunk into absolute insignificance in comparison with the great objects to be realized. Alas, for those sons that are without *Christian* mothers to bestow upon them this indispensable nurture! Alas, for those Christian mothers who are so derelict in duty as to permit their sons to pass the limit of early childhood without causing their youthful hearts to comprehend the nature and to feel the power of the elementary principles of religion!

The Dutchess circuit first appears in the Minutes for 1788 with only *ten* members. This comprised the sum-total of Methodism north of the Highlands on the Hudson River at that time. Benjamin Abbot was then just commencing his wonderful career. A son of thunder, he ranged through the country and assaulted the strongholds of wickedness, as though he had received a special commission from Heaven to storm the very citadel of hell itself. In 1789 he was stationed upon Dutchess circuit, and at the close of the year 1790 the one circuit had expanded into *four*, and the ten members had multiplied into nearly one thousand and four hundred! There had been sown "a handful of corn in the earth upon the top of the mountains, and the fruit thereof *shook* like Lebanon." Revivals broke out in every part of the circuit. The power of God was displayed in a wonderful manner. The most hardened and haughty were softened and subdued by the power of the gospel. Many of the vilest, the most wicked, men were converted, and became exemplary members of the Church. Some of these lived to a good old age, glorifying the Lord Jesus by a good confession, and at last dying in the triumphs of faith.

Mr. Hedding, who was then a lad of nine or ten years, ever after retained a vivid recollection of some of those early scenes. In later years, when tempted and buffeted by Satan, he often adopted the language of the psalmist,—"I will remember the years of the right hand of the Most High. I will remember the works of the Lord: surely I will remember thy wonders of old."

Among the subjects of this great revival were his mother, grandmother, and several other relatives.

A class was established in the neighbourhood; and his mother became not only a member, but also a regular attendant. On such occasions young Elijah accompanied her, so that he was often in class-meeting. On preaching days the preacher was accustomed to meet the class after the public congregation had been dismissed. At one of these meetings, when about nine or ten years old, he was the only person present who was not a member. After Mr. Abbot had spoken to the members he paused a moment, and looked earnestly upon young Hedding, and said,—"Well, my boy, do you know that you are a sinner?" He replied, "Yes, sir." Then, with great vehemence and deep feeling, Mr. Abbot continued,—"There is many a boy in hell not so old as you are;" and then exhorted him with tremendous power to get religion. This event not only frightened him, but produced real religious concern. The impression made upon his mind lasted for several weeks, but finally wore off without producing any lasting fruit. Soon after this he fell into the company of wicked boys, and by degrees learned their language and acquired similar habits. His religious feelings passed away, and the powerful impressions that had been made upon his mind were at length so far effaced that he ran greedily and thoughtlessly in the way of sin. But that impression was not altogether lost, for in the midst of his folly and wickedness his conscience was often terribly aroused, and the fear of death and hell gat hold upon him. Thus in the midst of seeming thoughtlessness, he was often the subject of the most intense concern with regard to his soul.

In 1791 the parents of young Hedding emigrated to Vermont, and settled in the town of Starksborough. This was a part of the country then newly and sparsely settled, and the family were consequently subjected to the exposures, privations, and hardships of frontier life. In all these, as well as in the severe labour incident to the subjugation of a wild country and the cultivation of a new farm, he shared largely and willingly. Familiarity with danger had begotten a daring that bordered upon recklessness. He was quick, decided, intrepid. Being a decided character, and also possessed of both mental and physical power, he became in some sort a leader of the young men who consorted with him. Yet was there something in him incomprehensible even to them; the suggestive remark upon some religious truth, or the striking admonition that would sometimes fall from him, often occasioned serious reflections amidst the wild and giddy scenes that occupied them.

From many of the moral dangers that beset young men in the crowded city and large town, the remote region and the newly-settled country are comparatively exempt. But the poison of infidelity spreads everywhere, and it may almost always be found among the restless, rash, adventurous spirits that usually become the pioneers in a new country. Thus in very many places infidelity preceded the gospel, in its introduction among the people, in our earlier history. From this cause young Hedding was more strongly tempted, and his principles and character more fearfully endangered during his youth, than from any other. Long before the institutions of the gospel had been established in the place of his residence, the various forms of infidelity had made their appearance. Infidel books were disseminated, and conceited and crafty men lost no opportunity afforded them for attempting to undermine the confidence of their neighbours in the principles of Christianity. Their puzzling questions, which a fool might ask; and their subtile sophisms, which puzzled the simple-hearted people not possessed of sufficient knowledge and intellectual acuteness to unravel their sophistry; and their bold assertion of the great lies of infidelity as so many conceded historical and scientific facts, were the means upon which they relied for the dissemination of the poison of their unbelief.

No wonder that the mind of young Hedding was deeply affected by these assaults. Deism appeared to him the most inviting form of scepticism, and long and earnestly did he seek to intrench himself within the creed of the deist. The form of deism then prevalent denied to man a future life; but the subject of our memoir, though he pondered long and deeply on the subject, and marshalled the specious objections in order before him again and again; nay, though he resolved again and again that he would let go his hold upon Christianity and be a deist, there was ever that in the very instinctive aspirations of his own nature which asserted his immortality; and, on the other hand, it seemed most unreasonable that a God of wisdom, power, and benevolence—as even the God of the deist must be—would create such a being as man, endow him with such rational faculties, fill his soul with such aspirations, and give to him such capacities for boundless improvement, and then cause him at death to go into utter annihilation. It was thus that his instinctive sentiments and his reason combined to deliver him from the toils of deism.

His effort to settle down upon atheism—the absolute denial of the being of God—was no more successful. It involved a mental conflict severe in its nature, but of short duration. The evidences of the Divine Being were too clearly seen in all his works to admit of a denial of his existence. As he looked upon the curious mechanism of his own body, the beautiful contrivances so obvious through all the animal and vegetable creation, and as he reflected upon the grandeur, harmony, and order of the heavenly bodies, and the nice adjustment of the various forces acting upon them to produce such grand results, he said within himself: "Here are facts the verity of which I cannot question. My eye sees them, my hand feels them, my perception and reason comprehend them. Here is contrivance, there is design. Here is the most exquisite adaptation of means or agencies for the accomplishment of specific and manifest ends; and there is an unseen, mysterious power *somewhere* that has executed, and which still continues to carry into effect these various plans. These facts I cannot question. My reason then tells me that there must be some unseen agency that has contrived, and some unseen power that has executed all this. To believe that it all could have happened without such an agency and power is ten thousand times more absurd, more contradictory to all the convictions of sound reason and judgment than the acknowledgment of the being of God, although clouds and darkness are around about him." But this was not all. The very instinctive sentiments of his nature warred against this delusion also. "My conscience," he says, "bore awful testimony, for it then was awful to me, that there is a God." Nor could he look into his Bible—taught in it as he had been by a mother's care—without everywhere seeing evidence that it was from God, and feeling that God was speaking to him through his blessed word.

Next he sought refuge from his consciousness of guilt and his fear of hell in Universalism. But he at once perceived that Universalism implied the non-existence of hell, and also of the devil; and he was already too well versed in the Scriptures not to perceive that hell was as much an existing fact, according to the Bible, as heaven was, and also that the person ality of the devil was as distinctly set forth as the personality of God, of Jesus Christ, or, in fine, of any existent intelligent being in the universe. Hence the denial of the fact of a hell and of the real and personal existence of the devil could not be made without a rejection of the Bible itself; and this would land him once more in deism, if not in rank atheism, both of which systems he had already satisfied himself were destitute of any substantial foundation.

These mental conflicts form an essential part of the biography of Mr. Hedding. They indicate his early intellectual character; they indicate the trials and discipline by which his mind was schooled into those habits of research and modes of thought which laid the foundations of his subsequent greatness in the Church of God.

Few have attained to eminence without the severe disciplining of mental conflict. This seems to be necessary to stir up the latent energies of the soul, and to give that intensity to its action which is necessary in order to grand results. The poet and the philosopher have their discipline in this respect; but none, as a class, go through a more severe mental ordeal than those who in the end become eminent for their attainments in piety, or eminent for their usefulness in the Church of God.

This was a critical period—the most critical period in the life of young Hedding. Satan, with his allurements, had already ensnared him in practical evil, and had perverted his heart to the love of sin; and now his devices were employed to shake the fabric and undermine the foundation of his religious principles. Had this latter device been accomplished at this period of his life, when his character was in a peculiar manner undergoing the process of formation, he would probably have become as firmly intrenched in sin as he afterward became in the Christian faith. For his deliverance in this season of temptation, and his complete victory over the enemy that had assaulted the foundations of his religious faith, he was unquestionably indebted to those religious instructions received from his mother's lips in early childhood, and also to the habit, formed under her guidance, of frequently reading the word of God, with special effort to understand its historical details and its prophetic records, as well as its religious teaching. These things proved a defence and a safeguard in the time of danger.

The little record he subsequently made of his feelings during this period of temptation is worthy of preservation. It at least shows the wretchedness of a soul warring against God and truth:—

"Notwithstanding my temptations to embrace the errors before alluded to, I believed the doctrines of Methodism, for I had understood them from the time I had heard Benjamin Abbot and other Methodist preachers preach on Dutchess Circuit. I believed I might be saved if I would turn to God; but my love for sin was so strong I would not give up my idols. Occasionally I had a faint hope that I might repent and obtain mercy on a dying bed; yet much of the time I was under a painful apprehension that I should be lost. I often *wished* that there was no God, or that he was such a God as would allow me to live in my sins and not send me to hell. I often wished I could be annihilated, or I would have been glad to be turned into a brute, that I might be free from the liability of punishment in another world. But, notwithstanding such vain wishes, the fearful conviction remained with me that I had an immortal nature and a sinful heart, and that my sins must be forgiven by the redeeming grace of Christ, or I could never be happy in another world."

About this period he had several narrow escapes from sudden death. One of these instances is worthy of note, not only because of the manifest providence of God in his deliverance, but also because it illustrates the practical recklessness of his external life and character, even while his mind was the subject of such deep convictions and such severe mental conflicts on the subject of religion; a case by no means singular. He was driving a yoke of oxen attached to a cart heavily loaded with wheat-sheaves from the harvest field. Having a steep hill to descend, he stepped before the oxen and attempted to check their pace; but by a sudden spring they knocked him down and trampled him beneath their feet, and one of the wheels of the loaded cart passed over his body. He must have been instantly killed had he not fallen, in the good providence of God, just below a large stone, over which the wheel passed and, by the bound, scarcely touched his body. He thus speaks of the thoughts and feelings that rushed through his mind while the oxen were trampling him beneath their feet, and the ponderous wheels were rushing apparently to his inevitable destruction:—

"It was an awful moment. I saw no possibility of escape, believed that I should be killed, and expected to be in hell in a few minutes. No language can express the awful horror that oppressed my soul during that brief moment. An age of horror seemed to be crowded into an instant of time. But God, in his providence, and in a singular and unexpected mode, delivered me."

No sooner, however, had the danger passed, than he leaped to his feet. There he stood, his heart still quaking with fear, and conscious that he had been delivered, as it were by a miracle, from the very jaws of hell. But he must needs show the men who were running from the fields that he was too courageous to be the subject of fear or of religious excitement, whatever might be the danger; and he laughed aloud, exclaiming, "Not dead yet! not dead yet!" Such is the presumptuous, Heaven-daring hardihood which ungodly men mistake for courage. How much nobler would it have been, and how much more of true manliness would it have exhibited, even in the sight of his companions, had he fallen down upon his knees and rendered thanksgiving for so gracious and wonderful a deliverance! This, no doubt, he would have done had he obeyed the better and truer impulses of his own heart; this he probably would have done had he been alone by himself; but the fear of man involved him in that snare which has led millions to perdition —the necessity of appearing reckless to avoid the suspicion of being religiously impressed. The event soon passed by, and seemed to leave no lasting impression upon his mind; but it could not be easily forgotten.

For four or five years after the Hedding family settled in Starksborough, the entire town remained nearly destitute of religious meetings and privileges. A Baptist preacher occasionally visited the place and preached a sermon, but with little effect. The Methodist itinerants, though ranging the country in every direction, had not as yet penetrated into this part of the state. About this time, however, a Methodist family moved into the neighbourhood. The man and his wife were both devotedly pious. Finding that there were no Sabbath meetings in the community, they invited their neighbours to meet at their house, and regular Sabbath services were kept up by them for two or three years, and until the appointment became regularly included within the newly-formed circuit of Vergennes, in 1798. The meetings were usually opened by singing and prayer, conducted by the man himself, and afterward one of Wesley's Sermons or a portion of Baxter's Call would be read by some one appointed for that purpose. Young Hedding was usually called upon to read on these occasions; and, though reluctant at first, the exercise soon became far from disagreeable—especially as the people seemed to listen with attention and interest. He says: "It was often a wonder to me that I was generally selected to read, for I was as wild and wicked as any of the young men around. There was nothing in my heart like love to God, or in my life like the walk of the Christian. But I suppose it was because I was a pretty good reader, probably the best among them." By this means he became intimately acquainted with this pious couple. They were thorough Methodists, experimentally and practically. They were intelligent, well versed in Methodist theology, and well supplied with Methodist books. In these books, which were loaned to him, young Hedding found a new source of mental improvement. They were read through and through, conned over and discussed, till he had not only read every book published by the Methodists, but absolutely mastered their contents. Thus did he early, and before his heart was renewed by divine grace, become thoroughly conversant with the system of Wesleyan theology; and, in preference to every other, he embraced it heartily and without the least mental reserve, as combining the grand truths embodied in the Bible. Yet all this while, he says of himself: "I lived as fond of my sins as ever, and was destitute of hope, and without God in the world."

We come now to the dawning of a new era in the religious history of the place as well as of the subject of our memoir. Methodism from the beginning has been a missionary system. Without waiting for a call from the people, and without any stipulations for recompense, like the apostles of old, they sought out the people and proclaimed to them, through every open door, the message of God's mercy to the lost and guilty sons of men. They went out everywhere. No pioneer could get beyond their reach. No fastness of the wilderness could become impervious to them. No prairie could be too expansive for them to traverse; and no people could be too poor, or too degraded, or too sinful to be sought out. Wherever the word took effect a class was organized, and a leader charged with its oversight and preservation, while the preacher pressed on to the regions beyond.* This pioneer sys-

* The following picture, taken from the Presbyterian Christian Herald, is certainly a true picture of early Methodism—more applicable, we fear, to its "heroic age" than to its present genius; but we thank God that the spirit of our fathers has not altogether departed from us:—

"No pioneer gets beyond the reach of the Methodist itinerants. Though he pass the Rocky Mountains, and pursue his game to the Pacific, he soon finds the self-denying, unconquerable, unescapeable Methodist minister at his side, summoning him to the camp-meeting and winning his soul to Christ! Thousands upon thousands of pioneers, scattered like sheep and almost lost from the world, in those far-off wilds of the West, have blessed God for raising up Wesley and the Methodists.

"The Catholics can do nothing with these stirring people. They are nonplussed, outstripped, and outdone by the simple and fervent Methodists. While Romanists are piling up their stone churches to last for ages, hanging their massive bells, fastening their images, and displaying their trinkets sent from Europe, the self-denying Methodist starts forth, caring little where he shall lay his head, erects his tent by the side of some stream in the wilderness, and *blows his horn* to call the hunter from the chase and the ploughman from his yet unfenced fields. The sounds of the gospel are impressive in those solitudes. The people gladly hear. God is there. They see his emblems in the majestic trees. They hear him in the winds. They see him and they hear him in the man of God, who has left all and come to them in love. Such love, and such manifestations of goodness are overpowering. Rough souls are melted down, hard hearts are subdued and converted, and huge hands are soon seen rearing up a house for God in the wilderness! Other settlers are now

tem taxed the itinerant with severe labour, exposed him to almost constant peril, and often reduced him almost to a state of destitution and want. Imbued with his high commission and filled with the spirit of his Master, he esteemed the reproach of Christ greater treasure than all the riches of Egypt. With his Bible, his Hymn-book, his horse, and his scantily filled saddle-bags as his companions, the young minister commenced at once his labours and his song:—

> "The love of Christ doth me constrain
> To seek the wandering souls of men,
> With cries, entreaties, tears to save—
> To snatch them from a gaping grave."

No other system and no other spirit could so well meet the wants of a new, sparsely-settled, and poor people. It seemed almost indispensable that the advent of the minister should precede the organization of the society and the erection of the church. If he waited for a

attracted around this spot; and presently here is a thriving Christian village!

"In the mean time, the minister has passed on and enacted similar scenes elsewhere. In a few years *several* Churches are formed, each nearly as numerous, it may be, and far more spirited and happy, than the one which the Romanists have collected from their bigoted immigrants, taught to count beads and to swallow down the Latin which is roared forth in their costly edifice from a European organ and a babbling priest!

"Thus it is that the Methodists have secured such large numbers in the mighty West. Spirit, energy, economy, and self-sacrifice have made them an overmatch for the Catholic host! They constitute the largest division of that great army which, I believe, God will use to make Protestantism completely triumphant in our country."

"call" from the people, Satan would preoccupy the ground. However such a system might answer for a densely-populated region, with societies organized and churches erected, to a new country the preacher must go *sent* of God, and not called by the people.

In the year 1798 the aggressive spirit of the Methodist itinerancy began to make systematic inroads into Vermont. The Vergennes Circuit was formed, and Joseph Mitchell and Abner Wood appointed to labour upon it. As it regards the geographical limits of the circuit, they were somewhat indefinite, and liable to incessant enlargement as the providence of God opened the way to new preaching places in destitute towns and villages. This much, however, we can say, that, as originally marked out, it included an immense sphere of travel and toil, of more than five hundred miles in compass, and required from four to six weeks to complete one round —the preacher, besides riding many miles, preaching once or twice on each week-day, and three times on each Sabbath, and at many of the appointments also leading class or conducting a prayer meeting. Mr. Mitchell continued on this circuit two years, enduring the privations and trials, and performing the Herculean tasks incident to a new field of labour, but effectually breaking up the ground for his successors. He was in every respect fitted for his work —a man of extraordinary natural powers—a natural logician, a shrewd wit; deficient indeed in scholastic education, but with all his faculties richly indued and acutely quickened by a most efficient practical edu cation. He was a most energetic and overpowering preacher. Like a flaming fire he ranged through the country, full of faith and of the Holy Ghost, preaching Christ and him crucified, in demonstration of the Spirit and with power. A memorable revival attended upon his labours. Up to this time, the mother of young Hedding and the pious couple of whom we have spoken were the only Methodists in the town of Starksborough. But now a host was raised up. The revival was remarkable not only for the number of its subjects, but also for the variety of their characters and the powerful manifestation of the Spirit of God in many of the meetings. Lorenzo Dow, in his Journal, relates an instance of Mr. Mitchell's power in the pulpit, which occurred at a quarterly meeting. His preaching produced such an effect that none of the usual ecclesiastical business of these occasions could be transacted; but the entire time was spent in public exercises and direct effort for the salvation of souls. When he began to exhort, a trembling commenced among the unconverted; first one, then another, fell from their seats, and began to cry for mercy. The influence spread till the cry became general; and for eleven hours there was no cessation of the loud cries and supplications of that smitten assembly. The wail of agony and the almost despairing cry for mercy, were not unfrequently changed into the shout of victory and the song of triumph on that memorable occasion. The most abandoned, profligate, and wicked men,—the cavilling, sceptical deist, the bold blaspheming atheist, and the brawling Universalist,—were alike humbled to the foot of the cross; and by the power of divine grace were at length renewed and clothed in their right mind. Many and bright stars, which now stud the crown of the devoted itinerant, were gathered here. When the two years of Mr. Mitchell were completed, in 1800, Vermont numbered six circuits, and a membership of one thousand and ninety-five. Truly God, in a short time, had accomplished a great work. Mr. Mitchell subsequently located and moved to the State of Illinois, where he finished his course in peace.

But let us return to the experience of the subject of our narrative. His first permanent religious impressions were made by the conversations of the pious Methodist woman—"mother in Israel"—already noticed. She perceived his promising talents and strong moral susceptibilities, and devoted herself to the task of leading him to God. Her mind was deeply impressed with the conviction that he would be called to important services in the Church of God, and she laboured the more earnestly to effect his salvation. She conversed with him frequently, earnestly, and often tearfully, on the interests of his soul; and succeeded at last in awakening in his mind a deep concern for his spiritual safety. All honour to this faithful, noble-hearted Christian woman.* She

* Her name was Bushnell. She had previously resided in Canaan, one of the north-western towns of Connecticut. Educated

was jealous for the cause of God, and yearned for the salvation of a soul that was lost. But little did she know how high an honour God was putting upon her, in making her the chief instrument in the conversion of one who was to win many souls to Christ, and become one of the great lights of the Church and the world.

During the first six months of the work of grace that was spreading through the region, young Hedding attended the meetings, but obstinately resisted the strivings of the Holy Ghost. This devoted woman however had singled him out as a special subject of prayer, and followed him with persevering effort till the great end was attained. One Sabbath-day after

in the Calvinistic faith, and accustomed to hear *Calvinism* preached, her mind had become perplexed and bewildered with regard to religious truth. Long perplexed and tried, without obtaining any relief, she had come to the conclusion that she was one of the *reprobates*. This often occasioned her great distress of mind. At length she heard that a Methodist preacher was to preach in her neighbourhood. This was the first time she had ever heard of such a people, and out of curiosity went to hear the novel preacher. The expectation of deriving any spiritual advantage from his ministry was furthest from her thoughts. He commenced the exercises by announcing and then singing the hymn beginning,—

"Come, sinners, to the gospel feast,
Let *every* soul be Jesus' guest;
Ye need not *one* be left behind,
For God hath bidden *all mankind.*"

It was a new but glorious doctrine to her. She said to herself,— "Can this be true? Has Christ indeed invited all mankind? Then *I*, even *I*, who have been so long buffeted by Satan, may come. I will come now." From that moment she sought salvation through the blood of the Lamb, and soon rejoiced as one of the *chosen* of the Lord. She was a woman highly gifted, and of deep and consistent piety.

he had been reading in meeting, this pious woman, when the congregation had separated, addressed him with such an earnest exhortation that his heart was deeply affected; and as he journeyed homeward he turned into a grove, and kneeled down by a large tree, and covenanted with God to cease from his follies and sins, to part with all his idols, and to devote himself sincerely and earnestly, and at any and every cost God might require, to the great work of his soul's salvation. Over fifty years after, and but a short time before he was gathered to his fathers, referring to this event, he said to the writer,—"In that hour I solemnly made a dedication of myself to God. I laid my all—soul, body, goods, and all—for time and for eternity, upon the altar, and I have never, *never* taken them back." He did not then, however, find relief aside from the conscious satisfaction of having done his duty; nor did he receive any satisfactory evidences of his acceptance with God. "This" said he, "was the first time in my life that I remember to have had the full consent of my will to part with all my sins for Christ's sake. My associates, hitherto, had been chiefly those who were fond of pleasure and mirth, and in their amusements I took special delight. Several times before, I seemed willing to give up everything except these social pleasures, but never until now while kneeling in the grove had this great idol of my heart been surrendered."

Not long after this, he heard a sermon from Joseph

Mitchell. It was a discourse of remarkable power, and disclosed to him, in a manner he had never before perceived, the exceeding sinfulness of sin, and the peril of the unrenewed soul. He was seized with unutterable anguish, and for several weeks sought God with strong cries and tears, night and day. "I was so overwhelmed," says he, "that I could not refrain from crying aloud. I could not breathe without an expression of anguish. Though I had long prided myself upon being perfectly fortified against childish feelings and tears, yet for six weeks I could not bear religious conversation or a prayer, nor could I read the Bible or any religious book, without being melted into tenderness and pouring out a flood of tears." In six weeks the itinerant evangelist came around again, and preached in the house where the youthful penitent had been accustomed to read the sermons of Wesley. After preaching, a class-meeting was held by the preacher, as usual, and young Hedding remained in the class. As the meeting was about being closed the preacher, perceiving the great distress of his mind, proposed special prayer in his behalf. The man of God and the pious cottagers bowed around him, and continued in supplication until God in great mercy spoke peace to his soul. His burden of guilt was removed, his conscience was now at rest, and peace and joy sprung up in his hitherto troubled soul. This was on the 27th of December, 1798; and on that very day his name was enrolled as a probationer in the Methodist Episcopal Church.

He appears not to have received at this time the witness of the Spirit to his adoption. Though he enjoyed peace, this great blessing was still wanting in order to the fulness of his joy. On this point he himself says,—"About six weeks after the time when I felt the burden of guilt removed from my conscience, during a conversation with Mr. Mitchell on the witness of the Spirit, the light of the Spirit broke in upon my mind, as clear and perceptible to me as the shining of the sun when it comes from behind a cloud, testifying that I was born of God. Then my heart was filled with joy and my mouth with praise.

'Jesus all the day long was my joy and my song.'

For several weeks after this, not a doubt, nor a fear, nor a moment's uncertainty clouded my spirit. Satan was not permitted to tempt me. It seemed as if the old adversary himself was chained, and my whole soul was love, and my whole time was employed in prayer and praise. As an evidence how completely the thoughts of religion occupied my mind and affected my conduct, it may be stated that during the winter I went to live with a man who resided in the town, and was distinguished for his knowledge of arithmetic,* that I might have a better opportunity of studying this branch of education; but my mind while under conviction, and after my conversion, and

* The possession of any competent knowledge of arithmetic, at that day, was more uncommon in the community than the mastery of the highest mathematical calculus at the present.

especially when I had received the witness of the Spirit, was so carried away by the all-absorbing power of divine grace, that I could give no attention to mathematics, but was wholly engaged in studying the Bible, learning religious hymns, and in the exercise of devotion. I who used to be sorry that I had a soul, and regret that I had been born into the world, continually rejoiced that I had been born to be born again."

The mathematician with whom he had gone to study was soon converted in a most striking and powerful manner. He was what would generally be called a moral man, but was proud and self-confident, and with reference to religion to all appearance thoroughly hardened and unfeeling. The power of God now got hold upon him; he went for some weeks with his head bowed down, and his countenance the picture of sadness and melancholy. He said little to any one about the state of his mind, till at length, at a prayer meeting, his feelings overcame him. He turned pale, his frame shook like an aspen leaf, and his soul seemed rent with contending emotions. At length he cried aloud and fell to the floor. In the greatest agony he cried out, "I am going to hell! I am going to hell!" He continued to cry out till he became almost exhausted. The people bade him look to Jesus the great Saviour, and wrestled mightily with God in his behalf. At length he was heard to murmur in a faint voice,—"Christ died for me." Then in a higher tone he repeated,—"He died for me;" and instantly sprung upon his feet and shouted aloud,—

"My sins are all forgiven; Christ *has* died for me. Glory to God in the highest!" Sudden and violent as was the transition of this man from sin to grace, his course thenceforward, for over forty years, and until he went up at the call of his Lord to receive the reward of the faithful, afforded the best possible evidence of the soundness of his conversion and the thoroughness of the work of grace in his heart.

We have now followed the subject of our memoir through his youthful career, and noted the various causes that combined to give peculiar development to his intellectual and religious character. We find him now a soundly-converted and deeply-devoted young man,—just about entering upon that career of toil and self-sacrifice, and yet of extended and honourable usefulness, which was continued through the lapse of more than half a century, and made his name immortal in the annals of the Church of God. It is well then to pause for a moment and take a brief survey of the special and signal agencies that deserve special recognition. Throughout, we cannot fail to see that God, by his gracious providence, was preparing a chosen vessel to bear the messages of his grace to dying men. Subjected to the hard labour of a new farm, and accustomed to the privations and dangers of frontier life, he acquired not only a hardy and vigorous constitution,—and, in fact, an almost gigantic physical development, being over six feet in height, and of fine manly proportions throughout,—but that daring of spirit, that ingenuity in overcoming obstacles and meeting emergencies, that power of endurance, and that indomitable energy and force of character, that were indispensable in the work for which Divine Providence was preparing him. No schools of human nor of divine learning could have supplied anything that would have answered as a substitute. He might have been possessed of the profoundest learning and the richest graces, but still, without this physical and mental adaptation he would have been inadequate to such labours and privations. He would most likely, as hundreds have done, have become discouraged and failed, or broken down in his work and gone to a premature grave.

We have also noticed the early effects of a mother's religious teaching in planting the seeds of religious truth in his young heart, and leaving there the ineffaceable conviction of religious duty. Then, too, stand worthy of notice the providential circumstances that gave him access to the ablest productions of John Wesley, Fletcher, and the other fathers of Methodism, when hardly any other books could be had to gratify his taste for reading. His controversies with sceptics and fatalists not only sharpened his logical powers, but led him to study thoroughly the great principles of the Wesleyan theology. His own mental conflicts, no less than the impulses of a mind naturally inquisitive, and possessed of great powers of reason and analysis, led him to survey, step by step, every foundation-stone in the great temple of the Christian faith. While all this was going on silently in his own mind, the necessity, in some sort, that was laid upon him to become the reader in the Sabbath convocations, not only developed his talents, and habituated him to their exercise in the presence of an assembly, but also proved an additional incitement to a more thorough mastery of the great teachings of revealed truth. Next comes the noble mother in Israel, illustrating by her life the practical beauty of religion, richly endowed with the wisdom that cometh down from God, breathing holy counsels into the heart of the young man, and sending up to heaven faithful prayers for his salvation. And then, when the way was all prepared, the flaming herald of the cross appears. He is sent by Heaven. His mission is in demonstration of the Spirit. The dry bones in the valley of death live. It is now that the mental discipline, the knowledge, and the doctrinal theories of the young man received their crowning glory in the sound and manifest renewal of his heart. Such was the school in which God prepared him for his great work. How wisely adapted were the agencies to the end they were designed to accomplish!

4

CHAPTER II.

COMMENCES HIS ITINERANT CAREER.

General Conviction of the People—Public Exercises—Talents and Graces developed by the Methodist Economy—Exercises of his Mind with reference to the Ministry—Receives an Exhorter's License—Holds Meetings—Lorenzo Dow—Leaves his Circuit—Young Hedding called out to succeed him—His Labours—Rowdies frightened—A Furious Bully—A Brother checked—Perplexed about his Duty—His First Sermon—The Question solved—Subsequent joyful Experience—The Retrospect—Called out by the Elder—Shadrach Bostwick—Admitted on Trial in the New-York Conference—His Companions—The Church—Circuits and Circuit Labours—Primitive Presiding Elders' Districts—Motives of Human Action—These Men and their Work—The Standard-Bearers in the New-York Conference—Appointed to Plattsburgh—The Circuit—Discouragements—His Colleague—His Studies—Thoroughness of his Investigations—An Illustration—Abundant in Labours—New Ground broken up—Still Another—Closes the Conference Year.

Very soon after his conversion, the conviction became very general among the people that God would in due time thrust the young convert out into the ministry. No doubt the subject presented itself to his own mind also, but it was not in the form of a distinct and unequivocal call from God. But his heart was too deeply engaged in the great work that was progressing for him to remain inactive. Soon after his conversion, he began to pray and to exhort in public.

The economy of the Methodist Church was well calculated to develop the talents of such young men. It trained them not in seminaries and colleges, but in the field of action. However indispensable the former have become in a later age—an age of more refinement and of more general intelligence—the latter was the only one that could meet the emergencies of those times. First, the simple narration of Christian experience—the tale of spiritual conflicts and triumphs, of sorrows and heavenly joys, uttered weekly among sympathizing and encouraging brethren in the class room; then the exercise of prayer in the social assembly, often gathered to mingle in songs of praise and fervent intercessions at the mercy-seat; next the exhortation in the public assembly; and finally, the ministration of the word to assemblies, convened often in private houses, rustic in their character, but hungering for the bread of life—such a training kept alive the holy fire in the heart, and at the same time developed that ready and effective practical talent admirably adapted to the times.

Such was the school in which young Hedding was being trained for the great work of God in which he was afterward to take so conspicuous a part. At first his own convictions in relation to his duty were not clear; and he determined that nothing should induce him to enter the ministry before he was clearly convinced that he was called by God to the work. The preachers sometimes told him it was his duty to preach, and once, at a quarterly conference, a license was offered him; but he uniformly replied that he was not satisfied that God had called him, and he was not willing to run before he was sent. His views of the great responsibilities of the minister's calling, and the necessity for eminent qualifications, as well as a special call from God himself for the work, and, withal, his views of personal unfitness, made him unwilling to believe it his duty whenever the subject was presented to him. Still he could not divest his mind of the impression that he ought to preach, and waited for God to make known to him his duty in such a manner as would remove all doubts. In the mean time he was constantly, and with absorbing interest, engaged in the study of the Bible. He continued also to exercise his talents in public prayer and exhortation as opportunity offered. The love of Christ fired his heart, and his fine and already somewhat exercised talents were often employed with powerful effect.

He had hardly been admitted into full membership in the Church, before he was persuaded by his brethren to receive an "exhorter's license." Now also he began to extend his labours beyond his own neighbourhood, and to visit the regions round about, labouring to persuade sinners to be reconciled to God. Sometimes he was induced to appoint meetings and conduct them himself; but most generally he accompanied or met the circuit preacher at his appointments, and delivered an exhortation at the close of the sermon. His word was often made the power of God in quickening and saving souls; and his brethren, especially the faithful ministers of Christ, rejoiced at the evidence of his growing gifts and graces.

At the conference in 1799 the Essex Circuit was

formed, and the eccentric Lorenzo Dow, then in the second year of his itinerant ministry, was appointed to labour upon it. The circuit was very large, and spread over a rough and wild country. It embraced the whole tract of country lying between Lake Champlain and the Green Mountains, and extending from the Onion River in Vermont northward some twenty or thirty miles into Canada. For a few months Dow travelled and laboured with incredible diligence, and his ministry was attended with great success; but at the end of this period he suddenly left his work. Imagining that he had received a special and divine mission to preach in Ireland, he immediately set sail for that country. All eyes were now turned upon the young exhorter as a necessary supply for the vacancy. Under great constraint, and in view of the necessities of the work, he at length consented, and, in the month of November, when but little over nineteen years of age, and within less than a year from the time of his conversion, went to the circuit. His labours here were of the most arduous character. It required not less than three hundred miles' travel to complete one round upon the circuit, which occupied four weeks. During this time he held regularly three meetings on the Sabbath, and met class at the close of each; and at least one, often two, on each day of the week, besides frequent prayer meetings. During this period young Hedding, being only an exhorter, conscientiously avoided the show or fact of preaching. He says of himself, that "instead of taking a text I delivered an exhortation usually about an hour long." His word was in demonstration of the Spirit and with power; revivals broke out, the work of God moved forward in every direction, "and much people was added to the Lord." It was now fully evident that he was a chosen vessel unto God to bear his name before the people and the Church. Having filled the time of his engagement, he returned home, and renewed his former occupation upon the farm.

While upon the circuit he encountered much opposition from the emissaries of Satan, who were especially busy whenever the attention of the people was powerfully awakened to the concerns of the soul. At one time, while holding an evening meeting in Canada, there came a number of young men who had banded together to break up the meeting. But the power of God got hold upon them; they became terribly frightened, and all of them, except one, fled with precipitation from the house. He was so mightily wrought upon that he had not power to go, and at length fell upon the floor, crying aloud for mercy. He drew out a large club he had concealed beneath his overcoat, and confessed with shame and horror the guilty intentions with which he and his comrades had come to the meeting. Then he besought the people to pray for him, for he was trembling over the very abyss of hell. The people prayed earnestly for his salvation; and that very night God spoke peace to his soul in so powerful and wonderful a manner that he shouted aloud, and went to his home praising God.

At another place in Canada, after Mr. Hedding had delivered his message, a young exhorter addressed the people. Two young men in the congregation were disorderly and disturbed the meeting, and were deservedly rebuked by the speaker. At the close of the public service, as the class remained, Mr. Hedding observed that the two young men remained in the house, and, believing that they tarried only for mischief, he desired the class to retire into another room. The young men went outside the door; but, unknown to those within, waited till the class-meeting was dismissed. As the exhorter, who was somewhat in advance of Mr. Hedding, stepped out of the door, one of them struck him and knocked him to the ground, and as he attempted to rise repeated the blow with like effect. Mr. Hedding then grasped the prostrate young man and drew him into the house, while the people closed in between him and his assaulter and prevented the repetition of the blows. The foiled bully then seemed to be enraged beyond all bounds. He ran out some twenty or thirty feet from the house, jumped up and down, and smote his fists together with great violence, cursed, swore, and blasphemed, and defied any one there to come out and fight with him. At that moment Mr. Hedding perceived a class-leader, formerly a noted boxer, but since powerfully converted, and now a real Christian, for a moment, under the great provocation, so far forgetting himself as to slip off his coat and prepare for a fight. He calmly laid his hand upon him and said:

"Brother, put on your coat. It won't do to fight. You are a Christian; and it is the Sabbath-day." The bully, however, showed himself too cowardly to stand even the appearance of an attack upon himself, and slunk away. Soon after the civil authorities took him up and fined him on five several indictments, viz.: for breaking the Sabbath, breaking the peace, assault and battery, cursing the king, and profane swearing.

Distrust of himself and of his capabilities was a prominent characteristic of Mr. Hedding in his early history, as well as in his subsequent career. He thus speaks of the embarrassment he felt when first thrust out into the work: "Thus far I had often been impressed with a belief that some time it would be my duty to preach, but believed that the time had not yet arrived for me to commence so great a work. I felt great reluctance to commence travelling as an exhorter, lest it should seem to others that I was too forward, and lest, on account of my youth and want of knowledge, I should hurt instead of helping the cause of Christ, which I so dearly loved. However, the solicitude of some of the preachers, the fewness of the labourers in the Lord's vineyard, and my strong desire for the salvation of mankind, led me to consent to the request of my brethren, and do what little I could in warning sinners to flee from the wrath to come." When he returned home from his engagement on Essex Circuit he seems not yet to have been fully satisfied in his own mind as to the line of duty.

He had never preached; that is, he had not yet discoursed from a text, though he had undoubtedly expounded the Scriptures in his exhortations.

His mode of reasoning within himself on the subject of his call to the ministry was thus expressed:—"I have no desire to be a preacher unless God require it. If he require it, he will let me know it. If he does not let me know it, he will never blame me for not preaching."

In this perplexed and doubtful state of mind he continued till Saturday, March 25, 1800. On that day, as he was engaged in his daily labour and thinking of an appointment he had as an exhorter, on the following day, the conviction that he ought to preach at that meeting, and the text he should use, and the manner in which he should preach, were so clearly impressed on his mind that he dared not refuse. He yielded to the impression, and preached with such comfort to his own mind, such enlargement of soul, and such manifest approval of the Divine Spirit, that from that time he never doubted but that he was called to the work of the ministry.*

From this time forth his course was determined.

* The author of the "Troy Conference Miscellany," Rev. Stephen Parks, says: "A humble cottage on the west side of Cumberland Head, about two miles from the village of Plattsburgh, has been pointed out to the writer as the place where this distinguished servant of God preached his first sermon." We incline to think this was his first "exhortation" after his entrance upon his labours on Essex Circuit, in 1799, and not his "first sermon;" but we are not certain.

The scruples which so strongly marked the conscien tiousness of the young man were now all removed. He was soon regularly licensed as a local preacher—no one doubting but that God had appointed him to the work of the ministry.

Up to this period his religious experience had been of a very clear and satisfactory character. He had preserved, from the time when first the Holy Spirit bore witness with his that he was born of God, the clear and indubitable evidence of his acceptance in the Beloved; so clear, indeed, that it had not been obscured by a doubt or a fear. The current of his religious feeling was deep, strong, and constant; like that of the mighty river, unaffected by drenching rains or withering droughts, it moved onward, with steady flow, to the great ocean where all his thoughts and feelings centred. But after his course for the ministry had been fully determined upon, and he had resolved to brave every hardship and privation that he might preach Christ and him crucified, there was a perceptible increase of his peace and joy. Amid the hard labour incident to a settlement in a new country, his joys literally abounded. The following passage will give us a glimpse of the state of his mind:—

"During the summer of 1800," says he, "I was engaged in some work a mile or two back in the woods, and, as I was often accustomed to do, kneeled down and prayed. My soul was so filled with the love of God, and I became so exceedingly happy, that I shouted the praise of God to the height of my voice. It seemed to me that I could not possibly breathe unless I shouted. For half an hour I made the woods ring with my loud shouts of glory to God in the highest."

Such were the feelings with which his heart overflowed when once the great question of duty had been settled. Scarcely less interesting were the feelings with which he contemplated his course when he viewed, in retrospect, the many years and severe hardships of his ministerial career. Said he: "Often the flesh has complained, my spirit has sunk within me, and, amid the privations, toils, and hardships of an itinerant life, worldly interests have pleaded for some other employment. But there has been a voice sounding continually in my soul, 'Woe is me if I preach not the gospel.' And however poorly I have performed the work for these many years, since the time I believed that God had called me to preach, it has been my delight to declare his message to dying men. And had I my life to live over again, and the choice of all the stations which earth could proffer, I would prefer to be a faithful, acceptable, and useful itinerant minister of the gospel of the blessed God."

Having been licensed as a local preacher, he continued to preach in his own and in neighbouring places during the summer of 1800. This position he was not permitted long to occupy, for in the ensuing fall he was called out by the Rev. Shadrach Bostwick, who had succeeded Sylvester Hutchinson as presiding elder of the district, to labour upon a circuit. On the 15th of November he commenced his itinerant career. At first he was placed upon the Plattsburgh Circuit, on the west side of Lake Champlain. Here he had his early friend and spiritual guide, Rev. Joseph Mitchell, as his colleague and superintendent. His labours on this circuit were blessed to the awakening and conversion of many souls. But his stay was short; for at the end of six weeks the exigences of the work required his removal to Cambridge Circuit, where one of the preachers had broken down. Here he had the Rev. Ebenezer Stevens as his colleague. His preaching was attended with some measure of success, and he continued to labour till the ensuing conference.

To the wise counsels, the kind care, and holy example of his presiding elder, the young itinerant was greatly indebted. Shadrach Bostwick was, in every respect, such a man as the young minister, in that early day, might look up to for counsel, and whose example he might safely imitate. He was one of "God's noblemen,"—a prince and a great man in our Israel. "He was a glorious man," said Bishop Hedding. He had been educated for a physician; and his talents were of a commanding order that would have secured him eminence in any department of life. As a preacher he stood foremost in rank, and through all the extensive regions of his labours he was famous for the intellectual and evangelical power of his sermons. His discourses were systematic, profound, luminous, and often overwhelming; his piety was deep and pure; his manners were dignified and amiable. Hundreds will rise up and call him blessed in the final day. His example and talents could not but fire the hearts and stimulate the energies of his young preachers. He had entered the travelling ministry in 1791, and his labours extended over Delaware, Maryland, New-Jersey, New-York, Connecticut, Massachusetts, and Ohio. He was eminently a pioneer. In 1803 he passed to the Western Reserve, in northeastern Ohio, then a remote settlement on the western frontier. Here he formed the first circuit; it extended through the sparse settlements, and required extraordinary labours and sacrifices. The roads he travelled were "Indian trails," and his guide-posts were marks on the trees. Indomitable as he was in energy of character, he was, nevertheless, often foiled in his winter travels by impassable roads and swollen torrents, over which there were no bridges. Amid such privations and toils he laid the foundation of Methodism in that fine region, and its healthiness to the present day attests the skill and faithfulness of the early workman. In 1805 he found it necessary to desist from travelling on account of domestic circumstances. He accordingly, after fourteen years' service, located and resumed the practice of medicine. Such were the men among whom young Hedding breathed the vital air of Methodism, and such the spirit that animated them.

On the 16th of June, 1801, Mr. Hedding was

admitted by the New-York Annual Conference on probation in the travelling connexion. Of the *fifty-five*, mostly young men, who that year entered the travelling ministry, but *two* survived him in that relation, and both of them had retired from effective service. The others, or most of them, long since ceased from their labours and entered upon their reward. Indeed, it is a striking commentary upon the privations and labours of that early period, that *twenty-nine* of the fifty-five retired from the ministry within the short period of ten years. It is painful to reflect how much talent has been lost to the Church, at every period of her history, in consequence of the severity of the labour and the insufficiency of the support.

At that period there were but eight annual conferences, three hundred and seven preachers, and seventy two thousand eight hundred and seventy-four members in our whole American connexion. The circuits were large, often requiring from three to five hundred miles to complete one round, and this round was to be completed in from two to six weeks, during which a sermon was to be preached and a class met daily; and often three sermons and three classes to be attended on the Sabbath. The journeys, too, were performed, not upon steamboats and railroads, nor yet in good carriages and by easy stages upon turnpikes; but on horseback, through rough and miry ways, and through wildernesses where no road as yet had been cast up. Rivers and swamps were to be forded. Nor could the journey be delayed. On, on, must the itinerant press his way, through the drenching rains of summer, the chilling sleet of spring or autumn, and the driving blasts or piercing cold of winter; and often amid perils, weariness, hunger, and almost nakedness, carrying the bread of life to the lost and perishing. And then, when the day of toil was ended, in the creviced hut of the frontier settler the weary itinerant, among those of kindred hearts and sympathies, found a cordial though humble place of repose. The subject of this memoir said that he had often lodged in log-houses where the stars could be seen through the roof above him, and that again and again, when he awoke in the morning, he has found the bed on which he slept covered with snow.

But this was not all. The people, though willing, were poor, and the support was often inadequate to meet the *necessities* of even a single man; but woe to the man and the family that were dependent for a livelihood upon the compensation received for such labours as these. And yet these were men—men sensible to suffering and want—men of tender sympathies for wives and children! And, alas! many of them broke down in the work and went early to their reward; others were compelled to retire from it; but here and there one of iron constitution and abiding faith toiled on, till, like our own Hedding, full of years and of faith, he has been gathered to those that had gone before. Such were the toils, hardships, and privations endured by our fathers in transforming the waste wilderness into a delightful vineyard, and mak ing it as the garden of God.

Nor was the presiding eldership any sinecure in those early days any more than now. The district which embraced the Essex Circuit, when Mr. Hedding was employed upon it, was of gigantic proportions. It embraced New-York city, the whole of Long Island, and extended northward, embracing the whole territory having the Connecticut River on the east and Hudson River and Lake Champlain on the west, and stretching far into Canada. In fact, it embraced nearly the whole territory now included within three annual conferences. This immense district was then travelled by Sylvester Hutchinson. He was a man of burning zeal and of indomitable energy. Mounted upon his favourite horse, he would ride through the entire extent of his district once each three months, visiting each circuit, and invariably filling all his numerous appointments. His voice rung like a trumpet's blast; and with words of fire, and in powerful demonstration of the Spirit, he preached Christ Jesus.

Into the fellowship of this noble company we have seen the subject of our memoir duly installed. The conference held its session in the old John-street Church, and Bishop Whatcoat presided over the deliberations of the body. It was a time of great interest to the young preacher. Never before had he seen so large a body of ministers gathered together. Many of them were already renowned for their talents and labours. There was Freeborn Garrettson, who was regarded as the apostle of Methodism within the bounds of the conference; a true Christian gentleman, a man of great influence in the connexion, and one whose life and labours are permanently interwoven with the early history of the Church. There was Daniel Ostrander,—a man of clear head and unbending integrity, a skilful debater, a logical sermonizer, an able preacher, and a godly man. There, too, was Thomas Morrell—formerly an officer in the revolutionary army, but now still more successful in leading the sacramental host of God's elect on to victory and heaven; a man of great talents and learning, and also of burning zeal in the cause of God. There also was John M'Claskey, a bold, brave, heroic man; wherever he went overwhelming power attended his proclamation of the truth. In that conference was Michael Coate,—remarkably prepossessing in his personal appearance, refined and attractive in his manners, easy and simple in his address, and justly ranked among the very best and most successful preachers of the day. Beginning to exhort the very night that God brought deliverance to his captive soul, in 1794, he continued through twenty years of incessant travels and labours sounding abroad the word of life, spreading his labours over vast regions, and founding societies and churches almost without number. There, too, was the eccentric Billy Hibbard,—a great wit, a man of shrewd parts, and also of great good sense; the inveterate and wily foe of

Calvinism, but a devoted and useful servant of Christ. There too was John Wilson, a thorough scholar, and who often manifested extraordinary energy, and was attended with peculiar unction in his pulpit exercises. Among that galaxy, too, was Samuel Merwin, whose transcendent eloquence for a long period chained the most crowded audiences in Philadelphia, Boston, and New-York. Many others also were there, scarcely inferior either in talents or success: such men were Aaron Hunt, and William Thatcher, and Mitchell, and Bostwick, and Brodhead, and Moriarty, and Chichester,—men known and honoured in the Church of God. Such were the men among whom Mr. Hedding was now introduced, and with whom he was to become a co-worker in spreading the knowledge of Christ. To be with them, and not be inspired by the same spirit that animated them, would have been a sure evidence of a want of appreciation of the nature of the work, and an unfitness for it. But to stand up as an equal among them, nay, to become an acknowledged leader among them, required an intellect and attainments of no ordinary grade.

At the close of this session of the conference, Mr. Hedding received his first appointment from conference, which was to the Plattsburgh Circuit. Here he had the Rev. Elijah Chichester for his senior preacher, a man eminently adapted to give to the young preacher judicious counsels, and to influence him by the purest and best example. The circuit lay upon the west side of Lake Champlain, extending from Ticonderoga on the south nearly to St. John's, in Canada, and from the shores of the lake to the wilderness and mountains of the west. Here, in this new and sparsely-settled country, he endured more than it is possible for us to describe of the toils and privations of the early itinerants. They had to travel over new and miry roads, and often their way to the remote settlements lay through unbroken and almost pathless forests. They had to face the piercing blasts of the cold winter, and to ford streams swollen by freshets and chilled by melting snows. They were often compelled to lodge in log-houses, whose creviced walls and roofs scarcely protected them from the driving winds, falling rain, or snow. A complete journey round the circuit was performed in each month. This required a travel of three hundred miles, and they were accustomed to preach at least once on each week-day, and three times on the Sabbath, besides meeting classes and attending prayer meetings.

At first, the prospects on the circuit were exceedingly discouraging. "For a season," said he, "we had hard times, as it respects religious things, and but little success seemed to attend our labours. Many of the members had backslidden, and it was necessary to expel some of them from the Church, so that everything wore a most discouraging aspect. Still we continued our labours with unabated zeal, and in the midst of our gloom confidently looked for an outpouring of the Spirit. In this we were not disappointed. The great Head of the Church encouraged us, by giving us in the latter part of the year a plentiful harvest. Revivals occurred at almost every appointment on the circuit; and many that were converted that year persevered for years, and at length died in the triumphs of faith."

Of his colleague during this year Mr. Hedding says: "Though he was a man of moderate learning, he had a deep understanding and a sharp and penetrating mind. What little he had time to read, he read and digested to the best advantage. He was a man of strict, upright moral life and conversation, of deep religious experience, was much in prayer, and delighted in heavenly meditations. He was a preacher of great industry, and faithful in every part of his duty. He was not what would be called a polished or popular preacher, but he was a good sermonizer, and preached and exhorted with great energy and success; for the Holy Ghost accompanied his word, and set it home on the hearts of the people. When we met, which was only occasionally, on the circuit, he manifested great kindness to me, gave me good counsel, and assisted me, as far as he was able to do, in my studies."

The difficulties and embarrassments in the way of study, at this early day, were very great to a Methodist preacher. His almost daily public labours, the long and often toilsome rides between his appointments, the great scarcity and high price of books, the difficulty of obtaining suitable accommodations for study, and the almost utter impossibility of obtaining any adequate help by way of instruction, were some of the difficulties that were to be encountered and overcome by him who would show himself to be a workman that needed not to be ashamed. With these difficulties Mr. Hedding resolutely grappled. The woods were often his study; the Bible, and "that elder scripture," also written with God's own hand, were the great text-books from which he drew forth the treasures of knowledge and truth. "I was glad," says he, "during the summer, to get into the woods, and find an hour or two to read my Bible and some other religious books that I could carry in my saddle-bags. In the winter, I was equally glad to get the same privilege by the fireside in a small log-cabin of but one room, and the fire surrounded by a family of children."

The peculiar cast of Mr. Hedding's mind, and the thoroughness with which he prosecuted his studies, even under his numerous disadvantages, may be illustrated by the following incident, which he himself related: "During that year I read Bishop Watson's Apology for the Bible. In his answers to Paine, I came to a place where Paine objects to a supposed contradiction in the Bible, namely, that Matthew says, chapter i, verse 16, 'Jacob begat Joseph the husband of Mary,' while Luke says, chapter iii, verse 23, 'Joseph was the son of Heli.' This Paine claimed to be an irreconcilable contradiction. On coming to the place in Watson, I found he did not know how to answer it, but slipped over it without giving a satisfactory solution. And not knowing how to answer it myself, I was troubled in spirit for several weeks. But, on coming to a friend's house in Ticonderoga, I found a copy of Mr. Wesley's Notes on the New Testament. I flew to the passage for an explanation of the difficulty; and here I found that Joseph was the son-in-law of Heli. I then perceived that Heli was Mary's father, and Jacob was Joseph's, and at once the difficulty vanished from my mind, and my spirit rejoiced." To remove any additional difficulty that may spring up in the mind of the reader in relation to calling Joseph, who was only the son-in-law, "the son of Heli," we have only to observe the fact that the Jews never permitted women to enter into their genealogical tables; and also that whenever a family-line happened to end with a daughter, instead of naming her in the genealogy, they inserted the name of her husband as the *son* of him who was, in reality, only his *father-in-law.** Joseph was considered, then, according to law, or, at least, allowed custom, to be the *son* of Heli. Therefore, in tracing the genealogy of Jesus through his maternal line, Luke pursued only the custom of the Jews when he called Joseph the son of Heli. Indeed, a second instance to the same effect occurs in Luke's genealogy, when, in verse twenty-seven, he calls Salathiel "the son of Neri," when he was actually the son of Jechonias, and only the *son-in-law* of Neri.

* See Adam Clarke, *in loco.*

It was thus, step by step, that young Hedding plodded his way along, using his little leisure and his few books to the best possible advantage. Whenever he encountered a difficulty, he ceased not to grapple with it till it was fully overcome; nor did he lay down a book until its contents had been thoroughly mastered, and, it will be scarcely too much to say, permanently stored away in his own mind.

He was not less ardent in his labours than in his studies. No man could surpass him in the amount of his labour, nor yet in the ardency with which it was performed. Not only was he ready to "enter every open door," but he was ready also to "lift the latch" in new places, to see if God would not open the door for the proclamation of the gospel to the poor and needy. Thus was he busily engaged in not only gathering into classes, and seeking to preserve those already converted, but constantly endeavouring to push on to "regions beyond."

The colleague of Mr. Hedding, going from one of his appointments to another, passed through a neighbourhood where they had not been accustomed to preach, and where, in fact, up to this time, there had been no preaching from any denomination. In the true spirit of his evangelical mission, he felt a desire to do something for the people. His mind was powerfully impressed with the conviction that God had a work for them to do there; but he knew no one in the place. He had just passed a house, when his mind was impressed to go back and inquire if they would allow preaching there. He returned, obtained the ready consent of the occupants, and left an appointment for Mr. Hedding in two weeks, his own appointments calling him to a distant part of the circuit. True to the time, the young itinerant hero appeared upon the new field of battle. It was a hot contest. The people were deeply affected. The work of the Lord broke out at the very first meeting; it swept with almost resistless power through the entire neighbourhood, and nearly all the inhabitants were converted to God. The whole place seemed to undergo an entire moral renovation. A society was organized, classes were formed, and regular preaching established. A good society still exists there; and for more than half a century the word of God has been preached in their midst.

Another incident, connected with the preceding, shows not only the pioneer character of the ministry, but also of the membership in those days. A young man, from a place several miles distant, was teaching the neighbourhood school at the time of this revival, and became one of its most clear and hopeful subjects. Soon after, he returned to his father's house, and reported what great things the Lord had done for him and for the people where he had been. He obtained his father's consent, and then invited the circuit preachers to visit and preach in that place also. Here too there had been no preaching of any kind up to that time. The preachers, utterly regardless of the weight it added to their already heavy burden, responded to the call and went. The father, mother, brothers, sisters, and many of the neighbours of the young man were soon rejoicing in the pardoning mercy of God, and one of the best societies in all that part of the country was speedily organized.

Such were the agencies by which the work of God multiplied and spread abroad at that early period. In the midst of such glorious labours and victories, with the work of God spreading out in every direction, and new openings for the ministry of the word revealing themselves in every quarter, young Hedding closed the first year of his regular itinerant ministry, by the approaching session of the conference for 1802.

CHAPTER III.

LABOURS ON FLETCHER, BRIDGEWATER, AND HANOVER CIRCUITS.

Does not attend the Conference of 1802—Appointed to Fletcher Circuit—Laban Clark's Description of it—Henry Ryan—Labours and Sufferings—Mode of crossing Rivers—Horse gives out—Walks half round his Circuit—Personal and Ministerial Characteristics—Application to Studies—Stackhouse's History of the Bible—His Colleague—Religious Condition of the People—St. Albans—Disciples of Thomas Paine—Persecutions—Two Young Women whipped—A Novel Scene—Infant Damnation—Anecdotes of Early Methodism—Ashgrove Conference in 1803—Ashgrove Society—Conference Services—Ordained Deacon—Appointed to Bridgewater—Extent of the Circuit—Promising Indications—Dangerously Sick—Effects on the Work—Given over to die—Revives—Attempts to resume his Work—Terrible Attack of Rheumatism—Spiritual Conflicts—Prospect of being a Cripple—Thrice tried—A Bright Example of Christian Charity—Resumes his Labours—Visits Saratoga—Incident on board a Sloop—Conference in 1804—Note to Bishop Asbury—Anecdote of Asbury—Hanover Circuit—Itinerancy of Single Men—Privileges of Study—Revolves his Plan—Studies English Grammar—Mode—Dictionary of the Language—Effects—Subsequent Studies—Successes of the Year.

We were a little before our story in saying in our last chapter that Mr. Hedding closed his first year's itinerant labour by the "*approaching*" session of the conference; for, in fact, he did not attend that session of the conference at all. It was not then as requisite for the young probationer in the conference to attend its sessions as it has now become since the introduction of a literary and theological course, attended with systematic examinations. Young Hedding, therefore, in view of the exigences of the circuit, chose to remain at home and prosecute the work progressing under such glorious auspices.

The session of the conference was held in the city of New-York, and commenced June 1, 1802. After its close, and while yet performing his rounds on the circuit as he had done during the year, Mr. Hedding was notified of his appointment to the Fletcher Circuit. This was the same circuit he had travelled as an exhorter in 1799, its name having been changed the preceding year from Essex to Fletcher. We have already given an outline of it as it was in 1799. The Rev. Laban Clark, in connexion with James Coleman, had been appointed to it in 1801, and he thus describes its form, extent, and the labours it involved. "Our circuit," says he, "was divided into two parts, nearly like a figure 8, containing two weeks' appointments in each, and bringing us together every two weeks; the whole distance about four hundred miles, including all that part of Vermont north of Onion River, and in Lower Canada from Sutton to Missisque Bay, and around the bay to Alsbury and Isle la Motte; embracing about forty appointments for four weeks."* Being a newly-settled country the roads were exceedingly bad, and to reach some portions of the circuit they were compelled to traverse extensive wildernesses, through which there were no roads.

Mr. Hedding had for his co-labourer and his senior in office this year the Rev. Henry Ryan. Of this colleague Mr Hedding says: "He was, in that day, a

* See Memorials of Methodism, Second Series, p. 146.

very pious man, a man of great love for the cause of Christ, and of great zeal in his work as a minister. He was a brave Irishman—a man who laboured as if the judgment thunders were to follow on each sermon. He was sometimes a little overbearing in the administration of discipline; but with that exception, he performed his duties in every part of his work as a minister of Christ as faithfully as any man I ever knew. He was very brotherly and kind to me—often speaking to me in a manner calculated to urge me on to diligence and fidelity in the great work. When we met at the place of intersection in the route of the circuit, he would occasionally salute me with his favourite exhortation: "Drive on, brother! drive on! Drive the devil out of the country! Drive him into the lake and drown him!" The author of the "Memorials of Methodism" says of this remarkable man: "He was characterized by an inextinguishable zeal and unfaltering energy. No difficulty could obstruct his course; he drove over his vast circuits, and still larger districts, preaching continually, and pressing on from one appointment to another. Neither the comforts nor the courtesies of life ever delayed him. In Canada his labours were Herculean; he achieved the work of half a score of men, and was instrumental in scattering the word of life over vast portions of that new country, when few other clergymen dared to venture among its wildernesses and privations. Not only did he labour gigantically, but he also suffered heroically from want, fatigue, bad roads, and the rigorous winters of those high latitudes." Such was the companion with whom Mr. Hedding was to be associated in the labours and privations of the second year of his ministry. He had but little suavity of manner to render himself agreeable to a colleague; but there was a heroism in his daring, and an invincible ardour in his movements that rendered him not altogether unprofitable as an associate.

They often suffered severely both from wet and cold in their journeys. Sometimes, during the wet seasons, they slept in log-huts so open and exposed that there was not a dry spot in them large enough for a bed. Mr. Hedding relates that on one occasion he occupied the same bed with his colleague on a cold winter night in Canada. When they awoke in the morning, they found, to their great surprise, that the feet of his colleague had been frozen while they were asleep. But this did not deter him a moment from his work. One of the greatest obstacles they encountered in travelling round the circuit was the difficulty of crossing the rivers. These rivers were generally without bridges, and often they were compelled to cross them when the waters were high and the current swift, thus exposing themselves to great peril. Sometimes they were ferried over in a canoe, holding their horses by the bridle while they swam; at other times they were compelled first to drive their horses over, and then to get over as they could on floating logs or fallen trees. On one occasion, Mr. Hedding rode his horse while he swam to the opposite side of the river, a distance of thirty or forty rods. But out of all their dangers the Lord delivered them.

Another incident in the labours of this year, which belongs to this connexion, is worthy of record; for while it finely illustrates the remarkable energy and perseverance of Mr. Hedding in prosecuting his labours, it also gives striking evidence of his devotion to the cause of Christ. At one time the travelling was unusually bad even for that country. There had been alternate rains and frosts. The roads were exceedingly rough, and frozen hard; all the pools of standing water were frozen over, but the weight of the horse would cause him to break through at almost every step, and he soon became so lame that it was impossible for him to proceed further. How should his appointments be reached? No one would risk a horse in such perilous travelling. When every other resort failed, the young itinerant, who had now reached the centre of his circuit, shouldered his saddle-bags, left his horse behind, and sallied forth to perform the round upon the northern part of the circuit on foot. In two weeks he actually travelled one hundred and fifty miles. Of this journey he said,—"Frequently I would break through the ice and the frozen mud in the swamps and woods, tearing my boots and keeping my feet wet most of the time; but I persevered, and got round to my appointments at the usual time, preaching once or twice a day with my other accustomed services. I lived through it, but the exposures and hardships of that tour I have never recovered from to this day."

Some of the personal characteristics of Mr. Hedding, at this period, may not be uninteresting to our readers. Raised amid the exposures and labours, and trained to all the hardy habits, of a new country, he possessed unusual physical vigour and hardihood. In physical strength and in power of endurance he was excelled by few, if any, of the young men of his time. Having enjoyed uniform health from his childhood, his constitution, naturally sound, was unimpaired. He was, in height, about six feet, of a large frame, erect and commanding in person. His voice, though by no means unmusical, was unusually sonorous; indeed, such was its volume and power, that, when speaking in the open air, he has often been heard at the distance of a mile. He spoke however with great ease, and with but little physical exhaustion. He was also an excellent singer, and generally led the singing in his congregations. His countenance bore striking evidence of decision and energy blended with meekness and benevolence; and, at the same time, his high, expansive forehead, penetrating eye, and intelligent expression, gave evidence of a high order of intellect. Even at that early day he was looked upon as a man of no ordinary character. His preaching was plain and practical. It exhibited no oratorical display—no transcendent flights of fancy—no succession of beautiful or startling ideas; but his sermons were well studied, and exhibited a rare and symmetrical combination of well-digested ideas. They were delivered with unction, which is, after all, the soul of eloquence, and with power. Upon controversial subjects his fine logical powers were often exercised to good purpose: the prevailing errors of the day—Calvinism, Universalism, and Infidelity—were often made to writhe under the invincible results of his reasoning.

Though abundant in labours, he did not forget or neglect his studies, but was a most diligent student During this year M'Ewen on the Types of Scripture was studied by him; and, at first, he was inclined to follow the example of some of the popular preachers of the day, in adopting his methods of illustration; but in after years he relinquished the practice. His great study, however, during the year, besides the Bible, which was always first, was Stackhouse's History of the Bible, comprising several octavo volumes. He found the work in the house of a friend, borrowed it, and carried it, volume after volume, in his saddle-bags, around the circuit. Every favourable moment for study was seized upon with an avidity that evidenced his thirst for knowledge. This work proved to be of great service to him, and added largely to his stock of Biblical knowledge. So thoroughly was it studied that he ever after retained a critical and ready knowledge of not only the positions taken upon the prominent points discussed, but also the data and the arguments by which those positions were sought to be sustained. The young theologian was, by the blessing of God, training himself manfully for his great work.

Mr. Hedding found his colleague as noble-hearted as he was brave; and they laboured together in great harmony. Indeed, they nobly vied with each other to excel in the abundance and efficiency of their labours Perhaps Mr. Ryan never had a colleague that it was more difficult to lead in these respects. Several very extensive and powerful revivals took place upon the circuit, and many precious souls were gathered into the fold of Christ.

The religious condition of the people, for the most part, was truly deplorable. Within the ample range of the circuit there was only one Congregational minister settled over a small society; and but two Baptist ministers, whose range of labour was also more or less restricted. The result of this destitution was not only great spiritual ignorance, but great moral degradation, and great insensibility to religious truth. Every form of pernicious error would spring up spontaneously in such a soil. The infidel works of Thomas Paine were just then taking the world by storm. They were circulated and read, and multitudes professed to believe their calumnies against God and the Bible. Mr. Hedding says: "When I first went to St. Albans, which was then included in this circuit, in 1799, though it was a considerable village, I could find but two individuals who professed experimental Christianity in the whole village. A large number of the inhabitants—both men and women, young and old—unblushingly professed to be the disciples of Paine. Many of them violently opposed Christianity. They would blackguard the preachers in the streets, and insult them even in their religious meetings. On one occasion a lawyer struck Elijah Sabin with the but of his whip, and knocked him down. At another time, another wrung the nose of Lorenzo Dow. No general revival had taken place at St. Albans previous to this year; but during the year we had a great revival. Infidelity was compelled to flee; and many of the disciples of Paine renounced their infidelity, and became the disciples of Christ." The seed that had been sown amid persecutions and privations then only began to take root. From that time forward the harvest has been growing more and still more abundant. Not only St. Albans, but all the region round about, has witnessed revival after revival, and many a glorious harvest has gladdened the heritage of God. The place where once only *two persons* professing godliness could be found, now holds a respectable position for its religious and benevolent institutions, while infidelity is scarcely known.

These faithful ministers of Jesus Christ, at this period, were not alone in suffering persecution. The faith of their young converts was often most severely tested in the fiery ordeal. The wives of ungodly men and the children of ungodly parents often suffered the most bitter and unrelenting cruelty from those who should have been foremost to aid and encourage them. "Some of the young people who experienced religion were turned out of doors by their parents; some of them were whipped cruelly. *Two young women were so whipped by their father that the blood ran down to their feet; and he then turned them out of doors, and they walked fifteen miles to a Methodist society.* That same father, eight of whose children experienced religion, drove six of them from their home, and continued cruelly to whip two younger boys for the crime of loving and praising God along with the Methodists. He did not, however, succeed in expurgating Methodism from his family, for some of their descendants are now among our wealthy and devoted members in that region."*

One or two other incidents illustrative of the times we shall draw from the same source. The first is from the pen of Abner Chase, one of the early co-labourers of Mr. Hedding, and gives a characteristic view of the annoyances they suffered in their meetings. It was a quarterly meeting, which was held in a large barn, the female part of the congregation occupying the floor, while the men occupied the "hay-mow." "While the prayer meeting on Saturday afternoon," says Mr. Chase, "was progressing in a good spirit, a wagon was driven up, in which was a number of persons of both sexes. They came in high glee, alighted from the wagon, and, after standing a while at the door, and listening to several prayers

* Troy Conference Miscellany, p. 41.

from some of the females, one of the young women from the wagon pressed through the crowd, declaring that she would pull down the next female that attempted to pray. Accordingly, as one commenced praying, she laid hold of her hair and drew her backward; and when another commenced she treated her in like manner. This produced a great excitement throughout the congregation, and yet no forcible means were used to compel the young woman to cease from her rudeness; but several of the females commenced praying that God would lay his hand upon her, and show her and her companions that he could vindicate his own cause and people. The spirit of these praying females seemed to be instantly diffused throughout the praying part of the assembly, as by a flash of electricity; and I have often thought that if I ever saw a company of people agreed, as touching one thing, it was on that occasion. While lips and heart were thus employed, this rude young woman seemed to be paralyzed, and stood like a statue; a death-like paleness came over her countenance; she trembled and fell to the floor as one dead. A loud shriek was uttered by her companions at the door; and after a short pause, two young men, who had accompanied her to the place, pressed through the crowd,—though with as much apparent alarm as though they had been approaching a loaded cannon ready to be discharged,—laid hold of her clothing and drew her through the congregation, and through the barn-yard, which had recently been wet by a shower;

tearing her garments in their haste, and besmearing them with mud and manure." In this ludicrous plight they threw her like a log into the wagon, pitched in themselves with all possible haste, and drove away at the top of their speed. "What became of her afterward," says Mr. Chase, "I never learned."

We add another incident which also goes to illustrate the lights and shades of itinerant life in this early day. The incident occurred not far from Starksborough, and is given on the authority of Rev. Ebenezer Washburn, who commenced his itinerant career the same year and in the same region with Mr. Hedding. "In this place," says he, referring to the vicinity of Hinesburg, "was a wealthy Dutchman by the name of Snyder, who had a large family. His youngest child, an interesting little girl about four or five years old, sickened and suddenly died. They called a Baptist preacher to attend the funeral, who preached a pointed Calvinistic sermon, which did not much please the Dutchman, he having been brought up to believe the doctrines of Luther. But when the preacher turned his address to the afflicted parents, he told them that there were at least nine chances for the child to be lost to one for it to be saved. The father's heart could bear no more. He stamped his foot and said, 'Hold your tongue; I will have no such talk in my house. I am so well satisfied where my little babe has gone, that, by the grace of God, I intend to do just so as to go to it.' He then turned to a member of the Methodist Church who was present, and said: 'Neighbour Norton, won't you bring a Methodist preacher to see me?' Brother Norton said, 'I will, if you request it.' 'When will you bring one?' said he. Brother Norton replied, 'I expect one at my house to-night; and I think it probable I can come here with him to-morrow morning.' 'Do,' said the afflicted father. The child was buried without further ceremony. The next morning brother Norton and I went to see him. The whole family were collected together, and I conversed with each one separately, gave a general exhortation, and prayed with them. I then left an appointment to preach there in two weeks, and went on my way rejoicing. When I came round again I found the man, his wife, and several of the children, earnestly seeking the salvation of their souls. I preached to them and a goodly number of their neighbours. The Lord was with us, and owned and blessed his word. The old gentleman, his wife, and some of the children experienced religion and joined the Church; and when I left the circuit, I left a flourishing class in that place, of which brother Snyder was the leader."

Incidents like the above give us a better insight into the prevailing temper of the times, the state of society, the agencies at work in it, and the prevailing features of the Methodistic movement, than could be obtained from any merely verbal description. Here the curtain seems to fall; that former age comes up to our vision, and passes in panoramic view before us. The "anecdotes of early Methodism" would not only fill a volume, but add an interesting and important chapter to its history. Indeed, not a little of the philosophy of Methodism, as it is with the philosophy of human life, would be found embodied and developed in its anecdotal history.

We come now to the celebrated session of the New-York Conference at Ashgrove, in 1803. Ashgrove was situated in the town of Cambridge, Washington County, New-York. It had received its name from a Mr. Ashton, an Irish emigrant, who, with others, had settled in the place, and planted Methodism there. The society was organized by Philip Embury, who had removed to the place after having founded a society and built a church in the city of New-York. This man, who is now everywhere recognised as the first Methodist preacher upon this continent, was a carpenter by trade, lived in humble life, and died here in 1775. In Ashgrove the first society was formed, and the first church erected, within the bounds of the present Troy Conference. The church was erected in 1788, and that year, for the first time, the little society was favoured with preaching by the appointment of the conference. It became, at an early date, one of the strongholds of Methodism in the country. "Around it cluster some of the most interesting associations of our early denominational history." Here repose the ashes of the sainted Embury, whose name has gone wherever Methodism has spread in its world-wide career. He sleeps in the company of a noble band of pioneers, with whom he took sweet counsel in the time of his pilgrimage.*

The session of the conference commenced July 1st. Bishops Asbury and Whatcoat were both present. Public preaching was had in the church every day at twelve o'clock; but the business sessions of the conference were held in a large private room of one of the members. Seats were made out of rough boards for the preachers, while two plain chairs near the window accommodated the bishops. The business of the conference was transacted with great despatch.† Nearly seventy preachers were present. It was a great and glorious time for the ministers, and also for the members, in all that region. The people gathered from all the adjacent country, so that on the Sabbath not less than two thousand persons had convened in and around the church to attend upon the ministry of the word and the ordinances of religion. The power of God attended upon the word, and great good was done. Mr. Hedding, having passed through his trial of two years, was admitted into full connexion; and, on the fourth of the month, was ordained deacon by Bishop Whatcoat.

At the close of the conference he received his appointment to the Bridgewater Circuit, in the State of New-Hampshire. No sooner had the announcement

* See "Troy Conference Miscellany," p. 24; also "Methodist Magazine" for 1827.

† See "Recollections of William Theophilus," (Rev. Wm. Thatcher,) a pilgrim of threescore. Published by Carlton & Phillips.

been made than, in the true spirit of the times, he mounted his horse with his saddle-bags, containing all his earthly goods—"real, personal, and mixed"—and started upon his long journey to find his circuit among the distant hills of a new state and a strange people. He had for his travelling companions the noble John Broadhead and his pious and estimable lady; and in their delightful intercourse beguiled many a long and weary mile.

Bridgewater Circuit lay nearly in the centre of the State of New-Hampshire. It had been recognised and the plan of a circuit struck out at the preceding session of the conference, with a membership of ten souls. In this hard field of labour the Rev. Reuben Jones had passed a year of toilsome and discouraging labour. The circuit comprised thirteen towns, and required about one hundred miles' travel each week, two sermons usually on each week-day, and three on the Sabbath. It was a rough, hilly, and rocky country, intersected by roads in the worst possible condition to be travelled. He had no colleague, but was left to bear the burden alone. Before labours that might have taxed the severe efforts of two able men he stood unappalled, and entered upon them with the firm resolve "to do or to die" for the Lord.

At the very commencement of his labours there were indications of a more general and sweeping revival than he had ever witnessed before. They were apparent in nearly every neighbourhood where he had an appointment. The whole population seemed to be moved as by some invincible yet unseen power. Mr. Hedding says of these times: "I never, before nor since, have seen such marks of an overwhelming and sweeping revival of the work of God. So deeply were the people interested to hear the preaching, that often we were driven to a barn or a grove, that they might be accommodated. And so wholly absorbed were they about their souls' concern, that the scattered population would collect on week day—men in harvest-time coming, on horseback, ten or fifteen miles to hear the word. The whole country seemed to think and talk of nothing but what they must do to be saved." This great movement among the people excited deeply his own feelings; and, having no fellow-labourer to aid him, he exerted himself beyond even his own herculean powers of physical endurance.

Hardly six weeks had elapsed before he was prostrated by a severe and dangerous attack of disease. There was not a single local preacher on the entire circuit, nor any other man capable of keeping up the meetings and carrying forward the work. Neither was there, at that time, any prospect that help could be obtained from any other circuit. The meetings were interrupted and, to a great extent, given up, so that the glorious prospect that had so lately cheered the hearts of all lovers of Zion, passed away without any of the promised practical results. The devil himself seemed to enter the field. Many evil and slanderous reports were spread abroad about the Methodists, and, in many instances, those who would once have plucked out their eyes, had it been necessary, to aid God's servants in their work, became their most bitter foes. This was the cause of inexpressible grief to Mr. Hedding, and fearfully aggravated his disease. To sicken and die away from kindred and home, among strangers and in a strange place, seemed not half so appalling to his feelings as to see the hosts of Zion recoil, and leave the field defeated and dispirited, when the shout of victory had already begun to ring along the victorious line. Can any one wonder that his mind was sorely tempted? Was it not a first, great, and profitable, though severe lesson, designed to teach him that the Christian minister *must walk by faith and not by sight?* and that he must *sow his seed, not knowing whether this or that shall prosper?*

His disease, which was at first a malignant form of dysentery, had progressed but a few days when his friends gave up all hope of his recovery, and became so convinced of the near approach of his dissolution that they privately sent a man thirty miles to meet the presiding elder at his quarterly meeting and get him to preach the funeral sermon. Happily for the Church and the world, before the presiding elder's arrival the disease had taken a favourable turn, and instead of lamenting the fall of a standard-bearer, they rejoiced in his deliverance from the very jaws of death.

When partially recovered, he attempted to resume his labours on the circuit. He rode fifteen miles and attended an appointment; but the effort was too much for him. He took cold. A terrible attack of rheumatism set in, affecting his whole system, and causing the most excruciating pain. He became entirely helpless, unable to move a hand or finger. Some of his joints were dislocated, and one of his wrists was not only drawn out of joint, but the hand stood out at right angles with his arm for four months, and was entirely helpless during all that time. By the use of bandages and splinters the doctor finally got it back nearly to its place, though it never became sound and strong as before. For six weeks he was unable to turn himself in his bed; and it was four months before he could walk across the room. The effects of that terrible attack were suffered by him through all his after-life.

During his first sickness his mind preserved a calm and comfortable reliance upon God, and he enjoyed great religious consolation and hope. But during the first ten days of his attack with the rheumatism, and while he was suffering great bodily distress, he was powerfully assailed by temptations from the devil. He was tried, like Job of old, in a most fearful ordeal; but he maintained his steadfastness, maintained his confidence in God, and came forth like gold tried in the fire. Referring to this scene of trial in his later years, he said, "The pain I suffered was beyond anything I had ever endured or conceived of before; and Satan took advantage of it to tempt me most violently. If I never had any other confirmation of the existence of the devil and his power to tempt men than what I felt in his severe assaults upon me at that time, I could never doubt his existence. He tempted me day and night to blaspheme, and would say to me, 'What have you ever done that you should suffer this? Curse God and die!' In my distress of mind I cried continually to the Lord, and prayed for deliverance and protection. I said to Satan, 'I will not, I will not!' But so great was my fear that I should be overcome that I held my teeth together, lest blaspheming words should escape from me. When this attack of my enemy had continued ten days, I obtained a complete victory over him, and my soul triumphed exceedingly in the Lord." Such was his fear lest in his weakness he had inadvertently yielded to the temptation and murmured against God, that it became a source of painful anxiety to his mind as he was recovering from his sickness. He earnestly desired the good woman who had watched over him in his sickness to tell him plainly whether he had murmured or repined under the chastening hand of God, and, to his great relief, she assured him that he had not uttered a single complaining word.

While recovering he was subjected to still another trial of his faith. He found himself crippled in his limbs, and his physician plainly told him he would probably be a cripple for life. This was to him a severe trial, and it was some time before he could become reconciled to it. His continual cry was, "Lord, help me to say, 'Thy will be done.'" At length he settled the matter thus in his own mind: "You don't now know certainly that you will be a cripple. You may yet, with the blessing of God, recover. To trouble your mind about it now is not only useless, but of evil influence. Wait, then, and see what God will do. If he afflict, when the sorrow comes you may at least claim the promise that *as your day is, so shall your strength be.*" He was now able to commit himself fully to the Lord, and came forth out of this second conflict with gushing joy in his heart and songs of praise upon his lips.

Thrice had he been tried in the furnace. First he was laid aside just as the fields were all white, and the reapers were going forth to gather in the harvest; and then, when he saw the whole harvest scattered and apparently wasted, was schooled into the submission, "Thy will be done." Again, when death seemed just ready to cut short his career, while yet in the first heat of the conflict, he was once more schooled into submission till he could say even here, "Thy will be done." But the trial of his faith was not yet ended. He was called once more to look upon the spectre of himself, a haggard, repulsive, useless cripple—a burden to his friends, an object of loathing to men—wearing away a miserable existence in inaction and dependence. The struggle was severe; but, with the faith almost of martyrdom, he was enabled yet a third time to say, "Thy will be done." Having undergone this trial of his faith, God brought him forth and planted his feet in a broad place; and henceforward we shall not wonder to find him possessed of that maturity of grace which seems almost to give exemption from the ordinary assaults of Satan. Like Abraham, he had been thoroughly proved, and henceforward, in a peculiar manner, was he to be known as "the friend of God."

One incident connected with his protracted sickness, for the honour of our common Christianity, must not be overlooked. We have already noticed that he fell sick far away from his home and kindred, and among comparative strangers. We hardly need state also that he was destitute of all means of support. Such was then the almost universal condition of the Methodist ministry. They went forth without purse or scrip; they trusted simply in God and his providence to open their way in labour, and to provide for them in misfortune and sickness. And rarely were they ever left without succour in the time of need. Mr. Hedding fell sick at the house of a Mr. Blodgett, at that time a deacon in the Baptist Church in Plymouth, New-Hampshire. He says of this man and his excellent lady, that they were like Zacharias and Elizabeth, walking in the ordinances of God without blame. A married son, who, with his wife, was a member of the Methodist Church, lived in the same house. They were exceedingly kind and attentive—ministering with the greatest tenderness and care to all his wants. Of their kindness Mr. Hedding bore a grateful recollection till the day of his death. Referring to it in later years he said: "The nature of my disease was such as to require much hard service; for six weeks it took four persons to turn me in bed, and this it was necessary to do every two hours. Mr. Blodgett and his family, and their neighbours, regularly and cheerfully performed this service the whole time. They sent for medicines and physicians; they procured watchers to be with me in the night; they could not have done more, or done it more cheerfully, or done it more heartily, had I been their own son. And for all this service and expense they utterly refused all fee or reward. May He that hath promised that a cup of cold water given to a disciple in his name shall not lose its reward, remember and reward them in that day." It does the heart good to record such noble and generous Christian hospitality. Mr. Hedding and his kind benefactor have, no doubt, ere this renewed the ties of Christian love in that land where there is no sickness.

It was eight months before Mr. Hedding had recovered far enough to enable him to resume his labours. Nor was it till the ensuing May that he was able to put on his clothes or get them off without help. He often prayed and preached sitting on a chair, when he could neither stand nor walk. His friends would help him on and off his horse as he rode from one appointment to another. His hands were of so little use to him that he was often compelled to hold his bridle between his teeth. In this crippled state he found it exceedingly difficult to guide or check his horse; and, to the great peril of both limbs and life, he was actually thrown from his back no less than ten times while travelling round the circuit. Yet he counted not his life dear unto himself so that he might fulfil the ministry of the grace of God which he had received. It was a year of great personal afflictions and trials, but one of great spiritual growth to his own soul, and not without some good to the people of his charge.

Finding the progress of his recovery slow, and evidently retarded by his efforts to perform labours for which he was entirely inadequate, he left the circuit some weeks before the session of the conference, crossed the Green Mountains on horseback, and spent several days at Saratoga, hoping to derive advantage from the medicinal properties of the waters. His stay, however, was too short to afford him any great relief. From Saratoga he passed on to Catskill, where he left his horse, and took passage on board a sloop for New-York city. This, at that time, was the usual mode of travelling on the river; and the boat was unusually crowded with passengers, many of them evidently rather "hard customers." By leave of the captain he preached to the people on board, and here sought to win some souls to Christ. The passengers and crew were respectful and attentive, but no manifest effects were produced. As they were passing through the Narrows in the Highlands, the crew, who were evidently of the "baser sort," thought to have some sport with the young preacher. They inquired whether he had ever before passed through the Highlands, and finding that he had not, claimed that, according to custom, he must treat them with a quart of whisky, or allow himself to be ducked in the river. He told them that he neither drank whisky nor furnished it to others, and that they need expect no such thing from him. They made a movement toward the execution of their alternative, when rising to his full height, and exhibiting an athletic frame and a development of muscle rather formidable to contend with, he told them it would be a question of skill and power whether he or they would be the first to go into the river. Things having taken a turn so serious to them, they retreated rather hastily and ingloriously from their meditated sport with the preacher, and thenceforward treated him with great respect, at least with as much as their rough natures knew how to treat him with.

The session of the conference for 1804 was again held in the old John-street Church, in the city of New-York. Bishop Asbury presided, and though it was, as usual, a season of spiritual profit to the preachers and people, nothing of special interest transpired. The feeble state of his health occasioned Mr. Hedding some solicitude in regard to his appointment. Accordingly, in a note addressed to the bishop, he stated his case, and requested that, in view of the benefit physicians thought he might derive from the use of the waters, he might be sent to the Saratoga Circuit, if the circumstances of the work would admit of such an arrangement. He heard nothing from his note till near the close of the conference, when, as he was sitting in his seat, Bishop Asbury came to him and in an intimate and friendly manner with both hands rubbed his ears briskly, and whispered, "John Brodhead says you must go back to New-Hampshire;" then turning abruptly, the bishop resumed his seat as the presiding officer of the conference. At the close of the session, he was appointed to Hanover Circuit, John Brodhead, who had travelled it the year before, having been made presiding elder of the newly-organized New-Hampshire District.

With his usual celerity Mr. Hedding was soon *en route* for his appointment. This was a comparatively easy circuit to travel. He says: "My presiding elder told me I was placed upon it for that reason, and I found it, indeed, a *resting place*, compared with those I had already travelled." His usual routine of labour he thus describes: "On one Sabbath I was accustomed to preach twice in the day time in the centre of the town of Hanover, in a Congregational meeting-house, where they had no settled minister. In the evening of the same day I would ride to the village where Dartmouth College is located, and preach in a private house or school-house. On the next Sabbath I preached in the town of Canaan, always twice and sometimes three times, thus keeping up preaching on alternate Sabbaths in these two towns." In addition to his Sabbath appointments, he had one week-day appointment in Lebanon, one in Enfield, and one in Hartford, Vt., besides frequent lectures in remote neighbourhoods both in Hanover and Canaan. Thus he usually preached six or seven times during each week, besides attending class and prayer meetings, preaching funeral sermons, and performing the pastoral labour of his charge. If this was a "*resting place*" for a disabled preacher in those days, what must have been the work of able-bodied men!

In these early times an unmarried Methodist preacher had no fixed place, even on his circuit, to which he could resort and say, "This is my home." He lived from house to house, as providence or friendship paved the way. His home was literally among the people. This *strict itinerancy*, though a sort of necessity in those times, and attended with some advantages both to the people and preacher, often subjected the latter to not a little inconvenience and embarrassment, and was exceedingly detrimental to his intellectual improvement. Among the people who entertained him, there would be a great variety in their modes of living and in their general habits; he would ofter suffer from the scanty provision made for his physical comfort. To gather a library, or even to expect access to any considerable or valuable collection of books, was entirely out of the question. Even the privilege of a separate room for study was a luxury rarely enjoyed, except when with his favourite book he retired to the sanctuary of the ancient forest to be alone.

Whatever Mr. Hedding had suffered in any of these

particulars in former years, on Hanover Circuit he was highly favoured. He found no lack of open houses and kind hearts ready to receive and entertain him. His opportunities for study also were better than ever before; and he was diligent in the improvement of them. It was here that he first began to give earnest attention to the structure of the English language, and laid the foundation of that critical knowledge and use of it that characterized him in after years. He never paid much attention to the acquisition of other languages than his own. His shrewd observation led him to the knowledge of the fact that many men who were accounted learned, and who really were learned in the ancient languages, and also well read in general literature and philosophy, were after all exceedingly deficient in the knowledge and use of their mother tongue. However skilled they might be in Cicero and Demosthenes, they could not analyze accurately and ascertain certainly a complicated sentence in Milton or Shakspeare. He thus reasoned: "Pleasing and important as may be the knowledge of ancient languages, it is of more importance to have a critical knowledge of our own. Just as a complete knowledge, and a mastery in the use of implements to be handled every day, and upon the right use of which success in life depends, are of more importance than the knowledge of the most complicated mathematical instruments to one who will seldom have occasion to use them; so the knowledge of our mother tongue is of first and vital importance." It is not to be inferred that he deemed a defective knowledge of English literature a necessary result of attention to classical studies, or that he underrated the value of such studies. Such was never the fact. But at his age, with such limited facilities, and such a work before him, he looked upon the mastery of the English language as the only thing within his power; and this he wisely determined to achieve. Inspired by this new determination, he first turned his attention to English Grammar. When a lad at school he had recited daily lessons in grammar, till a good portion of the text-book in use had been committed to memory. But grammar, as a system, he knew nothing about; it had never been explained to him; and he says, "I do not believe one of my teachers understood it." He had to study without teachers, only as he now and then fell in with a person versed in the subject, and by questioning him, drew forth suggestions and principles that solved his difficulties. He bought a copy of each of the grammars then in use, that he might gather knowledge by comparison; but he mainly relied upon Webster's. To obtain time, he omitted reading other books, except on the Sabbath; he also omitted making new sermons, and preached over those he had made in previous years. He carried his grammars in his portmanteau, and seized every moment, early and late, in his room and upon horseback, to study them. Whatever he could not understand in one book, he searched out in the others, comparing them together till he had solved the most abstruse questions, and had obtained a complete mastery over the rules and principles of the system. To increase his own skill and perfect his knowledge, whenever among those who prided themselves upon their knowledge of grammar, he would bring forward the most difficult sentences in order to exercise their skill in analyzing them. By these various means he made himself master of the system in about three months. From the raw state he had so advanced that he could analyze and parse understandingly any legitimate sentence in the English language. The effect of this study upon his habit and style of speaking he thus describes: "For a while, after I had *devoured* the grammar, it was an embarrassment to me in public speaking, for I had to correct certain sentences I had been in the habit of using; but after a few months a correct mode of speaking became familiar to me, and all the difficulty vanished."

He had no sooner finished the study of grammar, than, in the prosecution of his purpose to become master of his own language, he undertook another work, which, though unusual in its mode, and which none but one of his energy and perseverance would have performed, he carried through with similar success. This was to become acquainted with the proper pronunciation and meaning of every English word found in the dictionaries of the language. Perry's Dictionary was at that time used in the principal colleges and schools, and was the standard for pronunciation and definitions throughout the country. He purchased it and commenced its study. His object was to correct any errors, either in the pronunciation or in the application of words, into which he might have fallen. As he read on in course, he was accustomed to mark the excepted words, and to write them off, and exercise himself upon them till his habit was thoroughly corrected. This reading and notes embraced not only the dictionary proper, but also the list of Scripture names, which he found afterward to be especially beneficial to him. Thus he plodded through the entire dictionary. Nor will it be out of place to remark here, that a few years later, when Walker's Dictionary, so different in its pronunciation, came into general use in this country, he went through a similar process, that he might not fall behind the more intelligent in the community in his use of language. Still later, he applied the same study to Webster's. As the result of this application, he could tell at once how any word was spelled and pronounced, and the nice shades of definition given to it by either Perry, Walker, or Webster. Nothing can more strikingly illustrate the keenness of his perception, and the almost unequalled tenacity of his memory.

These studies of the year produced a great improvement in his general style of address. Those who knew him only in the later years of his ministry were often struck with the chasteness, simplicity, and correctness of his style, whether in the pulpit or in social intercourse. To such it cannot but be pleasing to learn the process by which that simplicity and accuracy were acquired. These studies, too, we should remark, were only stepping-stones to others in the higher departments of English literature,—such as rhetoric, logic, criticism, intellectual and moral philosophy, political economy, and the like.

Though these studies occupied much of his time, his duties as a preacher and pastor were not neglected. There was nothing of remarkable interest in the work upon the circuit during the year. For two or three years preceding it had been favoured with great revivals, and many had been gathered into the Church. This year was chiefly devoted to building up and establishing the young converts in the faith. There were some conversions, however; and the members of the Church generally attended to their duty, and lived in the love of God, and in fellowship one with another. The meetings were well attended, and were pleasant, edifying, and joyful. Wherever Mr. Hedding went he was cordially received, and listened to with attention and deep interest. He prospered in his own religious enjoyment; and nothing occurred upon the circuit to diminish the joy or mar the fellowship of the members.

CHAPTER IV.

MR. HEDDING UPON BARRE AND VERSHIRE CIRCUITS.

Mr. Hedding in the New-England Conference — Leading Men of that Conference — The Lynn Session in 1805 — Examination of Character — Finances — Public Exercises — Progress of the Work in New-England since 1790 — Difficulties and Opposition — Appointed to Barre Circuit — Dan Young, his Colleague — Mutual Assistance — Condition of the Circuit — Prosperity of the Work — Mr. Hedding as a Disciplinarian — Singular Trial of his Skill — Obstacles opposed to Methodism in Vermont — A "Tithing-man" in a Methodist Meeting — Session of the Conference for 1806 — Yearly Change of Preachers in Early Times — Appointed to Vershire Circuit — Its Situation and Extent — Emigration — Loss of Official Members — Theological Biasses of New-England — Doctrinal Discussions — Onset with a Doctor of Divinity — Results — Characteristic Labours of Methodist Pioneers — Tour of a Young Itinerant through Northern Vermont — Dialogue with a Poor Woman — Powerful Conversions — Mrs. Bishop — Spirit and Agencies of the Methodistic Revival — First Six Years of Itinerant Labour.

By a change in the boundaries of the New-York and the New-England Conferences, that part of the work in which Mr. Hedding was engaged, and the preachers also, were transferred to the latter conference. The New-England Conference at that time, though composed chiefly of young men, embraced some of the noblest spirits found in the itinerant ranks. Mr. Hedding, though removed by this change of relation from immediate association with men for whom he entertained a strong and lasting affection, still found himself in the companionship of a band of heroic men of equal talent and of like unquenchable ardour in the cause of God. Among the leading men in the

New-England Conference were George Pickering, Joshua Taylor, Daniel Ostrander, John Brodhead, Daniel Webb, Epaphras Kibby, Elijah R. Sabin, Joshua Soule, Ebenezer Washburn, Thomas Branch, Philip Munger, Asa Kent, Peter Jayne, Samuel Merwin, Martin Ruter, Oliver Beale, &c., several of whom, with Mr. Hedding, had been transferred from the New-York Conference.

The session of the New-England Conference commenced at Lynn, July 12, 1805. Bishop Asbury presided, and about forty preachers were present. "The records of this session afford abundant evidence of the continued vigilance of the conference over its members. The notices appended to the names which passed under review are remarkable for their brevity, but also for their explicit frankness. One candidate is pronounced, 'useful, firm, perhaps obstinate, contentious, well-meaning.' Another is said to be 'useful, but unguarded in some expressions:' he seems to have been somewhat in advance of the times, for there was 'some objection on his denial of visions and spiritual influences by dreams,' though he 'averred his firm belief of the Scriptures in these respects.' Another is said to be 'unexceptionable, useful, and devout;' another, 'pious, unimproved, impatient of reproof, not acceptable,' and is ordered to desist from travelling. True Glidden is recorded to be 'sick—near to death—happy.' One is charged gravely for marrying indiscreetly, and 'suspended one year from performing the functions of a deacon;' another is pronounced 'weak in doctrine and discipline, but as a preacher, useful, sincere, pious.' Lewis Bates is said to be 'plain, good, useful;' Zalman Lyon, 'pious, faithful, but of small improvement.' D. Young, 'pious, capable, rough, improving.' Elijah Willard, 'faithful, diligent.' One is said to be acceptable, useful, zealous—perhaps indiscreetly so—sincere, ingenious;' another 'pious, useful, weak.'"*

There were but two committees appointed at the conference. One of them was upon finances; and its report is a striking commentary upon "the inadequacy of ministerial support" in those times. The aggregate deficiency on the small pittance allowed the preachers was $2,800; and the collections to supply only $373. Soule's deficiency was $107; Brodhead's, $91; Willard's, $56; Washburn's, $50; Bates's, $45; Hedding's, $41; Ostrander's, $40; and so on, some more and some less. On these deficiencies appropriations were made, in sums ranging from thirty-five dollars down to four dollars, according to the claims of each. Mr. Asbury says: "We had a full conference, preaching at five, at eleven, and at eight o'clock. Sitting of conference from half-past eight o'clock till eleven in the forenoon; and from two until six o'clock in the afternoon. We had great harmony, and order and strict discipline withal. Sixteen deacons and eight elders were

* See Memorials of Methodism in New-England. To these volumes we are indebted for much information relating to this conference.

ordained." Among the latter was the subject of our memoir.

The public exercises of the conference were held in a pleasant grove, in the rear of where the parsonage of the Lynn Common Church is now located. Bishop Asbury calls it, "a beautiful, sequestered spot, though near the meeting-house." The religious exercises of the occasion were attended with extraordinary power, and produced extraordinary results. The Sabbath was a "high day." The people came in from all the surrounding country, and assembled in the grove, hungering for the word of life. The multitudes bowed before the power of the word as trees before a resistless tempest, and "the slain of the Lord were many." In all these exercises Mr. Hedding took an active part. "The excitement was so great," says he, "that many cried aloud in the congregation. One night, after I had been in meeting praying and exhorting until midnight, and had gone to my lodgings and retired to rest, I was called up to pray again for those who were wrestling with the Lord for mercy. There was great opposition to the work: many of 'the baser sort' came from Boston and Salem to make disturbance. But, notwithstanding all the opposition, God carried on his work, and many were converted at these meetings who continued steadfast in the gospel, and died in the hope of a better resurrection. A few are still living, after a lapse of almost fifty years, honouring the Lord who saved them at that time." The author of the Memorials of Methodism says, that "during the public labours of this session, great displays of the Spirit of God were witnessed; scores were awakened, some fell as dead men to the earth, many cried aloud with anguish, while others wept in silence, or rejoiced with thanksgiving for the pardon of their sins. A great noise went abroad, and hundreds flocked to witness the scene: the rabble raged and made threatening demonstrations; but the power of the word prevailed against all opposition." It was altogether a remarkable season; and both preachers and members were baptized anew. It is said that many old Methodists in that region still remember the remarkable scene, and call it up in their recollection as the great day of their lives.

Only fifteen years had elapsed up to the session of this conference from the time that Jesse Lee, in 1790, first took his stand upon a table beneath the shade of a gigantic elm in the centre of Boston Common, and commenced his first religious service in the region in the presence of four persons. From small beginnings and by the most gigantic effort on the part of Lee and his coadjutors, Methodism had continued to move forward till at this period it had penetrated every New-England state, and extended east into the province of Maine beyond the Penobscot River. The "New-England Conference," as then organized, embraced all these states except the western portions of Connecticut, Massachusetts, and Vermont. It comprehended five districts, forty-eight stations and circuits, seventy-seven preachers, and eight thousand five hundred and forty members.

This work had been accomplished in the face of obstacles and opposition that would have appalled ordinary men. All New-England was then controlled by an ecclesiastical organization that had commenced with the Puritan fathers, and was completely interwoven with all the traditions, prejudices, and habits of the people. Under its influence society had been moulded; and nothing could be more uncongenial to the prevailing spirit of the times than the simple, warm, and energetic worship of the Methodists. The parish pulpits were closed against them; and they were denounced, even in public assemblies, as "wolves in sheep's clothing." Sometimes they found access to court-houses, dancing halls, and school-houses; and here they were often left to warm and light the rooms, and also to ring the bells, or use such other methods as they could to get the people together. The ordinary hospitalities of society were often denied them; they were hooted at in the streets; their meetings often disturbed; and their lives frequently endangered. Calvinism has ever been the sturdy theologic enemy of Methodism; and against this iron system the Methodist itinerants continually levelled their heaviest artillery. They assailed it with Scripture, argument, and common sense; and so successfully did they assault this stronghold of error that its very foundations were soon dissolved. But after all, the great secret of their success lay in their powerful ministry of the gospel of the grace of God; appealing directly to the hearts and consciences of the people for an immediate settlement of the great question at issue between them and God. By this powerful ministry of the word they stormed the strongholds of Satan, and levelled his defences to the ground.

At the close of this conference Mr. Hedding was appointed to the Barre Circuit, in Vermont. This circuit lay nearly in the middle of the state, and extended over thirteen towns, including Montpelier, the present capital of the state. Mr. Hedding had for his colleague the Rev. Dan Young. Of him he says: "He was a young man of superior talents, and of great piety and zeal. He travelled a few years, and laboured with great success on other circuits afterward. He then located, and lived a few years in New-Hampshire; and then became a member of the state senate. Afterward he removed to Ohio. We laboured together with great comfort, and were happy in our own souls in the love of God, and saw the people happy under our ministry."

The hearts of these young men were knit together like those of David and Jonathan. They entered into a mutual agreement to aid each other in mental and religious improvement. They adjusted their work so that once a fortnight they would meet in the middle of the circuit, on a week day, and preach in each other's presence—one in the afternoon and the other in the evening. "We agreed," says Mr. Hedding, "to tell each other all the faults we discovered in our preaching,—either in doctrine, pronunciation, gesture, or otherwise. We next agreed to tell each other all the faults we discovered in private life, and all that we feared of each other; and then we agreed to tell all we heard, and all the people said of each other. This mutual agreement was the source of much profit to us, and we continued to practise it to the end of the year; nor was it the occasion of any ill feeling between us." Nothing can more strikingly attest the desire of these young men to improve themselves in all that pertains to a workman that needeth not to be ashamed; nothing can more finely illustrate the confidence they had in each other, and the mutual affection that subsisted between them.

The religious condition of the circuit was very encouraging when they first entered upon their work. A faithful labourer, Oliver Beale, had preceded them; but especially during this year gracious revivals prevailed in several places on the circuit. Multitudes were converted to God; and it is said that, even at the present day, many aged saints within the range of that circuit still cherish the name of Hedding as the messenger of Heaven, by whom their youthful feet were guided into the path of life.

In a few instances, during the year, the firmness and skill of Mr. Hedding, in the administration of discipline, were severely tested. Exceedingly kind and forbearing toward the penitent, the unfortunate, and the ignorant; on the other hand, he was alike decided and vigorous toward the wilfully stubborn and wicked.

A singular instance in the way of discipline occurred during the year, in one of the societies in the circuit. It had relation to two brothers-in-law, who were also connected in family relation with nearly all the members of the society. A dispute concerning some property had existed between them for a long time; and not only continued to increase in violence, but also involved, at length, most of the members of the society. Mr. Hedding collected the society together—some thirty or forty in number—to have the dispute between them settled. Both of them were fiery, impulsive, ungovernable men. The object of the meeting was to procure an amicable and brotherly adjustment of the long-pending dispute, or, at least, to devise some method of settlement. Mr. Hedding sat between the two men, and the wife of each sat beside her husband. They began to talk over the subject of dispute, when one of them suddenly warmed up and called the other a liar. Instantly both started to their feet, and rushed at each other; the females screamed, and a general alarm ensued. Mr. Hedding proved himself equal to the awkward emergency. He rushed between them, seized each by the collar of his coat; and with his herculean frame and strength held them at arms' length, face to face, but unable to strike each other. They struggled for a moment, but found themselves as though clutched in the jaws of a vice. Holding them at arms' length, he commenced to lecture them in round terms; he shamed them about the meanness and wickedness of the act their unbridled passions had prompted them to commit, in the presence of their wives, their family relations, the religious society of which they were members, their pastor, and especially in the presence of God, whose servants they professed to be. He told them of the scandal they had brought upon the Church, and the reproach cast upon the cause of God, by the course they had pursued toward each other. From the hearing of this entire lecture there was no escape, and they writhed under its withering power. After they had got somewhat calmed, Mr. Hedding suddenly exclaimed, "Let us pray!" and kneeled down, bringing the two men with him to their knees upon the floor. Still retaining his grasp, he prayed for them in a most fervent and powerful manner. When he had closed, he shook the one he held by his right hand, saying,—"Pray, brother, pray!" Soon he commenced praying and weeping, confessing his sins, and beseeching God and his brother to forgive him. When the first had closed, Mr. Hedding shook the other, and called upon him to pray. He was the most pugnacious of the two; and it was hard work for him to clear his throat so as to give utterance to words. "A thousand frogs seemed clogging his speech;" but he at length broke through his difficulty, and earnestly prayed God and his brother to forgive him. When he said "*Amen*" Mr. Hedding relinquished his grasp, and they all rose to their feet. "Now, shake hands, brethren," said he; "and live as brethren, and love each other as long as you live." They immediately embraced each other, and almost as quickly settled their dispute; the only difficulty seemed to be in their effort to see which should concede most to his brother. The difficulty was effectually settled. The two men ever after lived on the best terms of fraternal and Christian fellowship.

We have already noticed the peculiar difficulties in the way of Methodism in the New-England states. The obstacles opposed to its progress in Vermont were perhaps scarcely rivalled by those of any other state. Referring to this period, the author of Memorials of Methodism says: "Every means, from perilous rencounters to petty artifices, were used to retard their progress; and when it was found impossible not to tolerate them, it was, at least, determined not to respect them. Their opposers, failing to discourage them by menaces and mobs, often resorted to annoyances and ludicrous grievances, which might tend to make them a public jest. Asa Kent mentions numerous instances illustrative of this. One of these, as illustrative of the times, we will put upon record. An important officer of 'the standing order' in that day was the '*tithing-man*,' who, armed with a long rod, at once weapon and staff of office, presided over the Sabbath congregations, with full power to remind unwary hearers, by a thrust from his wand, of any undue disposition to sleep, or other indiscretion. 'In one of the towns,' says Mr. Kent, 'the population was sparse; but they had the shell of a meeting-house, with rough boards for seats; and having no minister, the Methodists were invited to occupy it on the Sabbath. Their preachers gave general satisfaction, except that some of them spoke *too loud.* But there was a sore grievance, which called for a speedy remedy. The Methodists, in those days, were often heard to respond to the preacher by an audible "Amen," and at other times to exclaim, "Glory to God!" and this was so different from the "still small voice," that it was judged by some to be an *intolerable disorder.* While some were devising a remedy, one, more wise than his fellows, intimated that, if he should be appointed "tithing-man," he would put a stop to such confusion. The next town-meeting appointed him to that office. He pledged his oath for his fidelity, and then requested the magistrate to give him definite instruction how to proceed. "Why," said the squire, "it is your duty to keep the people still in time of religious worship." "But what if they will not be still?" inquired the young officer. "Then have your staff, and rap them on the head." This was satisfactory, and he prepared his staff, which was the badge of his power. These staves were sometimes six or seven feet in length, that the officer might reach the offender without leaving his place. As there were no pews, the men sat together on one side of the meeting-house and the women on the other. Sabbath came, and the newly-appointed *tithing-man* walked in, staff in hand, and took his seat in the midst of the brethren. This was an eventful hour. Like modern *office-seekers*, he had come "pledged" to office, and was about to make his début under the scrutinizing eyes of his constituents. To add to his calamity it was quarterly-meeting, and the members were in the habit, in those days, of travelling a great distance on such occasions. Bostwick was the presiding elder, himself a host when the God of Sabaoth was in his message; and I think Joseph Mitchell was the circuit preacher. When prayer was offered, all the Methodists fell upon their knees; but our young officer stood up, staff in hand, to suppress all disorder. A brother said "Amen,' and was instantly rapped on the head. Another, and then another, said "Amen;" and each felt the rap. There was a shower of salvation before the preacher closed his prayer, and some shouted "Glory," and others "Amen," but each, in his turn, felt the rap; and to do his duty, the *tithing-man* sometimes reached as far as he could to the right, then as far as he could to the left; for they were kneeling around him so closely that he could not move. He had, in fact, as much as he could do to punish those within his reach, leaving those beyond to transgress with impunity. This exhibition was fine sport to a certain class of the congregation, while our members seemed to care nothing about it. But during the preaching our lover of order had new difficulties to contend with. When they had kneeled, with their eyes closed, he stood and wielded his authority with great adroitness; but now he is *seated* with them, and even his love of order is not sufficient to induce him to *stand* and rap the heads of the disorderly. But when a faithful officer cannot do *all* that he would, he will not readily yield the point until he has done what he could. The "tithing-man" accordingly fixed his eye upon one of the *most disorderly*, and determined to bring him to a better mind. The brother was a man of an ardent spirit and a warm heart; and although he had crossed the line of the "Old Bay State," he never dreamed that the Vermont statute prohibited shouting, and of course felt himself perfectly at home among his brethren. He sat upon the seat before our officer, and about the length of his rod from him, the end of which he placed under his side; and whenever the brother shouted, he would give him a jerk under his short ribs. This could be done without exposing himself to the congregation generally. The power of God was present to quicken and to sanctify his children, and great was their rejoicing. The poor brother selected as the victim of the "tithing-man," altogether unconscious of his august presence, sat gazing at the preacher, the tears flowing from his eyes, and often gave vent to an overflowing heart by shouts of "Glory;" while our *friend of order* gave him a faithful jerk for each transgression.'

"This ludicrous persecution continued some time to the amusement of the lookers-on, and the annoyance, doubtless, of the worshippers. But the latter, not comprehending it, took the most effectual means of rebuking it. They prayed directly in behalf of the 'tithing-man.' The supplications of a Methodist prayer-meeting were perilous to the gainsayers. The 'tithing-man' was foiled; he retreated from his office; the jests of his associates were turned upon him, and he appeared no more, with his staff of office, to compel the Methodists to keep the peace."*

The session of the New-England Conference for 1806, commenced in the town of Canaan, N. H., June 11th. This place was included in the Hanover Circuit, which had been previously travelled by Mr. Hedding. Bishop Asbury—the untiring apostle of Methodism—having completed over five thousand miles' travel in little over a year, reached the seat of the conference the day before it opened, and presided over its deliberations. The most memorable thing that transpired at the conference was a sermon preached by the bishop on the Sabbath. The word of the Lord was like a two-edged sword to the hearers. Both preachers and people shouted aloud for joy as they felt its power. Some were awakened and converted during the session of the conference; and in many respects it was a refreshing time. Mr. Asbury, however, says of it: "We went through our business in haste and peace, sitting seven hours a day. We did not, to my grief, tell our experiences, nor make observations as to what we had known of

* Memorials of Methodism, Second Series, p. 271.

the work of God; the members were impatient to be gone, particularly the married townsmen."

In those early times the preachers were almost universally—especially the unmarried men—moved yearly. Continuance the second year on the same circuit was the exception, and not the rule, as usage has made it in the present day. Accordingly, at the close of this conference, Mr. Hedding was removed from Barre to Vershire Circuit, which was also in the State of Vermont. This circuit was in the eastern part of the state, stretching along on the banks of the Connecticut River, and embracing ten towns. He was without a colleague, and the work was so arranged that he was to pass through these towns, and preach from one to three times daily within the limits of each every two weeks. Thus he was almost incessantly engaged either in preaching, or in the pastoral work—hunting up his scattered flock in their homes, and instructing and encouraging them and their families in the path of well-doing.

Prudence and discretion, combined with decision and energy, were prominent traits in Mr. Hedding's character. In the most sudden and trying emergencies, these rarely failed to carry him safely through. This year he was subjected to a peculiar trial. Ohio, with its mild and genial climate, its luxuriant soil and its inexhaustible "bottoms," its ample and inviting hunting-grounds, and its opportunities for wild and daring adventure, was then just opening to the people. The fever for emigration raged through all the Eastern

States, but especially in Vermont; and hundreds were leaving their homes in the east to make their abode in this new El Dorado of the west. Under this excitement, Mr. Hedding lost nearly every official member of the Church upon the entire circuit, and that too nearly at the same time. Indeed, of all the official body, only one leader remained. This was a serious embarrassment. They were the men who had sustained the religious meetings, transacted the business of the circuit, and provided homes for the preachers. Painfully trying as were his circumstances, he pushed forward the work, nothing daunted. New places of entertainment were thrown open to him in every town; the best men were sought out, and their services enlisted as stewards and leaders; the classes were reorganized, and soon the whole circuit was in working order. The dark cloud that hung so heavily over it passed away, and a clear sky, with a bright and shining sun, appeared. Notwithstanding the great losses of the circuit by emigration, a year of considerable prosperity was enjoyed.

In most parts of New-England, at this early day, the inhabitants were decidedly Puritanic. They were generally enterprising and economical in their habits, strict in their moral conduct, somewhat intelligent, and always inquisitive; and in religious faith—except where Universalism or Unitarianism had developed itself—rigid and unyielding Calvinists. Universalism and Unitarianism—the natural results of the reaction from the repulsive features of high-toned, though hon-

honest Calvinism—had sprung up in their midst. Methodism was from without; it came not by stealth, but in the open day; singlehanded, and alone, it openly assaulted Calvinism in its stronghold, and unquestionably proved the great moral antidote to the two principal forms of scepticism then developing everywhere among the people of New-England, and poisoning all the well-springs of her theology. Most of the Congregational clergy, especially in the country parishes, were of the ultra Calvinistic or Hopkinsian school; and they not only received the doctrines of this school, but they preached them openly, everywhere, and without palliation or disguise. No "sugar coat" had then been devised to conceal the nauseous taste of the pill.

Of course, wherever Methodism went the two systems were brought into direct conflict, and the way was opened to the most exciting discussions upon the subject. It was quite a common thing, after the Methodist minister had finished his sermon, and before the congregation had retired, for the settled minister, or a deacon, or some wordy, self-confident zealot for the faith of the fathers, to assail some doctrine of the preacher, or some supposed doctrine of Methodism, as heretical and pernicious. It was often the case that such adventurers engaged in the enterprise before they had counted the cost. Most of these early Methodist preachers were naturally very shrewd men, and their natural parts had been rendered still more acute and ready from constant exercise. They, too, were thoroughly posted up in all the peculiarities of Calvinism,—knew its salient points, were completely posted up as to all its logical consequences, were familiar with all the Scripture passages that were the strongholds of its reliance, and also with all the Scripture and logical stumbling-blocks of the system. In fact, this was a sort of forensic gladiatorship, in which the Methodist minister, from the very necessities of his work, was almost daily exercised. Unaccustomed to such contests, and relying upon the presumed ignorance of their antagonists, the men who assailed them rushed blindly into the conflict, and generally left the field only after suffering a most inglorious defeat. These discussions, when public, not unfrequently contributed largely to the advancement of Methodism.

Mr. Hedding, being possessed of great logical acuteness, a ready command of language, and thorough and ready knowledge of the phases of the whole controversy, was well armed for any emergency in this line. One day, in the midst of a snow-storm, while riding through one of the towns in his circuit, he fell in with a stranger travelling in the same direction. They had a short but interesting conversation on indifferent subjects. Mr. Hedding soon learned that his travelling companion was the settled clergyman of the town,—settled by vote of the town and paid from its treasury,—and also that he was dignified with the title of D. D. Before they parted, the clergyman obtained from Mr. Hedding a promise to pay him a visit at his earliest convenience. Accordingly, Mr. Hedding, two weeks later, taking a friend, a layman, with him, called upon the clergyman. The first salutation of the clergyman was: "Well, Mr. Hedding, I suppose you have come to discuss questions at issue between us, have you?" Mr. Hedding replied, "I have come, on your invitation, to pay you a short visit, and am willing to converse with you upon any subject most agreeable to yourself." "Very well," said the doctor; "we will take dinner first, and then we will go into the study and try the matter out." Accordingly, after dinner, the old man called his divinity students—of whom there were several under his private tuition—along with his guests into the parlour, and soon after began to question Mr. Hedding about the doctrines believed and taught by the Methodists. In a few words, Mr. H. gave him a formal statement of them. The suavity of the old man's spirit and manner seemed to abate very much during the statement; and no sooner had Mr. H. concluded, than, with a frowning brow and dogmatic manner,—as though his dictum was the end of the law,—the old man denounced these doctrines as fatally heretical and terribly pernicious, and closed by saying, "These were the doctrines of John Wesley, and I have no doubt he is now in hell for teaching such abominable heresy."

Mr. Hedding took the matter very coolly, and in turn questioned the doctor with reference to the doctrines he believed and taught. The doctor, with not a little precision and formality, explained the whole system of Hopkinsianism, and declared it to be his creed, and also most consonant with both reason and Scripture.

Mr. Hedding then said,—

"It appears that you believe God decrees and wills everything that comes to pass—even all the wicked conduct of sinful men."

The doctor admitted it was so.

"But," says Mr. Hedding, "God forbids that sinful conduct. He says, 'Thou shalt not steal,' &c. How do you make God's will and commands agree? or, if he *wills* one thing and *commands* another, is not God divided against himself?"

The doctor, who was now fairly placed upon the defensive, replied,—

"We have nothing to do with the will of God. All we have to do with, is his commands. We are bound to keep his commands, though he may have willed to the contrary. And it is perfectly just in him, under all and any circumstances, to punish us for disobedience to known commands."

In a similar manner they continued their conversation and arguments until sunset. Finding that he had *a man* to cope with,—a man well read in theology, thoroughly versed in all the tactics of polemic theology, and, withal, of great self-command both as to his spirit and language,—the doctor repressed the dogmatism that appeared at the outset, and treated him with marked respect throughout the subsequent stages of their controversy.

The following colloquy closed the discussion:—

Mr. Hedding asked, "Will all of God's elect finally be saved?"

The doctor answered, "Yes."

Mr. H. Will any others be saved besides God's elect?

Dr. ——. No.

Mr. H. Will all the elect be converted and pardoned while they remain in this world?

Dr. ——. Yes.

Mr. H. Are all of the elect convinced, before they are pardoned, that they are sinners, and in the way to hell?

Dr. ——. Yes.

Mr. H. Does the Holy Ghost convince them that they are in danger of going to hell?

Dr. ——. Yes.

Mr. H. Does the Holy Ghost always teach truth?

Dr. ——. Yes.

Mr. H. Now, sir, let me put your answers together, and see how they will read. You have said all the elect will be saved; none of them can possibly be lost; also, that while they are in this world, they are convinced they are in danger of going to hell. Now, how can they be in danger of going to hell, if God has decreed they shall be saved, and it is impossible for them to be lost?

Dr. ——. O, while they are under conviction they think they are in danger; but it is not so in fact.

Mr. H. Hold! You told me the Holy Ghost teaches them, and that the Holy Ghost always teaches truth."

Dr. ——. Well, after all, they are in danger.

Mr. H. Stop! You told me it was impossible for them to be lost; and how can a man be in danger of an impossibility?

Dr. ——. A man may be in danger of impossibilities sometimes.

Mr. H. Very well; you believe that a man may be in danger of falling up to the clouds. Good-by, sir."

The two men parted very cordially, notwithstanding the sharp controversy they had carried on in relation to their respective creeds. The old man was evidently deeply and favourably impressed; and a few years after, when he became more acquainted with Methodist doctrines and usages, his views and feelings toward them were greatly changed. He often invited the Methodist preachers to preach in his pulpit, and as often preached in theirs. Thus a mutual good understanding and cordial Christian fellowship subsisted between them.

But while the noble band of Methodist pioneers were thus wielding the polemic battle-axe, they did not cease to imitate their Lord and Master in his efforts to seek and save the lost sheep of the house of Israel. They went from house to house; went into the new and sparse settlements; visited the log-cabins, and made personal application of their message to the high and low, rich and poor. About this period the Rev. Ebenezer F. Newhall, then a young man, and not yet entered upon the regular work, made a tour on foot through parts of Vermont, and extended his travels beyond the line into Canada. His soul was stirred within him as he witnessed the moral and religious destitution of the people, and he commenced exhorting them to flee from the wrath to come. "Often I rested my weary limbs," said he, "by sitting down and reading in my Bible, and kneeling in prayer. Soon I came to a small opening —found a log hut—stopped—talked, read, sung, and prayed with them; and then inquired if there was a house two or three miles ahead where I could stop over night and hold a meeting, and was informed that there probably was. So on I went, calling on every family and praying with them: all seemed glad to see me, and promised to follow on to the meeting. As I came to the third opening I called at the first log hut, and found it inhabited by a very poor woman. I invited her to go to the meeting. She said, 'I have no clothes but these that I have on, and they are not suitable for such a place.' I replied, 'Don't stop for that; just wash you clean and go: God may meet you there, and wash away all your sins, and clothe you with salvation.' 'But I have no shoes,' she continued. 'No matter; God may put on your feet the gospel shoes.' 'Then I have no bonnet.' 'Well, God can put on your head a crown of life.' 'Neither have I any cloak.' 'Dear woman,' said I, 'make no more excuses; throw a sheet over your shoulders, and if you find Jesus, as you may, you will not be sorry you went, even if you should go ragged and barefoot, since it is the best your poverty allows.' I then passed on to the next house. With cheerful looks they welcomed me to the hospitalities of their house, sent notice of the meeting the other way, and thanked me for inviting the people as I came along. They soon assembled from several miles around; and the poor woman was among them, with rags sewed on her feet, a sheet doubled and flung over her head, and her children by her side. How easy it was to talk to a people hungry for the bread of life! My soul was happy, and praised God. In the morning I passed on in my journey through the woods, feeling that God was my support and comfort. I tarried a few weeks—held some meetings. The Lord moved upon the hearts of the people, and many were brought to rejoice in God." Such were the agencies by which Methodism was spread, and the souls of men, in the waste and destitute places, sought out and saved in this early day. Such were the agencies by which, especially in New-England, infidelity and its kindred heresies received a stern and formidable check, while the spirit of genial and vital godliness was revived among the people.

If the agencies for the spread of the work were peculiarly marked as agencies of God's own raising up, many of the conversions were not less strikingly marked with evidences of its being his own peculiar work. The first Methodist preachers that visited Lancaster, N. H., having been expelled from the village by a mob, Joseph Crawford resolved to visit the place, and preach in defiance of opposition. Under his first sermon there a Mrs. Bishop was powerfully awakened. "Her emotions were so great as to overpower her physical strength. Her husband procured immediately a physician and nurse, and her symptoms were medically treated for some time. But her agitation increased. Her neighbours were greatly interested, as she was highly esteemed among them; but neither friendly sympathy nor medical skill availed anything, for the arrows of the Almighty had sunk deep into her soul. Some days after, as she was pleading for mercy, the Lord set her soul at liberty, and she shouted his praise with the voice of triumph. Her nurse was startled at first, but soon exclaimed, 'Why, Mrs. Bishop, I now know what has ailed you all this time! You have been under conviction! I never thought of such a thing!' The Lord healed both soul and body; and such were the overflowings of her grateful heart, that she was ready to say with one of old, 'Come and hear, all ye that fear the Lord, and I will tell you what he hath done for my soul.' This singular sickness and strange cure induced numbers to call and satisfy themselves, and she rejoiced to tell them of redeeming grace and dying love."* The husband of this woman subsequently became converted. For a number of years

* Memorials of Methodism.

their house was the "preaching place," and also the "home" for the itinerant. Still later, her husband was called into the work of the ministry; and his wife was a noble help to him in the work. Says an old preacher* of her: "Mrs. Bishop was one of the most powerful female exhorters I ever heard. There was a chastened modesty in her manner, with a pleasant voice and affectionate address, by which she found access to the hearts of stubborn gainsayers." After travelling a few years her husband located; but they lived many years to illustrate the grace of God which so powerfully brought salvation to their house.

These and similar cases, scattered along the early Methodistic history, sufficiently illustrate the spirit and agencies of that great revival of experimental and practical godliness, to which we find the subject of our memoir consecrating the warmest affections of his heart and the holiest energies of his nature. That consecration was complete. He lived only to preach Christ Jesus, and him crucified. For this he endured privation and want, sacrificed ease and home, traversed mountains and forests; and yet counted it all joy if so be that he might win souls to Christ.

We have now traced his progress through the first six years of his itinerant life, while he traversed the immense circuits of early Methodism in new fields of labour. We must now prepare to trace his course in a new sphere, and, if possible, one of higher responsibilities, and, in some respects, of severer toil.

* Rev. Asa Kent.

CHAPTER V.

MR. HEDDING ON NEW-HAMPSHIRE DISTRICT.

First Conference in New-England — Jesse Lee's Mission to the Eastern States — His First Auxiliaries — Results up to the Fifteenth Anniversary — Session of the Conference for 1807 — Mr. Hedding appointed to New-Hampshire District — Charles Virgin — One of his Preachers won over to Calvinism — Effort to save him — Temporary Success — Finally secedes — Cause of Withdrawals — Inadequacy of Support — Enormous Proportion of Locations — Causes of Inadequacy of Support — Preachers partly chargeable — Influence of the same Causes at the Present Day — Deficiencies in the New-Hampshire District — Mr. Hedding's Receipts — His Conflicts of Mind — Finds an Associate of his Youth — A Temptation overcome — A Singular Charge preferred against him at Conference — The Disposition made of it — Results to the person preferring it — Session of the Conference for 1808 — Returned to New-Hampshire District — Elected a Delegate to the General Conference — Session of the General Conference — Question of a Delegated General Conference — Failure of the Plan by the Opposition of the Middle Conferences — Excitement and Dissatisfaction — Mr. Hedding's Labours to prevent a Rupture — The Subject reconsidered — The Plan adopted — Dr. Bangs's Remarks upon it — Proposed Increase of the Number of Bishops — Conference determines to elect one only — M'Kendree elected and ordained — Close of the Conference — Mr. Hedding returns to his District — Jesse Lee revisits New-England — His Remarks on Pews — His Character drawn by Rev. A. Stevens — An Admirable Pioneer — His First Labours — Present Condition of the Work — A Triumphal Tour — The Parting Pledge.

The first conference in New-England was held at Lynn in 1792, when Bishop Asbury said of the place, "We have the *outside* of a house completed;" and of the conference, "It consisted of eight persons, much united, besides myself." Not a single member of that conference was a native of New-England. Jesse Lee, the great apostle of Methodism in the East, was a native of Virginia, and his attention had first been directed to the New-England states while travelling with Bishop Asbury in South Carolina. Here he fell in with a clerk, who was a native of Massachusetts, and from whom he learned much concerning the general character, the social and religious condition of the people in the Eastern States. From that moment his soul burned with inextinguishable ardour to carry the blessings of the gospel to them; nor was he satisfied till he opened his mission in New-England by the first sermon he preached in Norwalk, Connecticut, on the 17th of June, 1789. Nearly a year later, when at Dantown, in Connecticut, he received the joyful intelligence that three preachers were on their way to join him. "I was greatly pleased at the report," says he, "and my heart seemed to reply, 'Blessed is he that cometh in the name of the Lord.' When I saw them riding up, I stood and looked at them, and could say from my heart, 'Thou hast well done that thou art come.' Brother Jacob Brush, an elder, and George Roberts and Daniel Smith, two young men, came from Maryland to assist me in this part of the world. No one knows, but God and myself, what comfort and joy I felt at their arrival. Surely the Lord has had respect unto my prayers and granted my request." Within the next two years new auxiliaries were sent into the field, and some already there were withdrawn and sent to other parts.

Who the *eight* were of whom Mr. Asbury speaks as composing the first New-England Conference, we cannot now fully determine. Only *five* appear upon the Minutes, so that they can positively be identified in this connexion. Their names are Jesse Lee, Menzies Rainor, Jeremiah Causden, John Allen, and Lemuel Smith. On the Hartford Circuit, however, we find the names of Hope Hull, G. Roberts, and F. Aldridge; and it is probable that these men were present at the New-England Conference, though their circuit appears in connexion with the Long Island District, of which Jacob Brush was then elder. Daniel Smith, after blazing for a little time with a glorious and useful light in New-England, had returned to the South. The membership of the Lynn District, which then embraced all New-England, not subsequently included in the New-York Conference, was only one hundred and sixty-seven.

As the *fifteenth* anniversary approaches, we feel inclined to survey the general field once more. Nor can we withhold the exclamation,—"What hath God wrought!" The little company of evangelists had grown up from five to eighty, and the membership from one hundred and sixty-seven to eight thousand three hundred and twenty-five. Instead of *one* district with *four* circuits, the conference now made an exhibit of *six* districts with *fifty-eight* circuits. Instead of being dependent upon missionaries from other parts of the work, there had been already raised up within its bounds such men as Joshua Soule, Timothy Merritt, Epaphras Kibby, Daniel Webb, and others well known in the Church. The conference was a tower of intellectual and moral strength,—united, compact, energetic,—rejoicing in past successes, and confidently trusting in God for the future.

The session of the conference for 1807 was held in Boston. Bishop Asbury was present, and presided. Bishop Whatcoat died in the previous July, and on Bishop Asbury again devolved "the care of all the Churches." It was necessary to despatch business. "It kept us busy," says Mr. Asbury, "to preach five times a day, ordain fifty-nine to office, and inquire and examine into characters, graces, and gifts, and appoint the numerous stations. I preached on Wednesday, and an ordination sermon on Thursday. And I must walk through the seven conferences, and travel six thousand miles in ten months." Nothing of special interest occurred at this session of the conference, only it appears to have been a session of great harmony and good feeling; and no sooner were the appointments announced, than the noble band were seen wending their way to their various fields of labour.

Mr. Hedding was this year made presiding elder, and appointed to the New-Hampshire District. The arrangement for the district was as follows: New-Hampshire District—*Elijah Hedding*, P. E. Grantham, Warren Bannister, Charles Virgin; Hanover, Dan Young; Bridgewater, Joseph Farrar; Pembroke, Hezekiah Field; Tuftonborough, Joseph Peck, Eben. Blake; Northfield, Zachariah Gibson; Centre

Harbour, *Paul Dustin;* Landaff, *Dyer Burge;* Lunenburg, John Green. It will be perceived by the above that there were but two ordained elders upon the entire district besides himself. Four were deacons, namely, Dan Young, Warren Bannister, Joseph Farrar, and Hezekiah Field. One, namely, John Green, was in the second year of his ministry; and the remaining four had just been admitted on trial, and now entered upon their first appointments.

The health of John Green failed, so that he could not enter upon the duties of his charge; and to meet the emergency, the elder found it necessary to remove Charles Virgin, and place him in charge of the circuit. This was a responsible charge for a young and inexperienced man. The circuit was principally in the northern part of Vermont, but extended many miles into Canada. It was one hundred miles distant from his first appointment. "The conflict of my spirit," says this young man, referring to his feelings when he received his new appointment, "for a while was indescribable; but I had put my hand to the plough, and dared not look back. To take charge of a circuit I could not think of but with great trembling. I had just performed a journey of one hundred and eighty miles, and my funds were nearly out. I had promised to put up that night at Deacon Sanborn's, of precious memory, in Unity. It was a sleepless night; I prayed and wept, wept and prayed, until the dawn of day. After breakfast and family prayer, I mounted my horse to go. In the family were three children, holy members of the Methodist Episcopal Church—one son and two daughters. They stood on the door-steps. As I came to the first, who was the son, and took his hand to bid him farewell, he put a silver dollar into my hand; the second gave me another, and the next a third. I was too much affected to speak. I turned away and got out of hearing as soon as possible, and then wept profusely, and, praying God to forgive me, resolved never again to distrust my heavenly Father."

Some idea of the extent of travel and amount of labour to be performed upon this district may be gathered from the fact that it embraced the whole state, except Portsmouth and its immediate vicinity and also some half-dozen towns in the south-western part of the state. It also embraced a portion of the State of Vermont. The circuits were all very extensive, and there was not a single station in the whole district. To complete his rounds during the year required a travel of not less than three thousand miles. At each quarterly meeting he preached twice, and generally three times, besides presiding in the quarterly conferences, conducting the love-feasts, and often labouring in the prayer-meetings. In addition to all this, he had his appointments scattered all along his route from one quarterly meeting to another; so that he often preached every evening in the week, except Saturday, for three months together.

His old rheumatic affection, with which he had been so terribly afflicted in 1803, returned upon him during this year, and caused not a little suffering. For whole nights he would be unable to lie down in his bed or to sleep; but, as he was somewhat relieved during the day, these afflictions were not permitted to interfere with his labours. The preachers associated with him were principally unmarried men; they were young in years and young in the ministry, of but little experience, and also, for the most part, of small literary acquirements. All these circumstances greatly increased his responsibility, and his solicitude for the success of the work in their hands. He says: "Some of them were men of excellent natural talents, and all of them were capable of preaching religious truth to the edification and benefit of the people. They were men, too, of deep piety and great zeal, and they laboured with all their power to advance the work of God; and the Lord gave his sanction to their labours, and great numbers throughout the district were awakened and converted."

During this year, one of his preachers—a young and somewhat unstable man, but of good talents and promise—was led to embrace Calvinism, and withdrew from the Church in order to become a Congregational minister. His determination to such a course had been somewhat suddenly formed, and his elder was entirely unapprized of it. But in passing around his district he fell in with the young man, and learned that he had been spending a day with his brother, who was a Calvinistic minister. After some conversation, the young man began to intimate his dissent from the doctrines he had received, and which were preached among the Methodists; and also his inclination to believe that he had been in error in rejecting the cardinal points of the Calvinistic theology. Mr. Hedding at once perceived the true cause of the difficulty, and upon interrogation found that his brother had had a twofold agency in unsettling his mind: first, being a man of great shrewdness and logical acumen, he had argued with the young man until he had become at least bewildered; and then he had plied him with an *ad hominem* argument, by comparing his forlorn condition and worldly prospects in the Methodist itinerancy with the comfort and respectability within his reach as a settled pastor. The young man evidently wished to do right, or at least to have such reason for his change of doctrinal views and Church relation as might satisfy his own conscience; but it was evident that he had not the moral firmness to withstand the temptation. Still Mr. Hedding felt it to be his duty to converse with him, and save him if he could; and still the more so, as the young man professed to be desirous of light. As they were to spend the day together, he proposed that they should talk over the celebrated "five points," and weigh them candidly in the light of Scripture and reason. To this the young man readily assented; and when they had discussed the matter till night—carefully examining every text that had a bearing on either side, and every argument drawn from the character of God and the principles of justice and truth, and also the various logical results of the Calvinistic theory—the young man acknowledged himself to be convinced that Calvinism was founded in error, and could be supported by neither reason nor Scripture. He now proposed to return to his circuit, and labour with renewed confidence and zeal in the proclamation of the truth. Over him, however, Mr. Hedding rejoiced with trembling; for he discovered that with all his fine talents, and even his piety, he was not made of that stern stuff so essential, amid the rigours of the Methodist itinerancy, to enable him to withstand the powerful temptations to other positions offering higher worldly honour, greater ease, and more adequate pecuniary compensation. The sequel proved the well-grounded nature of Mr. Hedding's apprehensions, and also illustrated his great insight into human character; for in three months the friends of the young man had converted him back to Calvinism. At the conference his name was recorded as "withdrawn" in the Minutes; and he subsequently became a Congregational minister.

It would be a very uncharitable insinuation, to intimate that the great body of those who have withdrawn from the Methodist ministry during her history have been actuated solely, or even mainly, by pecuniary considerations. But, unquestionably, the Church has suffered immensely from the inadequacy of the support given to her ministry. Many of the noblest heralds of the cross in her early history, after a few years' service, were compelled by the necessity of their families to retire from the regular work. During the first fifty years, more than one-half of all who entered the Methodist ministry sooner or later *located;* and many of those who died in the work were compelled, at some time during their ministry, to locate and make provision for their families. This inadequacy resulted in part from the new state of the country and the societies, as also from the poverty of the people. Another cause is to be found at the door of the preachers themselves; they often made it a matter of public boasting that they asked no salaries—sought not the money of the people, but the people themselves; and all this was done in a way that gave the people to understand that the Methodist religion was "a cheap religion"—was to cost the people but very little. Thus they not only failed to teach the people the Christian duty of giving, so far as they were able, a competent support to those who were called to preach the gospel to them, and who were to "live by the gospel," but many of them, by unguarded speeches, indirectly encouraged a spirit that would make beggars of ministers and paupers of their families. It is not too much to say, that that political and spiritual error of the fathers has been entailed, in many of its consequences, upon their children. "The fathers have eaten sour grapes, and the children's teeth are set on edge." At the present day, the influence of this evil in the Church—the inadequate support of the ministry—is manifested not so much in the number of locations, as in its prevention of many, who are called of God and who are not without gifts and graces, from entering into the field, where there is so little inviting to a young man in the line of personal comfort or family support. Were the Churches all poor and unable to do better, the case would be quite different; the responsibility would then lie wholly upon him who, when called by God, refused to obey: nor do we design to excuse or palliate the turning aside from the ministry on the part of any individual who has been called by God, merely on account of the poor prospect of needful support. It is safest and best to do our duty at all times and in all places. We only speak of facts that do exist. It is vain to deny them; it is unwise to close our eyes against them; and it is equally absurd to attempt to dispose of them altogether, by attempting to minify the value—the piety or talents—of these young men who are thus deterred from entering the ministry. It is an evil that requires not scorn, but cure. And then, on the other hand, we are to avoid with equal care holding out worldly inducements—in the way of ease, wealth, or honour—to the ministry, lest the Church of God become cursed with selfish and worldly-minded men in this office, to which the great motive should be the love of God and of the souls of men.

Perhaps in no part of the work where Methodism was organized was the support so inadequate as within the bounds of Mr. Hedding's district. The country was new, and mountainous, and sterile; the work was new, the people poor—many of them very poor indeed. It will seem almost incredible, and yet such is the fact, Mr. Hedding's receipts during his first year upon this district, besides his simple travelling expeness, which made but an inconsiderable sum, were $4 25! His horse broke down through excessive labour during the year; clothing, books, and other little necessaries, all were to be provided for out of this four dollars and twenty-five cents! While we cannot wonder that many of the noblest and purest spirits in the Methodistic reformation were compelled to retire from the itinerant work, that they might be able to provide for their children, we are filled with admiration that even the single men, with no families to provide for, were not disheartened. At times Mr. Hedding's mind was deeply affected, especially as he found himself cramped and straitened almost beyond endurance, and then could see no prospect of relief ahead. One passage of Scripture, however, was ever present with him in these times of mental misgiving: "To him that overcometh will I grant to sit with me in my throne." Cheered and comforted, he would go forth again heartily to his work. And as he went, his lips would often chime,—

"No foot of land do I possess;
No cottage in this wilderness:
A poor wayfaring man,
I lodge awhile in tents below,
Or gladly wander to and fro,
Till I my Canaan gain."

An incident, by which his mind was momentarily affected, he thus describes: "Having heard that an old associate of my youth resided a few miles out of my route on the district, I went to see him. I found him in good health, and that he had become quite rich. He was not a professed Christian. After taking me over his farm, and showing me all his many things for comfort and ease, and the taste and skill with which he had enriched and beautified the natural resources of the place, he said to me, 'I take great comfort in all these, and also in thinking that I shall leave at least one spot on the earth better than I found it.' At first the contrast between his temporal condition and my own—the ease and affluence in which he lived, and my own toilsome and poverty-stricken sphere—especially when I knew that my own prospects were at the outset as good at least as his, produced a deep depression in my mind. But it was only for a moment. Recurring to the fact that the man after all seemed to derive his happiness not so much from the enjoyment of the good things of life that surrounded him, as from the idea that he would leave behind him a cultivated spot where he had found a wilderness, I said to myself,—'If he finds comfort in thinking that the world will be better for his having lived in it, how much greater source of happiness have I, who am devoting all my time and energies to doing good in the world!' This thought had no sooner passed through my mind, than the rising disquietude of my heart was completely stilled; my soul was filled with consolation, and I was ready to exclaim:—

> "'Tis all my business here below
>   To cry—Behold the Lamb!
> Happy, if with my latest breath
>   I may but gasp his name;
> Preach him to all, and cry in death,
>   Behold, behold the Lamb!'"

The only formal complaint ever entered against Mr. Hedding at conference was from this district, and the occasion for it occurred during this year. On one of the circuits resided a certain physician; he was a man of good talents and great shrewdness, but at the same time a man of very narrow views, and exceedingly bigoted in his character. He made a formal complaint to the presiding elder against one of the preachers on the circuit, and demanded a council for his trial. The charge was, "*Superfluity of apparel;*" and the specifications were—"1. The preacher wore silver knee-buckles in his small clothes; 2. The preacher allowed his wife to wear a veil," which, by the way, was a mourning veil, worn on account of the death of some relative. These the doctor alleged were great grievances to himself, his wife, and many others of the Church; and also a great scandal to the cause of religion. Mr. Hedding plainly told him that these were small matters, not of sufficient magnitude to call a council to try a preacher for; and all that he could do would be to advise the preacher to cease wearing the silver knee-buckles, if their use was a stumbling-block to any, and to use strings in their place; and also to advise the preacher's wife to lay off her mourning veil for peace' sake. Mr. Hedding accordingly gave the advice to the preacher and to his wife, and there rested the matter. But when he reached conference, he found that the persistent physician had forwarded a bill of charges against him, signed by himself and wife, and accusing him of refusing to administer the Discipline against an offending preacher. The doctor's letter was read to the conference, when they instantly dismissed it as unworthy of notice. This, however, was not the end of the case, so far as the stickler against silver buckles and mourning veils was concerned. The society, learning that he had forwarded such charges, were indignant, and finding that while, like many others, he had tithed mint, and rue, and cummin, he had neglected the weightier matters of the law,—while he had been zealous against knee-buckles and mourning veils, he had not been so careful to preserve truth and righteousness, but had actually uttered falsehoods,—they called him to trial, found him guilty, and expelled him from the Church.

The session of the New-England Conference for 1808 was held in New-London, and commenced April 18th. Bishop Asbury was present and presided. The preachers came up from the different parts of the work, bringing the glad news of continued success and triumphs in the cause of Christ. They reported a membership of eight thousand eight hundred and twenty-five, and a gain of five hundred. The session of the conference was harmonious, and the public ministrations were attended with good results. The business of the conference had to be expedited on account of the General Conference, then just at hand. Bishop Asbury says: "The conference sat till Friday; we wrought in great haste, in great order, and in peace, through a great deal of business. There were seventeen deacons, travelling and local, ordained; and nine elders ordained in the Congregational Church, before fifteen hundred or two thousand witnesses. I know not where large congregations are so orderly as in tho Eastern States. There was a work of God going on during the sitting of conference. The General Conference hastened our breaking up, the delegates thereto requesting leave to go."

Mr. Hedding was returned again to the district, upon which the appointments were as follows:—NEW-HAMPSHIRE DISTRICT, *Elijah Hedding*, P. E.; Grantham, *Caleb Dustin*, *Paul Dustin;* Hanover, David Carr; Bridgewater, William Hunt; Pembroke, Hezekiah Field; Tuftonborough, *Lewis Bates;* Northfield and Centre-Harbour, Joseph Peck; Landaff, Zachariah Gibson; Lunenburg, Ebenezer Blake. This year there were three elders besides himself upon the district; also three deacons; and also three who were in the second year of their ministry.

The New-England Conference at its session elected seven delegates to attend the ensuing General Conference. They also passed resolutions in favour of making the General Conference a delegated body. The delegates elected were George Pickering, Joshua Soule, Elijah R. Sabin, Oliver Beale, Martin Ruter, Elijah Hedding, and Thomas Branch.

The session of the General Conference commenced May 1st, in the city of Baltimore. This General Conference having some of the fundamental principles of our economy to settle, its session was of no ordinary importance, and excited no ordinary degree of solicitude throughout the entire Church. Up to this time *every ordained elder* was entitled to a seat in this highest council in the Church. There were now present one hundred and twenty-nine members, distributed among the seven annual conferences as follows:—New-York Conference, nineteen; New-England, seven; Western, eleven; South Carolina, eleven; Virginia, eighteen; Baltimore, thirty-one; and Philadelphia, thirty-two. Bishop Asbury and many of the preachers had become convinced of the necessity of a delegated Conference. The reasons were obvious: the great extension of the work and the multiplication of elders; the difficulty, loss of time, and great expense attendant upon the gathering of so many from remote portions of the work; the preponderance that would always be in favour of the central annual conferences, among which the General Conferences would generally be held;* the practical inutility of

* This was strikingly manifest in the General Conference of 1804, in which all the elders were entitled to a seat. The conference representation, accordingly, was as follows:—

Border or remote conferences, namely: New-England Conference,

gathering so large a body of men to transact the business of the Church, when it could be done as well, if not better, by a delegated number; and, finally, the necessity of it as a bond of union among the annual conferences. This was, in fact, the great question of the conference. The interest of the Church had been thoroughly awakened upon the subject; for as early as 1806 Bishop Asbury had submitted a paper to the annual conferences, beginning with Baltimore, recommending a called session of a General Conference, or convention, of seven delegates from each annual conference. But the plan failed in consequence of the non-concurrence of the Virginia Conference.

The subject was brought before the body by a memorial from the New-York Conference, and referred to a committee of fourteen from each annual conference. The committee reported in favour of the memorialists; but the plan of a delegated conference proposed by them was, after considerable discussion, rejected by a vote of fifty-seven for, and sixty-five against it. The remote conferences were generally in favour of it; but the central ones, such as Baltimore, Virginia, and Philadelphia, were opposed to it. When the vote announcing the failure of the plan was declared, great dissatisfaction was mani-

four; Western Conference, three; South Carolina Conference, five; New-York Conference, twelve: making, from four conferences, a total of twenty-four.

Central Conferences, namely: Baltimore Conference, twenty-nine; Virginia Conference, seventeen; Philadelphia Conference, forty-one: making, from three central conferences, a total of eighty-seven.

fested; and fears were at one time entertained, that the conference would break up without establishing any general bond of union among the widely-scattered portions of the work. Many of the preachers from the remote conferences resolved to leave immediately, and return home. It was a crisis in the affairs of the Church, then in the infancy of its organization. "Had they left at this crisis," says Mr. Hedding, "it would probably have been the last General Conference ever held." All the members from the New-England Conference, except himself, were making arrangements to depart. In this emergency he entreated them to remain; and declared his own determination to remain till the close of the conference, whatever might happen. Mr. Asbury also exerted his influence, and detained them; and also the members of other conferences who were about leaving. The delegates from the central conferences now saw the necessity of some action, if they would preserve the integrity of the Church. The vote was reconsidered; and after mature deliberation, and considerable debate, the general plan of a delegated General Conference was agreed upon. It was to be composed of one delegate for every five members of an annual conference, and was to meet quadrennially on the first day of May. A constitution, in the form of restrictive provisions, by which its actions should be regulated, was adopted. This plan was adopted almost unanimously, and thus peace and harmony were restored to the body.

Though not brought before the body in so prominent a manner as some others, yet in this matter Mr. Hedding proved himself to be a wise counsellor, and a safe and judicious man. He exhibited that clear insight, that calm spirit, that dispassionate manner, and that sound judgment which so marked his character in subsequent years. Mr. Asbury was not a little indebted to him for the influence he exerted in checking the action of the more violent spirits on that exciting occasion.

In relation to the settlement of this great question, Dr. Bangs, in his History, says: "Before this, each General Conference felt itself at full liberty, not being prohibited by any standing laws, to make whatever alterations it might see fit, or to introduce any new doctrine or item, in the Discipline, which either fancy, inclination, discretion, or indiscretion might dictate. Under this state of things, knowing the rage of man for novelty, and witnessing the destructive changes which had frequently laid waste Churches, by removing ancient landmarks, and so modifying doctrines and usages as to suit the temper of the times, or to gratify either a corrupt taste or a perverse disposition, many had felt uneasy apprehensions for the safety and unity of the Church and the stability of its doctrines, moral discipline, and the frame of its government; and none were more solicitous on this subject than Bishop Asbury, who had laboured so long, with an assiduity equalled by few, if indeed any, and suffered so much for the propagation and establishing of these important points. He, therefore, greatly desired, before he should be called home, to see them fixed upon a permanent foundation." This action of the conference was received with lively satisfaction by both ministers and people throughout the entire connexion; and the experience of half a century has attested its wisdom, notwithstanding the modifications and infractions that have taken place.

Having settled this fundamental question in the economy of the Church, the body proceeded to the regular routine of business. Bishop Whatcoat had died; Dr. Coke was still in Europe, and proposed, with the consent of the conference, to remain there; it therefore became necessary to strengthen the episcopacy by the election of a new bishop. Indeed, it was proposed to elect seven bishops—one for each conference, having Bishop Asbury as a general superintendent; and thus either do away with the presiding eldership altogether, or at least to greatly modify it. The plan was advocated by some of the ablest men on the floor of the conference; but was finally rejected by a strong vote. A motion to elect two additional bishops was also negatived; and the conference finally determined upon the election of one. The election took place on the same day; and upon counting the ballots it was found that one hundred and twenty-eight votes had been cast, of which ninety-five were for William M'Kendree, who was therefore elected. The balance of the votes were cast for Ezekiel Cooper and Jesse Lee; the former, according to Bangs's History, having twenty-eight of that number. M'Kendree was a member of the Western Conference at the time of his election. He commenced travelling in the Virginia Conference in 1788; and from that time forward, by untiring devotion, arduous labours, signal successes, and acknowledged piety, prudence, and zeal, had made himself worthy of such distinguished honour and confidence from his brethren. On the 17th of May he was consecrated by Bishop Asbury, assisted by Rev. Messrs. Freeborn Garrettson, Philip Bruce, Jesse Lee, and Thomas Ware. He was fifty-one years of age at the time of his consecration, and continued to serve the Church with eminent ability in the episcopal office for nearly twenty-seven years; when, at the advanced age of seventy-eight, "he fell asleep."

Having surmounted the obstacles in the way of a general and harmonious organization, the subsequent doings of the conference were characterized by great harmony and good feeling. And in this spirit, having accomplished its great work, it adjourned on the 26th of the month. This settlement afforded unfeigned satisfaction to Bishop Asbury: his hope for the future of the Church now rested in abiding confidence; and he lived to realize, in a degree, the consummation of his hope in the assembling and transactions of the General Conference of 1812.

At the close of the General Conference, Mr. Hedding immediately returned, to resume his labours upon the New-Hampshire District. The labours of the year were much the same as those of the preceding,—much travel, continual preaching, and withal refreshing showers from the presence of the Lord. There were extensive revivals on the district, and many were added to the Church. Mr. Hedding, through determined effort, greatly improved the finances of his district, and secured more adequate support for the preachers.

Even at this early day, it was found necessary in New-England to pew the principal Methodist churches that were erected; such were the prevailing habits and tastes of the people. This was somewhat of an annoyance to Jesse Lee, who returned this year to survey his old field of labour. He says of the church in Newport, where Samuel Merwin was stationed that year: "The house has a steeple, with a pretty large bell; it is fitted up with large square pews, so that a part of the people sit with their faces, and others with their backs toward the preacher; and these pews are sold to purchasers. Males and females sit together. Is not this a violation of Methodist rules?" A few days after, we find him in Boston, preaching in the new church, then lately erected in Bromfield-street. He says: "This new meeting-house is large and elegant; I think eighty-four by sixty-four. It has an altar round the pulpit, in a half circle, and the house is fixed with long pews, of a circular form, to be uniform with the altar. The front of the gallery is of the same form. It looks very handsome, and will contain an abundance of people;

but is not on the Methodist plan, for the pews are sold to the highest bidder." Travelling on as far as Portsmouth, he preaches in another "meeting-house, fitted up with pews." We know not how many other churches of this character had been erected within his old field of labour; but it is evident that Methodism, in the short time that had elapsed from his departure till his return on this visit, had been acquiring strength, and the people were not altogether inattentive to the architecture of their churches, plain and even uncouth as some of those old churches appeared in subsequent years, when the general style of building, and especially of church architecture, had greatly changed.

We have already had frequent occasion to allude to the pioneer labours of Jesse Lee in New-England. The great Methodistic movement in the Eastern States, in which Mr. Hedding had now become one of the leading spirits, could not be well understood without at least a brief survey of the labours and character of this truly apostolic man. For this reason, and not because of any direct personal intimacy, we have made frequent references to his travels and labours. As he is now about to take his final leave of New-England, it is fitting that his character and the results of his labours should be briefly reviewed. Says the author of the Memorials of Methodism, speaking of Lee at this point in his career: "We cannot take our final leave of him without lingering a few moments in the contemplation of his rare career. He is the great man who achieves great results by great endeavours. History will accord to Lee no ordinary share of such fame. He possessed no preëminent intellectual faculty. His literary attainments were not above mediocrity. His only publication—the 'Short History of the Methodists'—though invaluable for its data, makes no pretensions whatever, except to industrious research and accuracy. His opinions on great ecclesiastical measures would not, we think, entitle him to the claim of superior legislative sagacity. But, with a good practical judgment for ordinary affairs, considerable general intelligence, a remarkably simple and pertinent Saxon style, strong sensibilities, which were easily kindled in discourse, and a rare native faculty of wit, he combined an executive energy which has few parallels in our history, except Wesley, Asbury, and, it may be, Garrettson. This energy was not impulsive; it was singularly cool and continuous. Its calmness was its most intrinsic and valuable trait. His great travels, his incessant preaching, the imperturbable persistence with which he brooked opposition and all obstacles, continually and tranquilly repeating his endeavours against them until they disappeared—these characteristics distinguishing a minister of thirty-three years, mark him as no ordinary man. The great results that have followed his labours will always entitle him to the reputation of greatness. His agency in the founding of Methodism in New-England will ever place him among the chief characters in the ecclesiastical history of those Eastern States." Mr. Lee, after this visit, continued to labour in the south some eight years, where he finished his long and eventful career in the joyful assurance of a better resurrection. He received his regular appointments to the last year of his career, but travelled more or less "at large." To the very last "he was characterized by the same unresting missionary spirit which prompted his earlier labours." He made extensive excursions into the remote parts of the south. He was also for several years chaplain to the Congress of the United States; and before the legislators of the nation it is said that "he preached with the same simplicity and power which attended his ministrations in the frontier wilderness, or on the highway."

From this outline of the character of this heroic man, it will be seen how admirably adapted he must have been, in the prime of his life, to pioneer work. But, without doing injustice to the memory of Lee, we think the necessity of a different class of men will also be seen; men of comprehensive and sagacious minds, of higher legislative and judicial capacities—such as were Hedding, Soule, Pickering and others—in order that the organic structure of the rising Church might be made harmonious, compact, strong, and lasting. Nineteen years before this final visit, Lee had entered New-England a solitary stranger: after more than three months' travel and labour, the first class, consisting of three women, had been formed at Stratfield, Conn. Now, on his return, he joyfully witnessed the spread of Methodism over all the land.

At the close of this ecclesiastical year, this scene of his former labours presented an array of one annual conference, six presiding elders' districts, fifty-seven circuits and stations, eighty-three stationed preachers, and an aggregate membership of ten thousand and ninety-six. No wonder that this last tour of Lee through New-England was a sort of triumphal tour, and that he was everywhere hailed by both preachers and people with the greatest delight. At the close of his meetings he was accustomed to give the parting hand to those who were determined to meet him in the better land. Multitudes there pledged themselves to him and to their God, and among them were hosts of the unconverted; and long before this most of them have, together with the heaven-honoured pioneer, entered into rest.

CHAPTER VI.

MR. HEDDING ON NEW-LONDON DISTRICT.

Session of the Conference for 1809—Mr. Hedding appointed to the New-London District—Preachers on the District—Its Extent—Camp-meeting—First one on the District—Solicitude—Wonderful Display of Divine Power—Five Hundred prostrate on the Earth—Results—Mr. Hedding's Marriage—Sketch of Miss Lucy Blish, afterward Mrs. Hedding—Her Parents—Early Education—Early Religious Impressions—Perplexed by Calvinism—Visits a Sister within the Bounds of Plattsburgh Circuit—Hears Methodist Preaching—Is converted and Joins the Church—Returns Home—Her Parents converted—A New Society raised up—Mr. Hedding's First Acquaintance with her—Their Marriage—Survives him—Mr. Hedding takes up his Residence in Winchester, N. H.—Reviews his Pecuniary Profits and Losses as a Single Man—The Session of the Conference at Winchester—How provided for—Bishops Asbury and M'Kendree—Returned to the District—Preachers with him—Removes to Ludlow, Mass.—Attempt to warn him out of Town—Employed by the Town on his Vacant Sabbaths—Invited by the Town to become the Settled Pastor—Declines—Subsequent Occasional Thoughts—Mr. Newhall's "Rich and Refreshing Meditations" when forcing his Way through Snow-drifts—Horse disabled—Travels on Foot—An Attack of Rheumatism—Crippled Condition—A Wayside Incident—A Singular Sweat—Unexpected Restoration—Conference approaching—Remarks upon his Ten Years' Labour—Difficulties encountered by Methodism—Its Great Successes—Progress of the Work on the District—Camp-meeting—Summation at the Close of the Year.

The session of the New-England Conference for 1809 commenced on the 15th of June, and was held at Monmouth, Me. Bishops Asbury and M'Kendree were both present. A camp-meeting was held during the time of the conference, in a grove about one mile distant. Many of the preachers devoted considerable time to its exercises; a great revival occurred, and many were converted to God. Many persons from a distance attended it; and its results extended to the societies throughout all that region. Mr. Hedding was an active participator in its exercises, notwithstanding his duties as a presiding elder, in the conference and the cabinet.

From this conference he was appointed to the New-London District, the organization of which was as follows: NEW-LONDON DISTRICT—*Elijah Hedding*, P.E.; Tolland, *Benj. P. Hill*, William Hinman; Ashburnham, *David Carr*, Robert Arnold; Needham, Benjamin R. Hoyt, Nathan Hill; Providence and Smithfield, Greenleaf R. Norris, Pliny Brett; East Greenwich, Theophilus Smith; Pomfret, Isaac Bonney, Samuel Cutler; New-London, Elisha Streeter, John Lindsey. It will be perceived that there were upon this entire district but two ordained elders besides Mr. Hedding. Three others were ordained deacons, namely, Norris, Brett, and Smith; while of the remaining eight, three had travelled one year, namely, Bonney, Hinman, and Cutler; and five, namely, Hoyt, Hill, Arnold, Streeter, and Lindsey, had just been admitted on trial. No less than *ten* preachers had located at this conference; most of them compelled to it from the necessity of providing for their families; and it was thus that their places were filled with new recruits.

The New-London District, at this time, embraced all that part of the State of Connecticut lying east of the Connecticut River, and all that part of Rhode

Island west of Narragansett Bay, including Providence; and also a belt across the State of Massachusetts, extending from the Connecticut River nearly to Boston, and a few towns in the south-western part of New-Hampshire. It was a year of great labour, but also of great success. Many of the circuits were visited with glorious revivals. Every circuit except one reported a good increase at the ensuing annual conference.

The first camp-meeting ever held upon the district was held by Mr. Hedding in Hebron, Conn., during the present year. It was a new thing in the country, and had no doubt been suggested to him by what he had witnessed at the camp-meeting in Monmouth at the previous session of the conference. Camp-meetings were first held in this country in the State of Kentucky, in the years 1801 and 1802, during the wonderful revival of religion that pervaded the Methodist and Presbyterian Churches in that region. In a few years, however, they became quite common among the Methodists in the south and west. In the east they were yet a novel thing. The fame of them, however, had spread everywhere; and when the time appointed for the meeting at Hebron arrived, the people flocked in from all the surrounding country. Many came the distance of fifty or sixty miles, provisioned for the week, and burning with desire to see the glory of the Lord. Such meetings were not then conducted with as much system as at the present time. There were at least four sermons each day; and the intermediate time, almost day and night without intermission, was occupied in meetings for prayer, exhortation, and the relation of Christian experience. Several things conspired to make Mr. Hedding feel an intense anxiety as to the conduct and results of this meeting. He knew that there was a strong prejudice in the community against such meetings, and many scandalous stories had been circulated about them. It was the first that had ever been attempted to be held on the district; and, in fact, he himself had but little acquaintance with the management of them, as he had visited but one, and that was the one held during the session of the conference at Monmouth.

He felt that a heavy responsibility was upon him; and he earnestly besought God that he would not permit his people to go up without his presence, and that the meeting might redound to the honour of true religion and the good of the Church. The result proved that these intercessions were not in vain; it was perhaps the most memorable camp-meeting ever held in New-England. From the very commencement there were signal indications of the divine presence and power. Often during the exercises individuals would fall prostrate to the ground. As the meeting progressed, the interest continued to increase. On the fourth or fifth day, during the evening sermon, the power of the Holy Ghost fell on the congregation with overwhelming force. The people began to fall on every side. Many who had come to the meeting out of mere idle curiosity, were stricken down to the ground, and cried aloud for mercy. Many of other Christian denominations, who were greatly prejudiced against the Methodists, and especially against such exercises, fell powerless to the earth, and afterward acknowledged the mighty hand of God. Quite a number of Methodists, also, who had never witnessed such scenes, and were strongly opposed to them, fell along with the others. It was an awful hour of the manifestation of God's power and grace. Within the space of a few minutes, it was ascertained that not less than *five hundred* lay prostrate by the power of the Holy Ghost. Although it was evening, the report of these events was spread through the town of Colchester, a few miles distant; and the people flocked in crowds to the scene. Physicians came, and passed around among the prostrate people, feeling the pulses of the helpless: they looked, as they passed around, as solemn as if they were just going forth to the judgment. The people were all amazed and confounded; the scoffer was silenced; the blasphemer turned pale and trembled; the infidel stood aghast. The universal voice of all was: "Truly this is the mighty power of God; let us adore and tremble before him." That night of glorious power was with multitudes the turning point that thenceforward shaped their destinies heavenward; and in the breasts of hundreds of Christians the holy fire was kindled anew into a more glorious and inextinguishable flame. Victory was now complete. The fame of this meeting spread far and wide, and exerted a powerful influence in favour of Methodism through all that region of country. It contributed not a little to swell the successes and the gains which we have already noticed for the year upon the district.

Up to this time Mr. Hedding had travelled as a single man; but on the 10th of January, 1810, he was united in marriage to Miss Lucy Blish, of Gilsum, Cheshire Co., N. H. Her parents were both members of the Congregational Church, her father being a deacon, and a man of good standing among his people. They had conscientiously and piously dedicated their daughter in her infancy to the Lord by the sacred rite of baptism. In very early life she was unusually thoughtful upon the subject of religion, and was often deeply anxious for the salvation of her soul: but little encouragement, however, was given at that day to induce children to become experimentally pious. She was also greatly perplexed with Calvinism. In this state of mind she continued till she was about eighteen years of age, when, in 1801, she visited a married sister residing within the bounds of the Plattsburgh Circuit. Here, for the first time in her life, she enjoyed the privilege of hearing Methodist doctrines and the Methodist ministry. These new doctrines immediately attracted her attention; she perceived that they solved all the difficulties which had so long perplexed her mind; and she at once embraced them heartily. But this was not all: her way was now opened to seek that which had so long been the conscious want of her soul: she sought the Lord with all her heart, and it was not long before pardoning mercy was revealed unto her soul, and she enjoyed a great and holy peace. As the ministry of the Methodist Church had been instrumental in leading her to God, and as she heartily believed all its doctrines, and believed that its institutions were peculiarly calculated to help her in the divine life, she soon became a member of that Church. From various causes, her stay with her sister was protracted to three or four years; during all of which time she enjoyed the ministry and the privileges of the Methodist Episcopal Church.

On her return to her father's house, she felt it to be her duty to converse with her parents and other members of the family upon experimental religion. The renewal of the heart was to them a new theme; and even her parents, though they had long been members of the Church, and her father was a deacon, confessed that they were not only inexperienced, but ignorant upon the subject. Anxious for the salvation of her parents, and solicitous for the cause of Christ in the neighbourhood, she obtained the consent of her parents to invite Methodist preachers—after giving a full and clear account of their doctrines and mode of preaching—to come into the neighbourhood and preach at her father's house. The result was that soon both parents, and also other members of the family, and some of the neighbours, were converted to God. Regular preaching was established, and a flourishing society raised up.

Mr. Hedding first became acquainted with this young woman when he was travelling the Plattsburgh Circuit, in 1801. That acquaintance had been renewed after her return to her father's in New-Hampshire. Having become satisfied of her fitness to be associated with him in the great work to which his all was dedicated, and that she would be a help and not a hinderance, whatever toils and privations they might be subjected to, he made proposals of marriage, and was accepted. It is a sufficient vindication of the wisdom of that choice, that through all the vicissitudes of an itinerant's career, for more than forty years, she was the constant companion of his toils, and the sharer of his joys and sorrows. Forty-two years and four months after their marriage we witnessed the agony of her bursting heart, as she came down to the brink of Jordan and saw the dark waters close over her sainted husband forever. An aged pilgrim, sustained and comforted by the undying faith that shed such a glorious halo over his last hours, she lingers yet a little while below, till her Master shall bid her come up and join her beloved in the better land. Calmly and peacefully may the shades of evening gather around her; glorious may be the unfolding of the morning of her immortality.

After his marriage Mr. Hedding took up his residence in the town of Winchester, New-Hampshire. He had now been travelling, including the period when employed by the elder, ten years. They were, as we have already seen, years of hard labour as well as effective service. They were, however, years of privation, as well as of toil and suffering. A short time before he died, referring to this period, he said to the author: "During that time I was a single man, and travelled, on an average, three thousand miles a year, or thirty thousand in ten years; and preached nearly every day in the year. All the pay I received for these ten years was four hundred and fifty dollars, or an average of forty-five dollars a year. One year I received on my circuit, exclusive of travelling expenses, three dollars and twenty-five cents; this was made up to twenty-one dollars at conference. My pantaloons were often patched upon the knees, and the sisters often showed their kindness by *turning an old coat for me!*" A man that could perform such labours and endure such privations, through so long a period, without murmuring and fainting, must have been deeply conscious of the imperative call of God that proclaimed woe to him if he preached not the gospel; and also deeply imbued with that divine love that led his Lord and Master to toil and suffer before him.

Let us pause for a moment in our narrative. A phenomenon rises before us demanding solution. The principles and motives of human action for the most part lie upon the surface, and may be known. The warrior, dyed with the blood of a hundred battles, goes forth at the summons of glory, or at his country's call. The stern Puritan forsakes the home of his fathers, and turns the prow of his bark toward the mighty sea; but we can gauge the magnitude of his mission: he goes to sow the seeds of liberty upon the virgin soil of a new world; he goes to build cities, to found nations, to people a continent, and to open up a highway to all the earth. The orator, in his divine eloquence, rushes with the impetuosity of a torrent, sweeping along with him the convictions and sympathies of men; but the ground of action no one can mistake: the interests of his country or of humanity are in peril, and he calls to the rescue. The man devoted to science toils with unceasing effort, his very frame shattered and shaken with the intensity of his thought; and we know that the love of science or of fame impels him to action, even while it is consuming all that is physical and mortal in his nature. The author delves into the deep, dark mines of thought: it is for him to speak to coming ages; his busy brain is shaping thoughts that shall live forever; preparing utterances that shall "fall like fire upon the hearts of men" in coming generations, and kindle in them new life and energy,—utterances that, by their sway over the realms of thought and emotion, shall exercise a vast and undying influence over the affairs of men, and the destinies of the world.

But what shall we say of this forlorn hope, this band of heroes, with a devotion more pure and ceaseless than that of the patriot, with an eloquence combining the elements of moral greatness and power, and with a hardihood that shrinks from no labour, and is intimidated by no danger,—toiling without prospect or hope of earthly reward,—sacrificing ease, comfort, home, health, and even life itself,—treading the waste places and the wildernesses, and traversing islands, continents, and oceans? Who are they? by whom are they sent forth? and what is the object of their toil? Let the Churches that have been planted all over the land, the missionaries that have been sent out to other lands; let the incessantly-increasing tide of influence that is rolling onward the kingdom of Christ to its complete and final triumph; and, above all, let the millions that have been brought to God, and are now decked with light and glory around the eternal throne; let all these respond and tell who these wanderers are, and for what they toil! Are they charged with being corrupt men and dissemblers? The purity of their lives vindicates them. Are they charged with being ignorant and blind fanatics? The results of their ministry, and the noble monument erected by their labours, are a full refutation of the charge. Is it said that they laboured only for selfish and mercenary ends? Their unselfish lives, their self-denials, and in most cases their poverty, attest that such were not their aims.

Roll back the tide of time through the lapse of eighteen centuries. I see a little band traversing the idolatrous, barbarous regions of Asia Minor. Their appearance marks them as of the land of Israel. They journey from city to city; they are inured to hardships and dangers; men despise and ridicule them; they are exposed to buffetting and stripes, imprisonments and death: but none of these things move them. I go and ask them why they toil, and suffer, and die. With united voice they respond, "The love of Christ constraineth us,"—"Neither count we our lives dear unto ourselves, so that we might finish our course with joy, and the ministry which we have received of the Lord Jesus, to testify the gospel of the grace of God." The same spirit that beamed out in the life of the missionaries of the primeval Church, though smothered for ages, burst forth again in all its primitive beauty and power in the early apostles of Methodism. The workmen were changed, but the work was one.

But, after all, was it not the fire of youthful enthusiasm, that would become rectified by age and experience? Shall we ask, then, how these labours, privations, and sufferings were regarded, when the time of labour was over, and life was hasting to its close? In the dismal cell of a Roman prison I see a prisoner: the walls of his narrow room, like a wall of granite, are enclosed about him; his locks are white, he is shaken with age; he sits down to write· with difficulty he traces his message upon the manuscript before him. It is a final charge to his son in the gospel. His own life has been spent in toil and suffering, and now he is in poverty and imprisonment, and soon to die like a common felon. Does he charge his son to seek exemption from toil and suffering?

Nay; he says, "Endure afflictions, do the work of an evangelist, make full proof of thy ministry." As he looks back upon the past, he says: "I am now ready to be offered, and the time of my departure is at hand. I have fought a good fight; I have finished my course; I have kept the faith." Then, as he glanced forward to the future, he added,—"Henceforth there is laid up for me a crown of righteousness, which the Lord, the righteous Judge, shall give me at that day."

And so our venerable Hedding—standing upon the brink of the grave, and looking back over the lapse of half a century—said: "I had laboured fifty years and one month in the ministry before my constitution gave way; I suffered a great deal; have been persecuted; the most abusive and slanderous stories have been circulated against me; men have come to my meetings armed with clubs, intending to assault me; the Methodists were poor, the fare hard, and the rides long and tedious: but *if I had fifty lives, and each afforded me an opportunity for fifty years' labour, I would cheerfully employ them all in the same blessed cause, and, if need be, would suffer the same privations.*"

Such were the feelings and views with which he entered upon the great work of his life; and such were the feelings with which he looked back upon that work from the sublime altitude from which he has so lately ascended to his God.

The New-England Conference, for the year 1810,

met at Winchester, the place which had lately become Mr. Hedding's residence. The conference met under circumstances somewhat peculiar. In the village of Winchester—or indeed near enough to it to entertain the preachers—there was but one Methodist family. At the preceding session of the conference, the head of this family presented himself before that body, and invited them to hold their next session in Winchester. When the brethren inquired how the conference would be entertained in a village where there was but one Methodist family, he requested that the conference would give themselves no concern as to that matter, but accept his invitation. His pledge was nobly redeemed. His own ample house was first filled to repletion, and abundant hospitality shown to all his guests. Then a number were quartered among his relations and friends in the village. Those that remained were provided with excellent board at his expense. The conference had never been more munificently entertained than at this session.

Bishops Asbury and M'Kendree were both present, and alternately presided over the sessions of the conference; and both took part in the public exercises of the occasion. The aggregate membership returned this year was eleven thousand two hundred and twenty, being an increase upon last year of one thousand one hundred and twenty-four. The ranks of the ministry were weakened by five locations, and recruited by fifteen admissions upon trial.

Mr. Hedding was returned to the district, the

organization of which for the year was as follows:—NEW-LONDON DISTRICT, *Elijah Hedding*, P. E.; Tolland, *Joel Steel*, Samuel Cutler; Ashburnham, *Philip Munger*, Stephen Wingate; Needham, *Isaac Bonney*, Robert Arnold; Providence and Smithfield, *Pliny Brett*, Elisha Streeter; East Greenwich, *Benjamin P. Hill;* Pomfret, *Theophilus Smith;* New-London, *Joel Winch*, E. Marble, A. Stebbins. Here we find seven elders besides Mr. Hedding on the district, and a much greater weight of experience if not of talent than on the former year.

To obtain a location more central to the district than Winchester, Mr. Hedding removed to Ludlow in Massachusetts. An incident connected with his removal to this place will show to what extent opposition to Methodism was carried in those early days, and what means were resorted to in order to throw reproach upon her ministers when opportunity offered. There was at this time a law in force in that state, providing that when a stranger moved into a place, if the authorities of the town warned him to leave it, and he did not, and afterward became a pauper, the town was not obliged to support him, but the expense of his support fell upon the state. When Mr. Hedding moved to Ludlow, some of the people were bitterly opposed to the residence of a Methodist preacher even in the town, and threatened, if he did not remove, to have him warned out. They seemed wonderfully excited with apprehension lest "the vagrant Methodist preacher," as they affected to call him, should become a pauper, and the town be compelled to support him. It should be borne in mind that this was not the voice of *the people*, but a few elect ones of "the standing order." But upon second thought, and a little more knowledge of the manner in which such a thing would be likely to be received by the public generally, his enemies abandoned their plan of operations, and were glad to hush the whole matter.

There was another law of the state which *required* each town to employ a minister and have preaching a certain portion of each year. When Mr. Hedding moved to Ludlow, the town was without any settled minister. About this time the town, in order to avoid the fine, appropriated a certain amount of money, and appointed a committee to supply the pulpit the requisite number of Sabbaths. The committee immediately invited Mr. Hedding to preach for them. Having but seven circuits on his district, he found it possible so to arrange his appointments as to accommodate them. He therefore made arrangements to supply the Congregational Church five Sabbaths in each quarter. The people not only soon became satisfied with the arrangement, but were greatly pleased with it: only one family in the whole town retained their opposition to it. The congregations were very large, and deeply interested in his ministrations; and it is believed that great good resulted from the incidental and somewhat anomalous relation. We opine that there are not many instances when the same individual, at the same time, has held the office of presiding elder in the Methodist Episcopal Church, and been settled pastor over a Congregational society. This extra labour was of material advantage to the finances of Mr. Hedding, as the district afforded him but a meager support.

How well his services were received in the town, their subsequent action will show. For the next year a town-meeting was called, and the town passed a resolution requesting him to locate as a Methodist minister, and to become settled as their pastor. They voted him an ample support, and appointed a committee to wait upon him, and make known their request at the ensuing conference. He had, however, become so thoroughly wedded to the itinerant ministry, and was so strongly convinced that, under God, it was to be the great instrument of spreading Scripture holiness over all these lands, that he could not for one moment entertain the idea of relinquishing his connexion with it. What, to him, were ease, worldly comfort, or worldly position compared with the accomplishment of the great mission which he had received to testify of the grace of God?

It may be that subsequently, when driving round his extensive districts, facing the chilling blasts and pelting storms of winter, or wading through drifts of snow to make a path for his horse, the flesh sometimes repined with more intenseness at the recollection of his rejection of so easy and so inviting a post. Perhaps these recollections would now and then give additional point to those "rich and refreshing meditations" the Rev. Mr. Newhall speaks of having when placed under similar circumstances. The process of getting through an immense snow-drift he thus describes: "I dismounted, and made my way through ahead of my horse, as far as I could without letting go of the bridle-rein; and then he would leap and wallow up to me, and wait till I had again made him a track. The storm was so severe that I found it difficult, at times, to catch my breath, and our path was filled as fast as we left it." In this way he was working more than two hours to get through a single drift—determined not to lose a single appointment except from the sternest necessity. While in this condition, he carried on the following dialogue with himself:—"*Q.* Who is that up to his arms in snow? *A.* A Methodist preacher. *Q.* Who is that in his snug study by a warm fire? *A.* The honourable settled minister. *Q.* What is the Methodist preacher doing? *A.* Making his way to his appointment, where he hopes to call sinners to repentance. *Q.* What is the settled minister doing? *A.* Hunting his library over, selecting portions, and adding, perhaps, some of his own thoughts, and writing out a sermon to read to the people the next Sabbath. *Q.* Which of them looks most like a lazy man; and which gets the most money, the most reproaches, or follows the example of Christ and the apostles nearest, in travelling, suffering, preaching, self-denials, watchings, fastings, and winning souls to Christ?

Here," continues he, "my mind looked back, and saw Jesus, weary, sitting on Jacob's well; Paul tossing on the rolling waves and shipwrecked at Miletus; and John on the desolate Isle of Patmos; and my full soul cried out, in the midst of the tempest, O Lord, permit me to wear out in thy service." To these feelings and these reasonings the heart of Mr. Hedding was no stranger; but never for one moment was he swerved from a full purpose to pursue to the end the path of duty that had been opened to him by the providence of God.

Toward the close of this year the energy and perseverance of Mr. Hedding were put to a rather severe test. His horse became disabled while passing round his district; and he was obliged to travel on foot a day or two before he could get another. The fatigue of travelling, together with a severe cold he had taken, brought on him another severe attack of the rheumatism. He was unable, without help, to mount or dismount from his horse, when he had procured one. He then obtained a chaise, but could neither get in nor out without aid; he could neither dress nor undress himself; nor could he stand to preach or kneel to pray, but would pray and preach sitting in his chair. In this crippled condition, and amid intense suffering, he rode all round his district, requiring a travel of over five hundred miles, and attended all his quarterly meetings, not omitting a single one of the duties he had been accustomed to perform.

While in this condition, he was one day riding

along a narrow road dug in the side of a hill. At a point where it was impossible for two wagons to pass in the road, he met a heavily-loaded team. Mr. Hedding told the man he was lame and unable to get out of his carriage, and requested him to help him out, and then to move his chaise to one side till he had passed. The Connecticut Yankee replied: "Sit still, sir, I can lift you and your chaise both out of the road;" and, suiting the action to the word, he placed his back under the axletree of the chaise, and actually lifted it up the hill-side so far that his own team passed without difficulty. Then he returned, and by the same means restored the chaise to its position in the middle of the road. Mr. Hedding acknowledged the favour and drove on, filled with wonder at the Herculean strength and the astonishing sleight which had enabled the man to perform with apparent ease what would have been deemed an utter impossibility.

Another incident connected with his affliction and final cure is worthy of record. Having broken his chaise in riding over the rough roads, he had been compelled to resume his travels on horseback. In one day he rode from Thompson, in Connecticut, to Warwick, Rhode Island. The next morning he had to call for help to enable him to get out of bed and to dress. At the hour of service he was enabled, by the help of crutches, to cross the street to a school-house, where he preached in a sitting posture; and afterward with great difficulty got back to his lodgings. At night, he said to his host he would never go to bed again until he was better or worse; and requested him to make a fire of large wood in the kitchen—one that would burn all night. This having been done, he lay down before it on the floor, with his clothes on; as near to the fire as he could get without burning. So completely exhausted was he with loss of sleep, and the bodily distress he had suffered, that he soon fell into a profound slumber, from which he did not awake till broad daylight. He then found that he had been in a great perspiration all night, and that his clothes were wet completely through and through. He arose, to his astonishment, without difficulty; and found that he could walk with ease and without pain. This was to him marvellous; but so completely was his cure effected by that sweat, administered in such a primitive mode, that he walked a mile to church, held a love-feast, preached twice, administered the sacrament, and then walked back without any inconvenience. He was troubled no more with the rheumatism that season.

Mr. Hedding was now drawing toward the close of the first ten years of his itinerant career, as a member of the conference. Just before their close, he made record of the following summary of his labours and trials: "I have averaged over three thousand miles' travel a year, and preached on an average a sermon a day since I commenced the itinerant life. During that period I have travelled circuits and districts that joined each other, through a tract of country beginning near Troy, New-York, and going north into Canada; thence east, through Vermont and New-Hampshire; and thence southerly, through Massachusetts, Rhode Island, and Connecticut, to Long Island Sound. I have never in this time owned a travelling vehicle, but have ridden on horseback, except occasionally in winter, when I have borrowed a sleigh, and also a few instances in which I have travelled by public conveyance or a borrowed carriage. I have both laboured hard and fared hard. Much of the time I have done missionary work without missionary money. Until recently I have had no dwelling-place or home; but, as a wayfaring man, lodged from night to night where hospitality and friendship opened the way. In most of these regions the Methodists were few, and comparatively poor; I was often obliged to depend upon poor people for food, and lodging, and horse-keeping; and though in general they provided for me cheerfully and willingly, yet I often felt that I was taking what they needed for their children, and that my horse was eating what they needed for their own beasts. I often suffered great trials of mind on this account; and have travelled many a day in summer and winter without dinner, because I had not a quarter of a dollar that I could spare to buy it.

"Through most all this region there existed strong prejudices against the Methodists, which greatly hindered their influence and usefulness. The principal objection was on account of their doctrines. They were regarded by many as heretics in theology. They were also despised and ridiculed on account of their poverty. The Methodist preachers were often represented as exceedingly ignorant and incompetent men. The itinerant system was also another ground of objection. The circuit preacher, coming as a stranger to a new people, would often find himself beset with the most scandalous reports of crimes and shameful acts, which it was alleged he had been guilty of on former circuits; and thus the enemies of Methodism would seek to undermine his influence and destroy his usefulness. Such are some of the difficulties the Methodist preachers have been compelled to encounter, especially in New-England, during the past ten years. But notwithstanding all, God has been with them, and given them favour in the eyes of the people, and great success in building up his Church. Revivals have spread through all the country; and multitudes have been added to the little and despised flock: nay, many who were once the greatest enemies of Methodism, and especially of Methodist preachers, have been converted, and are now become their greatest and truest friends."

During this year there were several revivals on the district. A camp-meeting was also held at Elliston, Connecticut. It was numerously attended; and, though not signalized for such wonderful displays of the power of God as that on the preceding year, the Church was greatly blessed, and many sinners were converted. The returns for the New-England Conference this year were eleven thousand eight hundred and sixty-eight, showing an increase of six hundred and forty-eight. The total membership of the Church in the United States and Canada, this year, amounted to one hundred and eighty-four thousand five hundred and sixty-seven, and the increase to ten thousand and seven. Thus had God been carrying on his work, by such instruments, and in spite of such obstacles as we have described, all over the country. The glad news of salvation by faith in Jesus Christ had been proclaimed not only through all New-England, but in the furthest south, and all along our frontiers among the teeming population of the far West.

CHAPTER VII.

LABOURS IN BOSTON, NANTUCKET, AND LYNN STATIONS.

New-England Conference for 1811—Mr. Hedding a Delegate to the General Conference—Appointed to Boston—Labours—The Embargo—Pecuniary Embarrassments of the People—Spiritual Prosperity—Conversion of E. T. Taylor—Mr. Hedding's Colleague, Rev. E. R. Sabin—The First Delegated General Conference—The Presiding Elder Question—The Question in the General Conference of 1808—In 1812—Its Subsequent History—The Question in 1816—Dr. Bangs's Account of the Discussion—The Question in 1820—The Compromise—Protest of Rev. Joshua Soule, Bishop Elect—Protest of Bishop M'Kendree—Attempt to reconsider fails—The Rule suspended—Finally rescinded—Mr. Hedding's Views—Change of his Opinion—Final Record of his Opinions on the Subject—The Question of Reserve Delegates—Surviving Members of this Conference—Session of the New-England Conference—War declared—Apprehended Evils—Mr. Hedding appointed to Nantucket—Origin of the Society here—Rev. George Cannon—Evil Results of Locating—Mr. Hedding's Reception on the Island—Excitement among the Islanders—Losses by the War—Condition of the People—State for the Church—Pastoral Labours—A Happy Convert—The Conference for 1813—State of the Work—Death of one of Mr. Hedding's Early Associates—Thomas Branch—Character and Labours—Departs for the West—Death—Mr. Hedding discovers his Grave in 1826—His Letter—Stationed at Lynn Common—Removal—Privations and Sufferings of the People—His Sympathy and Labours for them—His Colleague—Results of the Year—Returned to Lynn in 1814—Labours of the Year—Detained from Conference by a Revival.

The New-England Conference for 1811 held its session at Barnard, Vt., in the month of June. Bishop M'Kendree was present and presided. The only thing of special interest that occurred at this session was the election of delegates to the General Conference which was to be held the next year, but before another session of this annual conference.

Two of the delegates—George Pickering and Elijah Hedding—received every vote cast, except one. On the announcement of this result, Bishop M'Kendree pleasantly remarked that it was well those brethren did not have all the votes, for then it would be known they had voted for themselves.

At this conference, Mr. Hedding was appointed to Boston. This place and Marblehead stand connected in the Minutes; but the arrangement was that Messrs. Hedding and Sabin should labour in Boston, while the third preacher filled the appointments and took the pastoral charge of the society in Marblehead.

This was a year of unusually hard service for Mr. Hedding. Rev. E. R. Sabin was so disabled by his broken health, that he could do but little beyond preaching on the Sabbath. The two congregations were connected in one pastoral charge; and, consequently, the whole care and labour of Church business, of attendance upon the sick and upon funerals, as well as general pastoral visitation for both congregations, fell upon Mr. Hedding. He had to preach three times on each Sabbath, and to deliver two week-evening lectures—one in each church—weekly. But he was not a man to stand appalled before labours and difficulties; nor was he a man that could leave any portion of his work undone so long as its accomplishment came within the range of possibility. The amount of labour he performed this year, in the various departments of his work, was perhaps unsurpassed by that of any other year of his ministry.

Another thing that added to his labour, and was an additional obstacle to his success, was the political and monetary state of the country. The passage of "the embargo" and "non-intercourse" acts had produced a general stagnation of business. These effects fell upon no place with greater severity than upon Boston. A large portion of its capital was employed in commercial enterprise; and now it became not only non-productive, but in many instances was subjected to fearful diminution. The whole community felt the shock. The labourer could find no employment; provisions of almost every kind were enormously high. The poor suffered greatly; and Mr. Hedding's sympathies were often put to severe trial by witnessing the sufferings of many families of his own flock. In addition to all his other labours, he found it necessary to devote no inconsiderable portion of his time in efforts to relieve the needy and suffering. He says: "I often found able-bodied men ready and desirous to work, but unable to get work, while they and their families were destitute of food, and suffering in the winter from want of fuel. In addition to the small collections the Church could make for their relief, I often had to go to those who had the means, and personally beg bread and fuel for the relief of pious people who were suffering." In this state of pecuniary embarrassment, the preachers, of course, suffered along with the people. Their support was very limited; scarcely equal to the stern necessities of life.

But crushed and afflicted in temporal matters as they were, the Church and the ministers were nevertheless alive to their great work. They laboured like men of God for the salvation of souls, and not without effect. They were blessed with quite a revival, and there were many powerful and clear conversions. Mr. Hedding remarks that "some of those converted this year have lived and died in the faith and gone home to heaven; others are still in the way, holding fast their profession."

It was during this year that a young sailor, dressed in sailor garb, with his glazed hat under his arm, ventured into the old Bromfield-street Church. He took his position in the gallery near the stairs, and attentively listened to a discourse from Mr. Hedding. The truth, which was presented with great clearness, power, and pathos, made a deep impression upon his mind. He remained to the prayer meeting. Several surrounded the altar for prayer. The power of God was there. His people rejoiced in his presence; mourners at the altar were comforted; and sinners in the congregation were constrained to acknowledge his mighty hand. Soon the young sailor was seen to rise and make a movement for the altar. Through the crowd he pressed his way, fell upon his knees at the altar, and cried aloud for mercy. The preacher pointed him to Christ—the Saviour of the sailor as well as the landsman; the Church joined in prayer to God for his salvation. It was evident that it was no half-hearted matter on the part of the young man. He struggled for light and salvation. The kingdom of heaven suffered violence, and the violent took it by force. That very night, and before he left the altar, he was redeemed from sin. He then also gave himself to the Church as well as to God. A few years later this young sailor was licensed to preach; and now, for many years, has had a world-wide reputation as E. T. Taylor, the sailor preacher at the Mariners' Church in Boston.

In his colleague Mr. Hedding found a congenial spirit; and though greatly disabled by disease, he rejoiced in having him as his colleague. Here is his record concerning him:—"My colleague, Rev. Elijah R. Sabin, was a first-rate, excellent man, both as to piety and talents, and we laboured together with the greatest harmony and love. During this year he was elected to serve as chaplain to the legislature. I knew him well. Our acquaintance commenced in Vermont, when we were both young in the ministry. He experienced religion among the Baptists, and commenced as a Baptist preacher, and served in that capacity for a few months. About that time the Methodists came into the part of Vermont where he lived. He heard some of their preachers, and became convinced of the truth of their doctrines, and joined them. Soon after, he went out as an itinerant preacher, and was ever beloved as a pious, talented, and useful preacher among us. His health failing him, so that he was unable to do the duties of a travelling preacher, he took a location at the end of the year after we were stationed together in Boston. He then removed to the State of Maine, were he served a few years as a local preacher; he then went to the south to recover his health, but he died at Augusta, Georgia, leaving a good testimony that he had gone to receive a glorious reward."

The first delegated General Conference of the Methodist Episcopal Church was held in New-York city, commencing May 1st, 1812. To this conference Mr. Hedding had been elected by the suffrages of his brethren of the New-England Conference. Owing to its being the first *delegated* General Conference, it was regarded with unusual interest by the whole Church. The conferences were represented as follows, namely: New-York, thirteen; New-England, nine; Genesee, six; Western, thirteen; South Carolina, nine; Virginia, eleven; Baltimore, fifteen; and Philadelphia, fourteen: total, ninety. Several new measures were proposed for the action of this conference; but none created greater excitement, or occupied more attention of the conference, than an effort to make presiding elders elective by the conferences. A motion to this effect had been first introduced into the General Conference of 1808, and was thoroughly discussed by the ablest men in that body; but it was decided in the negative, by a vote of fifty-two in favour to seventy-three against it. The measure was thus defeated by the decisive majority of twenty-one. At this session of the General Conference, the subject was again introduced by a motion from one of the New-York delegates. As before, it elicited a great deal of discussion. Able and eloquent speeches were made both for and against it. The measure was again lost, though by a decreased majority,—forty-two voting in its favour, and forty-five against it; making a majority of only three. It appears that the delegates from the Philadelphia, New-York, and Genesee Conferences were unanimous in its favour. The New-England Conference delegates, we believe, were mostly in favour of it; but the southern delegates were generally united in opposition to the measure.

As this is a measure with which Mr. Hedding has been somewhat associated, it will be proper at this point to present the different stages through which it passed, till it received its quietus at the General Conference of 1828. In 1816 the subject again came before that body. The following is the resolution upon which the vote of the conference was finally taken: "The bishop, at an early period of the annual conference, shall nominate an elder for each district; and the conference shall, without debate, either confirm or reject such nomination. If the person or persons so nominated be not elected by the conference, the bishop shall nominate two others for such vacant district, one of whom shall be chosen; and the presiding elder so elected and appointed shall remain in office four years, unless dismissed by the mutual consent of the bishop and the conference: but no presiding elder shall be removed from office during the term of four years, unless the reasons for such removal be stated to him in presence of the conference, which shall decide without debate in his case." In another paragraph it was provided that the presiding elders, thus selected, should form a council to assist the bishop in stationing the preachers.

Dr. Bangs, to whom we are mainly indebted for this account, says:* "Perhaps a greater amount of talent was never brought to bear on any question ever brought before the General Conference, than was elicited from both sides of the house in the discussion of this resolution. Some of the speeches were deep, pungent, and highly argumentative, the speakers throwing their whole souls into the subject, and winding themselves up to the highest pitch of impassioned eloquence, often concluding with a tremendous appeal to the understandings and consciences of their antagonists; both sides invoking the future prosperity of the Church as an auxiliary to their arguments." The measure was finally lost, by a vote of thirty-eight in its favour to sixty-three against it. This was the heaviest majority—twenty-five—as yet obtained against it; and the question was thus settled for the next four years.

It should, however, be remarked to the honour of the majority of that body, that though decided in their opinion they were not proscriptive; for when they came to the election of bishops, one of the two

* History of the Methodist Episcopal Church, vol. ii, p. 330, &c.

elected was well known to be in favour of the proposed change in the mode of selecting the presiding elders.

At the General Conference of 1820 the measure was again brought forward, and again defeated. The state of the vote in this case we have not the means of determining; but the rejection of the measure excited so much feeling that a committee of six—three in favour and three against it—was appointed to confer with the bishops, and to report "whether any, and if any, what alterations might be made to conciliate the wishes of the brethren upon the subject." The committee were Ezekiel Cooper, Stephen G. Roszel, Nathan Bangs, Joshua Wells, John Emory, and William Capers. The bishops were William M'Kendree, Enoch George, and Robert R. Roberts. Bishop M'Kendree's health was such that he was unable to participate in the deliberations of the committee. After conference with each other, and with the two effective bishops, the committee, with the concurrence of the two bishops, unanimously recommended to the conference the adoption of the following provisions, to be inserted in their proper place in the Discipline: "1. That whenever in any annual conference there shall be a vacancy or vacancies in the office of presiding elder, in consequence of his period of four years having expired, or the bishop wishing to remove any presiding elder, or by death, resignation, or otherwise, the bishop or president of the conference, having ascertained the number wanted from any of these causes, shall nominate three times the number, out of which the conference shall elect by ballot, without debate, the number wanted;—provided, when there is more than one wanted, not more than three at a time shall be nominated, nor more than one at a time be elected. Provided, also, that in case of any vacancy or vacancies in the office of presiding elder, in the interval of any annual conference, the bishop shall have authority to fill the said vacancy or vacancies, until the ensuing annual conference. 2. That the presiding elders be and hereby are made the advisory council of the bishop or president of the conference in stationing the preachers."

This report was submitted to the General Conference on the 20th of May; and after some little conversation was very hastily passed by that body. It obtained the decisive vote of sixty-one in its favour to twenty-five in the negative, giving a clear majority of thirty-six.

It was now supposed that this question, which had so long agitated the Church, was finally settled; and many, both friends and opponents, congratulated themselves that they had now attained some common ground upon which they could rest. These congratulations, however, proved rather premature. The Rev. Joshua Soule, who had been elected to the episcopal office on the 13th, declined consecration in consequence of this action; stating to the conference his deep conviction that these provisions were unconstitutional, and as a bishop he could not, consistently with his views, be controlled by them. To add to the perplexity of the conference, and to unsettle the minds of the members, Bishop M'Kendree, three days after the passage of the resolutions, came to the conference room, and, "after assigning sundry reasons, entered his objections against them as unconstitutional, and, as he apprehended, subversive of the grand system of an efficient and general superintendency and itinerancy." The conference had perhaps been but little affected by the opposition of the Rev. Joshua Soule, bishop elect, as they accepted his resignation, which he tendered in consequence of the passage of the resolutions; but when Bishop M'Kendree—so justly respected in consequence of his long and laborious services, his age and experience—entered his solemn protest, it was brought to a dead stand. The more experienced thought it wise to pause and reconsider the subject. Many who had originally favoured the measure, or been subsequently led to countenance it, were now in serious suspense in respect to its expediency. All were interested in the stability and prosperity of the Church; and the singular and anomalous state of things produced a profound sensation. The conference, however, was not prepared to retrace its steps, and the effort to reconsider the obnoxious resolutions failed. Finally, it was proposed to suspend the operation of these rules for four years, and that in the mean time the government of the Church should be administered as heretofore. At the subsequent General Conference in 1824, if the opponents of the measure were not strong enough to secure the repeal of these resolutions, they succeeded in having the suspension of them continued another four years. At the end of this time they were rescinded, with but feeble opposition; and up to the present time the subject has rarely been agitated in the Church.

From the commencement of the agitation of this subject, Mr. Hedding had been in favour of making the presiding elder's office elective by the conference. He was among the advocates of the measure at the General Conference of 1812; and continued to sustain it, both by his arguments and his votes, till the measure was carried in 1820. But later in life he saw, as he believed, good reason to change his opinions upon the subject; and became satisfied that the perpetuity of our itinerancy and the harmony of its workings, required that the preachers should be appointed to the presiding eldership by the same authority that fixed their appointments in the circuits and stations. Nor was he alone in the change of opinion. Other advocates of that measure, as they advanced in years and acquired a wider experience, discovered reason in the workings of our economy to change their ground. It is perhaps owing to this quiet change of opinion in the old advocates of the measure—a change brought about, not by discussion, but by experience and observation with regard to the workings of our economy—that the subject has slumbered so quietly for over thirty years.

A short time before his death Bishop Hedding put his views upon this subject on record; and though it is not strictly in the chronological order of our narrative, it will best preserve the harmony of the subject to give them in this connexion. That record was made in view of his final departure from the Church, and but a few months before that event took place. It may, therefore, be regarded as his dying testimony upon this point. They are the ripe convictions of a long life of varied experience: the circumstances under which the record was made preclude the idea that any other purpose than the good of the Church and the glory of God could have prompted it. He says:—

"There is one point in our economy upon which I think it expedient here to record my opinion.

"The time was, when, with many others, I fully believed that the election of presiding elders by the annual conferences, and making those presiding elders an efficient council with the bishops to fix the appointments of the preachers, would be an improvement on our system, and a benefit to the itinerant work; but observation and experience have taught me that I was under a mistake.

"The majority of annual conferences, generally, have not sufficient age and experience to judge of the qualifications necessary for the office of presiding elder; and to submit the appointment of that office, so frequently as such appointments must be made, to an election in an annual conference, would be introducing and perpetuating a spirit of electioneering, and of party strifes, which would be injurious to the best interests of the cause of Christ. I have known instances, when men were proposed for presiding elders, when I was urged by many members of the conference to appoint them, when I knew that majorities of the conferences would have elected them, had they power to do it; when I knew the men better than the conferences knew them; when I knew, as well as I could know a thing of that sort, if they were appointed presiding elders, they would employ the influence of that office, not for the benefit, but for the injury of the Church; for they were not the friends of the Church, but the leaders of parties. In those instances, my judgment and my conscience forbade my appointing them. I suffered reproach and persecution for so doing; but I am thankful to the Head of the Church that he afforded me an influence that led me to do as I did.

"I have known enough of the bad effects of electioneering, in selecting delegates for the General Conference, to impress deeply on my mind the conviction that that mode of appointing presiding elders would not be a benefit, but an injury to the Church. In the election of delegates for the General Conference, I have known the young men combined to prevent the men of age and experience from being elected, and elect young men, some of whom understood neither the doctrine nor discipline of the Methodist Episcopal Church; and yet these were the men to appear at General Conference and make rules and regulations for the Methodist Episcopal Church, to hear and try appeals, and even to judge the bishops. Such men would sometimes be appointed presiding elders, if the conferences had power to elect them.

"Further, as strong reasons can be offered for the people to have the right of electing their preachers and their class-leaders, as can be offered for the election of presiding elders; and let the electing business go to this extent, and what becomes of the *itinerancy*, and of the moral discipline of the Church? Will it be said the presiding elder has so much power over the preachers of his district that they ought to have a voice in electing him? The same would be said by the people respecting the power of the preacher over them; for notwithstanding all the talk that has been made respecting the power of various officers in our Church, the greatest power that exists among these officers is in him who acts in the capacity of preacher in charge."

Another question arose at the opening of the session of the General Conference which elicited much debate, and which Mr. Hedding advocated as a wise prudential arrangement. The New-England Conference had appointed reserve delegates, in case those primarily appointed should be prevented from attending. One of this latter class was unable to be present, and the reserve came in his place. As no other conference had appointed reserves, it was long discussed whether the one from New-England should be allowed a seat. It was finally settled to admit him, and it was afterward established as a rule; and the several conferences since that time have appointed reserves in the place of others unable to attend.

Of the members of this conference few survive. There are some, however, whose names are like household words in the Church. Such men are Nathan Bangs, Aaron Hunt, and Laban Clark, who then represented the New-York Conference; Joshua Soule, Asa Kent, and Daniel Webb, then of the New-England Conference; David Young, then of the Western Conference; Lovick Pierce, then of the South Carolina Conference; and John Early, then of the Virginia Conference.

Immediately on the close of the General Conference, Mr. Hedding, with his co-delegates, hastened home to attend the session of the New-England Conference, which commenced on the 20th of June, at Lynn. It was characterized, as were most of the conferences of that day, by peaceful concord and strong brotherly love. The portentous cloud that had been lowering in the political horizon had awakened deep solicitude, and many were the prayers offered that God would avert the threatened storm. This, however, could not avert the evil. War against Great Britain had actually been declared on the 18th; and news of it reached Lynn not long after the assembling of the conference. This caused great excitement among both preachers and people. Many of them regarded war as utterly and irreconcilably opposed to the gospel of peace; and others were in danger of drinking in the spirit of the times to a degree that would seriously peril their Christian character. It was apprehended that partisan feelings would be aroused; that still more severe temporal embarrassments would be experienced; and above all, that in connexion with the "war spirit," a reckless, licentious feeling, and a depravation of public morals, would be engendered; and that thus the great political events of the day would work serious injury to the cause of religion, and peril the souls of many men. The state of public affairs thus became a subject of profound and absorbing interest in the conference. In all these feelings Mr. Hedding participated in an unusual degree. The sufferings he had witnessed and tried to alleviate, in Boston, during the preceding year, he regarded as premonitory of greater evils now certain to ensue.

Mr. Hedding was appointed at the close of the conference to Nantucket. So far as we can gather from the scanty documents within our reach, the society in this place was organized by the Rev. George Cannon, about the year 1797 or 1798. Mr. Cannon entered the travelling ministry in 1790, and after travelling four years in the south, came to reinforce the work in New-England. He was here successively stationed at Orange, Provincetown, and Marblehead, and located at the conference of 1797. Something of Mr. Cannon's mettle may be gathered from his ministry in Provincetown. Soon after his arrival there as the stationed preacher he took measures for the erection of a church. The lumber for that purpose was collected, when the "town-meeting" formally voted against the erection of a Methodist church in the town, and thus so obviously invited the wickedness, that the rabble took the hint, and not only destroyed the lumber, but consumed along with it a tarred and feathered effigy of the minister. The energy of the pastor of the society, however, was equal to the emergency. New material was speedily procured; the new temple was pushed forward to its completion; and in about four months they entered it with songs of praise and thanksgiving. After Mr. Cannon's location he removed to Nantucket, where as a local preacher he preached with considerable success, and succeeded in introducing Methodism. The prospect appearing flattering, he applied to the conference for a preacher; and, in 1800, the Rev. William Beauchamp was sent to his aid. Mr. Beauchamp was thus the first stationed preacher in Nantucket. He had not been in the station more than six months when a society of between seventy and eighty members was raised up; and before he left it a large and commodious church was erected.* From that time forward the society enjoyed the services of a regularly stationed preacher; and among the predecessors of Mr. Hedding were Messrs. Wm. Beauchamp, Joshua Wells, Joshua Soule, Truman Bishop, Joshua Crowell, and others of the leading men of the conference.

Having noticed the introduction and prosperity of Methodism in Nantucket, it will be well for us to

* See Methodist Magazine for 1825.

recur again to the agent of its introduction, Mr. Cannon, for the purpose of admonition and warning, as well as for the sake of historical truth. The author of the Memorials of Methodism says of him, that "the abandonment of the ministry produced, in his case, the usual results of such deviations from duty: he became absorbed in secular cares, fell into doctrinal errors, and retired from the Church. Frequently, in his hoary age, might this once useful man have been seen trembling under the discourse of his old fellow-labourers, in the midst of the Church which he himself had formed. He clung, however, to his errors—a species of Universalism—and was suddenly summoned to his final account; falling backward, 'his neck broke, and he died.'" What a sad warning to those who are tempted by worldly considerations to desist from the work to which God has called them!

Immediately on the close of the conference, Mr. Hedding shipped his goods, and took passage on board of a sloop for Nantucket, hastening his departure in order to escape the British privateers which it was expected would soon be scouring along the coast. Though isolated from the mainland, and from ready communication, Nantucket was one of the "green spots" in the conference. "We had scarcely reached the island," says Mr. Hedding, "before we were received and greeted with a cordiality and manifested friendship such as I never had received from any other place to which I had been appointed. We were immediately taken to a friend's house, and while engaged at dinner other brethren had taken our goods out of the sloop, and removed them to the house provided for us, and set them up in order. What was lacking in furniture was supplied, and also a good stock of groceries provided; so that we were completely settled in the parsonage, with all the conveniences for house-keeping, the same night." How cheering such a reception to the minister of God, as he goes from a society endeared to him by mutual sympathies, to make his home once more among strangers! How different this from what was often experienced in that early day, and which indeed is sometimes experienced even at the present time, when the preacher would go with his family to his charge, and find that no parsonage had been provided, and no one was interested to provide one; and also that no brother's door was cordially opened to give them even a temporary home! Such are the receptions that chill the heart; and, crushed in heart by them, many a preacher has exclaimed within himself: "*Were it not that God has called me to preach, I would instantly locate.*" No marvel if preachers enduring such things become dry and feeble. The fact is, all the sympathies of the heart become shocked and crushed; and the intellect is not only cut off from the aliment necessary to nourish and invigorate it, but it is dwarfed by the necessity of making the means of living and supporting a family a daily study and care.

This year was one of great excitement among the islanders on account of the war. The British ships of war and privateers were often in sight; and it was often apprehended that they would land and burn the village. They had no fort for their defence, and few of the munitions of war; and were so far from the mainland that no help could be expected from it in an emergency. The fears of the people, however, proved groundless, for though boats often landed from these cruisers, it was only to get supplies, and these they paid for; and, in fact, the people suffered no material injury during the whole war, except in the loss of their vessels taken upon the "high seas." In this latter respect they suffered greatly. At the commencement of the war they owned over one hundred vessels—many of them large whale ships. A large proportion of these were captured or destroyed during the war. This occasioned incessant anxiety for friends and property exposed to the enemy upon the great deep; and the loss of their vessels occasioned great pecuniary embarrassment. But, compared with what Mr. Hedding had witnessed in Boston the preceding year, they suffered nothing. "Notwithstanding," says he, "the terrors about the war, the people of Nantucket appeared to me to be a community the richest and happiest I had ever met with. A drunkard or a pauper was a creature rarely to be seen. On one occasion I asked one of the stewards if they did not make a collection at sacrament for the poor; and he replied, 'No, we have nobody here as poor as the preachers; we give all we can raise to the preachers.'"

The Church at Nantucket found in Mr. Hedding just the man that the exigences of its condition required. During the preceding year there had been gathered into it a large number, chiefly young persons, who were soon found to be unworthy of such a relation. Under the influence of a remarkable excitement, produced by extravagantly bold, noisy, and violent efforts in preaching and exhortation, they had united with the Church without proper instruction, and without giving those evidences which the Discipline requires. It is probable the greater part of them were never converted. Mr. Hedding had full exercise for all his gifts of head and heart. Some of them became haughty, proud, and dictatorial. Some, when the excitement died away, were found as worldly and careless as they had ever been; and others had to be arrested, tried, and expelled for gross crimes. In fact, a large portion of those who joined the preceding year had, in some form or other, to be made subjects of discipline. Among them, however, were a few instances of genuine and manifest piety. For this difficult and painful duty Mr. Hedding was eminently fitted. He had a heart to sympathize with the ignorant and unfortunate, and a forbearance and patience that greatly encouraged their penitence and their attempts at reformation; and had also discrimination and decision to deal plainly and firmly with the disobedient and stubborn. But little revival took place this year; it was chiefly devoted to pruning and sifting the unworthy from the good. "Among the older members of the Church," he says, "I found a noble, pious, and gifted company, true friends and supporters, who sustained me faithfully in the difficult work of administration that I was often compelled to discharge."

In visiting the sick, and in giving them counsel and comfort, he had a superior gift; and in no department of his work were his labours more appreciated. He found great satisfaction in being at their bedside, and imparting consolation and instruction to the sick and dying. He could relate instance after instance of such as had been converted, or through his prayers had been greatly consoled and strengthened, while upon a sick, perhaps a dying bed. The following is one that transpired while he resided at Nantucket. He says: "During this year I became acquainted with a young married lady who was sick with consumption, and whose husband was at sea. She was well educated, and in all respects a real lady. She had usually, when in health, attended the Methodist meeting, though her mother was a Quakeress; and now she resided with her mother. I visited her almost daily during her sickness; and she was brought under deep conviction for sin, and of her need of regenerating and pardoning grace. I conversed with her, and prayed with her, and instructed her as well as I knew how; but her mother, who knew nothing of experimental religion, endeavoured to counteract everything I said or did. She would often address her as follows: 'Daughter, thou need not weep so on account of thy sins; thou need not be so afraid to die. Thee has always been good from a child, and always kept the commandments; and when thee dies, thy Lord will receive thee. Therefore dismiss thy fears, wipe up thy tears, and quiet thyself.' But the daughter would reply: 'Ah, mother, you don't know my heart as I know it. I know my heart is sinful and wicked, and in the sight of God I have been a great sinner. I dare not die as I am. I know I cannot get to heaven as I am. I must be pardoned and born again through Jesus Christ, or I shall go to hell.' Thus she continued for two or three months. At last the Lord spoke peace to her soul; and she came out as clear as the sun without a cloud, and as happy as any one I ever saw, delivered from the fear of death. She praised God, and continued in the light, without a doubt or a fear, for two or three weeks, and died in the triumphs of faith. A brighter conversion I never witnessed."

The New-England Conference for 1813 had been appointed to meet at New-London, Connecticut; but as several British ships of war were lying near the harbour, and it was expected they would bombard and take the place, the bishops moved the seat of the conference to a place called Salem, about twenty miles northeast of New-London. As the British cruisers were all about the seas in the neighbourhood of Nantucket, Mr. Hedding found it exceedingly difficult to get a passage off the island. He finally succeeded, and embarked in a small open boat, in which he proc ,eded the first day to Holmes's Hole, Martha's Vineyard, where he made harbour for the night. The next day he proceeded, and landed safely at New-Bedford, Massachusetts. Thence he went by land through Providence, Rhode Island, to the seat of the conference. Bishops Asbury and M'Kendree were both present, and, though war and excitement raged without, the session of the conference was remarkable for peace and quietness.

Notwithstanding the deleterious influence which the war had exerted upon the morals and the religion of the people throughout the entire bounds of the conference, the preachers generally brought in a good report concerning the condition of their charges. The war spirit had not extinguished the vital spark of religion in the hearts of their members; and many places had been favoured with excellent revivals. There were, however, but two new charges made within the bounds of the entire conference; and upon the aggregate membership there was a decrease of one hundred and ninety-two. Other portions of the country were less affected at this stage of the war; and the returns from the whole Church showed an aggregate of two hundred and fourteen thousand three hundred and seven members, and six hundred and seventy-eight preachers, being an increase of eighteen thousand nine hundred and fifty for the year.

During this year one of Mr. Hedding's intimate friends and early associates in the ministry died.

We allude to Thomas Branch; and we specially refer to his decease here, because of an incident that connects Mr. Hedding with the account of his last hours, and of his last resting-place. He was a native of Preston, Connecticut, and is reported to have been altogether a noble man. He joined the New-York Conference with Mr. Hedding, in 1801; and was with him transferred to the New-England Conference, by a change of conference boundaries. He filled important stations, was everywhere a popular preacher, and was reported by his preachers to be *the best presiding elder they ever knew.* This last is saying a great deal, in times when Elijah Hedding, Joshua Soule, G. Pickering, Elijah R. Sabin, and John Brodhead were in the field. His health had failed two years before; and he had been placed on the supernumerary list at the conference of 1811. "The zeal of his spirit," says the author of the Memorials of Methodism, "could not be checked by the infirmities of the body; he had thoroughly consecrated himself to his work, and was resolute to die in it. Unable longer to sustain the inclemencies of the climate of New-England, he proposed to go to the southwest, and labour while his dwindling strength should last in the Western Conference—the only conference then beyond the Alleghanies. It extended from Detroit to Natchez, and was the great frontier battle-field of Methodism, where Cartwright, Finley, Young, Blackman, Winans, Lakin, Quinn, and other giant men, were bearing on the cross in the van of emigration, and travelling vast circuits, over parts of which they had to be protected by escorts of armed men. Besides the various choice of climate which this immense field afforded, there was, to the devoted mind of Branch, a romantic if not heroic attraction in its adventurous life, and the triumph with which the itinerant ministry was spreading the truth in its wildernesses; for though it had been organized only about twenty years, it already ranked as fourth in numerical strength among all the conferences, and comprised more than twenty-seven thousand members. Its white membership, indeed, was larger than that of any other conference." In this vast and inviting field Branch proposed to spend the remnant of his physical strength. Accordingly, at the conference of 1812, he was made effective, and appointed (*transfers* were then unknown) to Marietta, in the Muskingum District, with David Young.

The arrangements for his departure were easily made, and on horseback he started for his new field of labour in the west; but this field he never reached. He passed along through the western wilds of New-York, travelling and preaching as his health and strength permitted, and crossed the line into Pennsylvania. But here he disappeared. News came to his brethren that he had died on his way; but when or where he died, and the circumstances of his death were not known. Only vague rumours concerning his fate reached his brethren, and for fourteen years a mystery hung over the subject. In 1826 Mr. Hedding, then bishop, to whom the memory of his early associate was still dear, was on a tour of episcopal visitation to the west, and purposely passed through the region where Thomas Branch had been last heard from in 1812, and made inquiries about him. The result of these inquiries he communicated to the Zion's Herald, in which paper they were published during that year. Writing from Ohio, he says: "He fell in the wilderness, on his way to this country in the month of June, 1812. His sepulchre is in the woods, in the State of Pennsylvania, near the shore of Lake Erie, between the states of New-York and Ohio. As I came through that part of the country, I made inquiry respecting the sickness, death, and burial of our once beloved fellow-labourer in the cause of Christ. An intelligent friend, who said he had frequently visited and watched with him during his last sickness, and attended his funeral, gave me, in substance, the following circumstances: When brother Branch came into the neighbourhood where he died, it was a new settlement, where there was no Methodist society, and but few professors of religion of any name. He preached on a Sabbath, and at the close of the service stated to the strangers that he was on a journey; that he was ill and unable to proceed; and desired that some one would entertain him till he should recover his strength sufficiently to resume his journey. There was a long time of silence in the congregation; at last one came forward and invited him home. At that house he lingered many weeks, and finally expired. The accommodations were poor for a sick man: a small log-house containing a large family, consisting in part of small children; but doubtless it was the best the place could afford. In his sickness, which was pulmonary consumption, his sufferings were severe; but his patience and religious consolations were great also. He frequently preached, prayed, and exhorted, sitting on his bed, when he was unable to go out, or even to stand. And so he continued labouring for the salvation of men while his strength would permit, and rejoicing in the Lord to the hour of his death. The above named eye and ear witness informed me that brother Branch frequently said to him: 'It is an inscrutable providence that brought me here to die in the wilderness.' 'But,' said the witness, 'that providence was explained after his death: for, through the instrumentality of his labours, patience, fortitude, and religious joys, in his sickness, a glorious revival of religion shortly took place, a goodly number of souls were converted to God, other preachers were invited to the place, and a large Methodist society was organized after his death.' That society still continues to prosper, and they have now a decent house for worship.

"After the soul of our brother had rested in heaven, his body was conveyed to the grave on a sled drawn by oxen. The corpse was carried to a log building in the woods, called a meeting-house; but the proprietors denied admittance, and the funeral ceremonies were performed without. As I came through the woodland in company with a preacher, having been informed where the place of our friend's interment was, leaving our horse and carriage by the road, we walked some rods into the forest, and found the old log meeting-house, which had refused the stranger the rites of funeral; but it was partly fallen and forsaken. Then following a narrow path some distance further through the woods, we came to a small opening, which appeared to have been cleared of the wood for a habitation for the dead. After walking and looking some time, a decent stone, near one corner of the yard, under the shade of the thick-set tall forest, informed us where the body of our dear departed friend had been laid. A large oak-tree had fallen, and lay across two of the adjoining tenants of that lonely place. We kneeled, prayed, and left the lonely spot, in joyful hopes of meeting our brother again at the resurrection of the just. The associations of the place carried my thoughts back to the northern parts of New-Hampshire and Vermont, where, many years since, I had ridden, walked, talked, and prayed in company with Thomas Branch.

"Two important reflections have often since impressed my mind. One is, in how many circumstances a faithful minister of Christ may be useful—even in his most severe sufferings, and under the darkest dispensations of Providence which he may be called to endure. Little did Thomas Branch think that the fruits of his last labours and sufferings would be so abundant after his death. The other is, how much good may be done by the remembrance of the virtues of a faithful Christian long after he is dead. The memory of the example of Thomas Branch, revived in my mind by visiting his grave, has been a means of quickening my desires to live as he lived, and of strengthening my hopes of finally reaching that heaven to which, I trust, he has gone."

While this sketch will show how tenderly the memory of Thomas Branch was cherished by the subject of our narrative, it will also exhibit traits in the character of Mr. Hedding that commend him still more strongly to our Christian confidence and sympathy. The following extract from the Conference Minutes for this year will show the estimation in which Thomas Branch was held by his brethren: "An Israelite indeed, in life and in death. Who ever saw him out of the gravity and sincerity of a Christian minister? always apparently collected and recollected; a child of affliction and a son of resignation: how loved and honoured of God and men! Rest, rest, weary dust! Rest, weary spirit, with the Father of spirits, and live forever!" Can we wonder that such purity of character, such sincerity of devotion, should have left behind them a memory fragrant with heavenly perfume? It seemed a hard fate that left him to die, almost unfriended and alone; and many an eye has moistened with heart-felt sorrow at his lonely and suffering end; but, blessed be God! the Sun of righteousness now shines with undimmed lustre upon his soul in that house where there are "many mansions."

At the close of this conference Mr. Hedding was appointed to Lynn, in connexion with Daniel Webb. There were two appointments in Lynn, and each was placed under the charge of a preacher, Mr. Hedding having charge of the Lynn Common Church. The arrangement was for them to exchange once on each Sabbath.

After conference Mr. Hedding returned to Nantucket for his family and goods. But, owing to the hazard of a voyage around Cape Cod to Boston, on account of the British ships of war, so frequent in those parts, he was compelled to embark with his wife and goods in a sloop for Hyannis, a place nearest on the outer-side of the cape; thence he crossed to Barnstable, and passed from thence in a sloop to Boston, and thence to Lynn.

Although stationed in one of the best societies of the conference, the war continuing to rage during the year, made it a very laborious, suffering time. The business of the place was poor. The congregations were frequently broken up by the sight of a British cruiser near the place. Sometimes the people were aroused and alarmed in the night from the fear of danger. Every article of provision was at an exorbitant price. The bread they ate was brought by land from Philadelphia. They were compelled to pay sixteen dollars a barrel for flour, and much distress was experienced by the people. Such a state of things made it a year very unfavourable to religion and to revival influences throughout the country; but it was especially so at Lynn, because the place was peculiarly exposed. Notwithstanding all these hinderances Mr. Hedding continued at his post, preaching, visiting the people, and by his exhortations encouraging them to attend to all their duties. Perhaps almost any other society would have been worse affected than the one at Lynn. It was the first formed by Jesse Lee in his tour to the east, more than twenty years before, and the first Methodist society in Massachusetts. It embraced some of the first citizens of the place for respectability and means. It had but few backsliders, and its members were remarkable for strict attendance to all their religious duties. Notwithstanding the severity of his labours, and the trials and sufferings of the people of Lynn, Mr. Hedding found many enjoyments during the year. His faithfulness in all his ministerial duties much endeared him to the people; and their steadfastness in their religious profession much endeared them to him. In fact, during this and the subsequent year he formed many attachments that continued and strengthened until the most of them, as well as himself, had passed to the Church above. To this day many of the most active members of the Churches in Lynn are found among those who were baptized by him during this period of his labours.

Mr. Hedding considered himself highly favoured in the colleague with whom he laboured. Daniel Webb, who was two years his senior in the ministry, and who is still living at an advanced age: in fact, he is now the oldest effective travelling preacher in the world—his ministry having extended through the period of fifty-seven years. His talents as a preacher were much above mediocrity. In his discourses he was clear, methodical, and earnest. In his intercourse with his people he was social and agreeable, and was pious and active in the discharge of all his duties. He had previously filled, and has since continued to fill, appointments in many of the prominent Churches in the conference. Mr. Hedding retained with great satisfaction, to the end of life, a pleasing remembrance of the intimate friendship established with Mr. Webb during this year.

The effects of the war upon the progress of religion were now beginning to be somewhat realized. The New-England Conference again returned a decrease of membership, which this year amounted to two hundred and seventy-four. In the whole Church there was a decrease of three thousand one hundred and seventy-eight, leaving the total membership two hundred and eleven thousand one hundred and twenty-nine; and six hundred and eighty-seven preachers, being an increase of nine.

The New-England Conference for 1814 met at Durham, Maine, and Mr. Hedding was returned to Lynn. He had for his colleague the Rev. Leonard Frost.

For about eight months of this year his labours were much the same as the past; nor was the condition of the society in Lynn much altered from what it had been the preceding year The excitement occasioned by the war, and the attendant pecuniary embarrassments and sufferings, still engrossed the thoughts of the people. What made these embarrassments the more vexatious to the people was, that many of the inhabitants of Massachusetts, especially in the maritime towns, were opposed to the war. During the month of February, 1815, the news reached Lynn of the conclusion of peace between England and the United States, and created a time of general rejoicing. But what was cause of increased rejoicing to Mr. Hedding, as well as to the Church in that place, was a great work of revival which commenced about the same time. He had been labouring for more than a year and a half, and though generally the Church maintained a walk consistent with their profession in such troublous times, he had found but few seriously inquiring what they must do to be saved: still he laboured in hope, and did not labour in vain. About this time, on a Sabbath evening, he preached a sermon from, "He that, being often reproved, hardeneth his neck, shall suddenly be destroyed, and that without remedy." It proved a word in season to one of his hearers. A young woman present was deeply impressed by the truth, and in a short time was converted. From this the work spread rapidly, and a number more were soon rejoicing in the Lord. Soon after this sermon was preached a woman died, and he was called to preach her funeral sermon. Her husband requested that it might be written, and read to a few friends. While hearing it read, a number of them were awakened, and soon after converted. This revival continued up to the time of the next session of the conference, and such was its interest, at that time, that Mr. Hedding did not feel himself at liberty to leave to attend that conference. Much as he prized these annual sessions, as favourable opportunities to perpetuate and strengthen his attachment to his brethren, he still felt, that while God was graciously outpouring his Spirit upon the people, "his servant should stand by and watch the offering and feed the sacrifice:" an evidence that he considered the salvation of souls of first importance.

CHAPTER VIII.

LABOURS IN BOSTON, PORTLAND, LYNN, AND NEW-LONDON.

Conference of 1815 — Bishop Asbury — His Feebleness — Subsequent Labours — Death — Conference Business — Mr. Hedding elected Delegate to the General Conference — Stationed in Boston — Daniel Fillmore, his Colleague — Their mutual Attachment — An Amusing Anecdote, or "Shallow Preaching" — State of Religion in the City — Niece of Hancock converted — General Conference of 1816 — Session of the New-England Conference at Bristol — Mr. Hedding and his Colleague returned to Boston — Debt on the Churches — Noble and Successful Effort to liquidate it — A Bequest to the Churches — Methodism planted in Dorchester — Also in Charlestown — Prosperity in Boston — Conference in 1817 — Progress of Methodism — Stationed in Portland — State of the Society — Conference in 1818 — Mr. Hedding in Lynn — Member of the General Conference of 1820 — Stationed in New-London — Disorganized Condition of the Society — Character and End of the Disorderly — Health fails — Reaches Conference.

THE conference met, June, 1815, at Unity, New-Hampshire. It was attended by the venerable Asbury. This was his last visit to New-England; before its next session he had ceased from his labours and gone to his reward. He landed in this country on the 27th of October, 1771, having been then ten years in the ministry, though but a little over twenty-six years of age. His first sermon in this country was preached in New-York on Tuesday, the 13th of November following. At the General Conference of 1784 he and Dr. Coke were unanimously elected superintendents of the Methodist Church in America.

He therefore exercised the episcopal office nearly thirty-two years—making the entire period of his effective ministry nearly fifty-five years. He was altogether an extraordinary man, and in labours he was abundant. In his great work on this continent he travelled, mainly on horseback or in a sulky, nearly one hundred and fifty thousand miles, regarding neither the summer's heat nor the winter's cold. He preached nearly eighteen thousand sermons, presided at more than two hundred conferences, and ordained probably more ministers than any other man ever did. Though pressed by age and infirmity, and often solicited by his friends to lighten his labours, his zeal would never permit him to rest; and he toiled on, travelling and preaching till within a few days of his death. At this session of the New-England Conference he appeared to be literally worn out. He was, to a great extent, unable to be present in the sessions of the conference; and it was with great difficulty, such were his bodily infirmities, that he could go through the usual public ordination services. But we still find him prosecuting his work with indomitable energy of spirit, travelling south as far as to South Carolina and visiting the annual conferences. In South Carolina he contracted an influenza. This was about the last of December, and was attended with an entire loss of appetite and the formation of ulcers upon his lungs. His already worn-out constitution rapidly yielded under this fatal disease. His indomitable energy of spirit and his zeal for the cause were however unabated; and he continued by slow stages to make his way north, hoping to be able to meet the General Conference which was to assemble in May, in the city of Baltimore.

He at length reached Richmond, Virginia, where he preached his last sermon on Sunday, March the 24th. His friends endeavoured to dissuade him, on account of his extreme weakness, from attempting to preach; but he was anxious once more to bear his testimony in that place. He was carried from his carriage to the pulpit, where in a sitting posture he spoke nearly an hour with much feeling and effect, though frequently compelled to pause to recover his breath. His text was: "For he will finish the work, and cut it short in righteousness; because a short work will the Lord make upon the earth." Romans ix, 28. Both the subject and the discourse were appropriate to the impressive scene. After the sermon, he was again carried from the pulpit to his carriage, and taken to his place of rest. Notwithstanding he was evidently in the very last stages of disease and liable to die at any hour, we find him on Tuesday, Thursday, and Friday still travelling toward the seat of the General Conference. On Friday night he reached the house of an old friend, twenty miles from Fredericksburg. The next morning it was observed that he had passed a night of great bodily suffering. His travelling companion, Rev. J. W. Bond, proposed to send for a physician, but he declined having one called, observing that his breath would be gone before the doctor could get there. He however survived till the next day. A short time before he died, his speech failed. After this, observing the agony of his travelling companion, "he raised his hand and looked joyfully at him;" thus expressing what language now failed to communicate. "Brother Bond then asked him if he felt the Lord Jesus Christ to be precious. He seemed to exert all his remaining strength, and raised both his hands as a token of triumph." In a few minutes after this he expired. Asbury sustains very much the same relation to American Methodism that Wesley does to the same cause in the British nation; and his name will never cease to be venerated in the Church of God.

We have already noticed the feebleness of Mr. Asbury at the session of the New-England Conference, which rendered him unable to preside over its deliberations. The business of the conference, however, proceeded with usual harmony and despatch. At this conference twelve delegates to the General Conference were elected; and we find the name of Mr. Hedding third upon that list. At the close of the conference he was stationed, the second time, in Boston, with the Rev. Daniel Fillmore as his colleague. Of this colleague Mr. Hedding says: "He was a good man, a good preacher, a good pastor, and a good colleague." Indeed, the mutual attachment that was formed between these two ministers was as lasting as it was sincere. Their personal correspondence, which was continued down to the last year of Mr. Hedding's life, gives striking evidence of the strength and sincerity of their attachment. As late as 1849, Mr. Hedding, after acknowledging the receipt of a letter from Mr. Fillmore, says: "I was truly glad to receive such a letter from my old, tried friend and colleague. I am thankful for the blessings of God upon you and your family. It is especially a blessing to you, that now at the age of threescore, you enjoy so good health. When I read your appointment to the place you now occupy, I was afraid you were crowded into a poor corner; but I should judge from your letter it must be a pleasant appointment, where you have a good prospect of being greatly useful. What you say of our passing away, and soon to be in the spirit-world, following Pickering, Steele, Merrill, and others, impresses me deeply, from day to day and from night to night; and I am striving and hoping to be ready to follow them to the world of rest."

Two years later, while suffering from that disease which finally terminated his useful career, he says: "We have had many blessed seasons together. I believe since the day I first knew you, in the year 1811, there has been nothing between us contrary to brotherly love. And I trust we shall live forever in another and a better world."

Of their ministry in Boston, Mr. Fillmore, in subsequent years, was accustomed to narrate the following rather amusing anecdote. As was the custom of the times in city circuits, they followed each other successively around the different churches. The great reputation and popular talent of Mr. Hedding occasioned many to follow him from church to church. The difference between his congregations and those of his colleague was quite perceptible. On one occasion, when a portion of Mr. Fillmore's congregation had been drawn away to hear their popular preacher, leaving his house rather thin, a good sister came up at the close of the meeting to comfort her minister. She assured him that she had no disposition to run after his colleague with the multitude. "True," said she, "he has the reputation of being a *deep* preacher; but, for my part, I like *shallow preaching.*" Mr. Fillmore, with illy-regulated risibles, thanked the good sister for her sympathy; but whether he enjoyed the narration of the anecdote then, as well as he did afterward, when his character and reputation were more firmly established, may admit of a doubt. Mr. Fillmore was admitted on trial in the conference in 1811. It is no small compliment to his talents as a minister, that in the third year of his ministry he was stationed as preacher in charge in the city of Portland; and in the fourth year in Boston, as the colleague of Hedding. To the same charge and in the same relation he was returned a second year; and from that time forward continued to fill many of the most important appointments in his conference, between thirty and forty years, till the growing infirmities of age compelled him to retire from the effective ranks.

A quarter of a century had now passed since Jesse Lee first opened his mission under the great elm-tree on Boston Common. During all this period Methodism had been struggling for existence in Boston, and its progress had been exceedingly slow, and in the face of obstacles rarely encountered elsewhere. Unitarianism exerted a controlling influence, embracing the wealth and fashion of the city, and, consequently, experimental piety was held in doubtful repute. Many excellent members had been gathered into the Church,—men and women sincerely devoted to the cause of Christ, and whose spirit and life were an honour to the Christian name. But in worldly resources they were limited,—the great portion of them being poor, and few if any among them that could be called rich. They were regarded as intruders, and their professions of faith in Christ set down to the score of enthusiasm or fanaticism. The dignity of Mr. Hedding's carriage, the amiability of his manner, and the strength and power of his ministry, attracted to the Methodist Church many persons of a high order of intelligence, and also of high social position.

During the year he received into the Church a lady, who, from the circumstances of her conversion, and from her subsequent connexion with the Church, is worthy of special notice. The incident also gives us some insight into the state of religion in the Church then exerting by far the widest influence of any in the city. It should be recorded also because of the light it sheds upon the character of Mr. Hedding as a pastor, and also upon his rigid adherence to the Methodist Discipline and usages. Let us take the account as we have it from his own lips: "Some time during the year, a lady came to my house, and requested religious conversation with me. She was the niece of Governor Hancock. She said that she was a member of a Unitarian Church, but that she had never experienced religion until lately; nor had she until lately any true ideas of experimental religion. She had recently read a volume of Wesley's Sermons, which belonged to a servant girl in her house, into which she had first looked from curiosity; but as she continued to read, they brought her to a sense of her sins and danger, and gave her a knowledge of the way of salvation, and ultimately led her to the experience of that religion that Mr. Wesley taught. She said that she had found it necessary to leave the Unitarian meeting, as they had brought in a new version of the Testament, and read it in the Church, and their preaching was not profitable to her soul; that on the preceding Sabbath she went to an orthodox Congregational meeting, but when she arrived, perceiving that the pastor was absent, and another minister in the pulpit whom she did not care to hear, she left the meeting before the service commenced, with the intention of returning home. Her way home led her by the Methodist Church in Bromfield Lane. She said to herself, 'I will go in here and see if they preach as Wesley did.' She went in and took her seat, and before the service was through she thought, This is Wesley's meeting, and this preaching [Mr. Hedding preached on that occasion] is according to Wesley's preaching; and here I will join, if they will receive me. 'And now,' said she, 'I have come to offer myself as a member of your Church.' She told me her name and residence, and referred me to a number of respectable persons, of whom I could inquire respecting her character. I explained to her our mode of receiving members, and told her we should have a meeting the next Sabbath for that purpose; that I would inquire respecting her character, and if I found it satisfactory would introduce her case to the Church, if she would be present at that time. I told her also, 'I perceive you are very splendidly dressed, but we hold to plain dress, and our members generally observe it; and, if you join the Methodists, you will have to lay aside that gay dress.' She said, 'I know it, and I intend to do it. I have read your Discipline, and I intend to conform to it.' After this conversation she left; and, accordingly, on the following Sabbath she came to the church dressed as plain and as neat as ever Methodist women were required to, and was received on probation in the Church. Soon after this she buried her husband; but she lived for some years after his decease, as devout, pious, uniform, and rational a Christian as I ever knew, and died in the triumphs of faith. After her death it was found that she had left in her will $2,000 to the Methodist Church in Boston, to be funded, and the interest to be paid forever to the poorest members of the Church; and $500 for brother Fillmore, and $500 for myself. Respecting Wesley, this was an example of the Scripture truth, 'He being dead yet speaketh.'"

In the spring of 1816 Mr. Hedding attended the General Conference, which met in the city of Baltimore. It was composed of delegates from the annual conferences, as follows, namely: New-York, sixteen; New-England, twelve; Genesee, ten; Ohio, nine; Tennessee, six; South Carolina, fourteen; Virginia, ten; Baltimore, fourteen; and Philadelphia, thirteen. Bishop Asbury, the great apostle of Methodism, was no longer with them. Mr. Hedding mentions, with profound feeling, the deep sense of loss the absence of Asbury created in their council.

Nothing special took place at this General Conference. Mr. Hedding was at his post of duty; and already, though comparatively a young member, by his prudent counsels and energetic business habits, he had come to be regarded as one of the most influential members of that body. At this General Conference Enoch George and Robert R. Roberts were elected and ordained bishops,—the former having on the first ballot fifty-seven, and the latter, on the second ballot, fifty-five votes, out of one hundred and six. Rev. Joshua Soule and Rev. Thomas Mason were elected book agents; and the publication of the Methodist Magazine—a monthly of forty octavo pages—was ordered. Two years, however, elapsed before the agents found it consistent to carry this order into effect.

At the close of the General Conference Mr. Hedding returned to Bristol, Rhode Island, where the session of the New-England Conference commenced, on the 22d of June. Bishops M'Kendree and Roberts were both present, and presided alternately over its deliberations. Its sessions were harmonious and pleasant—the spirit of brotherly love prevailing in an unusual degree. Not only a common bond of interest, but the *fellowship of suffering* united the hearts of Methodist preachers in those early times. The business of an annual conference was then limited, compared with what has to be transacted in the present day; and much of the time, therefore, was devoted to the public religious services. Thus, the session of an annual conference was a signal for special efforts for the outpouring of the Holy Spirit, and for labours for the conversion of sinners. Mr. Hedding remarks that "our mode of conducting the business of conference in those days was much more social, and less under the discipline and forms of parliamentary rules than in later times." The New-England Conference this year returned a membership of eleven thousand nine hundred and seventy-four, being an increase of eight hundred and eighty-nine. The total membership of the Church was two hundred and fourteen thousand two hundred and thirty-five, showing a net gain of three thousand and seventy; preachers, six hundred and ninety-five, showing a decrease of nine.

Both Mr. Hedding and his colleague were returned

to Boston. There were two churches in the city at that time: one of them was located in what was familiarly known as Methodist Alley, and had been occupied by the society since 1794; the other, which was larger, and more substantially built, had been erected in 1806, and was located in Bromfield-street, on the same site, we believe, as the present Bromfield-street Church. These two churches were held by one board of trustees, and on them both there was then a debt of $18,000. This had been incurred mainly in building the second church; but had been increasing from year to year, till the society now groaned under it as an intolerable burden. Their affairs were now brought to a sort of crisis; for their creditors became importunate and demanded their money, and the trustees were of the opinion that if a forced public sale of the property was had, it would not at that time bring the amount of the encumbrance. For a time their affairs appeared to be in a desperate condition; and it was feared that both churches would have to be sold, and both congregations be left without a house to worship in. Nor would this be the extent of the calamity. The Methodists would be disheartened, and the financial credit of the Church would be destroyed. This greatly distressed the preachers as well as the people. At one time Mr. Hedding could see no way of averting the calamity; but he was not the man to yield to so crushing a misfortune, so long as there was any possible chance of averting it. To raise the money by any of the ordinary modes was impracticable, and so thoroughly convinced of this were both preachers and officiary that it was not attempted. Deliverance, however, was wrought out. Colonel Amos Binney, one of the best financiers in the Church, with whom the preachers counselled in this emergency, and who felt if possible still more deeply than themselves, finally proposed that if the two preachers would go through the city and persuade the people to take the unsold pews at their original valuation,—for enough of them still remained unsold to pay the entire debt,—he would take the notes of the people thus subscribing, payable in any articles of trade, or in any kind of labour that might be most convenient to those drawing them. Also, that he would give sufficient time for the payments, and run all risks in the case; and as soon as a sufficient amount was secured on these conditions, he would assume the Church debt, and take these notes in payment. This was a noble offer; but it imposed heavy conditions on the preachers, whose hands were already quite full. There were only about three hundred members in the city. Many of these had already taken pews; nearly all of them were poor. How then could so large a sum as $18,000 be raised? Fearful odds were against them; but Mr. Hedding was not without hope, and he possessed an energy of character equal to the emergency. He and his colleague, therefore, accepted the conditions, and hope again revived in the hearts of the people. The two preachers now applied themselves to their Herculean task. Except on the Sabbath, every day in the week, early and late, they travelled the city from end to end and from side to side, presenting the subject to every one with whom there was the least prospect of success. Thus many people who were not in the habit of attending any Church became enlisted in the enterprise, and were led to attend upon the Methodist ministry; and many of them subsequently became valuable members of the Church. After three months' unremitting labour, the necessary number of pews had been taken; and, on an afternoon appointed, the persons interested assembled in the Bromfield church, bid for their choice of pews, and gave their notes in accordance with the conditions of the subscription. All passed off harmoniously. The requisite sum was reached. The notes were transferred to Colonel Binney, who gave his check for the money, and the debt was paid. It was a time of great rejoicing among the people. God had brought them out of their troubles, and set their feet in a broad place. The number of regular attendants in the congregations was increased, and the Churches were placed upon a footing they had never before enjoyed. A great and glorious work had been accomplished.

During this year the society also received another benefit, for which it was undoubtedly indebted to Mr. Hedding. A Mr. Boardman, a member of the Church in Boston, but residing in Cambridge, was taken sick, and after some time died. During his sickness, Mr. Hedding was accustomed, though it required a walk of some three miles, to visit him twice or three times a week, to converse and pray with him. After his death, it was found that he had left in his will $4,000 to the Methodist Church in Boston, the use of it to be reserved to his wife during her life-time. She was a member of the Baptist Church, and a good Christian woman. Immediately after the death of her husband she paid over the entire amount to the trustees, generously and nobly relinquishing her right to the use of it. She lived nearly thirty years afterward. These events constituted a bright era in the early history of Methodism in Boston.

It was now a quarter of a century since Methodism was first planted in Boston; and it is not a little remarkable that, up to this time, no regular Methodist preaching had been established in any of the neighbouring towns excepting Lynn. But during this year Mr. Hedding and his colleague commenced preaching first in Dorchester, and afterward in Charlestown.

Mr. Arthur Otheman, a merchant in Boston, had removed to Dorchester, and thus opened the way for the establishment of preaching there. At first Mr. Hedding or his colleague preached once a week in Mr. Otheman's house; but he soon erected a small church near his residence, and preaching was permanently established there. In 1819, it appears upon the Minutes in connexion with Boston; and the succeeding year B. Otheman was appointed to it as an independent station. Here in 1820, Jotham Horton, who had that year been received on trial in the conference, commenced his ministry. Here also, thirty-three years after, he terminated his labours, breaking down in the midst of a gracious revival with which he had been blessed. His dying testimony was, "All my hope is in Christ; I look at nothing else. My transgressions, my labours, my righteousness, and unrighteousness, I lay at the feet of Christ. I trust only in him, and say with Mr. Wesley—

'I the chief of sinners am,
But Jesus died for me.'"

At this time there are two stations in the place, regularly supplied from the conference.

The removal of a few members to Charlestown opened the way to preaching in that place. Mr. Hedding and his colleague might have excused themselves from this extra labour on account of their arduous duties in Boston, and thus left these members of their flock to stray away into other folds, or to backslide; but they were not the men to shrink from labour, especially when a great and effectual door was opened. At first they preached once a week on a week evening in some private house. The seed very soon took root. A class was formed, and quite a revival took place. Two years later the society purchased a house on High-street; and Mr. Hedding, then stationed in Lynn, preached the dedication sermon from the text—"*And I am sure that when I come unto you, I shall come in the fulness of the blessing of the gospel of Christ.*" Romans xv., 29. In 1819 it became a station in connexion with Boston, and Wilbur Fisk, of glorious memory,—then in the second year of his ministry,—was their first pastor. The next year it was made a distinct charge, and Mr. Fisk was reappointed to it. From that time forward the little vine continued to grow and spread, till in Charlestown we have two well-established stations, with a membership of between three and four hundred.

But while these noble men were labouring so successfully to free the churches in Boston from their crushing debt, and also to plant Methodism in these two important new points, they were not neglectful of the spiritual interest of their charges in the city. The work of God steadily advanced, and at the ensuing conference they reported a membership of four hundred and three, being a net increase of sixty-five. So great was the impression made during that year by Mr. Hedding, that up to the present time the few surviving members continue to look back upon it as a great era in the history of Methodism in the city of Boston. For the second time in his ministry, Mr. Hedding felt constrained to remain with his flock on account of the religious interest that prevailed, instead of going to conference.

Concord, in the State of New-Hampshire, was the seat of the conference in 1817. Its session commenced

May the 16th. The progress of Methodism in the east was still onward. An increase of one thousand four hundred and thirty-three was reported, making a total membership in the New-England Conference of thirteen thousand four hundred and seven. The increase in the whole Church was ten thousand six hundred and eighteen, and the total membership two hundred and twenty-four thousand eight hundred and fifty-three. The number of travelling preachers was seven hundred and sixteen, being an increase of twenty-one. The celebrated Jesse Lee this year closed his long and eventful career in triumph. His labours extended almost from one end of the United States to the other. His best eulogy is found in the results of his labours.

At this conference, Mr. Hedding was appointed to Portland District. But his health being poor, and unequal to the arduous labours of a presiding elder, he was released by the bishop and stationed in Portland, and the Rev. N. Bigelow, who had been stationed there, succeeded him on the district.

The Methodist society in Portland was quite numerous, and a large part of very respectable character; but, for a few years previous, the Church had been much disturbed by some of its members, who were greatly in favour of noisy and boisterous meetings. Those who were the advocates of such extravagant meetings were few in number, but very zealous and furious in maintaining them, to the great annoyance of the larger part of the Church. It was the cause of considerable trouble and labour to Mr. Hedding; but by prudent and faithful efforts he prevented any open rupture during his stay among them. But the division in feeling and sentiment prevented any great work of revival. A rupture in the society, however, was only delayed. In the subsequent year, the few advocates of noisy meetings withdrew from the Church, and commenced a separate meeting, which they continued for a year or two, after which they were wholly broken up, and some of their prominent leaders became infidels or open backsliders. After this secession, the prudent and sober part of the society who remained had peace, and prospered more than before. The effects of it, however, were felt for several years; and the flourishing society of two hundred and twenty-four members which was there in 1816 was gradually reduced to one hundred and forty-two in 1819, and then it began to revive and increase. The esteem in which Mr. Hedding was held in Portland will appear from a letter from Rev. Joshua Taylor, then a located preacher connected with the charge. He says: "Brother Hedding spent one year with us here in Portland, and we were in hopes to have had him another year; but he was so loudly called for at Lynn that we lost the privilege. While he was with us he was highly esteemed and very useful, although no special revival took place; but his wise and judicious management saved the society from an eruption, or rather division, which afterward took place, and which I think would have been avoided could he have remained with us the second year."

The increase in the New-England Conference for this year was seven hundred and eighty-two, giving an aggregate of fourteen thousand one hundred and eighty-nine members. The increase in the whole Church was four thousand seven hundred and seventy-four, the aggregate two hundred and twenty-nine thousand six hundred and twenty-seven; number of travelling ministers seven hundred and forty-eight, increase thirty-two. The session of the conference was held at Hallowell, Maine.

In 1818 and 1819, Mr. Hedding was stationed again in Lynn. His former connexion with the society there had greatly endeared the people to him. Many of them had been converted under his ministry, and received into the Church by him. The appointment was peculiarly pleasing to him, and the people received him with open arms.

During the second year of his ministry there he was much afflicted with ill health; and during the winter was able to preach but little, and, indeed, for a good portion of the time he was confined to the house. The people were, however, unabated in their kindness. He supplied his pulpit as best he could; and in spite of all the disadvantages under which he laboured, it was a year of considerable success. Many, who, for years after, were among the most worthy and useful members of the Church, were that year converted to God.

The session of the conference for 1819 was held in Lynn, where Mr. Hedding was stationed. The membership reported at this conference was fifteen thousand three hundred and twelve, increase one thousand one hundred and twenty-three; total membership in the Church two hundred and forty thousand nine hundred and twenty four, increase eleven thousand two hundred and ninety-seven; total number of travelling preachers eight hundred and twelve, increase sixty-four.

Mr. Hedding was again elected a delegate to the General Conference, which was to assemble in the city of Baltimore on the first of the succeeding May. It was composed of delegates from the annual conferences, as follows, namely: New-York, thirteen; New-England, ten; Genesee, seven; Ohio, eight; Tennessee, six; South Carolina, nine; Virginia, eight; Baltimore, nine; Philadelphia, fourteen; Missouri, three; Mississippi, two. Important measures relating to the vital organization of the Church, and also to the multiplication of her agencies and the enlargement of her operations, were discussed at this conference. Some of them were radical in their character, and elicited much warmth of feeling in debate. In these questions Mr. Hedding took a deep interest, and participated in the debates that ensued; but the suavity and courtesy of his manner, the manifest sincerity and honesty of his opinions, and especially the plain, practical manner in which they were presented, challenged the respect, if not admiration of even his opponents. A large number of his brethren wished to present his name as a candidate for the episcopal office, as it had been determined to elect an additional bishop; but this he absolutely declined. The Rev. Joshua Soule was finally elected; but, as we have already seen, resigned before ordination, in consequence of the action of the conference upon the presiding-elder question. The conference accepted his resignation, but did not elect any other in his place.

After the close of the General Conference, Mr. Hedding, with his colleagues, returned by land to New-York, and thence sailed in a sloop to Nantucket, which was to be the seat of the New-England Conference for that year. Bishop George presided. A membership of seventeen thousand seven hundred and thirty-nine was reported, exhibiting the large and encouraging increase of two thousand four hundred and twenty-seven. It was a year of prosperity in the entire Church. The whole membership was two hundred and fifty-six thousand eight hundred and eighty one, increase fifteen thousand nine hundred and fifty-seven; number of preachers nine hun-and four, increase ninety-two.

Mr. Hedding was stationed in New-London. He sailed from Nantucket to Boston by sloop, travelled thence by land to Lynn, sent his goods by water to New-London, and with his wife proceeded by the stage to his appointment.

Some ten years before he had travelled the New-

London District, and had then formed a general acquaintance with the society in the city. At that time the society, though not large, was composed for the most part of excellent and truly devoted people. Since then large additions had been made. Among these were some excellent members; but many, who had more recently joined, were not regular and orderly Methodists. They had been the occasion of much difficulty in the Church, and affairs were now tending rapidly to a crisis. This class of persons made high professions of piety, were disposed to take a prominent part in all public meetings, and in all Church matters—except raising funds for its support. They were exceedingly boisterous and irregular in their religious exercises, impatient of all restraint or reproof, censorious in their spirit, and intolerably uncharitable toward every one—not even excepting their minister—who did not coincide with them in all their visionary notions, and participate in all their irregular and noisy demonstrations. The reader will now assent to the fact that a "fit appointment" had been made in sending Mr. Hedding to the place. His keen insight into man, his wisdom, and skill, and prudence, and firmness, all were brought into requisition.

Mr. Hedding soon comprehended the nature of the case, and resolutely set himself about the cure of the great evils that had sprung up in the society. This was a most delicate, difficult, and painful task. In fact, as it proved in the end, the evil had been so long tolerated that it was past cure. The irregulars did nothing toward the support of the preacher, or toward meeting the incidental expenses of the Church, and upon the faithful few the burden fell heavily; but they endeavoured to bear it like Christian men. It was impossible to conceive the many modes in which these deluded persons would annoy both the preacher and the faithful portion of the Church; it seemed as though the devil was ever present to help them. After Mr. Hedding left the charge this faction continued to annoy and distract the society, till at length, by violence, they obtained possession of the church. Here they now run riot in their fanaticism; but they soon quarrelled among themselves, and in the end came to naught. Some of them turned out to be immoral and grossly licentious; others wholly renounced Christianity, and became avowed infidels. The old society, for a time, occupied another place of worship, but eventually recovered their old church by a process of law; and being purged from the corruption that had tainted them, they became a well-established society. But Methodism received a severe shock in the place, from which it did not recover for many years.

During the latter part of this year Mr. Hedding suffered from an attack of the dyspepsy, and his health was so completely prostrated that he was compelled to relinquish his charge. He now began to fear that his itinerant work was done; and, much as he had suffered in that work. the idea of being compelled to desist occasioned the most painful feelings. Under advice, he determined to try the effect of travelling on horseback, though it was with the greatest difficulty that he could mount or dismount, or even hold his position after he had mounted. Accordingly he purchased a horse, and prepared for his journey. The first day he was able to progress but a few miles; the next he increased the distance. Thus he continued to travel for several weeks, his health gradually improving all the while. In June of that year he reached Barre, Vermont, in season to attend the session of the conference, which commenced on the 20th. Bishop George presided at this conference. His experiment in horseback exercise encouraged him to hope that he might stand the work a few years longer, if he could have such work as would require much out-door exercise, especially on horseback. The state of his health, and his desire as to the nature of his work, he made known to the bishop; and at the close of the conference he was placed upon the Boston District. The increase in the New-England Conference this year was one thousand nine hundred and eleven; and in the whole Church, twenty-one thousand two hundred and fifty-six. Seventy-three were also added to the number of travelling preachers.

CHAPTER IX.

MR. HEDDING ON BOSTON DISTRICT AND IN BOSTON—FROM 1821 TO 1824.

Boston District—An Inhospitable Methodist—State of the Work—Camp-meetings—Conference at Bath—Stationed in Boston—Mr. Hedding's Conference Sermon—Measures to establish Zion's Herald—Mr. Hedding's Colleague, Ephraim Wiley—Conference of 1823—Returned to Boston—Colleague—John Lindsey—Review of Mr. Hedding's Labours—Progress of Methodism—Elements of its Success—1. Revival of the Old Doctrines of Christianity—2. Appeal to Man's Consciousness of his Relations to God—3. A Conscious Personal Salvation—4. Individualizing Characteristics of Methodist Preaching—5. Peculiar Provisions of Organic Methodism—Perpetuity of these Elements—Confidence reposed in Mr. Hedding by his Brethren.

We have already noticed the appointment of Mr. Hedding to the Boston District. Though small in extent when compared with the earlier districts, and also when compared with some at that time, it embraced quite an extent of territory. In the north, it extended to Cape Ann and Newburyport; in the south, it included New-Bedford, Plymouth, and all of Cape Cod, also Nantucket and Martha's Vineyard. This, one would think, was a rather laborious field for a sick man. But no sooner has the conference closed, than, having fixed his family residence among his old friends at Lynn, he mounts his horse, and proceeds to a first survey of his extended work. His health continued to improve gradually; but it was nearly a year before he was fully recovered.

In the month of March, an incident occurred which laid the foundation of a severe cold, and came very near terminating his useful labours. While journeying to one of his quarterly meetings, on Cape Cod, he put up for the night with a certain physician, who was a member of the Church, and quite a wealthy man. A "north-east storm" of unusual violence came on. These storms, especially at that season of the year, are always severe along the sea-border of New-England; and along the bleak coast of Cape Cod they have full sweep. Mr. Hedding, finding in the morning that the violence of the storm was unabated, said to his wealthy host that, as he would still have time to reach his quarterly conference at Provincetown, he would not contend with the elements, but would remain in-doors for the day. The doctor gruffly replied, "You are neither sugar nor salt." The offensive expression was uttered in such a manner as to give unmistakable evidence that, such was the meanness of his nature, he would prefer that the minister of Christ should be exposed to the inconveniences and sufferings of the storm, and the danger that might result to his health and life, than be at the expense and trouble of entertaining him another day. Mr. Hedding immediately mounted his horse, and faced the pelting storm till he came to a more hospitable place of entertainment. By this exposure he contracted a cold, which settled upon his lungs; and though he visited his quarterly meetings, he was not able to preach again till after the next annual conference.

Mr. Hedding at this time gives the following short account of the condition of the work in his district:—"The societies throughout the district were generally orderly, steady, and religious. There were several very gracious revivals during the year. The society at Newburyport was young, and struggling with many embarrassments; but it prospered notwithstanding its difficulties. In Salem the Church had but just commenced, and hardly had the breath of life. In Lynn and Marblehead there were old and well-established societies, steadily advancing in numbers and influence. There was an overwhelming revival in Boston. The societies in Malden and Cambridge, but in their infancy, were doing well. Dorchester, though small, was continually increasing. New-Bedford, limited in numbers and strength, bid fair to make a good and useful Church. On Martha's Vineyard there were several small societies, but composed of devoutly religious members. Nantucket had a very large and flourishing Church. All over Cape Cod the societies were an interesting body of plain and faithful Christians; the Methodists had preoccupied that ground. Provincetown, at the end of the cape, was one of the oldest and best Churches on the district."

During this year he held two camp-meetings,—one at Wellfleet, on Cape Cod, and the other near New-Bedford. The former was one of signal profit to the people, and very many professed conversion. At the latter he preached the opening sermon. It was a sermon of great power, and was long remembered by many who heard it. His text was, "Speak unto the children of Israel, that they go forward."

The session of the conference commenced June 29, 1822, at Bath, Maine: Bishop Roberts presided. The increase in the New-England Conference this year was only three hundred and seventy-four, making a membership of twenty thousand and twenty-four; in the whole Church, sixteen thousand four hundred and seventy-six, making a membership of two hundred and ninety-seven thousand six hundred and twenty-two; in the itinerant ministry, one hundred and twenty-nine, making the total number one thousand one hundred and six.

Mr. Hedding says: "At this conference, on account of my ill health, resulting from a severe cold I had taken in the March preceding, I requested to give up the district, and asked the bishop to give me some small place, where the labour would be less, and I should be enabled to recover my health. But, in the council as presiding elder, I soon discovered that the bishop had set me down for Boston. I again requested to have some small place; but the bishop said no. 'Then,' said I, 'put me on the district; for it will be better for my health than to have so large and arduous a charge.' But the bishop persisted, and I was appointed to Boston."

The conference, at its preceding session, had requested Mr. Hedding to preach a sermon at this conference on the Divinity of Christ. This sermon gave great satisfaction, and the conference requested a copy for publication. It was published in the seventh volume of the Methodist Magazine. This sermon is not distinguished so much for grace of style and felicity of expression as for clear statement and sound Scriptural elucidation of Bible truth. The text taken for the occasion was, "In the beginning was the Word, and the Word was with God, and the Word was God. The same was in the beginning with God." John i, 1, 2. After a brief notice of the errors that had crept into the infant Church, and which the evangelist here sought to correct, the author proceeded to develop what was asserted in the text concerning Christ. This he shows could mean nothing less than that he is the Supreme God. The arguments are less novel than substantial. They exhibit not only an acquaintance with the best theological writers, but an amount of close Biblical research creditable to the author, and giving invincible strength to his positions. The following are his closing remarks, which we give as an example of the direct and forcible character of his style, as well as for the interest of the subject:—

"The subject, then, is brought to this point: we must either renounce the Bible, and go back with the pagans to the dim light of nature to be instructed respecting God and religion, or we must believe what it declares of Jesus Christ our Lord. Now, my brethren, what say you? Are you prepared to give up the Bible? Are you willing to be pagans or deists? No! you are Christians,—Christians by conviction and choice. You believe that the Almighty Being who made you has redeemed you. You believe in the *unity* of the Godhead,—not that there are two gods, nor three gods; but that Father, Son, and Holy Ghost are *one God:* one in essence, though three in persons, or modes of existence. You are, therefore, consistent *Unitarians;* for a Unitarian is a believer in one God. Whereas those who deny the supreme divinity of Christ, and yet believe the Bible, are not Unitarians. For they must believe that Christ is God in some sense, if they suppose him such only by office: and if they believe he is God in any other sense whatever than that in which we have proved him to be, then they believe in at least two gods,—a Supreme God, and a secondary god!

"The faith we entertain in our Lord and Master is perfectly consistent with his whole life. It is true, that in a few instances, when speaking of his human nature, or of his office as Mediator, he represents himself less than the Father; but he always does this in such a manner, or in such circumstances, as to make it appear that he speaks of his humanity, or of his office as Mediator; showing us, at the same time, that what he says on this point is not inconsistent with his supreme divinity. Take an example: 'My Father is greater than I.' These are suitable words for the *Eternal Word* to use in the time of his humiliation. But for the highest creature in the universe it would be a haughty piece of humility to say, *God is greater than I.* What should we think of Moses, Isaiah, or Paul, had one of them said so? And if Jesus were only a man, as some say,—admitting him to be higher than any man on earth, or any angel in heaven,—how would he appear saying, *God is greater than I?* What comparison can there be between the *Infinite God* and any creature?

"The conduct, conversation, and preaching of Christ were calculated to lead the people into a belief of his divinity. He wrought his miracles in his own name. He used the same language respecting himself, that the God of the Hebrews had done concerning himself: '*Before Abraham was, I am.*' He claimed equal honours with the Father. He professed to be able to do what none but God could do. '*The Son quickeneth whom he will. The dead shall hear the voice of the Son of God, and they that hear shall live. All that are in the graves shall hear his voice, and shall come forth.*' He could lay down and take up the life of his body at pleasure, by his own power: '*I have power to lay it down, and I have power to take it up again.*' He spoke of this power as an evidence of his divinity. 'If I do not the works of my Father, believe me not. But if I do, though ye believe not me, believe the works; that ye may know and believe that the Father is in me, and I in him.' He speaks of himself as being of the same essence with the Father, by saying, 'He that believeth on me, believeth not on me, but on him that sent me.' 'If ye had known me, ye should have known my Father also.' '*He that seeth me, seeth him that sent me.*'

"Christ prohibited the people serving any other but the true God: 'Him only shalt thou serve.' Yet he frequently required them to serve him, love him, &c. He commanded them to place the same confidence in him they placed in the Father: 'Ye believe in God, believe also in me.' And all these duties he enforced, by promising to give them the greatest possible blessings—blessings which none but God could give: 'I will give you rest—*I will receive you unto myself.*' 'If ye shall ask anything in my name, I will do it.' '*I give unto them eternal life. I will raise him up at the last day.*' 'He that believeth on me, though he were dead, yet shall he live.'

"He speaks of himself as having authority to send the Holy Spirit: 'But if I depart, I will send him unto you.' 'He shall glorify me; for he shall *receive of mine*, and shall show it unto you.'

"Consider how Christ uniformly condemned ostentation, and recommended humility. Hear him say to his disciples, '*Be not ye called Rabbi—neither be ye called masters.*' Then hear him speak of himself: 'For one is your Master, even Christ.' 'Ye call me Master and Lord, and ye say well; for so I am.'

"If Jesus Christ be God, all these declarations respecting himself appear consistent, rational, and sublime. But call him a mere creature, and you change the character from the highest state of glory to the lowest state of degradation and wretchedness. For then, instead of appearing to us as that merciful and powerful God he represented himself to be, he comes forward only as the son of Joseph and Mary, only as Jesus of Nazareth—a mere man! yet assuming the authority of God, claiming all the honours and services God claimed, professing to do all that God did, promising in his own name all that God promised, even blessings which none but God could bestow—making himself equal with God! In this view of him, it is impossible for us to believe that he was even a *good man.*

"Further, viewing him as a mere creature, if we could believe he was a good man, and if we could keep our souls from being chilled with horror at his high-sounding pretensions, what excellence could we see in him superior to that of many other servants of God? If he were but a creature, he made no atonement for sin, which, I believe, all allow who deny his divinity. Take away the divinity and the atonement, and wherein, I ask again, is he superior to the other servants of God? Leave him destitute of these excellences, and he falls at once into a level with his *fellow-creatures.* He taught no more than Moses had taught before him; he brought no new light into the world, though *he said he was the light of the world.* Is it said, He set a good example? So did other servants of God. You reply, He laboured for the good of mankind. Moses did more for the Hebrews than he did; Paul laboured more abundantly. Jesus preached three or four years; Paul preached about thirty years. Jesus preached only through Palestine; Clement says, Paul preached in the east, and to the uttermost bounds of the west. Did Jesus work miracles? Paul probably wrought more, for he lived longer; and if both were only men, both were equally dependent for the power by which they wrought them. 'But Jesus died for sinners.' Hold! This strange doctrine says *he did not die to atone for sin, he died only as a martyr!* So did Isaiah; so did Paul. But it is further stated, 'He is the Son of God." God has other sons besides him; and if he be only a man, we do not believe our heavenly Father placed him so much above his brethren, as he represents himself to be; Paul was a son of God also. Finally, making Jesus the character to which we have alluded, Paul did more for the salvation of mankind than Jesus did; and we are under greater obligations to Paul than to Jesus! Exclude the divinity and the atonement, and everything that is said in the Bible about salvation by Christ is a mere sound of words. Paul saved us in the same sense Jesus did, and suffered more to accomplish the work than Jesus did!

"Again, supposing Jesus to have been the mere creature many imagine he was, it is no wonder the Jews were offended at the high pretensions he set up. They understood those pretensions to be blasphemy, often accused him of that crime, and supposed their law (Lev. xxiv, 16) required them to put him to death. And if he were only a man, who can prove that the Jews had not good reasons for attempting to kill him, *because he made himself equal with God?* Such are the shocking consequences of denying the divinity of Christ.

"But, my brethren, we are not led away with these derogatory views of the Son of God. We believe *he is that Rock on which the Church is built*, and by which it is supported, so that *the gates of hell shall not prevail against it.* 'For other foundation can no man lay than that which is laid, which is Jesus Christ.' Then let us cleave to him with all our hearts, *holding the beginning of our confidence steadfast unto the end.* Believing Christ was what he professed to be, we respect the faith of the apostles, and admire their conduct when they worshipped him, and preached him to the world as an Almighty Saviour, *able to save them to the uttermost that came unto God by him;* and when they wrought miracles in his name, calling on the people to believe in him, encouraging them to expect he would pardon their sins, send down the Holy Spirit to sanctify their natures, and save their souls. These views of Christ carried the apostles among Jews and heathen, by land and water, through prisons, blood, and fire, among wild beasts, crosses, and gibbets, to pluck human souls as brands from the fire. By these views, the faithful servants of God, from the apostles down till now, have been animated and rendered successful in preaching *Christ crucified* to a dying world.

"Then, my brethren, let us go forward, in the name of our Almighty Master, and vindicate his injured honour; and, by the best of our ability, to the end of life, maintain his cause, by doing all in our power to be the means of saving the souls he purchased by his blood."

The conference requested the publication of this sermon as early as June, 1822; its publication was not commenced till the August number of the Methodist Magazine for 1824. It was then completed in two numbers.

At the conference of 1822, the question of establishing a religious newspaper was brought before the body; and, after full discussion, it was determined to go forward in tho enterprise. The conference appointed a committee to carry its purpose into effect. Mr. Hedding was an active friend of the measure, and one of the committee. The paper was to be issued from Boston; and, as Mr. Hedding was the only one of the committee in that vicinity, the burden of the enterprise fell upon him. The result was the establishment of the Zion's Herald, the first weekly religious newspaper established under the patronage of the Church; and, indeed, among the first established in the country.

Mr. Hedding's colleague in Boston this year was Ephraim Wiley, who had also been in the city the preceding year in connexion with Rev. S. W. Wilson. Mr. Wiley was received on trial in 1818, and during the first two years of his ministry was stationed in Wellfleet, the third in Malden, and the next two in Boston. Mr. Hedding says of him: "He was a pleasant, useful, and popular preacher; and we laboured together in great harmony. Although the year was not characterized for great revivals, there was a good state of religious interest in the Churches; it was a year of profit and some ingathering." Mr. Wiley continued many years an efficient and popular minister; but was finally returned superannuated in 1839. Two of his sons graduated at the Wesleyan University: one of them became a physician, and the other is the Rev. E. E. Wiley, D. D., President of the Emory and Henry College in Western Virginia.

Bishop George presided at the conference in 1823; and its sessions commenced in Providence, Rhode Island, June 12th. The work was still advancing in New-England. Places heretofore inaccessible, on account of their remoteness, or on account of the invincible wall of bigotry and prejudice that defended them, were constantly invaded, and the standard of Methodism planted in their very midst. The old circuits, too, as the society became strong in numbers and in ability, were constantly contracting their borders by the excision of parts, which were organized into new stations or circuits. The summation for this year was twenty thousand nine hundred and twenty-six,* increase nine hundred and two; membership in the whole Church, three hundred and twelve thousand five hundred and forty, increase fourteen thousand

* The General Minutes for this year make it twenty-one thousand nine hundred and twenty-six, an error of one thousand made in adding.

nine hundred and eight; travelling ministers one thousand two hundred and twenty-six, increase one hundred and twenty.

Mr. Hedding was reappointed to Boston, with the Rev. John Lindsey as his colleague. Mr. Lindsey was a native of Lynn, Massachusetts, and was among the early fruits of Methodism in that place, and entered the travelling ministry in 1809. Mr. Hedding says of him: "He was a true friend and a good preacher. We laboured together during the year in great brotherly love—preaching, praying, and visiting the classes." The Christian affection established between these two men of God at this early day, continued unabated for more than a quarter of a century; when Mr. Lindsey fell, while yet in the heat of the battle, with his armour still girded upon him. The following extract from a letter, written by Mr. Hedding after the death of his old colleague, will show his estimate of his character and life: "His religious experience was deep and genuine. His spirit and manner of life were devout, and religiously upright. He was a man of industrious habits, and manifested that industry in all the departments of his duty. He was a man of more than ordinary talents, and by industry and perseverance he acquired a large amount of useful knowledge. He was really a sound and learned divine. He had great resolution in the pursuit of his labours and the prosecution of his duties. Many of his appointments required great mental effort and bodily labours; but he braved the summer's heat, and the winter's cold and snows, and, like a good soldier of Jesus Christ, accomplished his work. His labours were frequently followed with blessings on the souls of the people,—both in edifying and strengthening the children of God and in awakening and converting sinners. He was a man by nature of a kind heart; and by grace that affection was sanctified and strengthened. He was an abiding friend to his friends, and he had a heart to forgive an enemy." Such was the character of Mr. Hedding's colleague in the last appointment he filled before his elevation to the episcopal office. One of his sons, the Rev. J. W. Lindsey, A. M., is now a professor in the Wesleyan University at Middletown, Connecticut.

Through the labours of Mr. Hedding and his colleague, a church was erected at what is now called East Cambridge, the corner-stone of which was laid by Mr. Hedding in the midst of a violent snow-storm. Such was the zeal of the people that the storm did not prevent their assembling; and the preachers were not a whit behind them in braving obstacles when a great work was before them.

As this year terminated Mr. Hedding's special connexion with the New-England Conference, by his election to the episcopal office, it may be well to survey the progress of the work during his connexion with it. As we have already seen, his first field of labour was in Vermont; and, with the exception of one year, all his subsequent fields of labour were included mainly in New-England. He went out first under the presiding elder, in 1799. The whole membership of the Church, then, was sixty-one thousand three hundred and fifty-one, of whom twelve thousand two hundred and thirty six—or about one-fifth of the whole—were coloured; and the whole number of preachers two hundred and seventy-two. In the territory subsequently included in the New-England Conference, there were then but two thousand nine hundred and seventy-five members, and thirty-one preachers. The aggregate, at the close of this year, was twenty-one thousand six hundred and twenty-five members, and one hundred and fifty-seven travelling preachers. Then there were very few churches, and but little provision made for the support of the preachers or their families; now churches had been established in almost every section of the work, and the people had become better able to make the preachers and their families comfortable. Then the societies were generally a mere handful, widely separated from each other on the extensive circuits, and could be reached only by long and fatiguing rides over bad and often dangerous roads; now the circuits had generally become contracted, so as to lessen the physical labour and exposure necessary in performing the services they required; and many of the societies that had become sufficiently strong had been organized into stations, and enjoyed the entire pastoral oversight as well as ministerial labour of the preacher. Then Methodist publications were very rare, and difficult to be obtained, and among the people there were few books except those published by Calvinists and of Calvinistic tendencies; but these few were greatly prized, and were read and re-read, and then loaned to their neighbours. Now the Book Concern in New-York had begun to develop its giant energies, and was rapidly increasing its list of publications, and in a still higher ratio the number of its issues; so that, by the efficient agency of the preachers, Methodist literature was diffused through all the land. Then the daring itinerant, who went forth into distant regions to "break up new ground," though in the wildest country and among the poorest people, was left to the chances of fortune or the providence of God for his support, and even for shelter for his head. Now the missionary spirit had been evoked in the Church, and a society had been organized, which, though still greatly inadequate, was doing a good work to help forward the cause in the waste places and in the frontier settlements. The broad foundations of a noble superstructure had been wisely and firmly laid. Many of the fathers had been gathered to their rest. Whatcoat, and Coke, and Asbury, and Wilson, and Branch, and Moriarty, and Michael Coate, and Jesse Lee, were no longer marshalled in the van of the sacramental host; but in their places God had raised up other standard-bearers—not less single in purpose, and not less valiant in the conflict. Thus, while the instruments were subject to the common frailty of earth, the work itself possessed a perpetuity that demonstrated its divine origin.

It will also be well to glance at the peculiar means by which such great results had been realized; or, in other words, to invite the attention of the reader to the grand elements of success in the Methodistic movement. Without at all denying the providential origin of Methodism, we may profitably search out the secondary causes—the instruments of Providence—by which its grand results have been realized. Such inquiries may not only discover to us the foundations of our strength, but also, if the spirit of our fathers in any degree remains, may lead us to seek after the "old paths." Isaac Taylor, by far the most philosophical writer that has ever essayed the problem of Methodism, says, that "the product of the Methodist ministrations was such as has no parallel, even in the most exciting moments of the Reformation; nor has it had any parallel in these later times."

The same writer adds: "In what proportion of instances the Methodistic movement, which affected so many thousands of hearers through its forty years of primitive energy, did in fact issue in producing a godly, righteous, and sober life, we are not now concerned to inquire; nor would such an inquiry, however laboriously instituted, yield any satisfactory result. What we have to do with is not that which can be known only in heaven, but that which is patent and unquestionable, namely,—that Protestant doctrine, proclaimed by men variously gifted and qualified, did, through a course of years, and where ever carried, affect the minds of thousands of persons, not in the way of a transient excitement, but effectively and permanently. The very same things had been affirmed, from year to year, by able and sincere preachers, in the hearing of congregations assenting to all they heard—not indeed altogether without effect; yet with no such effect as that which ordinarily, if not invariably, attended the Methodistic preaching. Nor, if we look beyond the pale of religious influence, had any previous ministrations of the same Protestant doctrines taken hold, as this did, or in any remarkable manner, of the untaught masses of the people—the non-attendants upon public worship—the heathen million that circulates every Sunday around churches and chapels. Let it be said—and we hold it as an undoubted truth, and a truth apart from which the facts before us must be wholly inexplicable—that the Methodistic proclamation of the gospel was rendered effective by a divine energy, granted at the time, in a sovereign manner, and in an unwonted degree; but this truth remembered always as it ought to be, the question returns,—What were the principal elements of that religious impression which Methodistic preaching so generally produced?"

The above sets forth precisely the question we have just proposed to ourselves; and also contains an acknowledgment and a lucid statement of the facts that will ever give a lively interest to this question in the mind of the Christian philosopher. We may not perhaps view the subject in the same light as Isaac

Taylor, for we contemplate it from an altogether different stand-point,—one, however, we believe, not less favourable to a candid and correct observation.

In the first place, then, we would say that in the Methodistic reformation there was the revival of the old doctrines of Christianity, which, if they had not been formally renounced, had become obsolete and powerless. The revival of these doctrines, or the planting of a doctrinal basis, however, could not alone have produced these results. The doctrines of universal atonement by the blood of Jesus, of justification by faith, of adoption and purification, and of the conscious testimony of the Spirit of God to our justification and adoption,—all might have been preached without any such result. They might have been drawn out with logical exactness, and demonstrated with mathematical precision, and yet have been—as they often were—so completely neutralized by cold formalities, and by the utter absence of that spirit which constitutes the growing power of all Christian teaching, as to cause them to fall powerless upon the dozing multitude. Thus a sound orthodoxy—the shell of Christianity—may be maintained, though vitalized by the breath of no living spirit. But these doctrines, *as* they were preached by the early heroes of Methodism, fell directly upon the hearts of men, and awakened that dormant religious consciousness, or innate sense of our personal relationship to Christ as our Redeemer and Saviour, and to God as our final Judge, which had well nigh been extinguished by the formalism of the age. Religion then became a *reality to the people.* The heart is always the stronghold of sin, and the conscience is the great avenger of wrong. These, however, can be reached, not by modes, and forms, and processes of reasoning, but by direct appeals coming from a heart powerfully quickened in its sensibilities, and a conscience all alive to truth and God. In ancient times, when a prophet came forth with a "Thus saith the Lord," into the temple or public assemblies of God's ancient people, there was something unexpressed and inexpressible in human language, that said to the hearts of the multitude, "This is God's messenger," and thus vindicated his authority. So in modern times, when a man has a special mission from God, and goes forth in the spirit of that mission, every movement and every word vindicates the authenticity of his message and the genuineness of his mission.

Again, this awakening of the consciousness of personal relationship to God had its correlatives. First, it completely annihilated the old Romish idea of Christianity—an idea also grafted upon the Church of England and developed in her organization and spirit—the idea that the Church is to lift from the individual his personal responsibility, and assume the responsibility of his safe conveyance to heaven. It assumes that all born within the pale of the Church, and all coming within that pale, belong to the Church; and whatever belongs to the Church is entitled, through the Church, to heaven. Methodism in contravention to this "Church idea," as it has been called, came directly to the sinner's heart and conscience, and brought up directly to his view, not the Church, but Christ as a refuge from his sins. And then again, having awakened the personal consciousness, it developed the elements of a new life—a permanent, spiritual, growing life.

Individualizing was a characteristic of all early Methodist preaching. Each man had his peculiar style: Wesley was sententious and solid, Whitefield was imaginative and impassioned, Coke was discursive and almost hypercritical, Nelson was untrammelled by any principles of logic or rules of rhetoric; and yet in the preaching of all these men, *individualizing* was a common, nay, universal characteristic. They spoke to the individual soul: "My message is to *thee*, sinner! I stand here to-day to bring *thee* to bethink thyself of thy past ways. *Thou* who dost now appear in the presence of thy God—loathsome in thy sins—I challenge and command thee to bow thy stubborn neck, to bend thy stubborn knee. Dost not thou—even thou, ungrateful as thou hast been these many years—yea, a hardened rebel from thy mother's breast even until now—dost thou not hear the Saviour calling to *thee* to repent and to turn? Was it not for thee that he shed his blood? Did he not carry thy sorrows on Calvary, even thine? Was he not wounded for *thy* transgressions? Did he not think of thee, of thy soul, and of all its abominations, that dark night when he lay in agony on the ground?

Yes. It was thine own sins that made him sweat blood in that garden. But now, with a purpose of mercy in his heart toward thy wretched soul, he calls thee to himself, and says—yes, he says it to *thee*—'Come now, let us reason together.'" Such is a faint semblance—for only a faint semblance can be transferred to paper—of the direct, pungent, personal, and awakening appeals carried home by the Spirit of God to the sinner's heart.

Following these philosophical and spiritual elements of Methodism were other elements, less fundamental, it may be, but scarcely less important. Their extemporaneous style of preaching—so completely adapted to the individualizing messages, as no other style could be—was equally novel and attractive. Nor did it lose any of its power to subdue and control, because of homely style and blunt phrases. It was a ministry of the heart, of power—to the heart, and to the masses of the people. The systematic organization of Methodism guarded against a useless expenditure, a waste of this power. Its conferences—general, annual and quarterly; its districts, circuits, and itinerancy; its social convocations, in which Christian experience was nurtured and Christian zeal was inspired anew; its school of constant exercise, where large use was made of the smallest talent and great gains realized from it,—these were some of the minor agencies that co-worked with the higher elements of the Methodistic reformation. Without those higher elements, these might have existed, but they would have been empty and unproductive. On the other hand, without these, those higher principles would have wasted their energy in spasmodic manifestations. Such is a faint outline picture of the genius of Methodism, providentially raised up by God to be an efficient co-worker in spreading Scripture holiness over all these lands.

Now if we carefully examine these elements, or even these organic provisions, there is not one in the whole series that may not exist in perpetuity. There is, then, no elemental cause, unless it be found in principles of our nature not here brought to view, why Methodism might not have retained its pristine energy and its aggressive conquests till God's purpose had been realized in the complete destruction of Satan's empire among men.

We can pursue this investigation no further. Our limits have allowed us only a glance at some of the most important aspects of the question, and of others we could give only fragmentary glimpses. We must now return to the thread of our narrative.

At the session of the conference for 1823, Mr. Hedding was elected, as he had been four times before, to represent that body in the General Conference. The vote for him had been uniformly almost unanimous. It is said that he never lacked more than two or three of the entire number of votes cast. The conference elected fourteen delegates, and among them are the names of Pickering, Merritt, Mudge, Merrill, Kilburn, Lindsey, Fisk, Hoyt, and others In the unanimity of the vote cast for him as a delegate by the members of his conference, and in the hearty and cordial support given to him for the episcopal office by his brethren, we have evidence of the estimation in which he was held by them—especially those who had known him longest and who knew him best. It will not be too much to say that his subsequent career abundantly proved that this confidence was not misplaced.

The General Conference of 1824 and the election of Mr. Hedding to the episcopal office, will form the subject of our next chapter.

CHAPTER X.

GENERAL CONFERENCE OF 1824, AND MR. HEDDING'S ELECTION TO THE EPISCOPACY.

Representation in the General Conference — British Delegation — Address of the Bishops — Educational Demands upon the Church — Religious Education of the Children — Seminaries and Public Schools — Missionary Society — Book Concern — Slavery and the "Tenth Section" — Memorials on Lay Delegation — Action of the Conference — Reasons Assigned — The Presiding-Elder Question — Ballotings for Bishops — Mr. Hedding's Election — His Reluctance to being a Candidate — Rev. E. Mudge's Account — Feelings after Election — Subsequent Resolution of the Conference — Accepts the Office and is ordained — Fitness for the Office.

The General Conference of 1824 commenced its session in the city of Baltimore on the 1st day of May, as usual. Twelve conferences were represented by one hundred and thirty-three delegates, distributed as follows: New-York Conference, seventeen; New-England, fourteen; Genesee, twelve; Ohio, fifteen; Kentucky, eight; Missouri, five; Tennessee, ten; Mississippi, three; South Carolina, eleven; Virginia, nine; Baltimore, fifteen; Philadelphia, fourteen. A large proportion of the strong men of the Church in that day are found in this list of delegates, and questions of great moment were to be discussed and decided by them. Bishops M'Kendree, George, and Roberts were present.

At the General Conference of 1820, Rev. John Emory had been appointed delegate to the Wesleyan

Conference in England, in order to promote fraternal relations between the two great Wesleyan bodies. At this session, Rev. Richard Reece, with Rev. John Hannah as his travelling companion, appeared as the representative of that body to the Methodist Episcopal Church in the United States. The first day of the session was spent mainly in the organization of the conference, appointment of committees, &c. On the second day the British delegates were introduced by Bishop M'Kendree, and the reading of the address of the British Conference was followed by a neat address from Rev. Richard Reece. Both these addresses evinced the kindest sympathy with the Church in this country, and a strong and sincere desire to preserve more intimate fraternal relations with it.

After this the address of the bishops was presented. Among the topics brought to the consideration of the conference, in this document, were the state and progress of the work, the necessity of increasing the number of superintendents, the division and changing of the boundaries of some of the annual conferences, memorials on the subject of our Church government, peculiar condition of the work in Canada, the Book Concern and the circulation of our books, the local district conferences, the financial system of the Church, the instruction and education of our children and youth, the importance of supporting the plan of an itinerant ministry, and of preserving the union and integrity of the Church. These subjects were referred to the appropriate committees.

The subject of education engaged the earnest attention of the conference. Multitudes of young people had been gathered into the church and congregations, or were connected with it as the children of its members—for the moral and mental training of which she could not but recognise her obligations. In the short period of fifty-one years her membership had run up from one thousand one hundred and sixty, with ten preachers, to three hundred and twenty-eight thousand five hundred and twenty-three, with one thousand two hundred and seventy-two preachers. Having "everything to do"—all her societies to organize, her churches and parsonages to build, and that too among a comparatively poor people—it is not a matter of surprise that, with such a rapid expansion of her work and her responsibilities, she should be found with inadequate provision to meet them. This conference seemed disposed to recognise the full measure of its obligation both as to the religious care of the children, and also the more general education of all young persons under the influence of the Church.

To meet the former want, it was proposed that every preacher should obtain the names of the children connected with his charge, form them into classes for the purpose of giving them religious instruction, and that, so far as practicable, he should instruct them in person. Had this provision been faithfully carried out in every circuit and station for the past thirty years, how vast the influence it would have had upon the character and destinies of the Church! Within this thirty years, what an intelligent membership should we have raised up! What multitudes of our children and youth, by being early instructed in the Scriptures and in Methodism, would have been prevented from growing up in frivolity, in indifference to religious things, and in sin! How many would have been prevented from growing up without any special ties of attachment, or feelings of veneration for the Church that should have been their "nursing mother," and thus left to wander away into the world, or perchance into other Christian communions! What a host of teachers in our Sunday schools and in our schools of general learning, of intelligent and active official members in the Church, and of ministers and missionaries, might have been raised up to do battle for God—even from among those now completely lost to us, if not to God and heaven! Thanks be to God! our Sunday schools are now doing a good work in these respects; but they can never answer as a substitute for either parental religious education, or that religious instruction which may be imparted so efficiently by one reverenced as is the pastor of a Church by the children of his flock.

To meet the second want, the conference renewed the recommendation of 1820, that every annual conference put forth its utmost exertions for the establishment of a seminary of learning within its bounds; and also that every travelling preacher keep in mind the importance of having suitable teachers employed in the instruction of the youth of our country, and to use his influence to introduce teachers into schools whose learning, piety, and religious tenets were such as would insure the right moral education of the young. The former recommendation may be regarded as the origin of that grand movement which has given birth to so many noble institutions of learning in almost every part of the Church. The second, owing to the constant change of our ministers in accordance with our itinerant system, was encumbered with some difficulties, as a new resident in a place cannot always command that local influence, even though he be a minister, nor can he possess that thorough knowledge of local interests which would be requisite in order to have the recommendation efficiently carried out. Nevertheless, it suggests an obligation of great practical importance, and one of which the minister of Christ should never lose sight.

The operations of the infant Missionary Society also claimed the attention of the General Conference; and among other provisions made, preliminary steps were taken for the establishment of a mission in Liberia and the appointment of missionaries to labour there.

The interests of the Book Concern were also carefully considered: Nathan Bangs and John Emory were appointed agents. The Magazine was continued, and authority given for the issue of a weekly paper, the Christian Advocate and Journal, which was commenced in 1826. Up to the present, this continues to be the most widely-circulated religious journal of the kind in the country, if not in the world.

The question of slavery, everywhere present in the councils of the Church and of the state, found its way into this body; and after no little discussion and feeling, the celebrated "TENTH SECTION" was elaborated and adopted precisely as it now appears in the Methodist Discipline.

Among the most exciting questions before the body at this session was that of "lay delegation" in the General and Annual Conferences. Memorials and petitions from local preachers and from lay-members had come up from different parts of the work requesting the privilege of a voice in the legislative department of the Church. This subject received the earnest attention of the conference. There was a strong desire to give a full hearing to the memorialists, and to weigh carefully the arguments they presented. But the conference became satisfied that so radical a change in the economy of the Church would be a hazardous experiment, and therefore declined to make it.

They deemed the subject, however, of so much importance as to send forth a circular to the petitioners and memorialists, showing the fallacies and misconceptions with reference to rights set forth in the memorials, and also the reasons which induced the body to decline the changes proposed. With reference to the reasons assigned for the proposed change, the conference says: "We rejoice to know that the proposed change is not contemplated as a remedy for evils which now exist in some infraction of the rights and privileges of the people, as defined to them by the form of Discipline; but that it is offered, either in anticipation of the possible existence of such evils, or else on a supposition of abstract rights, which, in the opinion of some, should form the basis of our government." Upon the question of abstract rights and privileges urged by some of the memorialists, drawn from the analogy instituted between the state and the Church, they reply: "If by rights and privileges it is intended to signify something foreign from the institutions of the Church, as we received them from our fathers, pardon us if we know no such rights—if we do not comprehend such privileges. With our brethren everywhere we rejoice that the institutions of our happy country are admirably calculated to secure the best ends of civil government. With their rights as citizens of these United States, the Church disclaims all interference; but that it should be inferred from these what are your rights as Methodists, seems to us no less surprising than if your Methodism should be made the criterion of your rights as citizens."

The main reasons assigned for the inexpediency of the proposed change are, in substance, that it would tend to create a distinction of interests between the itinerancy and the membership of the Church—that it presupposes that the authority of the General Conference, or the manner of exercising it, is displeasing to the Church, whereas the reverse appeared to be the case—that it would involve a tedious procedure, inconvenient in itself, and calculated to agitate the Church to her injury—and finally, that it would give those districts which are conveniently situated, and could therefore secure the attendance of their delegates, an undue influence in the government of the Church. Many of the memorialists on further reflection, and upon carefully weighing the reasons assigned by the General Conference for not granting their request, became satisfied that the change was of less importance to themselves than they had at first supposed, and that the objections to so radical a change in our economy had not been by them fully comprehended, and they were therefore contented to remain in the Church and to sustain its organization as it was. Others subsequently withdrew from the connexion and organized the Methodist Protestant Church.

But the most exciting of all questions, and that upon which the conflicting parties in the conference were more nearly balanced, was "the presiding-elder question." The measures adopted by the General Conference of 1820, as we have already seen, were suspended for four years. Those opposed to them were not sufficiently confident of their strength at this conference to attempt their repeal, and therefore moved a continuance of the suspension for four years longer. Then came the "tug of war." Every member was on the alert. Warm and earnest was the discussion. When the vote was about to be taken, it was recollected that one of the delegates, by the appointment of the conference, was then preaching in a church three-quarters of a mile distant. A messenger was despatched post-haste, and finding him in the midst of his sermon, he came behind him in the pulpit, twitched his coat to arrest his attention, and then hastily communicated the call for his presence in the General Conference. Leaving the messenger to make his apology to the congregation, and also to close the services, the preacher hastened to his post in the conference. Here he arrived, panting for breath and bathed with perspiration, just after the decision in favour of postponement had been announced. As this decision accorded with his views, he was content to let the matter rest.

This question entered largely into the canvass for the election of bishops. The conference having determined upon the election of two, each party brought forward their strong candidates. On the one side Joshua Soule and William Beauchamp, and on the other Elijah Hedding and John Emory, were brought forward for the suffrages of their brethren. On the first ballot there were one hundred and twenty-eight votes cast, requiring sixty-five for an election. Joshua Soule had sixty-four, Elijah Hedding sixty-one, William Beauchamp sixty-two, John Emory fifty-nine, and ten scattering. On the second ballot Joshua Soule had sixty-five, and was elected; Elijah Hedding sixty-four, William Beauchamp sixty-two, and John Emory fifty-eight, and five scattering. Rev. John Emory then withdrew his name from the canvass; and, on ballotting a third time, Elijah Hedding received sixty-six votes, and was elected. On this ballotting William Beauchamp received sixty votes, and there were two scattering.

In 1820, many of his brethren had desired Mr. Hedding's consent to be placed in nomination for the episcopal office; but this he absolutely refused. Early in the session of this conference the minds of a large portion of his brethren seemed to centre upon him again. It was, however, with extreme reluctance that he allowed his name to be used. This reluctance was sincere and unaffected. The Rev. Enoch Mudge says: "I believe I was the first who named to him at the General Conference that a number of his brethren had determined to bring him forward as a candidate for the episcopal office. Although it is a true saying that *if a man desireth the office of a bishop he desireth a good work*, it is certainly not what he desired or sought. I well remember how it affected him. He wept, remonstrated, and urged a number of objections against the movement. I urged such considerations as appeared to me to be valid, and in view of which I thought he ought not to object. He yielded in the end, but only because he was constrained to do so by the united and urgent solicitations of his northern brethren." After the chair had announced his election, Mr. Hedding says: "Many of my dear brethren rejoiced, and presented me their kindest congratulations; but my heart sunk within me, and a gloomy impression that I had consented to undertake what I could never accomplish overwhelmed me." His main objections seemed to be, first, a deep conviction that he was not possessed of either the piety or the administrative qualifications requisite for the office; and, secondly, the infirm and uncertain state of his health.

At a suitable time, Mr. Hedding expressed his feelings and convictions upon the subject to the conference. So great was the sense of unworthiness and unfitness that had come upon him, that he doubted whether he could consent to be ordained; and requested time to consider the subject, and to pray for divine direction. After making this statement with tears, he retired from the Church. Immediately after his departure the following resolution was presented and unanimously passed by the conference:—

"*Resolved*, That we do entertain unlimited confidence in the integrity, ability, and ministerial worth of our beloved brother, Elijah Hedding; and he having signified to the General Conference some hesitancy of receiving episcopal ordination, arising, as we believe, out of his own humble views of his qualifications, as well as on account of impaired health, we affectionately request him to submit himself to the call of Providence and of the Church, and receive ordination to the office of a bishop.

(Signed,) "W. CAPERS,
W. WINANS."

This resolution being introduced by brethren who differed from him on the great question that had agitated the body, and being so cordially sustained by those who coincided with them on that question, removed any objection that existed in his own mind on that score, and made it still more conclusive that his call to the episcopal office was a providential call. He then returned to the body, and stated that he must receive the voice of the Church as the voice of God in the matter, and therefore would submit himself to their direction.

Subsequently a similar resolution was passed in relation to Bishop Soule, both parties generally concurring. Rev. Joshua Soule and Rev. Elijah Hedding were, on the 28th of the month, duly set apart and consecrated to the episcopal office.

Bishop Hedding brought to the episcopal office a sound and deep piety, whose ardour had not been abated through a period of nearly twenty-six years—most of which had been spent in laborious service, and in the midst of many trials and privations in the cause of Christ. His mind, naturally clear and discriminating, had been well matured by reading and study, by intercourse with men, and by a large and well-improved experience. He was possessed of great simplicity and sincerity of manner—a peculiar and confiding openness in his intercourse with his brethren, that at once won their confidence and affection. At the same time, his natural dignity and great discretion made him an object of reverence as well as of affection. Also his great shrewdness, and his almost instinctive insight into the character of men, guarded him from becoming the dupe of the crafty and designing. His heart was as true as it was large in its sympathies. His brethren never in vain sought his counsel or his sympathy. It was evident to all that he had one object in view—the salvation of men and the glory of God. In the exercise of the episcopal functions he developed those rare qualifications that had distinguished him as a presiding officer, and especially as an expounder of ecclesiastical law. The soundness of his views upon the doctrines and discipline of the Church has been so fully and so universally conceded, that in the end he became almost an oracle in the Church in these respects; and his opinions are regarded with profound veneration.

CHAPTER XI.

FIRST QUADRENNIAL OF EPISCOPAL LABOUR.

Division of Episcopal Labour — Bishops George and Hedding attend the New-York Conference — Bishop Hedding makes Lynn his Residence — New-England Conference — Joshua Randle — Bishop George's Opinion of his Colleague — Genesee Conference — Cazenovia Seminary — Proposed Tour in Canada — Excitement there — Rate of Travel — Incident in Toronto — Hardships — A Log-cabin Tavern — Difficulties compromised — Henry Ryan — Close of Conference — Progress of the Church during the Year — Sickness — A Hard Ride — Reaches Home in March — Difficulties of Travel — Starts for Philadelphia — Desponding Letter — Philadelphia, New-York, New-England, and Maine Conferences — State of the Work in Maine — Journey to Northern New-York — Letter to his Wife — Genesee Conference — Canada Conference — Progress of the Work — Summation for the Year — Returns Home — A Wayside Incident — Winter of 1825–6 — Meeting of the Bishops in Baltimore — Failure to appoint a Delegate to the British Conference — Philadelphia and New-York Conferences — Genesee Conference — Letter to his Wife — Pittsburgh Conference — The "Radical Movement" — Mr. Hedding's Address to the Conference — Plain Talk in the Cabinet — Changes two Presiding Elders — Letter to Mrs. Hedding — The Ohio Conference — Return to Lynn — Results of another Year — Starts again — A Letter — Philadelphia and New-York Conferences — Difficulties in Stationing Preachers — An Illustrative Instance — The True Course for a Young Preacher — New-England Conference — Fever and Ague — Journey to Portland — Maine Conference — Journey Westward — The Canada Conference — Prevailing Drought — Sickness of Preachers — Visits the Indian Mission Stations in Canada — Interesting Anecdotes of Converted Indians — Reading the Testament without learning the Letters — Indians at Rice Lake — Visit to Grape Island — Bark Canoe — Novel Mode of Landing — Captain Beaver — Preaches to the Indians — Sermon of Peter Jones — Church Labour with an Erring Brother — Curious Questions — Estimate of the Work among the Indians — Journey to Troy — Dedicates State-street Church — Reaches Home — End of the Year — Maine Wesleyan Seminary — Bishop Hedding's Interest in our Educational Movements.

There were now five bishops in the Church, and fifteen annual conferences. Bishop M'Kendree, however, was too feeble, by reason of his age and his bodily infirmities, to perform the regular work of a superintendent; and the General Conference had requested him to perform only so much as he found consistent with his health and strength. At his suggestion the following division of labour was agreed upon for the year: Bishops Roberts and Soule were to take the supervision of the Baltimore and Kentucky Conferences, and all the conferences south and southwest of them; while Bishops George and Hedding were to take the Philadelphia and Pittsburgh Conferences, and all the conferences north and northeast of them.

Accordingly, after the close of the session of the General Conference, Bishop Hedding, in company with Bishop George, proceeded to New-York city to attend the New-York Conference, which was to be held in the Wesleyan Seminary. They agreed that, as far as possible, they would attend the conferences assigned to them in company, and mutually share the labours and responsibilities of each conference.

At the close of conference they left for Barnard, Vermont, where the New-England Conference was to meet on the 22d of June. Leaving his colleague to go by a more direct route, Bishop Hedding made a detour to Boston, where he had been stationed the preceding two years, in order to settle up his affairs preparatory to the conference. Having determined to make Lynn his residence,—so far as it was possible in those days for a Methodist bishop to have any local residence,—he packed up his goods in the short time he had, and sent them on to be stored in that place, till a respite from his official duties should allow him an opportunity to prepare for housekeeping. Then, accompanied by his wife, he started to meet Bishop George at the seat of the conference.

The session of the conference proved a time of unusual religious interest. The Sabbath was a high and glorious day. The people poured in from all the surrounding region. Bishops George and Hedding both preached with great power to the assembled multitude, in a grove near by the church. Twenty-seven travelling, and several local preachers, were ordained deacons. Among the former were A. D. Merrill and A. D. Sargeant, long and favourably known as eminent ministers of the cross of Christ; also Melville B. Cox, who, not many years after, offered himself a noble sacrifice on the altar of Africa's redemption; and also Orange Scott, whose noble powers were subsequently betrayed into a warfare against the Church in whose lap they had been warmed into life. Eight travelling and several local ministers were also ordained elders. Among these were Jotham Horton, Phineas Crandall, and Charles Baker—the first of whom ceased from his labours in 1853, at which time the other two were still in the effective ranks, one on the Worcester and the other on the Springfield District, in the old New-England Conference.

Mr. Hedding was greeted by his brethren in the conference with every manifestation of affection and confidence. The following resolution was proposed and unanimously passed, expressive of their great satisfaction at his election to the episcopal office:—

"*Resolved*, That this conference hereby express their cordial and entire approbation of the election and ordination of brother Elijah Hedding, one of the members of this conference, to the episcopal office. We also request Bishop Hedding to locate his family within the bounds of this conference, and spend as much of his time among us as he can spare, without interfering with the duties of his office."

At this conference Joshua Randle was tried for heresy, and suspended, for the time being, from the exercise of his ministerial functions. The singular theological dogma he had assumed was, in substance, that *while Christ died to atone for original sin, he made no atonement for actual transgressions; but for these the transgressor might be pardoned without an atonement.* Two years before, at the session of the conference held in Bath, Maine, he had been convicted of holding and teaching this dangerous heresy, and required by the conference to cease advocating such doctrines, whether publicly or privately, so long as he remained a minister among us. During the year preceding this conference the old man could not keep quiet, but agitated his peculiar notions among the people and preachers. The conference found it necessary to take away his parchments, and from this decision he appealed to the next General Conference; but, in 1826, we find him returned "expelled" on the Minutes of the New-England Conference. This subject attracted more than usual attention a few years after, from its appearance in another relation before the General Conference. Mr. Randle defended himself before the General Conference; and the action of the New-England Conference was vindicated by Dr. Wilbur Fisk in an overwhelming argument. The General Conference confirmed the decision of the New-England Conference by a vote of one hundred and sixty-four to one.

Bishop Hedding had now exercised his new duties at two conferences, in company with Bishop George, who, in a letter to Bishop Roberts, under date of June 6th, says of him, "My colleague does excellently in his new office."

After the close of the New-England Conference the two bishops journeyed across the Green Mountains, visiting the Churches at Lansingburgh, Troy, Utica, and many other places on their way to Lansing, on the east side of Cayuga Lake, where they met the Genesee Conference on the 25th of July.

The Genesee Conference at this time embraced all, or nearly all, that territory now included in the Genesee, East Genesee, Oneida, Black River, and Wyoming Conferences. That great and promising field was cultivated by a noble band of men; among whom were George Lane, George Gary, Elias Bowen, George Peck, Abner Chase, J. B. Alverson, Z. Paddock, John Dempster, I. Chamberlayne, Seth Mattison, G. Fillmore, and others known throughout the Church. At that time there was in this whole region a membership of twenty-four thousand one hundred and sixty-one, and one hundred and thirty-five travelling preachers; at the close of 1853, on the same territory, there were five annual conferences, embracing eighty-one thousand six hundred and thirty-two members, and six hundred and ninety-one preachers. Bishop Hedding was now among brethren with whom he was comparatively unacquainted. His first endeavour was to become personally acquainted with as many of them as possible. His remarkably tenacious memory was here put into very successful requisition; for he says, "In a few days I found that I could recognise and call by name nearly every brother upon the floor."

This year the plan proposed by the General Conference for the promotion of education in the Church, was carried into effect within the bounds of this conference by the establishment of the Cazenovia Seminary. It was incorporated by the state legislature, and commenced its career under the most favourable auspices. This was the opening of a new era for Methodism; and the visions of good to the Church, seen only by the faith and hope of the noble few who were fully alive to the importance of our educational interests, have been fully realized in the result. It has given a host of strong men to the Church, and exerted an influence on Methodism in all that region. Now, after a lapse of thirty years, though its territory has been abridged by the formation of new conferences and the establishment of similar institutions, yet its success has been unabated. It reflects honour upon those who founded and have sustained it, and hundreds if not thousands cherish its memory with the warmest affection.

This conference having closed its session, the two bishops started for the Canada Conference, which was to meet at Hallowell, Upper Canada, on the 24th of August. For the sake of encompassing as much of the work and visiting as many of the societies as possible, they separated, Bishop George going around the lower end of Lake Ontario and Bishop Hedding going around the upper end of it; each visiting the Churches in their route, and preaching as often as circumstances would allow.

The preachers and people in Upper Canada up to the last General Conference had constituted a part of the Genesee Conference. This relation had proved unsatisfactory to both preachers and people. They laboured under many disabilities on account of their ecclesiastical connexion with the United States. The people regarded their movements with suspicion, and the civil powers were desirous of discouraging such connexions. Under these circumstances, they petitioned the General Conference to set them off as an independent Church, with the privilege of electing their own bishops and regulating their own affairs. This the General Conference could not do, but erected them into a distinct conference, bounded by the boundary lines of Upper Canada, and to be under the general superintendence of the Methodist Episcopal Church. The General Conference also addressed a circular to the preachers and members in Upper Canada, expressive of its interest in their prosperity, and urging the importance of maintaining union among themselves. With this decision, many of the people and preachers were dissatisfied. Prominent among the dissentients were the local preachers. They sent circulars into every part of the province, and before the time for the session of the Canada Conference arrived, they held a general convention, organized an independent Church, and sent forth a declaration of their rights, grievances, and newly-proposed mode of operations among the people. This had created a great excitement among the Methodists all over the province, distracting and dividing societies, and sometimes even members of the same family. The intelligence of this unhappy state of affairs in Canada reached Bishops George and Hedding while at the Genesee Conference.

The route of travel they had proposed enabled Bishop George to enter Canada near the lower end of the province, and thus he could range through the societies in that section and do what he could to correct misrepresentations, and to allay the excitement among both preachers and people. Bishop Hedding was to do the same in the upper section of the conference; and both agreed that it would be best to invite all the local preachers they could to meet the conference, in hope of effecting a general reconciliation of parties. Bishop Hedding was accompanied by Rev. Nathan Bangs, then principal book-agent in New-York. Dr. Bangs, when first received into the travelling ministry in 1802, had been sent as a missionary into Upper Canada, and had laboured there five or six years with great efficiency and success. Many of the societies had been formed by him, and many of the prominent Methodists, both members and ministers, had been converted to God through his instrumentality. He therefore knew the people, and they knew him; and to Bishop Hedding he proved a most timely and efficient assistant in his delicate and arduous work.

On both routes the bishops found they had an unpleasant and, in some instances, a painful work on their hands. The people had been thoroughly prejudiced against them. Some, however, treated them kindly; but others treated them with contempt and even insult. At Toronto, such was the state of affairs that Bishop Hedding deemed it advisable to call a meeting of the society. He found them, however, perfectly impracticable: his explanations of the measures proposed for the good of the work in Canada, and his earnest warnings against the divisions and contentions that were creeping in among them, distracting their peace, enfeebling their moral power, and tending to the ruin of the souls of men, were attentively listened to by many, and some seemed to be deeply affected; but the leaders in the seditious movement were unmoved, and one of the most prominent among them took the lead in opposition. He plainly told Bishop Hedding, "We don't want you here; we don't want *any* Yankee bishops; we can take care of ourselves." Such was the spirit which they encountered in many portions of the work. It must have been exceedingly painful to Dr. Bangs, who had toiled and suffered so much to carry the glad news of salvation among them, when they were dwelling in log-huts and were in poverty and want.

This journey was not only attended with trials of mind, but also bodily hardships. The bishops often found it difficult, in their journey through the new settlements, to procure suitable food for themselves and their horses; and still more difficult to obtain comfortable lodgings. One day they had been unable to procure anything to eat. Jaded and hungry, they at length came in sight of a log-cabin with a tavern-sign hanging out. Their courage revived, and they drove up to the door and asked if they could have entertainment. The landlord looked at them quizzically, as if he would say, "What *kind* of entertainment do you want?" They inquired, "Can we have hay for our horses?" The laconic reply was, "No, have none." "Oats?" say they. "No, have none," was the reply. "Pasture?" "No, have none." "Well, can you furnish *us* anything to eat?" "No," replied the landlord; "have nothing to eat in the house." "What have you then?" they inquired. "O, plenty of whisky." Satisfied with their colloquy, the hungry and weary travellers resumed their journey, and at length found a hut where they could obtain hay for their horses and food and rest for themselves.

Bishop Hedding and his colleague met at Hallowell, Upper Canada. At their instance, a large number of local preachers, and, indeed, many of the prominent lay members, were present at the seat of the conference—particularly those who had been foremost in the disorderly and radical movement. The various questions of rights, privileges, disabilities, &c., were discussed with frankness and candour, for the most part, in the conference. After a long series of negotiation between the parties, those who had commenced their revolutionizing movement agreed to retract what they had done; and all agreed to preserve the peace and integrity of the Church till the next General Conference. Bishops George and Hedding, and Dr. Bangs, on their part, agreed to use their influence with the next General Conference to have the Methodists in Upper Canada set off into an independent Methodist Episcopal Church, if it could be effected consistently with the principles of the gospel, and the government of the Methodist Episcopal Church. Thus they succeeded with great effort in calming the agitation, and in healing the divisions; and the Church in that section had comparative peace for the ensuing four years.

The leader in this movement was none other than the bluff old Irishman who had been Mr. Hedding's colleague on the Fletcher Circuit, in Vermont, twenty-two years before. Crooked and quaint notions had possessed him, and he had unfortunately become soured toward the Church. Of course he could not be satisfied with any peaceable adjustment of the difficulty. The next year he took a superannuated relation, and two years later withdrew from the Church. Afterward he attempted to organize a distinct Church. By way of derision, his followers were called "Ryanites;" and after a sickly existence of a few years the societies he organized became extinct. Poor, mistaken man! How lamentable to see a man, after such long and generally useful service, and in his old age, becoming the victim of Satan's devices, and thus marring his own peace of mind, and bringing injury to the cause of God! An old Methodist preacher, imbittered in his feelings, and soured toward the Church, is a sad spectacle. We thank God it is a spectacle so rarely witnessed.

This great question disposed of, the ordinary business of the conference proceeded with harmony and despatch. The best feelings existed: six preachers were admitted on trial; three were ordained deacons, and five elders. The total membership of the conference was six thousand one hundred and fifty, and the number of travelling preachers thirty-six.

This is the last conference included in the Minutes for the present year. The results of the year gave an increase of fifteen thousand nine hundred and eighty-three members in the whole Church, making a grand total of three hundred and twenty-eight thousand five hundred and twenty-three. The whole number of travelling preachers was twelve hundred and seventy-two, showing an increase of only forty-six.

Bishop Hedding was very much exhausted by the labours and anxieties to which he had been subject in Canada, and at the close of the conference was taken down with the bilious remittent fever. This, thought he, was a hard induction into the episcopal office,—anxiety that had almost deprived him of sleep for more than a month; travel, exposure, and privation, that had completely exhausted his physical energies; and now, to complete the series of trials, he was taken down with a severe and dangerous disease, not only far from home, but in a place where few comforts could be afforded to a sick man, and where medical assistance was uncertain and unreliable. Finding that it would be inconvenient for the family where he had been entertained for him to remain with them, he determined, sick as he was, upon a removal. One of the preachers took charge of him, got him on board of a steamboat, and accompanied him to Kingston. Here he found a *home* with a family by the name of Armstrong, where he was confined over six weeks. "This," says he, "was an excellent Christian family; their hospitality and kindness I shall have cause to remember as long as I live."

After he had been with this kind family for so many weeks, a brother of his, living on the west side of Lake Champlain, hearing of his sickness, came to see him, and if possible to take him back with him to his home. The bishop says: "I had but partly recovered, but was able to sit up all the day. I sent for my physician and consulted him whether it would be safe for me to start on the journey, situated as I then was. He said, 'By no means; it would be at the risk of my life.' But I asked him for my bill, and paid it, and said, 'I must go, and trust Providence for the consequences.' My brother took me on board of a steamboat next morning, down the River St. Lawrence seventy miles, to Ogdensburgh. We were twenty-four hours making the passage. From Ogdensburgh he carried me in his wagon, one hundred and twenty miles, across the country to his home. It was a hard journey, through mud and mire frequently covering the hubs of the wagon, over a wilderness and rough country; and we had to proceed through rain and storm. A sad way of operating for a sick man. But, through a good Providence, instead of dying, as the doctor thought I would, I continued to improve through the journey, and was much better at the end of it than when I left Kingston."

Here he met his wife, from whom he had been absent about four months. After remaining with his brother a few weeks he crossed Lake Champlain into Vermont, and visited a sister residing in that state. Here an accident occurred to Mrs. Hedding, from being thrown out of a sleigh, which confined her to the house for two months. They did not reach Lynn before the ensuing March. But Mr. Hedding was not idle in the mean time; for wherever he was delayed he visited the societies for several miles around, and preached to them. This was the more interesting to him as it was chiefly in the country where he had first commenced his labours in the ministry, a quarter of a century before. A number of the older members of the Church remembered him when on his first circuit; but the Church since that time had greatly increased in numbers and influence, and the mass of them had been gathered into it since he had left those regions for other fields of labour.

We can hardly appreciate the labour and fatigue of travelling in those days, when, even on the great inland thoroughfares, it was to be performed only by the slow and tiresome progress of the stage-line, or by private conveyances. Now, we can whirl away hundreds of miles in twenty-four hours, and, such are the facilities for travel and the accommodations for rest, scarcely feel wearied by the transit. But, during this spring, Bishop Hedding speaks of one journey of only fifty miles, which, upon bad roads and in stormy weather, occupied no less than three days. A journey from Lynn to Philadelphia, which was the seat of Bishop Hedding's next conference, ordinarily occupied nearly a week.

He was at home but a few days when he started for Philadelphia, visiting the societies, as far as he was able, along the route. The session of the conference was to commence on the 14th of April. He reached the city on the 13th, but the night before had been taken with a violent attack of fever and ague, so that he was confined to his room, and for the most part to his bed, till after the session of the conference closed. This was a great mortification as well as trial to him. On the 19th he found a little respite from the severity of his distress, and indited a letter to his wife. After giving an account of his sickness, and his inability to meet the conference, or even to see many of his brethren, he acknowledges the kindness of the family whose hospitality and care he enjoyed, and then despondingly adds: "I see but little prospect of my being able to perform the journeys my station requires, my health is so broken. I have been sick a week, so as to be unable to write till to-day. I was attacked about twenty miles from this place, on my way here, much as I was last year in Canada. I feel very forcibly the need of being prepared for death, for I am conscious these repeated strokes, if continued, must soon bring me to the grave. Though I am hardly able to hold my pen, my soul is full of heavenly peace."

A week or two after the close of the Philadelphia Conference, his health was so far recovered that he started for Troy, where he rejoined Bishop George, and the two presided alternately at the session of the New-York Conference, which commenced on the 3d of May. From thence they proceeded by different routes—so as to visit the societies as extensively as possible—to East Cambridge, where the New-England Conference commenced its session on the 8th of June.

This conference had been divided by the preceding General Conference; and the three districts included in the State of Maine, with nearly seven thousand members and forty-six preachers, had been organized into the Maine Conference. This latter conference held its session at Gardiner, Maine, commencing on the 7th of July. On their way to the Maine Conference they preached in Portland, and also attended a camp-meeting at Gorham. Of the work in Maine at this time he says: "It was the most laborious field of labour in New-England. We had only about forty preachers to supply the entire state, embracing generally a new and sparsely-settled territory, and having larger circuits, on an average, than any other part of the eastern work." But here, as in other portions of the work, a noble band of heroes were in the field, who counted not their lives dear unto themselves so that they might fulfil the ministry which had been given to them to testify of the grace of God. Among them, as veterans, stood Philip Munger, and Eleazer Wells, and Joshua Hall, and David Kilburn; while among the junior preachers were Heman Nickerson, Ezekiel Robinson, and others, who have long stood as pillars in the work. Since then, the work has continued to spread and increase in the state, till the one conference has become two, the forty-six preachers have become one hundred and ninety-two, and the six thousand nine hundred and fifty-seven members, twenty-one thousand four hundred and seventy-three, or more than there were in all New-England at the time of the division.

Returning from Maine, the two bishops travelled in company as far as Madison, New-York, where they parted—Bishop George bound for the Pittsburgh Conference, and Bishop Hedding for the Genesee. From Albany Bishop Hedding wrote to his wife under date of August 2, 1825:—

"Through the goodness of Providence I have been preserved in tolerable health, amid fatigue, and heat, and dust. My situation in life is an occasion of many trials of mind as well as labours of body; but our good God supporteth me with great peace, and glorious hopes of a life of rest and peace in heaven. Let us keep this great object in view, and prepare to live where parting and sorrow will be no more."

After parting from Bishop George, Bishop Hedding continued his journey to Lansing, where the Genesee Conference assembled August 17. This was a village in the same town where the conference met the year previous. A camp-meeting was held near by during the session of the conference. It was one of the largest ever held in the county. The ordination services were performed at the camp-meeting. Some most powerful sermons were preached, and many were converted. It had been a year of unwonted success. In the Ontario district, of which George Lane had been presiding elder, the net increase had been about one thousand, and in the whole conference two thousand seven hundred and seventy-nine.

After the close of the Genesee Conference, Bishop Hedding crossed Cayuga Lake, visited the societies in Geneva, Canandaigua, Buffalo, and several other places. From Buffalo he crossed into Canada, and met the Canada Conference on the 14th of September at Fifty Mile Creek, in Saltfleet township. The condition of the work in Canada he found much better than he expected. An increase of seven hundred and twenty-five was realized: the preachers and people were living and labouring in harmony, generally contented to abide by the stipulations they had entered into the preceding year.

The general recapitulation this year exhibited an increase of nineteen thousand six hundred and seventy-two, making the total membership three hundred and forty-eight thousand one hundred and ninety-five. The number of itinerants was one thousand three hundred and fourteen, being an increase of forty-two.

After the close of the Canada Conference, Bishop Hedding, wearied and worn with his journeyings and labours, took the most direct route to Albany, and thence crossed over the country to Lynn, where he hoped to enjoy a little rest. In all his cares and anxieties he found the Lord ever present to sustain and comfort him, and of his mercy he made grateful acknowledgment. He had been remarkably sustained by the grace of God, and rejoiced exceedingly in witnessing the growth and spread of Methodism throughout the land.

Few men could enjoy with a higher relish the little

amusing incidents of travel than Bishop Hedding. Speaking of his journey home, he says: "At Pittsfield, Mass., I called upon a located preacher, and told him I was a Methodist preacher. He asked me if I was a travelling preacher. I said, 'Yes.' He said, 'What conference?' I said, 'Not any conference in particular.' He said, 'What circuit or station?' I said, 'Not any in particular.' He asked, 'Are you a presiding elder?' I said, 'No.' Again, he said, 'Are you a missionary?' I said, 'Well, I travel about as missionaries do; but I am not called a missionary.' 'Well, how is this?' said the man, with a puzzled and confused expression of countenance; 'how can you be a travelling preacher, and not belong to any conference, nor to any circuit or station, and are not a presiding elder or a missionary?' I saw that I was about being suspected as an impostor, and said to him, 'I am one of those they call bishops.' Light flashed upon the mind of my proposed host, and the whole matter was explained. I scarcely need add, that I received a hearty welcome and good entertainment."

The winter of 1825–6 was spent mainly in visiting the Churches in the eastern part of Massachusetts, and attending to such other duties as were incident to his office. Early in the spring, however, he left home and travelled by way of New-York and New-Jersey to meet the other bishops at Baltimore. The object of their meeting was to carry out the resolution passed by the General Conference, that, in 1826, the bishops should appoint some person to go as a delegate to the British Conference. The action of this meeting of the bishops was such as to throw some light on what were then the views of Bishop Hedding on the question of slavery and its relations to the Church. Bishops M'Kendree, George, Soule, and Hedding were present. Bishop Roberts was unable to attend. When they came to nominate a delegate, Bishops M'Kendree and Soule nominated William Capers, of South Carolina, and Bishops George and Hedding nominated Wilbur Fisk for that office. The appointment of Mr. Capers was objected to on account of his connexion with slavery. It was urged that the views of Mr. Wesley, and of the Wesleyan Conference after him, on the subject of slavery, being well known, it would not be respectful to them to appoint a slaveholder as a delegate; and further, that such a man would be in danger of not being favourably received, and, at all events, would be greatly embarrassed in his mission on account of his connexion with slavery. "The two bishops," says Mr. Hedding, "who had nominated Rev. W. Capers, refused to yield their nomination, or to concur in ours, alleging that slaveholding should not be a bar to any office in the appointment of the Church. In this state of things, neither side being willing to yield, and being equally divided in our choice, we agreed to adjourn till the following year, when the absent bishop could meet with us. The next year we all met, and it was found that those of us who had been together the year before remained of the same mind. The other bishop was unwilling to take the responsibility of the casting vote, and after two days' delay, decided that we had not authority to make the appointment in 1827, since the General Conference voted it should be done in 1826; and we adjourned without sending a delegate." From the above facts, the intelligent reader will infer that the aggressive movements of slavery, which finally led to the disruption of the Church, were not wholly without episcopal sanction at a very early date.

After this meeting, in company with Bishop George, Bishop Hedding attended the Philadelphia and New-York Conferences. At the close of the New-York Conference they parted, Bishop George leaving for the eastern conferences, and Bishop Hedding for the western.

The Genesee Conference met June 15th at Palmyra, and Bishop Hedding was present and presided. From this place, under date of June 15th, he wrote to Mrs. Hedding as follows: "My manner of life is exceedingly trying. My only support is in the consolations of religion, and the hope that I may be the means of some little good to mankind. Whatever may befall us in this state of pilgrimage, let us try to make a sure preparation for a better life. This, by the grace of God, I am determined to do." After the conference, he spent some weeks with one of the presiding elders in attending camp-meetings in that region, and then went to Washington, Penn., where he met the Pittsburgh Conference on the 22d of August. This was his first visit to the Pittsburgh Conference, which was one of the new conferences organized in 1824. It comprised eighty-two travelling preachers, and twenty thousand four hundred and thirty-two members, being an increase of two thousand four hundred and seventy for the year. Some of the choice spirits in the itinerant ranks were to be found in this body: such were Thornton Fleming, Charles Cooke, Alfred Brunson, Charles Elliott, William Stevens, Ira Eddy, Hiram Kinsley, and others of whom we have less knowledge. Here, also, was Asa Shinn, a talented, zealous, laborious, but radical man, and a great disturber of the peace and quiet of the Church. Here, too, was the great orator of the West, H. B. Bascom, who had but recently returned from the East, where he had filled the minds of the people with astonishment at the transcendent displays of his eloquence. He was now in the full flood-tide of popularity; and having fully embarked in the radical movement with Mr. Shinn, the two, in connexion with Rev. George Brown, and some few others, had produced no little excitement within the bounds of the Pittsburgh Conference. Mr. Shinn had been presiding elder of the Pittsburgh District, Mr. Brown presiding elder of the Monongahela District, Mr. Bascom "conference missionary." The three had, therefore, been favourably situated for the propagation of their radical views in relation to the economy of the Church; and when the conference assembled, it was openly claimed that the radicals were in the ascendency. The radicals, too, had adroitly drawn in Bishop Hedding, by representing that he was in favour of their views, not only on the question of electing presiding elders, but also on the question of lay delegation in the Annual and General Conferences, and the other radical measures they proposed. The wisest and best men in the conference were perplexed and alarmed. The state of affairs was laid open to the bishop at an early date in the conference by one of the presiding elders yet living, and also the representations that had been made concerning his views. The bishop was sorely afflicted at the state of affairs, and was indignant at the unwarrantable statements that had been made concerning himself. His firmness, decision, and ability, however, were equal to the task before him. It was not long before occasion was given to call him out on the subject. Then, in a most masterly speech to the conference, he exposed the unfounded assumptions of the radicals, the evils that would inevitably result to the Church should they succeed, and especially the wickedness and baseness of the report that had been fabricated and circulated, that he in any measure countenanced the course of those men whose action would rend and destroy the Church. It was a masterly vindication of the Church, and also of himself. It carried consternation into the hearts of the radical leaders. They ventured no reply, but in silence saw the downfal of their hopes.

But the bishop did not stop here. He carried the matter into the cabinet, and told the presiding elders plainly that he could appoint no man to that office who was not sound in his views of Church polity, and true in his allegiance to the Church. "This," said he, "is not a personal matter with me; I have no personal interests to look after in the matter, no friends to favour, and no enemies to punish; but to this course I am shut up by my most solemn official duty to the Church." He therefore gave them to understand, that the two elders who were known to be leaders in the radical movement could not expect to be returned to their districts. Accordingly we find Thornton Fleming and William Stevens returned to the two districts that had been occupied by Shinn and Brown. Mr. Bascom was this year stationed in Uniontown, Pa. An attempt was made to establish the Madison College in this place during the succeeding winter, and Mr. Bascom was subsequently elected president of it, but retained his post only about two years. He then accepted an agency for the American Colonization Society, and was soon after transferred to the Kentucky Conference, which conference he represented in the General Conference of 1832. In 1830, Asa Shinn and George Brown are both returned as having withdrawn from the connexion. The decided and judicious course pursued by Bishop Hedding completely discomfitted the leaders in the radical movement and thwarted their designs. It was an opportune effort. Many who were on the very edge of the precipice were enabled to see through the designs of the movement and to comprehend the result, and they started back with alarm. After the bishop had taken his position and expressed his views, there was no disposition to bring the matter to a test before the conference, much as the radical party had boasted previously of a certain and large ascendency. Such a discomfiture, however, could not but produce intense feeling among them. This feeling they vented in the most malignant attacks over anonymous signatures in the "Mutual Rights," published in Baltimore.

Under the date of September 1st, Bishop Hedding wrote to Mrs. Hedding as follows: "The Pittsburgh Conference closed its session on the 29th ult. After I wrote to you last I came to the town of Erie, Pa., near the shore of Lake Erie; thence on my way to Pittsburgh sixty miles; then turned west to a camp-meeting, near the line between Pennsylvania and Ohio. There we had a great time; about one hundred tents and about eight thousand people were on the ground. Fifty or sixty professed to be converted. Rev. Shadrach Bostwick was there; it was within about twenty-five miles of the place where he lives. He preaches as a local preacher, and practises as a physician to a great extent. He looks old as well as I, and has lately buried his wife.

"From that camp-meeting I bore west some distance into the State of Ohio, then south, then east into Pennsylvania, and struck the Ohio River at the mouth of the Big Beaver, then up the Ohio thirty miles to Pittsburgh, thence southwest twenty-six miles to Washington, thence northwest thirty miles to this place. Here I am on the west bank of the Ohio River, about three hundred and fifty miles nearly west of Philadelphia, and have upwards of two hundred miles yet to go southwest to get to the Ohio Conference. The country I have travelled for fifty miles before I arrived at Pittsburgh, and from that to this, and all about here, is as hilly as New-England, but not so rocky; generally good land to the tops of the hills, good water, and healthy. I have got along thus far without a horse; and, if I can find means of conveyance, I shall go from the Ohio Conference to Sandusky, take the steamboat through Lake Erie to Buffalo, and thence through the canal to Albany.

"I am told that part of the country I have to go through to get to the Ohio Conference is sickly; but I believe the same God rules there as at Lynn, or here, and that he will keep me in health as long as he sees best I should have it, and that he will keep me in life as long as he sees my life will be of any use to me or any one else. I feel safe in his hands, in one country as in another; I feel that my great business is to get ready to go; for this I am daily striving and praying, and I know my God is the only proper judge when is the best time and where the best place to call me hence. The time seems long to be from home; but why should a living man complain?"

The Ohio Conference assembled at Hillsborough on the 4th of October. This conference then numbered thirty thousand six hundred and eighty-three members and ninety travelling preachers. Among the ministers received on trial that year were George W. Walker and Adam Poe; and among the ordained deacons was Augustus Eddy. Among those in the conference who were then, or have since become well known to the Church, were Martin Ruter, Russel Bigelow, W. H. Raper, John Sale, James Quinn, James B. Finley, John F. Wright, David and Jacob Young, Leroy Swormstedt, J. P. Durbin, J. H. Power, and others. Twenty-eight years later the same territory comprehended not less than four annual conferences, six hundred and seventy travelling preachers, and one hundred and nine thousand six hundred and six members, exclusive of a portion that had been dismembered from the Church by the Southern organization. In this first visit to the Ohio Conference, Bishop Hedding made a most favourable impression, both as to his ability as a presiding officer and a preacher, and as to his sincerity and integrity of character.

It was not till in the month of December that he reached Lynn, having been absent from home about nine months. He was much worn by the fatigues of travel and the labour and care of his official duties, and greatly needed the short respite now allowed him to recruit his exhausted energies.

The year had been one of general though not

remarkable prosperity in the Church. The number of members reported was three hundred and sixty thousand eight hundred, increase twelve thousand six hundred and one; number of preachers one thousand four hundred and six, increase ninety-two.

Early in March, 1827, Mr. Hedding left his home for Baltimore, to attend a meeting of the bishops, where, among other business, another abortive attempt was made to appoint a delegate to the British Wesleyan Conference.

On his way to Baltimore, under date of March 24, he wrote to his wife from Philadelphia:—"I arrived in this city yesterday in tolerable health. My old afflictions follow me, as I expect they will do till the grave conceals me from them; but I have got along as well as I expected. I met with a cordial reception in New-London, and spent about a week there. I had no idea that the people of New-London would be so glad to see one who was not worth seeing. Many of them expressed a great deal of sorrow that you did not come. At New-York and Brooklyn I had a pleasant visit. The work of the Lord in those places is in a state of prosperity. After coming from New-York, I visited New-Brunswick, Trenton, and Burlington, New-Jersey. I am continually humbled and often pained by the respect and attention the people show me from place to place: humbled, because I know myself to be so unworthy; sometimes pained, because I think it cannot be the man but the office they respect. I always enjoyed the love of the poor, and the fellowship of the saints; but when the great, the rich, the learned, the wise, the aged come round me, and talk and act as though they think I am somebody, I feel like creeping away somewhere out of sight. But, if there were any pleasure in these things, I have enough of the opposite—enough of clamour, enough of hard questions to settle—to try me to the last drop of my patience, and to make me feel as though I am nothing."

After this meeting in Baltimore, Bishops George and Hedding took their course across the Chesapeake Bay, and through the eastern part of Maryland, and proceeded to Smyrna, Del., where the Philadelphia Conference held its session April 12th. When this conference was over, they went in company to Troy, N. Y., and held the New-York Conference May 9th.

In the work generally, it was found that the preachers for the most part made but little disturbance about their appointments, and, when they were made, received them like men of God. A few exceptions, however, were met with in almost every conference. Certain men seemed vastly more solicitous about where they were to go than how they should serve and benefit the people where they might be appointed. With this class of men the bishops often had great difficulty. They annoyed them with private applications and interviews, and not unfrequently they would petition to be sent to an appointment from which the bishop had advice that the people would not receive them at all; and then, when they failed in getting the appointment they desired, they would charge the whole blame upon the bishop, who had to stand between them and the people. Some, in their over-estimate of themselves, pleaded that their gifts had not been duly appreciated, or that they had been shut up in narrow places where they had not room for the exercise of them. Others, having located their families on a farm or in some village, would seek an appointment near by, and demand it even to the detriment of the work. Some, having got into debt, wanted an appointment where large salaries were paid to the preacher, in order that they might be able to pay their debts—forgetting that, as a general thing, the expense of living increases in a higher ratio than the salaries in the more popular places. These are some of the things that have ever embarrassed the superintendents, and clogged the wheels of our itinerancy. We can, perhaps, hardly wonder that they exist. Nay, considering all things, is it not a wonder that for the space of three-quarters of a century the work has been so little embarrassed by them; and that the great body of our preachers, believing in the providential arrangement of our itinerant economy, have gone with the utmost cheerfulness to their appointed fields of labour?

At this session of the New-York Conference one of the preachers, who was wanted for Vermont, came to the bishops and desired to be appointed elsewhere, alleging that it would be inconvenient for his family, and that his wife was then with her parents on a circuit quite down toward New-York. He therefore asked to be appointed near to her. Desiring, as much as possible, to accommodate him, the bishops sent him to a circuit in that region. It appeared subsequently that he wanted to go to the circuit where his wife was. After the conference had adjourned and the bishops had retired to their lodgings, the preacher came stamping and frowning into their room, and said, "I thought you were to give me an appointment to accommodate me near where my wife is." Bishop George replied, "We could not appoint you to the circuit where your wife is, but we appointed you as near as we could." The preacher said, "You have not accommodated me at all; I cannot go to the circuit." Bishop George then said, "Go home, then, and take care of your wife, and stay with her." The preacher replied, "And what will you do with the circuit then?" Bishop George answered, "Never mind the circuit; we'll take care of that; you take care of yourself, and go home and take care of your wife." The preacher turned on his heel, and, grumbling, went away. But, on sober reflection, he concluded to go to his circuit, and notified the bishops to that effect.

Bishop Hedding possessed a naturally tender and sympathizing heart, and it was often the cause of the greatest grief to him, when, after having done all that the demands of the work would allow, to gratify preachers in any special request, they would attribute his action to indifference, or perhaps hostility to them, because he was unable to do just as they desired. On this point the bishop had in his possession sundry letters, the rehearsal of which would make the ears of certain living men tingle, and prove a warning to younger brethren. But it is best they should slumber, and that the kind veil of Christian charity should be thrown over the entire subject. We would say, however, with all the earnestness of spirit we possess, to our junior brethren,—*the best possible way to secure better appointments is to make yourself more than equal to those you now have.* The man that will do this will have no occasion for anxiety about good appointments.

When the New-York Conference had closed, Bishop Hedding proceeded east, journeying through the western part of Vermont, to attend the New-England Conference, which was to meet at Lisbon, N. H., June 6. When he arrived at Middlebury, he awoke in the night with a terrible attack of the fever and ague. This disease followed him for about two months; the fits coming on regularly once in about two days, and lasting about twenty hours, confining him to his bed in great suffering at each attack. He was unable to continue his journey by public conveyance, but procured the aid of friends, who assisted him on his way, between the attacks, until he arrived at the seat of the conference. When this conference commenced its session, he was wholly unable to attend its sittings; and, indeed, had become so weak that, with great difficulty, he performed the ordination services on the Sabbath.

From Lisbon he was conveyed by Rev. D. Kilburn in his private carriage to Portland, the seat of the Maine Conference. The journey was performed with great suffering. They had about three hundred miles to travel, and were obliged to stop, wherever they were, when the attacks came upon him. The intervals between the attacks, however, they improved to the best possible advantage—often rising at midnight to resume their journey. They reached Portland the week before the session of the conference was to commence. Immediately on his arrival, he sent for an eminent physician who had seen much of the fever and ague in the West India Islands. He said he could cure him, and made preparations to do it, commencing by internal remedies, and the application of bottles of hot water to his feet and back, a short time before the attack was expected to come on. By these means he kept it off for almost two hours. "Then," says the bishop, "I suddenly felt as if I had been plunged into cold water; and, as I was told by those present, a violent fit of the disease ensued, which lasted twenty hours. In the shock I lost my reason, and knew nothing the whole time. The physician now took another method, and, by the use of a different remedy, gradually wore off the attacks; and in about a week or ten days they entirely left me."

Only partially recovered as he was, he managed

to preside part of the time in the conference and to attend to his other episcopal duties. From Portland he returned to Lynn; but in a few weeks started for the Canada Conference. His health was quite infirm; he was able to walk only a short distance without resting; but he did not feel at liberty, such were the pressing necessities of the work, to be absent from the session of the Canada Conference, if by any possibility he could reach the place. By stage he went across the country to Troy and Schenectady; thence by canal-boat to Buffalo. Here he crossed into Canada, and thus succeeded in reaching Hamilton, about four miles from Lake Ontario, and near Burlington Heights, where he opened the Canada Conference, August 30.

At this time a great drought was prevailing in the country. So severe was it that all the wells and springs in the neighbourhood failed, and the only water that could be obtained had to be drawn from the neighbouring swamps, where it had been standing among leaves and rotten wood. Many of the preachers became sick from its use, and were unable to attend the sessions of the conference. Bishop Hedding also suffered, but he toiled on through the labours of the session. During the session of the conference, he was greatly afflicted by the necessity which existed of bringing the Rev. Henry Ryan to trial before the body. He had been forward in producing dissension among the people, on account of the action of the last General Conference in respect to the Canada Conference. What made it peculiarly painful to Bishop

Hedding, Mr. Ryan had been one of his first colleagues in the ministry, and was then a zealous, devoted, and true-hearted Methodist preacher. The case finally terminated by the withdrawal of Mr. Ryan from the Church.

According to previous arrangements, it now became Bishop Hedding's duty to journey around the Canada side of Lake Ontario, and visit the Indian Missions scattered through the wildernesses of that country. Scarcely recovered from the fever and ague with which he had been so severely attacked, especially when taken in connexion with the unhealthy condition of the country at that time, it was a hazardous experiment; but the interests of the Church required it, and he did not for a moment hesitate about compliance. His travelling companion was Rev. Wm. Case, at the time superintendent of these missions. It was but a few years since the missions to these aboriginal inhabitants had been begun. The work of grace among them had been carried forward most powerfully, and great multitudes had been converted. Already many of them had learned to be farmers and mechanics, and adopted the habits of civilized life. This journey, though a laborious one, was full of interest; and many incidents occurred illustrative of the simplicity of the habits of the Indians and of the reformation of their lives. We shall be justified in introducing a few of these incidents, narrated by Bishop Hedding:—

"On Monday morning, a converted Indian came

to me and said: 'Yesterday I crossed the River Credit in a canoe, and the salmon were thick all around me; and he no run away, for he know Christian Indian would not catch salmon on Sunday.'

"I saw among these natives an Indian who could read quite well, especially in the New Testament. He said, and others confirmed it, that he did not know his letters. I found, on inquiry, that he had been so anxious to learn to read that he carried a New Testament with him constantly, and asked every boy or girl he met what was the name of any particular word he would point out. Thus he learned the word by its shape; just as a child learns the name of a chair, or a spoon, or a hat, before it learns its letters.

"I visited the Indians that belonged to Rice Lake. I asked one of the chiefs, 'How many belong to your tribe?' and he said, 'Three hundred.' I asked him, 'How many have left off drinking whisky?' and he said, 'All but one.' I inquired, 'How many have experienced religion?' He replied, 'All but one.' I continued, 'How many of them pray?' and he said, 'All but one.' I then said, 'Why does not that one pray?' 'Ha!' said he, 'he no feel Him in here,' putting his hand on his breast. On further inquiry, I learned from the missionary that his story was a true one; that all the Indians, with one exception, in that region, had apparently and professedly been converted to the Lord.

"I visited the Indians on Grape Island, an island in

Bay Quinte, where there was a mission established. I went to this island in company with Rev. Wm. Case, and Rev. Mr. Reynolds and wife, and the two Indians who managed the canoe. Our boat was an Indian bark canoe, and the distance seven or eight miles. Before arriving at the island the wind arose, and the waves rolled quite high, which made it quite unpleasant, if not dangerous. As we approached the island the Indians—men, women, and children—came down and stood by the water to see us land. The bank at the water's edge was eight or ten feet perpendicular, and the waves rolled so high that I feared we should not be able to land without getting wet. The expertness and skill of those with me in the canoe, and those on shore, saved us from this. The Indians had cut rude stairs in the ground, to go up and down to the water. No sooner had the bow of the canoe struck the shore, than the two preachers and the two Indians jumped out; at the same time two rows of Indians came running down the bank, some of them in the water to their arm-pits, and all seizing the canoe by its rim, carried it, with the wife of the preacher and myself in it, high and dry upon the bank; and then, according to their custom, I went through the ceremony of shaking hands with all the tribe—men, women, and children.

"On this island there were about three hundred Indians, and nearly all of them who were old enough professed religion; and they appeared to enjoy its spirit and power. Here I had a large, stout, fine-looking

Indian, who had been an old warrior, for my interpreter. They called him Captain Beaver. He appeared to be solemnly engaged in religion, and deeply affected with its great truths. Before his conversion he had been a great sinner. The people told me that he had killed one wife, and, in a drunken frolic, had thrown a child out of doors into the mud, and stamped it to death. On one occasion I preached to them on the intercession of Christ. The whole congregation were greatly affected, and cried aloud, so that I was obliged to stop for some time before they could hear me. Captain Beaver, my interpreter, became so affected that he bowed himself nearly double, and cried aloud, 'O! O!' I was told afterward by the missionary that this doctrine of the intercession of the Saviour had probably not been taught them before; and it was the discovery of it then, for the first time, which so wonderfully affected them.

"During my visit to these Indians, I had an opportunity to hear Peter Jones preach to them in their native tongue; and though I could not understand his speech, I saw that his congregation were wonderfully affected by what he said; and as the people went to their houses, in their village, they cried and sobbed aloud.

"An incident had occurred just before my visit to them that showed how strong had become their hatred of whisky drinking. A Christian Indian had gone out in the bay in a canoe, and been driven off in a storm; and, in his danger, had been picked up by a steamboat. The poor Indian was almost exhausted, and the captain of the steamboat made him drink a glass of whisky. When he came back to the village, the Indians were so afflicted that he should, under any circumstances, drink whisky, that they took up a discipline with him; and for one whole afternoon and evening, alternately, one would exhort him and another pray for him, and then they would make him promise that he would drink no more whisky.

"I had a meeting of the Indians, to allow them to ask me any questions they might desire. It was astonishing, and sometimes amusing, to hear the questions they proposed. A squaw said she heard her boy read in the Testament that a man and his wife were one; now, supposing that the squaw is converted and her husband is a drunkard, when they die will the Indian go to heaven with the squaw, or must she go to hell with her husband, seeing they are one? I was afterward told that the husband of that squaw was a drunkard, and the only unconverted person on the island.

"The work of God among the Indians through that province was the greatest, all things considered, I ever saw among any people. Before their conversion, they were almost universally drunkards, both men and women. They were miserably poor and filthy, living in wigwams, and getting but a scanty support by hunting and fishing. But when they were converted, they became sober and regular in their lives, and a devoutly religious people. They abandoned their old sinful habits, drunkenness and all, and became farmers and learned mechanical trades. Their children were educated at the mission schools. A number of them became powerful and successful preachers; and, altogether, they became a respectable religious community, and continued so to the last of my visiting them. From the best information I have been able to get since, they have generally persevered in sobriety and Christianity."

Bishop Hedding's journey home from Grape Island was anything but pleasant. With the horse he had borrowed, he worked his way down to Kingston, where he took steamboat to Ogdensburgh. From this place he designed, by public conveyance, to cross the country to Lake Champlain; but, it being a new country and late in the season, and the roads in bad condition, the stages had all stopped running. It was deemed impossible to get through with a carriage of any sort. His only resort, then, was to hire a horse, and obtain the aid of a preacher to go with him and bring the horse back. In this way they wallowed through the mire to Lake Champlain, a distance of one hundred and twenty miles. Here he took a horse that he had left two or three years before, and, crossing Lake Champlain into Vermont, proceeded as far as Middlebury.

It had now become late in November, and his horse trotted so hard that he found he would be unable to endure that mode of travel. He accordingly sold his horse and took stage for Troy, which he had engaged to visit on his way home.

The object of his visit to Troy was to dedicate the new Methodist church which had been erected in State-street. The dedication took place on the 1st day of December, on which occasion Bishop Hedding preached a powerful and appropriate sermon from Isa. ii, 1–3. Being now too much exhausted and in too feeble a state of health to attempt a passage in the stage across the country to Lynn, he embarked on a boat for New-York city. The river, which had been closed by ice for several days, had just been opened by a sudden thaw; consequently the boat was filled to repletion with passengers. The crowd was so great he could find no place to lie, and scarcely a place where he could sit. The weather was exceedingly cold and stormy, and the river full of floating ice. The passage from Albany to New-York occupied a day and a night.

From New-York, Bishop Hedding wrote to his wife:—"I have passed over many rough waters and rough lands, and it is a wonderful and kind Providence by which my life and limbs have been preserved so long. I owe a debt of gratitude to the Author of all good for temporal as well as for spiritual mercies. O that I may in the end be found ready to render an account to my God for an improvement of all his mercies!" From various causes he was delayed so that he did not reach home till the last of December, having been absent, with the exception of one short visit, nearly ten months.

The year had been one of general prosperity in the Church. Every conference in the connexion reported an increase of members. The greatest increase was in the Genesee Conference, which amounted to three thousand two hundred and seventy-nine. The whole increase in the Church was twenty-one thousand one hundred and ninety-seven, making the total membership three hundred and eighty-one thousand nine hundred and ninety-seven. The number of travelling preachers reported this year was one thousand five hundred and seventy-six, being an increase of one hundred and seventy.

During this year the Maine Wesleyan Seminary was established at Readfield, Maine. "Father Sampson," an old and wealthy member of the society in that place, had given an eligibly located farm, valued at $10,000, for this purpose. A manual labour department, embracing agriculture and the mechanical arts, was connected with the institution. This department proved of immense advantage to many indigent students, as well as to many others whose constitutions were too feeble to endure the confinement of close study without the physical exercise it secured, and thus tended to build up the institution. But, on the whole, it was difficult to maintain it, and after an experience of some ten or twelve years it was given up. The seminary, however, from the beginning, has continued to flourish, and has sent forth a large number who are now prominent ministers in both of the Maine Conferences. Others have been carried, by the Providence of God, beyond the bounds of the state, where they also are doing good service for the cause of Christ. Twenty-three years ago,—dating from the spring of 1854,—a rustic boy, we ascended "the Hill of Science," as we students were wont to call the place, and became a member of the institution. Here, under the tuition of the lamented Merritt Caldwell, we spent a little over three laborious and happy years. Through all changes of life they will not be forgotten. Grateful will we ever be, that at this early date there was a Methodist seminary in the land, where, under the genial influences of her economy and her spirit, the soul might rise in virtue as in knowledge. We have long since in our heart forgiven the good but mistaken old preacher, who, on learning our purpose to acquire, if possible, an education, said, "Ah, Davis, I fear you will get too proud to be a Methodist preacher!"

In all these early educational movements, Bishop Hedding took a deep and abiding interest. He looked upon them as pillars of strength in the Church. Even then, he felt and said: "The time will come when our ministers will need a higher degree of education than at the beginning, and we must have our own schools so that they may be educated aright. Our people, too, will be educating their sons and daughters, and if we do not have schools they will send them elsewhere, and then they will be in danger of being lost to the Church. If we would keep our people and make them stable and strong as Christians, we must provide books, and periodicals, and schools for them."

After spending a little more than two months at home, and in visiting the societies in its neighbourhood, Bishop Hedding left on a tour of visitation to the Churches, and finally met Bishop George in Philadelphia, where that conference convened on the 1st day of April, 1828. This closed the first quadrennial division of his long and important service as a bishop.

CHAPTER XII.

SECOND QUADRENNIAL OF EPISCOPAL LABOURS.

Goes to the General Conference — Doubts about the Duty of Continuing in the Office — The General Conference — Progress of the "Radical Movement" — Changes sought for — The "Union Society" — "Mutual Rights" — Dr. Bond's "Appeal" — Church Trials in Baltimore — Memorial to the General Conference — Report of the Committee — Asa Shinn moves its Adoption — Nine-tenths of the People opposed to the proposed Change — Bishop Hedding misrepresented in the "Mutual Rights" by "Timothy" — Seeks Redress — "Timothy's" Anonymous Certificates — Bishop Hedding brings the Matter before the General Conference — Action of the Committee on the Episcopacy — Testimony of the Pittsburgh Delegation — Confession of Rev. George Brown, the Real "Timothy" — Triumphant Vindication of the Bishop — Progress of the Work during the Four Years — Close of the General Conference — Route to New-York — Perils upon Lake Erie — Parts with Bishop George for the Last Time — Their Association and Attachment — Dr. Bangs's Portraiture of the Character of Bishop George — Outline of his Life and Labours — Responsibility that had rested on Bishop Hedding — Route into New-England — Perilous Accident — Visit to Canada — The Independent Organization of the Canada Conference completed — A Dying Father's Charge to his Son to maintain "the Family Altar" — The Result — Close of the Ecclesiastical Year — Progress of the Work — Increase in the Church during the "Radical Movement" — Prophesied Ruin of the Church not realized — Bishop Hedding spends the Winter of 1828–9 in Lynn — Sermon on Dancing — Philadelphia, New-York, and New-England Conferences for 1829 — Excitement on Masonry — Maine Conference — Tour of Visitation to the Churches — Refused Entertainment by a Wealthy Methodist.

In company with Bishop George, Bishop Hedding proceeded from the seat of the Philadelphia Conference to Pittsburgh, to attend the session of the General Conference. Under date of March 25, he wrote to his wife from Philadelphia: "I go to General Conference under great anxieties of mind respecting what I ought to do about continuing in my office. My inclination is strong to resign; but the preachers say, Go on. Let me do whichever I will, I expect to linger out the remains of my poor life in suffering. If I desist from travelling, my infirmities will provide sufferings for me; if I continue to travel, the time of my suffering will, perhaps, be shorter. The great object with me is to know, in this respect, what will be most acceptable to Him whose I am and whom I serve; for I think I desire to know and do his will in all things. Some people, and perhaps some preachers, think my situation in the Church very pleasant; but it is because they are ignorant of its labours and its trials. I feel great need of help from above. I desire your prayers that I may be directed aright. The Lord bless you."

In this General Conference there were one hundred and seventy delegates, representing seventeen annual conferences. So great was the ratio of representation that the New-York Conference had eighteen delegates, also the Genesee; while the New-England had seventeen and the Philadelphia fifteen. The five bishops were present; and the opening services of the conference were conducted by Bishop M'Kendree.

Several subjects of very grave importance came before this body for consideration. The relation of the brethren in Canada was adjusted to the mutual satisfaction of the parties as nearly as it could be. But, perhaps more than all, the radical* controversy and movements claimed the attention of the conference. This had now grown to be a serious difficulty in the Church, producing not only suspicion and alienation of feeling in it, but secession from it. As early as 1820, a periodical called the "Wesleyan Repository" had been started in Trenton, New-Jersey. Its object was to effect a change in the economy of the Methodist Church, so that lay delegates might be introduced into the General and Annual Conferences; and so also that, in some way not clearly defined, the functions of the episcopacy might be essentially modified. It was patronized by a few travelling preachers and a few lay members; but the local preachers were its principal supporters. Very few of its correspondents were known to the public, their articles being generally published over fictitious signatures. To further their designs, the "Union Society" was organized in 1824 in the city of Baltimore, and a committee of correspondence appointed, whose special duty was to correspond with the disaffected in different parts of the Church, and to secure the organization of auxiliaries to the "Union Society" wherever it could be effected. The movement, which had hitherto been inchoate, now assumed an organized and somewhat formidable shape. Soon after, the publication of the "Mutual Rights" was commenced in Baltimore. It was exceedingly violent and denunciatory, of not

* We use this as a convenient term, and do not intend it in an offensive sense.

only the economy of the Church, but also of the officers of the Church. Its writers generally assumed fictitious signatures; but several of them were known to be prominent travelling preachers. In this crisis of affairs Dr. Bond's masterly "Appeal to the Methodists, in Opposition to the Changes proposed in their Church Government," was published, and produced a powerful effect, especially upon those who had not already committed themselves to the new and perilous movement. But before the General Conference of 1828, matters had proceeded to such a degree of open violence against the Church, on the part of the more radical, that the Rev. Mr. Hanson, then preacher in charge of the Baltimore Station, was compelled to cite several local preachers and several lay brethren to trial on the charge of "inveighing against our Discipline," "speaking evil of ministers," &c. On this charge they were severally convicted; and after laborious but ineffectual effort to bring about some adjustment of the difficulty, they were expelled from the communion of the Church. The withdrawal of others followed, and the separatists formed themselves into a society called the "Associated Methodist Reformers," and finally assumed the title of the "Methodist Protestant Church." In the month of November, 1827, a General Convention of the "reformers" was held in Baltimore, and a memorial, setting forth their rights, grievances, and claims, sent up to the General Conference. This memorial was referred to an able committee, of which Dr. Emory was chairman. Dr. Bond was also present, and corresponded freely with the committee in their deliberations. Having been resident at the "seat of war," and having in fact been foremost in the heat of the battle in all its successive stages, no one was so thoroughly acquainted with all its phases, and so completely posted up in all matters relating to it. The report of the committee was able and conclusive. It was presented by Dr. Emory, as chairman, and immediately adopted by the General Conference. It is a singular fact that the Rev. Asa Shinn moved the adoption of the report, and also that five thousand copies of it be printed immediately.* This was the final settlement of the question, so far as the government of the Church was concerned. The radicals claimed to give utterance to the *voice of the people* in the demands they made; but the General Conference, from data then in their possession, and which subsequent facts abundantly verified, were satisfied that they did not represent *one-tenth* part of the Church, and that yielding to their demands would not only peril the future success of the Church, but be acting contrary to the views and feelings of *nine-tenths* of all its members, both lay and ministerial.

We have seen how Bishop Hedding was compelled to breast the storm of this radical innovation at the Pittsburgh Conference in 1826. Of course, it could not be otherwise than that the bold and decided stand he then took should bring down upon him the

* See the "Itinerant" for April 15, 1829.

maledictions of the reformers. His address before the Pittsburgh Conference was misrepresented and perverted by several who heard it; and a member of the conference, the Rev. George Brown, over the signature of "Timothy," wrote for the "Mutual Rights" a violent article, assailing the course of the bishop, and misrepresenting his action, and also his address. In the spring of 1827 Bishop Hedding, being in Baltimore, called upon the editors of the "Mutual Rights," and requested the name of the person who had assailed him in their columns over the signature of "Timothy." This the editors declined giving except on two conditions, namely,—that the bishop should make his request in writing, and that they should obtain the consent of the author. Accordingly the bishop wrote them a note requesting the real name of "Timothy," and stating that the representation made by him of his address before the Pittsburgh Conference was a misrepresentation throughout. This communication the editors published in their paper, and also forwarded to the Rev. George Brown. To vindicate himself before the public, Mr. Brown procured the signatures of about a dozen of the radical members of the conference to certificates testifying to the correctness of the representation of the bishop's address made by "Timothy." These several certificates were published conspicuously in the "Mutual Rights," though without appending the names of the signers; and thus an impression exceedingly prejudicial to the moral and ministerial character of the bishop was sought to be made upon the public mind.

Bishop Hedding desired to meet the question before the Pittsburgh Conference in 1827, but his official duties rendered it impossible for him to be there. Consequently the earliest point at which his vindication could be reached was at the session of the General Conference in 1828, which fortunately was at Pittsburgh, and within the bounds of the conference before which his address was delivered. Accordingly he took an early opportunity to state the facts to the General Conference, and to invoke their action in the case, saying that if the accusations against him were true, he ought no longer to be a bishop or even a minister in the Church; but if they were not true, it was due to him, to the Church, and to the cause of truth, that he should receive a vindication; and to this end he desired a full and impartial investigation. The matter was, accordingly, referred to the Committee on the Episcopacy. We are in possession of a certified copy of the report of that committee, taken from the General Conference records in 1852, and which we here give entire:—

"The Committee on Episcopacy, to whom the letter of the Rev. E. Hedding to the General Conference was referred, submit the following:—

"An article having appeared in the 'Mutual Rights,' over the signature of 'Timothy,' purporting to be an address to the junior bishop, E. Hedding, in relation to an address delivered by the bishop to the members of the Pittsburgh Annual Conference in August, 1826, which the bishop considered unjust—a misrepresentation throughout, and a base slander upon his character, as he declared in a note to the editor of the said 'Mutual Rights,' which note was published in that periodical; and several anonymous certificates having also been published in said 'Mutual Rights' justifying the representations in 'Timothy,' and of course contradicting the contents of the bishop's note. These various circumstances the bishop conceived had already operated to his injury, and might so operate in future; and he therefore felt himself called upon to lay the matter before the General Conference, and to invite investigation. This he did in a written communication, which, after being read before the conference, was referred to the Committee on the Episcopacy. That committee, having taken the same into consideration, resolved to procure a meeting between the bishop and the delegates of the Pittsburgh Annual Conference in the presence of the committee, and in presence of the writer of the article signed 'Timothy,' in order, as far as possible, to ascertain the character of the address delivered by the bishop to the Pittsburgh Conference.

"The plan pursued to attain this object was for the members of the said delegation, severally, first to state their recollections of that address, and then to answer the questions proposed to them on the subject. After all those delegates had thus communicated to the committee their recollections, a paper was read containing as accurate an outline of the address of the bishop as he had been able to make out from his own recollection. The recollections of the delegates from the Pittsburgh Annual Conference, and of Bishop Hedding, were not only substantially, but, in a remarkable degree, circumstantially concurrent.

"The bishop then pointed out the injustice, misrepresentation, and slander of his character, which he considered as pervading the address signed 'Timothy.' After which the author of that article, having been permitted to address the committee, acknowledged, that in not properly distinguishing in two instances, he had done injustice, giving the general character of the bishop's address—that some of the inferences he had drawn were unjust—and that, as his premises were incorrect, all the inferences drawn from them might be erroneous.

"Your committee beg leave, therefore, to declare, as the result of their investigations in this matter, that they consider the view presented in the bishop's note to the editor of the 'Mutual Rights,' of the article signed 'Timothy,' to have been strictly correct.

"The committee would further declare, that, in their opinion, the address of Bishop Hedding, as recollected by himself and the delegates of Pittsburgh Annual Conference, not only was not deserving of censure, but was such as the circumstances of the case rendered it his official duty to deliver.

(Signed,) "S. G. Roszel, *Chairman.*

"Pittsburgh, May 15, 1828."

The report of the committee was adopted by the conference without dissent. This complete vindication of Bishop Hedding was regarded by his friends as still more triumphant, because in the Pittsburgh delegation there were at least two individuals who had all along sympathized with the radical movement, and had, at the outset, placed the same construction upon the bishop's address that "Timothy" did in his article; and, in fact, stimulated him to the course he pursued, and which eventuated in his withdrawal from the Methodist Episcopal Church. We refer to the Rev. Asa Shinn and the Rev. H. B. Bascom.

At this General Conference two new annual conferences were organized, namely, the Oneida and the New-Hampshire and Vermont. But as the Canada Conference now ceased to be an integral portion of the Church, there was an increase of only one annual conference. The progress of the work, however, in almost every part of the country had been great beyond precedent during the four years. This may be seen from the actual increase, which was no less than one hundred and six thousand five hundred and ninety-nine members in four years, and five hundred and three ministers.

At the close of the General Conference Bishops George and Hedding started for New-York city, where they were to meet the New-York Conference on the 25th of June. Having experienced a rather rough journey on their way out across the mountains, they determined to take another route home. Accordingly, they took a steamer down the Ohio to Beaver. Here the captain found it more convenient to land his passengers on the side of the river opposite to Beaver in the woods. They were landed about midnight; it was both dark and rainy, and the party had to grope their way for a long time before they could find a place of shelter. They, however, made the best of it, and early the next day took stage from Beaver for Ashtabula, on Lake Erie. "It was a desperate road," says Bishop Hedding, "through mud and swamps." They at length got through tho "swamps," but this was by no means the end of their troubles; for, when they reached Ashtabula, the wind was so high that no steamer could land. Quite a company having been detained here, they chartered a schooner to take them to Buffalo. But no sooner was the vessel out upon the lake than she tossed about and careened in a such a manner that Bishop Hedding at once suspected she was without sufficient ballast to make her safe, especially as the wind was blowing a gale; and, upon looking down through the hatchway, he found to his dismay that there was neither ballast nor freight in her hold. He soon after made another discovery which added nothing to his comfort: he found that both captain and crew were half drunk, and well supplied with brandy for the voyage. The wind, however, was in the right direction, and the vessel ploughed through the water at a terrible rate, sometimes veering to so as to head in toward the land and shake all the wind out of the sails, and at others falling off so that the main-boom would sweep across the deck with a force that made the whole vessel quiver as though she would break in pieces. "In this way," says Bishop Hedding, "we tumbled over or ploughed through the waters for over two hundred miles, in most imminent danger the whole voyage." They, however, reached Buffalo in safety, and from thence had a pleasant passage by canal-boat to Albany, and by steamboat to New-York.

Here they enjoyed a pleasant session of the New-York Conference; and an increase of two thousand three hundred and seventy-seven, making a total membership of thirty-one thousand nine hundred and forty-one, attested the continued prosperity of the work. After this conference Bishops George and Hedding parted to meet no more on earth. Bishop George left to meet the Holston Conference, which was to hold its session in Jonesborough, Tenn. He had proceeded on his journey as far as Staunton, Va., when he was attacked with the dysentery. The attack, from the first, was very severe, and throughout defied all medical skill. Its work was accomplished in a few days; and on the 23d of August, with the exclamation "Glory to God!" still lingering on his tongue, Bishop George ceased from his labours. His sudden and unexpected death gave a shock to the whole Church. Few, however, felt it more deeply than Bishop Hedding. For four years they had been intimately associated together; in company they had travelled many thousand miles, and presided over a large number of conferences. During these labours a mutual and strong attachment had sprung up between them. "Bishop George was a man of deep piety, of great simplicity of manners, a very pathetic, powerful, and successful preacher, greatly beloved in life, and very extensively lamented in death." Such is the testimony of his contemporaries concerning him. We judge that he was a man of deep sympathy and feeling, and that in this is to be found the secret of his success in the pulpit.

Bishop George was a native of Virginia, and was born in 1767. He entered the travelling connexion in 1790, travelled principally in Virginia and Maryland till 1816, when he was elected to the episcopal office. He was therefore forty-nine years of age, and had travelled twenty-six years when he was elected bishop: which office he filled twelve years, and died at the age of sixty-one.

On the 23d of July, Bishop Hedding met the New-England Conference at Lynn; and on the 14th of August, the Maine Conference at Vienna. From this place he crossed New-Hampshire and Vermont on his way to Upper Canada, where he was to meet that conference. On his route he visited the societies as far as he could; and when he reached the shores of Lake Champlain, he turned aside from his course a few days to attend a camp-meeting at Charlotte, not far from Burlington. He was now in the region of his early home. Here he had experienced religion, and here commenced his ministry. At this camp-meeting he met many of his old associates and friends, and with them talked over the scenes that had transpired thirty years before. It was to him a precious and refreshing time. As they together recounted the mercies of God, his soul was filled with unspeakable joy.

Shortly after this, while prosecuting his journey, he met with a somewhat serious accident which well nigh terminated his labours. He was in the midst of a forest, and as the sun was setting, he felt in haste to reach the settlement before night closed around him. While riding at a rapid pace over a bridge thrown across a deep ravine, his horse broke a plank, and both his fore feet went down through the opening. The shock was so sudden that Bishop Hedding was thrown out of his sulky some eight or ten feet over the head of his horse, and for some time lay insensible. When he came to, he found himself lying upon the very edge of the bridge, below which yawned a chasm twenty feet deep, down which, had he fallen, he must inevitably have been dashed to pieces upon the rough rocks at the bottom. After rendering thanksgiving to God for his preservation, he looked around for his horse, and found him out of the hole, but entangled in the harness and lying broadside upon the bridge. With great difficulty he disengaged him, got him up and resumed his journey. When he reached Chazy, N. Y., he wrote to his wife, under date of September 20: "Through the mercy of God I am yet alive. My good friend and fellow-traveller, Bishop George, is taken and I am left; I feel myself solemnly admonished to be ready also; I seem to myself like one walking on the brink of the grave." After giving an account of the accident that occurred to him, he says: "The sudden shock shook the poor old building with such violence that it had well nigh gone to pieces; but I am now gradually recovering." He then sends his love to "all who may inquire after a wandering pilgrim," and adds: "Some people think it a wonderful privilege to be a Methodist bishop; but if they had to drag around with me one year, I think they would alter their opinion."

From Chazy Bishop Hedding passed across the country to Ogdensburgh, on the St. Lawrence River, and proceeded by steamboat to Kingston. Here, in company with several preachers, he hired a lumber-wagon with two horses, and proceeded through a rough wilderness country to Ancaster, the seat of the conference.

We have already mentioned the desire of the brethren in Canada, on account of civil and political relations, to dissolve their ecclesiastical connexion with the Methodist Episcopal Church in the United States, and also the action of the General Conference looking toward such an event. This, therefore, was to be the last session of the Canada Conference in its present ecclesiastical connexion. Bishop Hedding had been mainly instrumental in preventing a violent disruption of the conference four years before; and now he was exceedingly anxious that the new ecclesiastical organization should come into existence under circumstances that would tend to perpetuate the union of feeling and sympathy between the Methodists on both sides of the line. He also desired that their act of separation should be such as would bear judicial scrutiny. Accordingly, after the usual conference business had all been transacted, resolutions were introduced and adopted by the body, declaring their ecclesiastical connexion with the Methodist Episcopal Church in the United States dissolved, and organizing themselves into a separate and independent Church by the name of the Methodist Episcopal Church in Canada. Bishop Hedding then, after congratulating them on their prosperity, and upon the amicable attainment of a result that, in their judgment, promised so much usefulness to themselves, vacated the chair; and thenceforward the "Canada Conference" became the "Methodist Episcopal Church in Canada."

While at this conference Bishop Hedding renewed an acquaintance with a family by the name of Sweetzer, whom he had known in Northern New-York twenty-eight years before. Mr. Sweetzer had recently died, and from the surviving widow he gathered the following interesting item of family history. A short time before his death, his son, an only child, had married and brought his wife home, and they lived with his parents. This son, though a moral young man, had been apparently indifferent to the subject of religion up to the period of his father's death. When his father was upon his dying bed he called his son to his side, told him that he was about to die, charged him to take care of his mother, and then tenderly addressed him upon the subject of his own soul's salvation. After this, he added:—"My son, I believe I am going to heaven; but I cannot leave the world in peace unless you will make me two promises. My house, you know, has always been a home for Methodist preachers, and the first thing I wish you to promise is, that it shall always continue to be so, and that you will take care of them as I have done. Again, my house has always been a house of prayer, and I cannot bear to think that family prayer shall cease to be offered in it. I want you to promise that after I am gone, and you become the head of the family, you will commence family prayer, and keep it up regularly, as I have done." With tears, the young man pledged himself that the dying request of his father should be fulfilled; and the old man, with a smile of satisfaction upon his countenance, died in peace. The son immediately commenced family prayer, and in a few days both he and his wife were converted. The house continued, as before, the home of the itinerants; and the young man regarded their presence, as his father had before him, a boon and a blessing. When the bishop saw them, the young man and his wife were happy in the love of God. "What a fulfilment," he remarks, "of the promise made to Abraham:—'I know that he will command his children and his household after him.'"

After the close of the Canada Conference, Bishop Hedding returned by way of Ogdensburgh, Plattsburgh, Middlebury, Vt., and thence across the Green Mountains home to Lynn.

Thus ended another year of toilsome labour in the great work to which all his powers were consecrated. It had been a year of great prosperity in the Church, notwithstanding some portions of the work had been greatly distracted by the radical excitement and the secessions produced by it. But how little the Church at large was affected by these excitements will be apparent from the fact that the increase for the year was thirty-six thousand four hundred and seven, making a total membership of four hundred and eighteen thousand nine hundred and twenty-seven.* The number of preachers this year was one thousand six hundred and forty-two, being an increase of sixty-six for the year. The other interests of the Church had also proportionably increased. The missionary cause had been greatly extended; new churches had been erected; new societies and circuits organized; and the cause of education had received a new and powerful impulse. And here we may as well remark,

* There is an error in the printed Minutes for this year, making the total membership four hundred and twenty-one thousand one hundred and fifty-six, or two thousand two hundred and twenty-nine more than it should be.

that each year during the excitement connected with the organization of the Methodist Protestant Church, there was a continued and large increase in the membership of the old Church. For instance, in 1829, there was an increase of twenty-nine thousand three hundred and five; in 1830, an increase of twenty-eight thousand four hundred and ten—even after deducting nine thousand six hundred and seventy-eight for the Canada Conference, which had then ceased its ecclesiastical connexion with us; in 1831, an increase of thirty-seven thousand one hundred and fourteen. The same is true of the principal cities where the "reformers" were most numerous, and which they made the centre of their operations. Omitting the coloured membership, which were affected but little either way by the movement, the following table, taken from Bangs's History, exhibits the condition of Methodism in these several cities by the statistics of its white members:—

	1827.	1828.	1829.	1830.	1831.
New-York	3,219	3,416	3,473	3,866	4,889
Philadelphia...............	3,633	3,882	4,440	4,678	4,859
Baltimore	3,631	3,886	4,119	4,295	5,059
Pittsburgh..................	737	655	676	630	700
Cincinnati..................	901	915	929	1,171	1,495
	12,121	12,754	13,637	14,640	17,002

It will thus be perceived that, so far from preventing the general progress of the Church, there was, during the five years of greatest turmoil and excitement on the part of the "reformers," a net increase in the five cities where their greatest power was centred of four thousand eight hundred and eighty-one, or almost one thousand a year. How strongly this result contrasts with the heated notions of men, when carried away with some visionary idea! To read over the denunciatory and prophetic pleas of some of these men as they now stand in the columns of the "Mutual Rights," one would suppose that, unless the General Conference yielded to what was erroneously called "the voice of the people," the Methodist Church would be rent in pieces, and would remain only as an old and deserted hulk stranded upon the shore. How widely different from this was the result! While these men were wasting their energies in their wild crusade, the great body of the ministers went steadily forward in their godlike work of preaching Christ crucified; sinners were converted, the Church was edified, and Christians, matured for heaven, crossed the flood with songs of joy, and joined the host of the redeemed above.

The winter of 1828–9 was spent by Bishop Hedding principally at home, though he answered repeated calls to visit societies, and to perform special services in various places in his vicinity. On the 25th of January he preached a sermon on dancing in the Lynn Common Church, which made a strong impression at the time and elicited much remark.

The "Lynn Mirror," under the title of "Bishop Hedding," thus notices this discourse: "On Sabbath evening, January 25th, Bishop Hedding, of the Methodist Episcopal Church, according to previous notice, delivered at the first Methodist meeting-house in this town a very ingenious and interesting sermon on *dancing:* text, Eccl. i, 1. The argument of the discourse was conducted in so artful a manner as to carry along with him the minds of the audience, and producing none of that revulsion of feeling which frequently arises when favourite notions are attacked without sufficient remark by way of exordium. The wound shrinks back from the rash hand of the surgeon; the muscles of the dislocate joint are rigid, and require to be softened down by gentle means before they will suffer the limb to be reduced to its proper place. Thus it happens to the man who would unceremoniously attack our prejudices and our errors—the precipitancy of the operator often insures defeat. The preacher evidently intended to direct the chief force of his battery against dancing, but chose first to make himself master of several out-posts before he came to the principal engagement. The excellence of true religion was set forth in a pleasing light, as tending to create the highest happiness, even in this world, without depriving its possessor of a single innocent gratification. Nevertheless, the passions must be controlled, and pleasure abandoned, when they dampen the ardour of piety and break all distinction between professed Christians and the mere *men of the world.* After showing that an attendance upon theatres, card-tables, &c., was not calculated to increase the work of grace in the soul, and illustrating his arguments by several well-told anecdotes, he proceeded to the more immediate object in view—*dancing*. To obviate any arguments which might be advanced in favour of dancing from the Scriptures, it was remarked that the Hebrew word translated *dancing*, according to some of the best critics, should be rendered *playing upon an instrument*, or *piping*. At all events, that this exercise, whatever it was, evidently must have been a religious act; and if the dancing of the present day was of the same nature as the dancing of David, then balls and assemblies should be held on the Sabbath as a religious exercise.

"The disposition of the argument offered by *physiologists* in favour of dancing, namely, that it tends to promote health, we think must have made a forcible impression upon the minds even of the friends of this amusement. So far from promoting health, the preacher thought that overaction, and late hours, and artificial stimulus, would have a contrary effect; but if otherwise, then dances should not be held once a month, but every night, or great benefit and great *cures* could not be expected; and facts were adverted to in proof that warm ball-rooms, excessive action, thin dresses, and the midnight air, have laid the foundations of disease, and have been the precursors of many a premature grave. Upon the whole, we think the numerous assembly, whatever private opinions had previously existed, must have been gratified with the adroitness of the discourse and felt the force of its arguments, and at the same time been pleased with the honest intentions of the speaker."

This year he met the Philadelphia Conference at Philadelphia, April the 15th; the New-York at Troy, May 15th. From Troy he crossed the country to Portsmouth, New-Hampshire, and attended the session of the New-England Conference on the 10th of June. At this session the New-Hampshire and Vermont Conference was formed—the preceding General Conference having left the division to be made by the conference, with the concurrence of the bishop.

During the three years preceding this there had sprung up quite a strong party feeling in some of the conferences in respect to Freemasonry. Already it had occasioned, both in the conferences and in some Churches, alienations and strifes injurious to the cause of religion. In the New-England Conference the excitement had reached a great height. The parties were about equally divided, and embraced many of the prominent men on each side. When the conference commenced, it was even feared that the agitation might cause a formal rupture of the conference. Bishop Hedding apprehended great difficulty, and, with characteristic zeal and prudence, set himself to work to prevent the threatened storm. He was well qualified for such a work. In former years he had been a mason, but for some time had ceased to attend their meetings, and these facts being known gave him influence with both parties. At length a large meeting of the principal men of the conference, embracing the leaders on both sides of the controversy, was informally held, and, after much discussion, resolutions of a conciliatory character were agreed upon. Subsequently, when introduced into the conference, they were carried unanimously. Thus the question was so fully and amicably settled, that a year or two afterward it had nearly ceased to be agitated among the people.

From Portsmouth he proceeded to Gardiner, Maine, where he met the Maine Conference, July 9th. This was the last conference assigned to him for the year, and having completed his labours here he returned home; and soon after, having his wife in company, he commenced a tour of visitation to the Churches in Massachusetts, New-Hampshire, Vermont, and part of the State of New-York. He had before him a large number of appointments, extending through a range of nearly two thousand miles, and requiring some three or four months' travel. This labour, however, he successfully accomplished, and reached his home near the close of the year.

In his travels in different parts of the country, he was occasionally the subject or the observer of amusing as well as painful incidents. Those who knew him are aware that he had a keen perception and enjoyment of the ludicrous, as well as things that were grave; and that however sudden, or strange, or even laughable, any event might be, he had the good sense and ready wit to turn it to proper account, and in no way to be disconcerted by it. During this last journey an incident transpired that is worthy of narration from the lesson to be derived from it, if nothing more. He was travelling in the town of Chester, Vermont, and stopped on Friday night at a public house. As he was wearied with travelling, he desired to spend the Sabbath with some Methodist society near by, and inquired of his host if there were any Methodists in the place. The landlord directed him to a place about three miles off, and gave him the name of the principal man in the society, where he thought the bishop would be well entertained, and where the people would be glad to have him stay and preach. Accordingly, on the following morning he started, and toiled up the hills to the house of this "principal man in the society." Leaving his wife in his carriage, he went to the door, and the gentleman himself met him. The bishop stated that he was a Methodist preacher on a journey, and would like to stay and preach among them if there was any place where he could be entertained. "Well," said the "principal man," "I want first to know if you are a mason?" "O!" said the bishop, "that is a question I don't want to meddle with; there is a great deal of excitement about it, and it is no matter whether I am or not." "Then," said the man, "I know you are one; if you are not, you would say you are not. We don't want to entertain you, or hear you, unless we know you are not a mason." "Well," said the bishop, "are there no other Methodists about here?" "Yes," said the man, "there is a poor widow down below, but she can't take care of you; she has enough to do to take care of herself." "Well, good-by," said the bishop. He thought he would drive to the widow's and make further inquiries. The "poor widow" and her two daughters were Methodists, and received them gladly. They prepared dinner for them, and then sent their hired man to a brother a short distance off. He came and took the bishop and his wife home with him, and entertained them kindly. He also made an appointment for him to preach in the school-house the morning and afternoon of the next day, and circulated it through all the neighbourhood. The people came out in crowds; even the strong anti-mason came, but looked quite sullen. The bishop preached with unusual unction and power, and made a very strong impression. After meeting, when he had returned to his host's, a number of the society came in to see and converse with the new preacher. While they were there, one of the number, remembering that Hedding was the name of one of the bishops, cried out, "O, it's one of the bishops! it's one of the bishops!" This discovery produced quite a commotion, and they crowded around him with new interest. He says: "I enjoyed my visit among this people very much, and was as heartily entertained as I ever was in any place, and was perhaps the means of doing them a little good." When the "principal man of the place" learned that the Methodist preacher he had so rudely repulsed from his door was none other than a bishop, his mortification was extreme. The bishop, having enjoyed the hospitality and brotherly love of the people through the Sabbath, resumed his journey early Monday morning, and saw them no more.

CHAPTER XIII.

SECOND QUADRENNIAL OF EPISCOPAL LABOURS—CONCLUDED.

Conferences for the Spring of 1830—Visits the Oneida Indian Mission—Sermon to the Indians—Journeys Westward—Review of Labours—A Week's Rest—Visit to Canada—Reaches Home after Nine Months' Absence—Summation for the Year—Baltimore Conference in 1831—A "Located Itinerant"—Submits to a Surgical Operation—Conferences attended this Spring—Leaves Home on a Western and Southern Tour—Letter to his Wife—Genesee Conference—Christian Hospitality *vs.* Hospitality to Office—A Cold Reception—Quartered among Apprentice Boys—Pittsburgh Conference—Journey to Mansfield, Ohio—Adventures with a Preacher who had "Time enough yet"—Meets the Kentucky Conference at Louisville—Journey from Louisville to East Tennessee—Reaches Athens—Rebuke of a Pompous Young Man—Holston Conference—Visits the Cherokee Nation—State of Society, &c.—Encounter with a Watch-Dog—Travels in Georgia—A Slave Auction—The Georgia Conference—South-Carolina Conference—Conversation with a Negro on the Roanoke—Hospitality of a Tavern-keeper—Virginia Conference—Philadelphia Conference—Arrives at the Seat of the General Conference—Progress of the Work during the Four Years—Educational Movement—Colleges—Seminaries—Missions—Among the Slaves—Liberia—Indian Missions—In Canada—At Green Bay—Rev. John Clark—The Wyandots—Rev. J. B. Finley—Visit to the East with Indians—Choctaws—Cherokees—Death of Ministers.

The opening spring finds Bishop Hedding again at the city of Philadelphia, where he met that conference on the 14th of April. On his return to New-York he wrote to his wife, under date of April 30th, as follows: "I have just returned from the Philadelphia Conference in tolerable health: had plenty of labour and care, but have been graciously preserved. The preachers are beginning to come for conference. They have had a good increase (two thousand five hundred and fifty) in the Philadelphia Conference, and the Churches generally in those regions are in a state of good prosperity. I have a great care and responsibility resting upon me; many important and difficult questions to decide—important in relation to the Church, the preachers, their families, &c.; but I make it my constant care to do right. Yet in this I grieve some and offend others, because some who are interested cannot see what *right is*. I hope so to conduct in this respect, as well as in others, as to be able to render an account to the Chief Shepherd. But O how much mercy I need to cover ten thousand failings! many of which, perhaps, I do not see. Lord, help me! Amen."

The session of the New-York Conference commenced May 6th, and at its close Bishop Hedding proceeded to New-Bedford, where he met the New-England Conference, May 20th. Then, visiting home on his way, he proceeded to Portland to meet the Maine Conference, which assembled on the 9th of June. Thence he crossed the mountains and attended the New-Hampshire and Vermont Conference, which assembled June 23d, at Barre, Vermont. Continuing his course westward, he met the Oneida Conference, at Utica, on the 15th of July.

After the close of the Oneida Conference he visited the Oneida Indian Mission, about twenty miles from Utica. The Oneida Indians had been settled on an Indian reservation in this part of the

State of New-York. They had been partly civilized, and some of them were cultivators of the soil, and had adopted the habits of civilized life. The Protestant Episcopal Church had established a mission among them several years before; but, so far as it concerns religion and morals, they were in a truly deplorable state. Like most of the half-civilized aborigines that skirted our states and territories, they were debased by habits of intemperance and other degrading vices. As a result of their vices, they were diminishing in numbers, and becoming more and more impoverished. While they were in this condition a young converted Mohawk came among them, impelled by his love for Christ and for the souls of men to make known to them the ministry of reconciliation. Being able to speak in their own language, he unfolded to them, from the fulness of his own experience, and with a heart all on fire with the love of God, the way of salvation. The people heard him gladly. A work of grace commenced among them, and upward of one hundred were soundly converted. These stray lambs in the wilderness needed tender care and great watching. A missionary was sent to them; a school was established for the education of their children, and also for the adult Indians who were desirous of learning. This Indian mission has been sustained in the Oneida Conference until the present day, and been attended with the best of results to the Indians. Several of these converted Indians emigrated to Green Bay, where they now form one of the most interesting and successful of all our Indian missions.

Bishop Hedding preached to the Indians through an interpreter. In his discourse an incident occurred that shows how difficult it often is to translate the strong figurative language of the Bible. He had occasion to quote the text, "He led captivity captive, and gave gifts unto men." The interpreter paused, and spoke to him in a low voice, "Captivity captive? captivity captive? I can't interpret that; I don't understand it." "Well," said the bishop, as he thought of the strange and wonderful imagery of the text, "if you can't interpret it let it pass."

After his visit to the mission he proceeded to Rochester, where the Genesee Conference assembled July 29th. At this point, reviewing his labours, he says: "At the close of the Genesee Conference I had attended seven conferences, alone, in about three months and a half. Several of them were large conferences, that required at least nine or ten days. I had travelled most of the way with horse and sulky, and in all my travel had been over fourteen hundred miles. I had been so pressed with conference business all that time, that I had often not half as much time to sleep as I needed. And I was now under an engagement to go to the Canada Conference to ordain their preachers, by a request of that conference, and by the consent of the General Conference.

To meet this engagement, from Rochester he crossed Lake Ontario to Canada. Having arrived at a friend's house in a retired place, and being worn down by such protracted and exhausting labours, he paused awhile to recruit himself. "For a whole week," says he, "I devoted myself to *rest*. I would lie down at any time when I felt sleepy, whether it was night or day, and at the end of the time felt much recruited." He then proceeded, visiting the Churches where he was acquainted. He went also to the mission station at Grape Island, where he had been a few years before, and found them in increasing prosperity. Then he attended the Canada Conference, at Kingston, not as its president, but as a visitor and friend, and ordained the preachers that were elected to orders by the conference, and gave them certificates appropriate to their relation to the Church in Canada. After this conference he crossed the St. Lawrence, a little below the lake, and visited Watertown. Thence he crossed the country in his sulky through parts of New-York, Vermont, and Massachusetts, to his home in Lynn.

He reached home about the last of November, having been absent, except a flying visit paid while on his way to the Maine Conference, nearly nine months. This was the most laborious year he had as yet experienced since he entered the episcopal office. He now retired into "winter-quarters."

The progress of the work during the year was of a very cheering character. The total membership reported was four hundred and seventy-six thousand one hundred and fifty-three, being an increase of twenty-eight thousand four hundred and ten; or, if we add nine thousand six hundred and seventy-eight, the membership of the Canada Conference, which was dropped from the record this year, the actual increase was thirty-seven thousand nine hundred and thirty-five. The number of travelling preachers reported was one thousand nine hundred, showing an increase of eighty-three.

About the last of February Bishop Hedding started on his episcopal tour for 1831. At the request of Bishop Roberts, who was detained by sickness, he met the Baltimore Conference in Washington, D. C., March 16th. The business of the conference was transacted in great harmony and with great despatch. Baltimore had been, from the beginning, one of the grand radiating centres of Methodism.

Here, however, as in other conferences, there were a few *located itinerants*, the accommodation of whom seriously embarrassed the work. One of this class, who was comparatively a young man, had married a rich wife, and, in addition to other worldly business, had for several years been keeping a store. To accommodate him, he had been appointed to the neighbouring circuits, till there was no circuit in all that region which was willing to receive him on any condition. He was this year appointed to a circuit quite up in the spurs of the Alleghany Mountains. When the appointments were read out in conference, the brother threw himself upon the seat, and, to the great amusement of the conference, roared aloud, "My German brethren told me it would be so! My German brethren told me it would be so!" The bishop, without appearing to notice the ludicrous exhibition, closed the conference and retired to his lodgings. While conversing with the family, a coloured boy belonging to the house came rushing into the room, so thoroughly frightened as to make a grand display of the white of his eyes, and screamed out, "O bishop, bishop, bishop! go up stairs quick, quick, quick! there is a man dying up in your room!" The bishop, followed by members of the family, rushed up to the room. There they found the veritable *located itinerant* on the bed upon his knees, with his face pushed into the clothes as far as possible, still bellowing out, "My German brethren told me it would be so!" The bishop, for a time, hardly knew whether to yield to the provoking or the ludicrous aspects of the case. He at length made the brother get up, then pointed out to him the impropriety of his former course as a minister, chided him for his present folly, and wound up by saying, "Now stop this bawling, and go to your appointment and labour like a man." He then dismissed him, supposing that would be the last he would hear from him. But a fortnight after he came to see the bishop in Baltimore, and renewed his complaint and sought redress. "But bishop," said he, "I don't blame you, I don't blame you; it is that Chris. Frye, my presiding elder. And now, bishop, if you will only hear him and me preach two bouts of twenty sermons each, if I don't beat him I'll give up!" The bishop, not fancying the adjustment of the case by such a trial, told the man that, so far as he was concerned, he could not in conscience change his appointment, and told him to go to it and labour like a man of God. In the fall of that year, when the bishop was in Lebanon, Ohio, he was one day called down from his room to see a gentleman who had called upon him. To his great surprise, he found he was honoured with a third call from his old *located itinerant* and his wife. The preacher gave the following account of himself: "I went to *that* circuit, and could find no house fit to live in, and no place suitable to board my wife; and I could not stay there alone so far away from home, so we concluded we would take a journey and see the world." The next day the bishop saw them leaving the place with a splendid carriage and span of horses. At the next session of the Baltimore Conference Bishop M'Kendree was present, and delivered an address before reading the appointments. Among other things, he said: "You have generally good circuits in this conference. It is true some of them are not quite so good as others; but," said he, looking the preacher who had travelled to see the world right in the eye, "there is not one of them so bad that it need make a *man cry*."

Immediately after the session of the Baltimore Conference, Bishop Hedding visited the city of Baltimore and submitted to a surgical operation. He had suffered great pain and inconvenience from a hemorrhoidal tumor for ten years. Its removal was a painful operation, and resulted in his confinement eight or ten days; but in the end relieved him of great suffering, and effected an almost entire cure of a painful and debilitating disease.

Before he had fully recovered from the surgical operation, he was compelled to resume his journey northward. The Philadelphia Conference was in session when he reached that city, having been opened by Bishop Soule on the 13th of April. In company they travelled to Middletown, Conn., and met the New-York Conference on the 4th of May; then to Springfield, Mass., and met the New-England Conference May 18th.

After the New-England Conference, by two days' hard travelling he was enabled to reach home, where he had three or four days to spend with his family before he would be under the necessity of starting on a tour to visit the western and southern conferences, which would require a long absence. These few days soon glided away, and we soon find him with his horse and sulky journeying along through the southern parts of New-Hampshire and Vermont, into the interior of the State of New-York, as usual attending camp-meetings, and meeting special appointments by the way.

From Lansingburgh he wrote to his wife under date of June 29th; and, after referring to the long journey and many exposures that were before him, he says: "But I consider God governs everywhere, and if he sees fit, can preserve me in one place as well as in another. While I am in the way of my duty I feel safe, for I know that my Master will let me live as long as he sees best. Though, if it were the will of God, I should much rather die at home in the presence of my wife, than abroad among strangers; yet, whenever I die, I hope to go to rest. A preparation for this solemn event is my daily concern. When I look at my imperfections, and compare myself with God's holy law, I am ready to ask, How can such a wretch get to heaven? But when I look at the blood of atonement, and hang on my Saviour, I feel that I have a sure foundation, and rest in a firm hope. Whatever may become of all other concerns, O let us strive to enter in at the strait gate!"

At Le Roy, N. Y., in conjunction with Bishop Soule, he met the Genesee Conference on the 28th of July. On the third day of the session, leaving Bishop Soule to finish the business of the conference, he started on his tour, journeying through Buffalo, Fredonia, Erie, Pa., &c., to meet the western conferences. Before leaving Le Roy he wrote again to his wife under date of August 1st: "The Genesee Conference has been in session three days besides the Sabbath. Bishop Soule is here. As yet I get no letter from Bishop Roberts, consequently I have to go to the Pittsburgh Conference. I purpose to start this day. I have felt more affliction about being away from home this journey than ever I did before, the time seems so long, and the uncertainty of life so great. But we have one safe way—to commit our lives and all our concerns to the care of God; he knows what is best, and will certainly do what is best. I desire you will pray for me, but give yourself no distressing anxiety about me; I feel myself safe in the hands of my heavenly Father."

Bishop Hedding was a plain and humble man. He chose only to be known as a Methodist preacher. He wore the garb, travelled in the style, and assumed the character of a Methodist preacher. Accordingly, when he stopped to seek lodgings with his brethren, he would announce himself simply as a Methodist preacher. If this did not always secure him as cordial a reception, and as grand an entertainment, as if he had announced himself "bishop" instead of "preacher," it, at least, enabled him to distinguish between Christian hospitality and hospitality to office.

While on this journey an incident illustrative of this occurred. One Saturday, toward noon, he reached a manufacturing village, and finding both himself and his horse much jaded, he concluded to remain over the Sabbath. The preacher and his wife being both absent from the parsonage, he went to the public-house near by. After dinner he inquired of the landlord who were the principal men among the Methodists in the place; intending to seek the hospitality of some one of them rather than remain at the public-house over the Sabbath. The landlord gave him the name and pointed out the residence of one, who, he said, was the principal man in the Church, and also in the village. The bishop immediately walked over to the house, and made known his wish to the lady. Instead of giving him a reply, she sent for her husband. When the man came in he introduced himself to him as a Methodist preacher on a journey, and said, that as he knew of no place he could reach before the Sabbath, he would like to pass it in that place if he could be entertained. The man made no reply, but turned the conversation to some other subject. After waiting a reasonable time, and no reply being made to his request, the bishop took his hat, and said, "Good afternoon, sir," intending to return and spend the Sabbath at the tavern. The man then said, in a cold and heartless manner, "I guess you'd better stay here." The bishop replied, that he would like to stay, if it would not be a burden to him or his family; but he did not like to make himself burdensome anywhere. "O, you can stay," said the man, with the same cold, apathetic indifference. "Well," said the bishop, "I have a horse at the tavern; have you horse-keeping?" "I have a barn and hay," replied the man, "but no grain." The bishop then said: "I can procure grain at the tavern, if you have good hay; but if your hay is not good, I will keep him there, as I have a long journey to perform." The man replied, with some little irritability, "The hay is good enough for your horse."

Upon this slender prospect of hospitality the bishop

went to the tavern, procured oats, brought them in his sulky, and put out his horse, and took care of him while he remained. When evening came his host said to him—"There is a prayer-meeting at the meeting-house: you can go, if you please; I can't go." The bishop went to the prayer-meeting, took his seat in the congregation, and, at a suitable time, prayed along with the other brethren. After the meeting closed he returned to his lodgings.

The house of his host was large, and elegantly furnished; but at the hour of rest they sent the bishop to a small, remote chamber—far from being clean. Here he had three apprentice boys for his companions—one of them occupying the same bed with himself.

In the morning, his host, in a half-inviting, half-repelling manner, remarked that there was to be a love-feast, and inquired if he would go. "O, yes, certainly," said the bishop. Soon after he had taken his seat in the congregation, the preacher came in. He observed his host go up and speak to the preacher, when both turned their eyes upon him. The preacher had seen him before, and instantly recognised him. A flame of fire seemed to overspread the face of his host, as he slunk away to a seat. At the request of the preacher Bishop Hedding took charge of the love-feast, and then preached for him. He also engaged to accompany the preacher and officiate for him at his afternoon appointment—almost glad of the opportunity to escape from his host at this juncture. As soon as the service closed, he left the church to get his horse. His host soon came up with him, took his arm, and—half-mad, half-gracious, and quite thoroughly confused—said, in a quick, impatient manner, "Why didn't you tell me you was a bishop?" "O," said the bishop, "I am a plain Methodist preacher." Both the man and his wife seemed completely overcome with mortification, and it was a relief to the bishop to get away.

Perhaps after that the man remembered the injunction of the good Book, "Be careful to entertain strangers, for some thereby have entertained angels unawares." At all events, he received an admonition upon the propriety of giving, at least, a decent reception and entertainment to the Methodist preachers.

Bishop Hedding met the Pittsburgh Conference August 17th, and from thence journeyed to Mansfield, Ohio, where he met the Ohio Conference, September 8th. While on his journey to Mansfield he had a little trial of his patience. Every one who knew the bishop is aware of the promptness and energy of his action. The management of a train upon a railroad is scarcely more systematic as to the time of arrival and departure from the different points, than were the movements of Bishop Hedding in carrying out his arrangements. On one occasion on this journey he put up in a village where the preacher was to leave in the morning for conference, and they arranged to start early and travel in company—the day's journey before them being between thirty and forty miles. With this arrangement the bishop was well pleased, as the country was new and he was ignorant of the way; and accordingly he was up with the lark in the morning, ate his breakfast, and had his horse fed and prepared for the journey. But when he came to the preacher's he found he had not been to breakfast; and upon suggesting the necessity of haste, he replied, "O, there is time enough yet." At length the preacher lazily got up his horse, when, lo! one shoe was off and another loose; "time enough yet," said he, "I will have him shod before I start." To the great annoyance of the bishop, and to the scandal of his punctuality, it was nine o'clock before they were fairly started on their journey. The preacher, being acquainted with the road, led the way; but he drove so slowly that but little progress was made before dinner. After dinner the bishop, having inquired the way, started off upon a brisk trot and continued to lead. The preacher followed after, but there being a flaw in one of his axletrees that he had neglected to have repaired, it at length broke down, and an hour and a half were spent in repairing it. Night came on before they had reached the settlement where they were to tarry, and in the darkness they could creep only at a snail's pace. The result of "time enough yet" was, that they did not reach their stopping place till eleven o'clock at night, and not only put the people where they stayed to an inconvenience, but lost the opportunity of having a good night's rest for themselves and their horses. The bishop excused himself from delaying for the brother, as his wagon must be mended before he could start, and was off in the morning while yet his fellow-traveller was taking his rest. The second day of the conference "time enough yet" made his appearance, having just arrived, and took his seat among his brethren. How the laggard ever got over the Alleghanies, and how he could keep the breath in his body in such a "go-ahead" atmosphere, was a mystery the bishop's philosophy did not attempt to unravel. He wrote to his wife from Mansfield, September 11: "I have had much hard toil and many bad roads; but the Lord in mercy has preserved me, so that no evil has befallen me. It is more healthy in this country than usual at this season; yet I frequently see people shaking with the ague. They humorously call it, 'taking a shake.' There have been great revivals of religion in many parts through which I have come—greater than any I have ever seen before. I am about eight hundred miles from home, and have travelled about one thousand miles to get here. I seem to myself to be far off, but a long way I have to go before I can see you again. Though I have sorrows, and afflictions, and toils, yet I have many comforts—the greatest of all my comforts is found in the love and service of my God, and the hope of obtaining a place in heaven, when I go from this world. O let us live for God and heaven, and then, through the merits of our Lord and Saviour, we shall be safe and happy, let what will befall us here."

In a postscript to this letter he speaks of the preachers being as fine a set of men as he ever saw, nearly one hundred and fifty in number, and that the increase for the year in the conference was over four thousand.*

From Mansfield he travelled in his sulky to Cincinnati; then, finding the mud deep in the roads and the travelling hard, he took his horse and carriage on board a steamboat, and went down the river to Louisville, which was the seat of the Kentucky Conference that year. Being a few weeks in advance of the conference, he crossed the river into Indiana, and visited several of the Churches in that part of the state. He had expected Bishop Roberts to be with him at the Kentucky Conference; but in this he was disappointed, as he did not arrive from the Indiana Conference, on account of his feeble health and the bad roads, till just after the former conference closed. The conference, which commenced October 13th, however, passed off delightfully; and Bishop Hedding was much pleased with the spirit and bearing of both preachers and people. He was especially pleased with the anti-slavery feeling that so manifestly pervaded the conference. That body then, though in a slave state, refused to elect local preachers who held slaves to deacon's or elder's orders.

From Louisville he travelled through Kentucky,

* The exact number of preachers was one hundred and forty-eight, and the increase was four thousand two hundred and thirty-three; making a total membership of forty-four thousand eight hundred and seventy-nine.

and crossed the Cumberland Mountains into East Tennessee. In crossing these mountains he was exposed to a new kind of danger. There was a distance of thirty miles where the country was uninhabited, only as it was roamed over by wild beasts and hunters—the latter being but little more civilized than the Indians, and living in much the same way. The brethren of the Kentucky Conference, knowing the difficulty and danger of the way, kindly employed a young preacher to accompany him. This young man rode on horseback and led the way, while the bishop followed in his sulky. They made every effort to get through by daylight; but night closed in upon them two hours before they reached a tavern. The night was so dark that none but an experienced traveller could have found the way; and the road, which was so rough as to be almost impassible by daylight, was now doubly dangerous in the darkness of the night. They were, however, protected by a gracious Providence, and reached the public-house beyond the mountains in safety. The landlord expressed his surprise that they had got through without being torn to pieces. He said that only a few days before a panther leaped at a man who was armed with a gun, but leaped so high as to pass over him; and when he turned to attack him in the other direction, the man, who was quick with his gun, shot him dead.

He reached Athens, Tennessee, where the Holston Conference was to meet, on the 10th of November.

Being some days in advance of the time, he sent out several appointments which he filled in the neighbourhood.

To a man of such real diffidence and true gentlemanly bearing as Bishop Hedding, any appearance of inflated self-confidence or of ill-mannerly impudence in a Methodist preacher was exceedingly offensive. No man knew how to level such persons with stern and cutting rebuke, or to wither them with silent contempt, better than Bishop Hedding; and no man could do it more effectually. One evening while at Athens, prior to the session of the conference, as he was sitting in his room conversing with a few friends, a young preacher came in, and with a bold, impudent air strutted up before the bishop, at the same time brushing up his hair with one hand, and then thrusting both into his pantaloon's pockets. "Sir," said he, "I understand you have an appointment to preach at brother B——'s to-morrow night. Is it so?" The bishop replied that he had an appointment there. "Well, then," said the young man, "I believe I shall go out and hear you, and see if you can preach any." The bishop regarded the young man for a moment with a commiserating expression that told in its effect, and then turned away without replying a word, and resumed his conversation with his friends. He made no further allusion to the subject, and took no further notice of the young man, who awkwardly retreated from his prominent position. The pointed and deserved rebuke was richly enjoyed by the spectators, and keenly felt by the young man. His perceptions however were not remarkably keen in those respects, nor were his sensibilities remarkably refined. It was not long before he discovered that he was altogether too great a man to be a Methodist preacher, especially as something always intervened to prevent his taking the position among his brethren to which, in his own judgment, he was fairly entitled. Accordingly he located, and became a political stump orator, and the editor of a political paper. He finally succeeded in getting elected to Congress; but still failed to convince the country that he was either a strong or wise man.

After the Holston Conference, Bishop Hedding crossed the Hiawassee River into the Cherokee country, where he visited the Indians, preaching to them in different places, and travelling about one hundred and forty miles in their nation. Thence he crossed the Chattohoochee River, and came out into the white settlements. The brethren of the Holston Conference were not to be outdone by those of Kentucky in their kindness to the bishop. They also sent a young man to escort him in all his travels in the Cherokee country. At this time he writes: "Since leaving home I have travelled one thousand eight hundred and twenty miles with my horse and sulky. The roads have been bad and the travelling difficult. Indeed, most of the way it has been mud and mire, alternating with stumps, and trees, and stones. I met with few bridges or ferry-boats, so that I had to ford most of the streams.

But my labours and cares have been much lightened by the great kindness of the people. A more friendly, pleasant, and hospitable people I have never met."

From Athens, Georgia, under date of December 12, he wrote to his wife: "Through the mercy of God I still live, and enjoy a comfortable state of health. Since I wrote you last, from the seat of the Tennessee Conference, I have travelled about two hundred and twenty miles, and have yet one hundred and thirty to travel to the Georgia Conference. I do not always take the most direct route; but frequently diverge from the straight course to attend quarterly meetings, four-day meetings, and to ordain local preachers. Since the first of August I have been in *the new countries;* and, except in the few cities and towns, (villages,) have struggled with various difficulties. The want of the comforts and conveniences of life, though they seem to be lightly regarded by those who have never had them, is to me a serious inconvenience. If my friends at Lynn knew what I have passed through, they would wonder that I am yet alive. For four hundred miles back I have seen but few country houses (I mean except in villages) which had a glass window in them. A farmer will have large droves of horses, cattle, hogs, and even negroes, and not a single pane of glass in his house. The windows are closed with board shutters; and consequently the windows or doors, or both, must be kept open in the coldest weather in order to have light in the dwelling. Not unfrequently we have four beds in the same room, occupied with quite a variety of sleepers. Other things are on much the same scale; but the kindness of the people is such that it makes up for other deficiencies. I am now getting into an older settled country, and have bidden farewell for the present to the scenes of frontier life." The bishop was evidently too plain and practical a man to enjoy the scenes of "frontier life" that he was called to witness. To many, such a jaunt would have been an era in their lives—storing their minds with a thousand images of the exciting, the novel, and the grand. But the bishop had already travelled too long and suffered too much to be smitten with the poetry of adventure; with him it was a plain prosaic affair.

Through all this region each family had one or more savage dogs, which were companions of the men when out on their hunting excursions, and general sentinels at home in the night. They were usually chained in the daytime, but set loose at night. One evening, as the bishop had been walking in the fields for meditation, and was returning to the house, he encountered one of these ferocious dogs that did not recognise his right to be there. He was without any means of defence, and none were accessible. He, however, held the dog at bay with his eye for a whole hour; when a member of the family discovered the predicament he was in, and came to his relief.

In this part of Georgia he travelled extensively, visited many places, and ordained quite a number of local preachers. The recommendation of the quarterly meeting and the approbation of the yearly conference for the ordination of local preachers to deacon or elder's orders having been obtained, at this day, they were often ordained in the interim of the annual conferences, as the bishop progressed in his rounds among the people. This was the work that mainly occupied him during the month of December. About the first of January, 1832, he reached Augusta, which was to be the seat of the Georgia Conference.

While waiting here, he rode out one day into the country; and on his return, hearing a loud noise he followed its direction, and soon came to the market-place, where a lot of slaves were being sold at auction. There was a great gathering of the people, and the auction had already commenced. The slaves, of whom there appeared to be a large number, had been the property of a planter lately deceased, and whose estate, after his death, was found to be insolvent. The bishop rode up as near as he could approach in his sulky, and for some time witnessed the scene. Husbands and wives who had grown old together, parents and children, brothers and sisters, were here severed from each other, probably forever. The most affecting scene of all was the separation of a mother from two interesting little children. It was a scene such as his eyes never witnessed before; and it moved his whole soul from its very depths. Just then he saw in the crowd a man from the East, whom he had known in Boston. Motioning to the man, he came up to him, as did also several members of the Church in Augusta who knew the bishop. Pointing to a female who was upon the auctioneer's stand for sale, the bishop said to his friend, "Don't that make your Yankee blood boil?" "*Yes*, SIR!" responded the man, with great emphasis. A few days after, one of the preachers came to the bishop, and told him that his conversation with the gentleman from Boston had been reported, and had occasioned great excitement in the town, and advised him to be careful what he said upon that subject. The bishop did not consider it unwise to follow the counsels of his brother preacher; but he did not hesitate, to the end of his life, to speak of that as one of the most revolting scenes he had ever been called to witness.

The Georgia Conference opened on the 5th of January, and the business proceeded with unusual despatch and harmony. "They were," says the bishop, "a lovely body of men, and many of them able ministers of the New Testament." Among the strong men of the conference at this time were Stephen Olin, then supernumerary, and a professor in Franklin College; James O. Andrew, elected a few months later a bishop in the Church; and George F. Pierce, then in the second year of his ministry, but twenty-two years later elected bishop in the Methodist Episcopal Church, South. The membership of the conference, including coloured, was thirty-one thousand five hundred and seventy-one; and the increase for the year was four thousand and nineteen.

From Augusta Bishop Hedding travelled to Darlington, South Carolina, where he met the South Carolina Conference on the 26th of January. He says of them, "A very agreeable body of preachers,—enterprising, devoted, and true-hearted." From this place he passed on northward to Norfolk, Virginia, where the Virginia Conference assembled, February 23d.

While on his journey through North Carolina, he had occasion to cross the Roanoke River. He was ferried over by a slave who had charge of the ferry-boat. He was a large and noble-looking fellow, and withal exceedingly talkative. No sooner had they left the bank than he began to interrogate his solitary passenger:—"Massa, where you going to?" The bishop said, "I am going to Massachusetts." "Why, massa, so far off from home? Why, massa, where you been?" "O!" said the bishop, "I have been down through Tennessee, and through the Cherokee nation of Indians, and through Georgia and South Carolina." "O, massa, massa! what for could you be away over all that country so far from home for?" "I have been preaching the gospel," said the bishop. "Ah, massa, that be a good business! Now I thought you were a minister, judge, or speculator," (that is, slave-trader.) "Speculators once used to come along dressed like dandies; but they got afraid we negroes would kill them. So now they dress like ministers or judges, so nobody would suspect them to be speculators." The coloured man seemed delighted to discover that the bishop was a real minister, and not a "speculator," —the grand terror of all his race.

The day he crossed the Roanoke he had an instance of hospitality to the *minister*, when the bishop was unknown. That day he travelled along the river for about forty miles, and during the whole route was unable to obtain any food for himself or his horse. Just at night-fall he came to a public-house. He found himself entirely exhausted, and giving his horse in care to the hostler, he made his way with difficulty into the house. The landlord, a very gentlemanly man, observing his condition, asked him if he would not take a glass of brandy and water. The bishop replied that he was a minister, and did not drink brandy.

"You a minister!" said the landlord; "of what denomination?"

"I am a Methodist minister."

"A Methodist minister?" said he; "my wife is half a Methodist."

Then running to the foot of the stairs, he cried out, "Wife! wife! come down quick. Here is a Methodist preacher."

She dropped her work, and came running down stairs as if she were hurrying to meet a father. Then both she and her husband welcomed him to their house; the best room was allotted to him, and the best entertainment that the place afforded provided. Subsequently, when they learned who he was, they expressed the greatest pleasure at seeing him; and by their urgent persuasions, he was induced to remain two or three days with them to recruit his exhausted energies before he resumed his journey.

At Norfolk, Bishop Hedding sold the horse and sulky with which he had made the circuit of almost the entire country, and took public conveyance to Baltimore, where he met the Baltimore Conference, March 14th. From thence he proceeded to Wilmington, Del., and presided over the Philadelphia Conference, which commenced on the 11th of April; then continued his journey to Philadelphia to meet his colleagues preparatory to the General Conference, which was to assemble in that city on the 1st of May.

Thus are we brought to the end of the second quadrennial of the bishop's labours in the episcopal office. Let us take a brief glance at the progress of the work during this period. Taking the summation at the close of this year as the basis of our calculation, and comparing it with the returns four years before, we find that the membership of the Church had gone up from four hundred and twenty-one thousand one hundred and twenty-six to five hundred and forty-eight thousand five hundred and ninety-three, making a total increase of one hundred and twenty-seven thousand four hundred and sixty-seven. During the same period the number of travelling preachers had increased from one thousand six hundred and forty-two to two thousand two hundred, making an increase of five hundred and fifty-eight. In the above membership are included seventy-eight thousand eight hundred and seventeen coloured members, principally in the South, and two thousand four hundred and twelve Indians, connected with the different mission stations.

The educational system of the Church was now receiving an auspicious development. The Wesleyan University had been established at Middletown, Conn., and Dr. Wilbur Fisk, of the New-England Conference, was at its head, and John M. Smith, of the New-York Conference, one of the professors. Madison College—now extinct, but whose place has since been supplied by Alleghany College—had gone into successful operation in Western Pennsylvania; J. H. Fielding had succeed H. B. Bascom as president, and H. J. Clark was one of the professors; both were members of the Pittsburgh Conference. Augusta College had been established under the patronage of the Kentucky and Ohio Conferences; Martin Ruter was president, and H. B. Bascom, J. S. Tomlinson, J. P. Durbin, and Burr H. M'Cown, were professors; all of them members of the Kentucky Conference except J. P. Durbin, who belonged to the Ohio. In the southwest, Lagrange College had been established; Robert Paine was president, and E. D. Simms one of the professors. In Virginia, Randolph Macon College had been established, and M. P. Parks, of the Virginia Conference, was one of its professors, and Stephen Olin was soon after placed at its head. Thus it will be seen that no less than *five* colleges had sprung into existence in an incredibly short time, and were already in successful operation under the supervision of the Church. Several conference seminaries also had been established; such were Cazenovia Seminary, the Maine Wesleyan Seminary, Wilbraham Academy, Genesee Wesleyan Seminary, Shelbyville Female Academy, and others, which were in successful operation in different parts of the Church. These institutions, then in their infancy, have from that time forward exerted a powerful influence in developing the intellectual and moral resources of our people. Up to this time the Methodist Church had been frequently charged with opposition to education; but the true state of the case was, that at first she had everything to do—societies to found, churches to build, her Book Concern to establish, and all the essentials of organized churches to obtain, while at the same time she was, of course, greatly deficient in resources. It was, therefore, natural that the wants first felt, and felt to be most pressing, should receive first attention. To one acquainted with all the circumstances, the wonder will be rather that she so soon and successfully engaged in the work of establishing and endowing seminaries and colleges for the education of her people.

The missionary work had also greatly advanced in the Church. Great good had been accomplished by the missions established in several places for the benefit of the people of colour in the South, and here an interesting and inviting field for missionary enterprise was opened to the Church. The settlement of free coloured persons, effected by the American Colonization Society at Liberia, in Western Africa, had for several years attracted the attention of the missionary board and of the authorities of the Church; but only this year had the way been opened for the establishment of a mission there, and Melville B. Cox, a native of the State of Maine, but at that time a member of the Baltimore Conference, was appointed to superintend it. Mr. Cox was one of the noblest missionaries ever sent into the foreign field; and though his career as a missionary was brief, yet in that short time he laid the broad and sure foundations of a noble work, and his name will forever be associated with Africa's redemption. He died at his post, a martyr to his work, exclaiming, "*Though thousands fall, let not Africa be given up!*" But perhaps the most interesting of the missions then under the care of the Church were those established among the Indians. We have already noticed the Indian missions in Canada. In 1831, when they were transferred to the superintendence of the Wesleyan Conference in England, there were no less than ten mission stations among the various tribes in that country, and one thousand eight hundred and fifty adult Indians under religious instruction, a large proportion of whom were members of the Church. We have also mentioned the introduction of the gospel among the Oneida Indians, and the establishment and progress of the mission among them. Some of this tribe had emigrated to Green Bay, and several of the converted Indians were of the number. When settled, they desired to have a missionary sent out to them, and

Mr. Schoolcraft, who resided there in the capacity of Indian Agent, favoured their wishes. Accordingly the Rev. John Clark was sent out to labour among them. He was not only a man of sterling integrity and purity of character, but he also possessed an indomitable energy and perseverance, and laid the foundations of a work in that region which has not ceased to produce grateful results to the present day. He was the intimate and personal friend of Hedding, and has recently been suddenly called to join him in the land of rest.* The writer witnessed a delightful interview between these two men a short time before the death of Hedding. The mission to the Wyandot Indians had been in successful operation for several years, and now numbered two hundred and forty-eight converted Indians as members. A short time previous, the Rev. J. B. Finley, who had long laboured among them with eminent success, visited the eastern cities in company with several of the converted chiefs, some of whom had become local preachers and class-leaders, and by this means excited a very general interest in behalf of the Indian missions. Equally successful had been the Indian missions in the South, some of which were visited by Bishop Hedding during his last episcopal tour. Among the Choctaws there were one thousand three hundred and twelve Church-members, embracing many of the chief men of the nation. In the Cherokee nation

* He died of an attack of Asiatic cholera, near Chicago, about the middle of July, 1854.

there were seventeen missionaries, including interpreters, and eight hundred and fifty Church-members. Several other Indian missions had been attempted with various success.

During these four years also death had been busily at work. God had been gathering home the ripened fruits to himself. No less than fifty-five preachers had fallen. Bishop George died shouting, "Glory to God!" Samuel Garrard, saying, "I have had my failings and imperfections in common with other men; but my trust is reposed in Christ alone, who died for me—by whose stripes I am healed:" Robert Minshall, exclaiming, "I have been a travelling man, my lot is in heaven. Glory, glory, forever and ever!" William H. Chapman, shouting, "Glory! glory!" Samuel Doughty, testifying, "Death has no terrors:" Thomas Everard, exclaiming, "All is well!" Nathaniel P. Deveraux, repeating,—

"I will not let thee go
Till all I have is lost in thee,
And all renew'd I am:"

John Fisk, when language failed, "making signs to his friends that all was well:" Henry Holmes, saying, "Yesterday I examined myself closely, and I saw my way before me as clearly as the rising sun:" Christopher Thomas, exclaiming, "Perfectly happy; death is my friend; I live in Christ, and Christ is all to me!" (laying his hands upon his breast,) "I have all I desire; Glory, hallelujah!" Simon L. Booker, saying,

"I want a conductor to heaven!" and pausing for a moment, he broke out, "I have one—a sublime one!" Moses Amedon, saying, "Willing, willing, willing!" Coleman Harwell, exclaiming, "Now, Lord, lettest thou thy servant depart in peace!" William M. Smith, crying out, "O death, where is thy sting? O grave, where is thy victory?" Wesley Deskin, shouting, "Victory, victory!" Peter F. Baker, testifying, "I know in whom I have believed:" Edwin Ray, witnessing, "The religion which I have professed and preached has comforted me in life, supported me in affliction, and now enables me to triumph in death;" and Ralph Lawning, exclaiming, "I am happy—praise the Lord!" Of the others, who were rational in their last moments, it is said that they "died in peace—in great peace;" "his end was peaceful and glorious;" "died in the triumphs of faith;" "with a bright prospect of eternal blessedness;" "rejoicing in God his Saviour;" "glorifying God in the patience of hope and the triumph of faith;" "strong in the faith of the gospel, and full of the hope of immortality;" "elevated in holy triumph above the sufferings of disease and the fear of death;" "without fear or alarm, but rejoicing that he had got so near home;" "heavenly light radiated his mind, and eternal glory beamed upon his path;" "died witnessing a good confession before many witnesses," &c., &c. *Let me die the death of the righteous, and let my last end be like his.*

CHAPTER XIV.

THIRD QUADRENNIAL OF EPISCOPAL LABOURS.

General Conference of 1832 — Representation — Character of the Session — Two Bishops elected — Bishop Hedding's Purpose to resign — Action of the New-York and New-England Delegates — He yields to their Judgment — The New-York Conference — Its Division — Law Questions — A Question proposed — New-England Conference — Ravages of the Cholera — Aspect in New-York City — The People rushing from the City — Passage up the Hudson — Reflections — NOTE: Distressing Case of a Widow and her Son — Letter to Bishop Roberts — Oneida Conference — Genesee — Efforts to reach the Canada Conference — Fails — Alarming Symptoms — Reaches Home — State of his Feelings — Statistics of the Year — Presides over the Virginia Conference in 1833 — A Few Days in Washington — Idea of the City — Old Age an Incurable Disease — Conferences attended — A Great Dinner — The Meeting of Old Friends — Prosperity of the Oneida Conference — Completes his Conference Visitation for the Year — Tax upon his Distinction as an Expounder of Ecclesiastical Law — Prosperity of the Church — The Oregon Mission — Educational Interests — Conference Labours for 1834 — Death of two Fellow-labourers — The Labours of a Bishop — Question involving the Administration of Presiding Elders — The Course of Study for Candidates in the Ministry — Action of the Bishops assailed — Letter of Bishop Emory — A Singular Question affecting the Marriage Relation of Slaves — Progress of the Church — Conferences in 1835 — Development of our Ecclesiastical Jurisprudence — Question upon electing Committees on Trials — Death of Bishop M'Kendree — Sudden Death of Bishop Emory — Returns of Members — Incident upon Long Island Sound — Attends the Virginia and Baltimore Conferences — Progress of the Church during the four Preceding Years.

THE General Conference of 1832 was composed of two hundred and twenty-three delegates, representing twenty annual conferences, as follows:—New-York, twenty; New-England, fourteen; Maine, eleven; New-Hampshire and Vermont, eleven; Oneida, twelve; Genesee, six; Pittsburgh, eleven; Ohio, fifteen; Illinois, seven; Holston, eight; Kentucky, thirteen; Missouri, three; Tennessee, thirteen; Mississippi, seven; Georgia, twelve; South Carolina, nine; Virginia, fourteen; Baltimore, seventeen; Philadelphia, eighteen; and Canada, three. The conference was opened in the usual manner, after which the address of the bishops was read. It is a concise, compact business document, congratulating the Church upon the great prosperity of the preceding four years, and upon the passing away of the troubles and dangers which seemed so portentous of evil; and then presenting before the body the various benevolent enterprises and provisionary arrangements that should claim their attention during the session. The business of the conference appears to have proceeded with great harmony and despatch; nor was there any topic that occasioned such excitement and elicited such discussions as had been witnessed in several preceding sessions. The presiding-elder question had been decisively settled, and even the radical controversy, after the withdrawal of most of the leading malcontents, had died away. Even upon the subject of slavery, a spirit of conciliation seemed to prevail; for the South, passing by the man who would have been the favourite candidate for the episcopacy but for his connexion with "the great evil," nominated Rev. James O. Andrew, and he, with the Rev. John Emory, was elected to the office of bishop on the first ballotting,—the former receiving one hundred and forty, and the latter one hundred and thirty-five out of two hundred and twenty-three, the whole number of votes cast.

We have already noticed the unaffected reluctance with which Bishop Hedding consented to enter upon the duties of the episcopal office. He had now continued in the office eight years, and during that time had presided in whole or in part over fifty-two conferences, and had traversed the whole country from Maine in the east to Indiana in the west, and from Canada in the north to Georgia in the south. In this work he had performed severe labour, and endured many hardships; but his success was abundant, and he had been steadily rising in the esteem and confidence of the whole Church. But it appears that from the outset he had been subject to great trials of mind with reference to continuing in the office of bishop. These arose in part from the great difficulties and responsibilities of the work,—particularly that of stationing the preachers; and in part from his humble estimate of his own personal qualifications for the office. These things, in connexion with his bodily afflictions, now made him doubt whether he ought any longer to continue in the office; and indeed he says, "I felt a strong desire to be released from its burdens." He, however, did not feel at liberty to offer his resignation of the office without first consulting his brethren—the delegates of the New-York and the New-England Conferences, by whose efforts he had been elected, and by whom he had been so cordially sustained. Accordingly he called a meeting of these delegates, and laid open his views and wishes fully to them, and told them it would be a great relief to him if they would consent to his resignation. After he had retired they canvassed the matter among themselves, and gave expression to their strong conviction in the following resolution:—

"*Resolved*, That it is the unanimous judgment of the delegates of the New-York and New-England Conferences, that Bishop Hedding ought wholly to relinquish the idea of ever resigning the episcopal office, or of discontinuing the exercise of it at any time, unless under some imperious dispensation of Providence compelling him so to do.

"DANIEL OSTRANDER, *Chairman*.
"W. FISK, *Secretary*."

"PHILADELPHIA,
May 8, 1832."

The leading brethren of these delegations also conversed with him privately, and gave their reasons in detail for objecting to his resignation. They were such as he could not resist, but at the same time such as often made him feel a crushing sense of his responsibility. Under the constraining influence of this advice, he yielded to the convictions of his brethren and the universal wish of the Church, and continued with unabated zeal and fidelity to exercise the episcopal functions till disabled by age and failing health.

Mrs. Hedding joined her husband, whom she had not seen for eleven months, at Philadelphia. After the adjournment of the General Conference they journeyed, in company with Bishop Roberts, to New-York city, where the New-York Conference commenced its session on the 6th of June. Remarkable prosperity had been enjoyed within the bounds of this conference during the year, and an increase of seven thousand seven hundred and ninety-eight was reported, making a total membership of forty-seven thousand and eighty-six. The General Conference had just provided for its division, and that division was to be carried into effect at this session. This rendered it a session of great importance and responsibility. The stations of the preachers would determine whether they should continue their ecclesiastical relation to the New-York Conference, or be included in the Troy Conference, now to be organized. The milder climate and peculiar facilities of the southern division, and also the local connexions, with many of the preachers, rendered it an object of great interest to fall into that section of the work. Under these circumstances, to fix all the appointments so as to secure the great interests of the work and satisfy the people, and at the same time to meet the wishes of the preachers, was a task not often encountered even in episcopal experience. Bishop Roberts being a comparative stranger, the duty of adjusting these questions fell mainly upon Bishop Hedding. With a patience that seemed to know no exhaustion he listened to every application, and carefully weighed the arguments by which each was enforced; and rarely failed either to grant the request, or to satisfy the brother making it that it could not be granted without injury to the work. By this means the appointments were finally so arranged as to give almost universal satisfaction. About eighteen thousand five hundred members and ninety-two preachers were thus set off into the Troy Conference.

Some years later than this, it was provided in the Discipline that the bishops presiding in an annual conference should be the official judges of questions of law. But at this time, and even earlier, it had become quite common for annual conferences to submit such questions to them for their opinion. Bishop Hedding had already acquired a reputation for his sound and able judgment in all questions touching the constitution and law of the Church; and whenever he presided, it had come to be quite common for the conference to ask his opinion on any such question in respect to which differences of opinion had arisen, or diversity of administration had taken place. At this conference a great debate arose on a law question. A local preacher had been expelled by a quarterly conference, and he appealed to the annual conference, not on the ground of injustice in the decision, but of illegality in the proceedings against him. The illegality he alleged was, that prior to the quarterly conference which expelled him, and preparatory to his trial by that conference, he had been arrested, examined, and suspended by an illegal court—the committee in the case being constituted of two local preachers and one class-leader; whereas he alleged it should have consisted exclusively of local preachers. The members of the annual conference were divided in opinion; some believed the trial was illegal, and others believed it was not. As it was a law question, a motion was made to refer it to the bishops. Bishop Roberts declined having anything to do with it. Bishop Hedding said he would decide the question, provided they would agree to abide by his decision and have no debate about it afterward; but he would not decide it otherwise. On these conditions the conference submitted it to his judgment. He decided that the court which suspended the local preacher was illegal, as alleged; that, in fact, he was not suspended, but went to the quarterly meeting under charges the same as if no previous step had been taken. The quarterly conference had original jurisdiction in the case. They tried and expelled him; and as he had not appealed on the ground of injustice in the decision of the quarterly conference, but only on the ground of illegality in the court that suspended him, he was legally expelled. His appeal therefore cannot lie, and the case is dismissed.

The New-England Conference commenced its session June 15th, at Providence, Rhode Island. Bishops Roberts and Hedding were both present. The conference statistics exhibited a good degree of prosperity, the increase being two thousand four hundred and nine. The total number of members was fifteen thousand five hundred and forty-six, and the number of preachers one hundred and twenty-nine. The exciting scenes of polemic disputation and of bitter opposition experienced while Methodism was first invading this territory had died away, and the sons were now carefully and wisely cultivating the ground which had been first taken possession of by their pioneer fathers. During the session of the conference, the alarming intelligence reached the place that the Asiatic Cholera had broken out in New-York and other cities, and was making frightful ravages. The news created a profound impression, and elicited much and earnest prayer; but the preachers seemed universally determined to stand at their posts, and commit themselves to God.

Bishop Hedding was now within about fifty miles of his home, from which he had been absent—with the exception of a single visit of three or four days—about sixteen months. But he was not even now permitted to visit it; for his duties required him immediately at the close of the conference to turn his face in another direction. He returned to New-York on his way to the northern conferences. In the city he spent only an hour; but this was enough to reveal to him something of the horrors of the scene witnessed there. The people were flying in every direction to escape the dreaded pestilence; men, women, and children were dying every hour, and that too, for the most part, with a transition from health to death as sudden as it was painful; gloom and comparative stillness pervaded the city, and the symbols of death were seen in every direction. Even on board the boat, some of the fugitives who were endeavouring to escape from the pestilence God had sent upon the land were stricken down, and the bitter cry of despairing agony broke the stillness that otherwise prevailed; for no one seemed disposed to conversation, and the necessary communications were made in suppressed and almost inaudible tones. Bishop Hedding felt that it was a time for the trial of his faith: he was travelling alone; was among strangers, each one of whom seemed intent only upon his own safety; he might die, and be shuffled into the earth; and in the haste and confusion no one ever ascertain his name, or apprize his friends of his death.*

*Such things actually occurred in repeated instances. One I will relate. A widow with her only son, a lad of ten or twelve years, started from the city on one of the over-crowded steamboats for one of the Hudson River villages, intending to find a place of refuge with an uncle back in the country. The passage up the river was made under the greatest excitement, as several of the passengers were smitten down with the pestilence, and a number died. The village was reached, and a large number of passengers were landed; but so frightful were the ravages of the disease among them, that many died before they reached their place of refuge, and were hurried beneath the sod. The little boy's mother complained of being unwell before landing, and when landed found herself unable to walk, and to procure a conveyance was impossible. She then directed her son to travel as fast as possible to the uncle's, and return with a conveyance. It was not till the next morning that he could return, and then no traces of his mother could be found. Several had died, and been buried; but the burial had been roughly and hastily done, just when the victim happened to breathe his last, and by whomsoever happened to be near, and to possess the courage necessary to perform the work. That lad, when he had grown up to man's es-

But in this hour of trial he committed his all to God; and felt great peace in the assurance that if his Heavenly Father had further need of his services he could protect and preserve him from all the dangers that beset his path. When he reached Albany, he found that city also in the greatest consternation from the same cause. His own mind, however, was calm and collected. He rested quietly through the night, and in the morning left for Utica by a canal packet-boat. All along the line of the canal, and at Utica, he witnessed the ravages of the same frightful disease.

A beautifully appropriate letter was written by Mrs. Hedding about this time to Bishop Roberts. From it the following extracts are drawn: "Since I saw you my health has been every day improving. I received a letter from Mr. Hedding, dated July 12th. He had not then decided about going to Upper Canada. He will write again soon. He is surrounded by the mortal pestilence, and whichever way he turns must face it; yet I believe God will preserve him.

"As for myself, I had more anxiety to know that my soul was fitted for heaven than usual; for I know that this mortal body must, ere long, return to its

tate, told me that the uncertainty which hung over the fate of his mother still occasioned him the most excruciating anguish; and that he had spent weeks, if not months, around the spot where he parted from her, and along the entire road leading to his uncle's, seeking from every man, woman, and child along the line some little token that might serve as a clue to the painful mystery. None was ever found.

mother earth. The Church fast was a blessing to me. The Lord is my portion. I am happy when in the Sabbath school. Blessed be the name of the Lord! May our good God prosper you on your way! Give my love to Mrs. Roberts, of whom I often think. Pray for me."

On his way to the Oneida Conference, Bishop Hedding visited the Indian mission, and was highly gratified at the permanent and progressive character of the work among these poor natives. The conference assembled at Manlius, July 12th. It had been a year of almost unprecedented religious prosperity. An increase of three thousand seven hundred and forty was reported, making a total membership of thirty-one thousand five hundred and sixty. Nor was this all. There had been a great and manifest increase of the work of God in the hearts of the preachers, many of whom came forward and told what great things God had done for *them*, as well as for their flocks, during the year. A deep devotional feeling pervaded the entire conference, and it was a session of unusual religious interest. God had not only given to his servants a good increase for their labours, but was preparing them for still greater things.

From Manlius he proceeded to Penn Yan, where he met the Genesee Conference on the 26th of July. He had engaged also to attend the session of the Canada Conference, and ordain the preachers who might be elected to orders. For this purpose he proceeded to Oswego, designing to cross the lake into

Canada. But here he found all communication broken off, in consequence of the ravages of the cholera. Unwilling to be foiled in the discharge of his duty, he took the stage for Watertown, intending to cross the St. Lawrence just below that place, and thus accomplish the object of his mission. On the 7th of August he reported himself, in a letter to his wife, as being twenty-five miles from the place where he expected to be able to cross the St. Lawrence, and eighty miles from the seat of the conference, which was to commence its session the next day; yet he expected to reach it before the Sabbath. But as he advanced he found the ravages of the cholera more frightful, and all the usual modes of communication broken up, or rendered so irregular that no reliance could be placed upon them. Under these circumstances he was induced to give over the effort, and turn his face homeward. The day after he started from Watertown he was seized with symptoms of cholera—an exhausting diarrhœa, with cold feet and legs up to his knees. Yet he continued his journey, stopping a day or two to recruit when he had become entirely exhausted. In this plight he travelled through northern New-York, crossed Vermont and New-Hampshire into Massachusetts, and at length reached Lynn. Then followed a long season of sickness and exhaustion, from which he had only partially recovered when summoned again from his home by the episcopal duties of the succeeding year.

The record of his feelings and views at this period

possesses a peculiar interest. "I have been led," says he, "to many serious and solemn reflections—apprehending that probably my public labours, if not my life, may be nearly at an end. But I thank my God that through the merit of my Lord and Saviour Jesus Christ I am supported with a glorious hope of rest in heaven! I have been comforted also with the reflection that my life has been spent, and my body worn out, in endeavouring sincerely, though imperfectly, to promote the cause of Christ; and after thirty-two years' employment in preaching the doctrines of the Methodist Episcopal Church, I am confirmed in the belief that they are the doctrines of Christ. And after seeing, for that length of time, the effects of our plan of spreading the gospel, and governing the flock committed to our care, and bearing my full share of the burdens and privations connected with this plan, I am satisfied it is the best I know of in this world for the benefit of the souls of men. If I could have another life, I would cheerfully spend it in this blessed cause."

The Church had been favoured with blessed prosperity during this year. Only two conferences, namely, Kentucky and Tennessee, had reported a decrease, the former amounting to one thousand five hundred and seventy-nine, and the latter to one hundred and seventy-six. On the other hand, several of the conferences reported a large increase—the New-York, seven thousand seven hundred and ninety-eight; the Ohio, four thousand two hundred and twenty-three; the Georgia, four thousand and nineteen; the Oneida, three thousand seven hundred and forty; the Illinois, three thousand two hundred and thirty; and others not as large. The aggregate of membership was now five hundred and forty-eight thousand five hundred and ninety-three, making an increase for the year of thirty-five thousand four hundred and seventy. The aggregate of travelling preachers was two thousand two hundred; increase, one hundred and ninety. Within the bounds of the New-York and the Oneida Conferences especially, there had been very extensive revivals. The ravages of that terrible scourge, the Asiatic cholera, instead of interrupting the progress of these revivals, seemed to deepen the religious interest, and was instrumental in bringing hundreds, if not thousands, of the thoughtless and wicked to deep concern for the salvation of their souls. Thus judgment and mercy were blended together.

On the 5th of February, with his health only imperfectly restored, Bishop Hedding left his home to enter upon the episcopal duties of the year. He reached Petersburgh, Virginia, on the 26th, and the next day opened the Virginia Conference. He was here assisted by Bishop Emory. After its close he returned to Baltimore, by the way of Norfolk and Washington, and met the Baltimore Conference on the 27th of March. At Washington City he rested a few days at the house of Dr. Sewall—a name of precious memory in the Methodist Church. The only thing that seemed to mar his comfort, was the number of "burdensome dinners and teas" to which his friends in the kindness of their hearts subjected him. "This city," says he, in a letter to his wife, "is the seat of fashion and folly. Here great speeches are made, and here great weakness and foolishness are exhibited. Here great talent, some wisdom, a little virtue, and great and glaring corruptions, are brought together from all parts of the nation." In a subsequent part of his letter, referring to his health, he says, "It has been gradually improving since I left home, but I am not yet as well as I was a year ago. I am getting what Dr. Clarke calls an incurable disease—that is, *old age*. I am daily reminded that I am hastening to my long home. It seems but a few days since I was a boy, and now I am an old man, just ready to drop into the grave. What a poor thing is human life! a dream, a shadow! But there is hope beyond the grave—hope of eternal life! Let us cleave to that hope, and hope on unto the end."

The session of the Baltimore Conference was quite protracted and laborious, owing to several trials, some of which were complicated, and consumed a good deal of time. Great success had attended the labours of the preachers, and an increase of five thousand two hundred and forty-nine was reported, making the total membership in the conference forty-nine thousand two hundred and thirty-nine. From Baltimore he proceeded to Newark, N. J., where he met the Philadelphia Conference on the 17th of April. The session of this conference was a season of unusual religious interest. Both preachers and people seemed to realize the presence and power of God in an unusual degree. Here also the large increase of six thousand and twenty-six was reported, making a total membership of fifty-five thousand and seventy-one. Philadelphia was now the largest conference in the Church. At Poughkeepsie, Bishop Hedding met the New-York Conference on the 8th of May; on the 7th of June following, the New-England Conference at Boston; and on the 3d of July, the Maine Conference at Bath.

An incident worthy of record occurred during the session of the conference at Bath. A prominent citizen of the place, an ex-governor of the state, made a great dinner, and invited nearly all the members of the conference, and also many prominent laymen. The tables were loaded with the choicest luxuries of the day, among which the wine-bottles that were scattered over them made a prominent figure. The gentleman took his seat at the end of one of the tables, and placed the bishop by the side of his lady at the end of another. After they had been seated a short time, their host rose, and turning to the bishop—at the same time filling his wine-glass—said, "Bishop, give me the pleasure to drink a glass of wine with you." The bishop, with his usual frankness and readiness, but with much decision, replied, "I pray you will excuse me, sir; I never drink wine except at the sacrament, or as a medicine." The gentleman, somewhat confused, then turned and solicited the whole company to drink with him; but not a single preacher, and only one or two laymen, touched the cup. Temperance principles had already begun to work powerfully among the people, and in that movement, as well as in all other philanthropic and benevolent enterprises, the preachers were leading the way both by precept and example. The liberal host, who thought to regale them with wine, as well as to feast them with food, was either not well posted up in the character of the temperance movement, or he thought, by betraying the preachers into indulgence in wine, to throw contempt upon the incipient reformation, and paralyze their moral power in the cause. If the blunder resulted from ignorance of the temperance movement, the politician got some light upon the subject; if through mischievous design, he met with a severe and just rebuke.

The next conference met by the bishop was the New-Hampshire, at Northfield, July 18th. Here he met many old friends not only among the preachers, but also among the laity. Many who had nobly stood by him nearly thirty years before, during the six years of his early toil in this region, now came miles to take him by the hand, and mingle their rejoicings with his at the prosperity of the cause of God, and over the glorious prospect of a re-union in the better land. The sight of these old veterans of the cross, some of them his old spiritual children, deeply affected the heart of the bishop, as they vividly called up the toils and trials of those early days. "Verily," said he, "it is bread gathered after many days. God has showed me that I did not labour in vain. How great is his mercy in blessing labours so feeble, and making them so fruitful. Those labours were often crossing to the flesh, and I sometimes almost repined as though mine was a hard lot. But O! if I were young again, and could buckle on the armour afresh, how would I rejoice to endure even greater hardships and to perform even harder labours, if I might be instrumental in accomplishing like results."

Soon after the session of this conference, he proceeded to Granville, N. Y., where he preached the dedication sermon in a new church which had been erected in that place. He also met the Troy Conference, in the city of Troy, on the 28th of August. Then he journeyed west, visiting again the Oneida Indian mission, and meeting the Oneida Conference at Cazenovia on the 25th of September. Another year of remarkable prosperity had been enjoyed within the bounds of this conference—the increase for the year being five thousand six hundred and twenty-seven. This conference first appears upon the Minutes, in 1829, with nineteen thousand three hundren and twenty members, and one hundred and ten travelling preachers. This was, therefore, its fifth session, and it now presented an aggregate of thirty-seven thousand one hundred and eighty-seven members, and one hundred and sixty-six travelling preachers—being an increase in five years of seventeen thousand eight hundred and sixty-seven members and fifty-six preachers. It was now the sixth conference in point of numbers.

From Cazenovia Bishop Hedding travelled to West Mendon, where he met the Genesee Conference on the 16th of October. After this he had several engagements, which so occupied him on his return home that he did not reach Lynn till the 10th of December. His episcopal tours and labours had occupied him between ten and eleven months this year. He had attended ten conferences, and, with one exception, had presided in all without the aid of any other bishop. Yet his health had greatly improved from what it was the preceding year, and God had greatly sustained and blessed him in his labours.

Bishop Hedding had already attained an enviable distinction as an able expounder of ecclesiastical law; but this honour was not worn without a heavy compensation, demanded in the form of solutions of law questions. These were propounded to him from all parts of the work, but more especially from the northern conferences; consequently, when he reached home he found a frightful accumulation of letters requiring answers. Many of these propounded grave and intricate questions, which required serious reflection and elaborate answers. Much of his time during the present winter was devoted to this private, but responsible and laborious, portion of the duties of a bishop in the Methodist Episcopal Church.

The Church had enjoyed another year of great

prosperity. The excitements and agitations growing out of the radical controversy had died away, so that the Church, enjoying peace within, had been left to turn all her forces against the powers of the kingdom of darkness without. The result was an increase of fifty-one thousand one hundred and forty-three, making the total membership five hundred and ninety-nine thousand seven hundred and thirty-six. The greatest increase in any one conference was in the Ohio, where it was six thousand five hundred and eighty-one. The total number of travelling preachers was two thousand four hundred; increase, two hundred. All the other interests of the Church had advanced in due proportion. The missionary work was progressing with uncommon interest. New missions had been established in destitute portions of the home work in different parts of the country; also several new missions among the Indians, and several for the benefit of the slaves in different parts of the South. During this year, also, Messrs. Rufus Spaulding and Samuel O. Wright, and their wives, together with Miss Sophronia Farrington, were appointed to the missionary work in Liberia, and sailed to carry forward, if it were the will of God, the work so nobly commenced by the martyred Cox. These appointments occasioned Bishop Hedding a great amount of anxiety, and he felt much solicitude about the result. The missionary cause had also received an additional impulse this year from the visit of four Flat-head Indians from beyond the Rocky Mountains, who had come as a delegation from their tribe, nearly three thousand miles, that they might obtain some knowledge of the true God, and the better forms of worship. In answer to the stirring appeals of Dr. Fisk, funds were soon raised; and two hardy and enterprising men, Jason and Daniel Lee, were appointed to the missionary work among the Indians in Oregon.

In the educational department the Church had done well this year. Two colleges—*Dickinson* and *Alleghany*—were added to the list: Rev. J. P. Durbin was appointed president of the former, and Rev. Martin Ruter, D. D., to the presidency of the latter. The Genesee Wesleyan Seminary was also established during this year, and commenced its operations under the most favourable auspices. Rev. Samuel Luckey, D. D., was elected principal. Bishop Hedding felt a deep interest in the establishment of these institutions; for no man in that day saw more clearly, or felt more deeply, the necessity of providing for the education of our own people. "Little did I think," said he, "thirty years ago, that I should live to see the day when the Methodist Episcopal Church would have her seminaries and her colleges in every part of the land, and when she would number more than half a million of communicants. Had any one predicted this when I first entered the work as a travelling minister, I would have thought him mad. Verily God has done great things for us. He has made a *great* people out of us who were no people. How great is our responsibility to the people, to the nation, and to the world! If we preserve the form of sound doctrine among us; if we preserve the simplicity of our manners, the fire and purity of our zeal, and the integrity of our institutions, Methodism will yet bless not only our own country but the whole earth. Who could have predicted that God would have accomplished such wonders by the instrumentality of Methodism! and who can tell what wonders he will yet accomplish by it in the earth!"

After a few months' rest he left home to resume his episcopal labours, on the 3d of April, 1834. This year he attended the following conferences, namely: Philadelphia, at Philadelphia, April 9th; New-York, at New-Haven, Connecticut, May 7th; New-England, at Webster, Massachusetts, June 4th; Maine, at Gardiner, July 3d; New-Hampshire, at West Windsor, Vermont, August 6th; Troy, at Plattsburgh, August 27th; Oneida, at Auburn, September 25th; Genesee, at Brockport, October 15th. He returned to Lynn the last of November, where he enjoyed a longer respite from conference labours than he had before been favoured with since his election to the episcopal office.

While at the Philadelphia Conference he says: "My heart was much affected by the remembrance of two of my old and intimate friends, who had died within the past year, Rev. Thomas F. Sargent and Rev. Joseph L. Inglis. They were talented, lovely, and heavenly-minded men."

After the session of the Maine Conference this year

he spent a short time at home, endeavouring, as he said, "to recruit both body and spirit from the exhaustion they had suffered." "Few persons," says he at this time, "can have any idea of the labour of body and mind the president of an annual conference has to go through at one of its sessions. At the Maine Conference I was closely confined to business, early and late, for nine days. Most of the time the weather was extremely hot and enfeebling. I presided on one trial eight and a half hours, without any intermission; and now, though ten days have passed since the conference closed, I am not yet recovered from my exhaustion. I do not yet feel like myself; a sense of fatigue hangs upon me. O, may I be prepared to rest in heaven, when my body shall rest from these journeys and labours, and my mind from these cares and anxieties!"

At the Oneida Conference a law question was presented for his decision, involving a point which, since the usage and the law of the Church had become so clearly defined, it is surprising could ever have been a matter of doubt. It involved the administration of two presiding elders, both of them leading men in the conference. The case was this. These two presiding elders, in the interim of the conference, and without obtaining the sanction of or even consulting a bishop, had changed men from one district to another. This had been the occasion of great dissatisfaction both among the preachers and some of the laymen. The question was raised whether a presiding elder had authority to make changes that would transfer a man beyond the bounds of his district. The bishop decided that the presiding elders had no authority to make such changes; and if they attempted to make them without authority, the preachers were under no obligation to submit to them. This prompt decision, which was acquiesced in on the part of all concerned, effectually cured an evil which had sprung up, and which, but for this timely check, might have been productive of the most serious consequences.

As early as 1816, the General Conference requested the bishops to prescribe a course of study for the candidates in the ministry. This was done; but the course was too limited, and the examinations too superficial, to meet for any great length of time the increasing demands for intellectual culture in their ministers on the part of the people. Bishop Hedding, with his keen, natural sagacity, had not been slow to discover this fact; and for several years it had occupied his mind with increasing force of conviction. At the Philadelphia Conference in 1833, Bishops Hedding and Emory prepared a special two years' course of study for the candidates for deacon's orders. It was unanimously adopted by the conference, and examining committees appointed to conduct the examination.* The same course was adopted by the Mississippi Conference; and, by their request, divided by Bishop Emory so as to extend

* This Course may be found in the Christian Advocate and Journal, May 10, 1833.

through four years, thus prescribing studies for the candidates for elder's orders as well as deacon's. This plan was adopted in course by other conferences till it became general, and received the sanction of all the bishops. The General Conference had directed the bishops to prescribe studies for the candidates for deacons' orders only, and beyond this they did not claim or exercise authority; but as the whole broad power of judgment, as to fitness or qualification, for the elder's office, and also of election to it, had been vested in the annual conferences, they judged the prescribing of such a course as being clearly within the legitimate functions of an annual conference, and it therefore had their hearty coöperation.

It would seem that the bishops here were acting within the most unquestioned limits of their authority; yet their course was subjected to not only strange misrepresentations, but the most virulent opposition, which degenerated into grave personalities in relation to Bishop Emory. A writer in the Christian Advocate and Journal, signing himself "Proficio," was the principal, and, in fact, almost the only assailant in the case.

After speaking of the good effect of putting candidates upon a two years' course, and subjecting them to a rigid examination, he adds: "I have thought also, that were a course of study prescribed for the *third*, and even fourth year, it would not be amiss; but as the General Conference has not provided for this, an annual conference, and much less an examining committee, has no authority to require it, and surely not as an indispensable condition of their reception to the office of elders. But as improvement is the order of the day, at some future time this may be provided for by those concerned. As, however, there are not many individuals bold enough to 'assume the responsibility' of acting above and without law, the limitation to two years of this mental discipline must be observed until the General Conference shall direct." This, of course, directly impugned the administration of the bishops, and especially of Bishop Emory, as well as the action of the conferences which had adopted the *four* years' course —representing it to be "above and without law." Bishop Emory replied, explaining and vindicating the action of the episcopacy and of the conferences in a calm and temperate manner. The editor contradicts this article with a sort of editorial vindication of "Proficio," whom, oddly enough, he calls "our correspondent," and informs him that the columns of the paper will be open to his use, "provided he writes in temperate and respectful language." This reply appeared in the following number, the signature "Proficio" having been dropped, and that of "A Member of the New-York Conference" assumed. In the end it turned out that "Proficio" and "our correspondent" were one and the same as the senior editor.

Bishop Hedding did not feel himself necessitated to make any public defence personally. First, because the insinuation about acting "without and above law" seemed more particularly aimed at Bishop Emory; then, also, he considered that the defence of their administration and of the conferences was in good hands; nor was he unwilling to leave the matter to be adjudged by the good sense of the Church, and especially by the proper constituted authorities. The following extract from a letter from Bishop Emory to Bishop Hedding, bearing the date of October 25, 1834, will throw some light upon this subject. He says:—"You have probably seen some communications from me in the Christian Advocate and Journal in defence of the third and fourth years' course of study for candidates for elder's orders, and how they have been treated. If there was anything in the matter or spirit of my articles to justify or require such rude personalities as have been heaped on me, I am unconscious of it, and certainly aimed to write otherwise. My last communication, too, was accompanied by a private note, assuring the editor that I was actuated by no personal unkindness, and proposing, if my communication should not be satisfactory, that we would agree on some short article to conclude with *in mutual respect.* The notes in the same paper with my article were the only answer I received. That a bishop degrades himself, and divests himself of the episcopal character, by defending publicly, in a grave and respectful discussion, any important measure of his administration, is to me a new doctrine, and I think a dangerous one. On the contrary, it is my opinion that, as general superintendents, we have a right, whenever we think the interests of the Church require it, to speak through the columns of the Advocate as our official organ; and, if we even be thought in error, the Advocate is not the proper medium for our correction. As to any personal attack on the senior editor, I certainly never intended any such thing, and thought, and still think, I said enough to assure him of that. If he had at any time disavowed intending to censure *the measure* adopted by the conferences with our sanction, it would have been sufficient; but this has never been done—even to this day. On the contrary, it has been averred that *the Advocate is against it*, which I think a perversion of the design of that paper. I consider the measure as now sanctioned, not only by at least eight conferences, but by *all* the acting bishops. A similar course was adopted by the Pittsburgh Conference in 1833, under Bishop Roberts's administration, and in 1834 under Bishop Soule's."

Unpleasant as was the opposition to the introduction of the four years' course of study—an opposition rendered more unpleasant in consequence of the source from which it originated, and the spirit in which it was manifested—it could not but have been gratifying to all the friends of sound ministerial education to know that the measure won its way among the conferences, and finally became the established policy of the Church by authority of the General Conference.

In the same letter from which the above extract was taken, Bishop Emory solicits the opinion of Bishop Hedding on a question singular enough—growing out of the peculiar relations of the system of slavery to the Church in the South. "The South Carolina Conference," says he, "requests the opinion of the bishops on the following question. I will preface it by stating that in Charleston the usage—sanctioned, as I am informed, by Bishop Asbury—has been, that when slaves have been admitted into the Church, the husband and wife then acknowledged by them is ever after to be so considered. But if the master send either away for life to such a distance that there is no reason to expect a return, then if, after a year or more, the bereaved husband or wife apply for permission to take another husband or wife, he or she may be permitted, not advised, so to do. If afterward the former husband or wife returns, the Church never interferes in the question who shall be the acknowledged husband or wife. You are aware, too, that among slaves in the South—such is my information at least as to the South Carolina Conference, although it is not exactly so in Maryland—the ceremony of marriage strictly is rarely performed; but the parties take each other with the permission of their masters and the knowledge of their friends. The question, then, is,—Suppose a wicked husband, clearly without just cause, deserts his wife—she being a member of the Church—and notoriously lives with another woman; or a wicked wife deserts her husband—he being a member of our Church—and notoriously lives with another man; may the deserted, after years of patient waiting, be permitted, on application, to take another husband or wife, as the case may be? The present usage applies only to cases in which the *master's* act causes the separation. The question now submitted is as to the propriety or expediency of the extension of the usage to any cases of separation by the acts of the parties. Among our brethren in the South, there are advocates for and against the extension, and the opinion of the bishops is required to settle it. You are aware that the decision will apply to similar cases in all the slave-holding states. Please let me know your judgment as early as convenient, that I may communicate it to the conference."

What Bishop Hedding's judgment in the matter was we have no means at hand to enable us to determine, nor are we curious to know. We give the item as a matter of historical interest, illustrating one phase of the relations of slavery to Christianity.

During this year the Church had not only enjoyed great peace, but great prosperity. The Pittsburgh Conference reported an increase of five thousand seven hundred and seventy; the Ohio, seven thousand three hundred and eighty; the Kentucky, four thousand six hundred and thirty-three; the Illinois, three thousand one hundred and three; the Indiana, three thousand five hundred and eighty-two; the Tennessee, five thousand one hundred and ten; the Alabama, two thousand eight hundred and seventy-nine; the Baltimore, three thousand two hundred and nine; the Oneida, two thousand five hundred and ten: and the general increase for the year in the whole Church was thirty-thousand and forty-eight in the membership, and two hundred and twenty-five in the ministry—making the number of members six hundred and thirty-eighty thousand seven hundred and eighty-four, and the number of traveling preachers two thousand six hundred and twenty-five. The cause of education in the Church was also strengthened this year by the establishment of M'Kendree College at Lebanon, Illinois; and also by the addition of several academies in different parts of the work. The publishing interests in New-York, and also at the branch in Cincinnati, had continued to rapidly develop the vast resources of their power.

In 1835, Bishop Hedding met the New-York, New-England, and Troy Conferences in company with Bishop Emory. During the session of the latter conference at Albany he visited Troy, and preached the dedication sermon of the North-Second-street Church, then newly erected. To Bishop Emory also had been assigned the Oneida and Genesee Conferences; but owing to sickness in his family he was compelled to return home, and Bishop Hedding visited those conferences in his stead. The first of these conferences he met at Oswego, September 24th; the last at Lockport, October 14th. He reached home in November, where he remained till the ensuing January. While at Oswego his health became quite poor, so much so that he was unable to preach; nor did he fully recover till some time after he had reached home.

The gradual development of our system of ecclesiastical jurisprudence may be frequently indicated by incidental occurrences, especially by law questions that came up for discussion and settlement. A question of this character, and one which even now is of general interest to the Church, came up at the session of the Oneida Conference this year. A preacher was charged with neglect of duty, or perhaps maladministration, in that he did not himself appoint the "select number" to try a member in a case of Church trial, but left it to the society to elect the committee. The preacher impleaded, in his defence took the position that he had a right to leave it to the society to elect, inasmuch as the rule does not say who shall do it. The accusers contended that the principles of the Discipline required that the preacher should select the number, and not leave it to the society, and thereby make it a matter of strife. They alleged that it was dangerous to make such a committee elective; because, if this were done, rich men, officious men, and leaders of parties would be likely to secure the election of such persons as would serve their own purposes, and thus the innocent might be condemned or the guilty be cleared. The conference finally referred it as a question of law to the bishop. He at once decided that it was the duty of the preacher in charge always to appoint the "select number" to try accused members. Among the reasons he offered to justify this opinion were, that formerly the preacher was the sole judge in the case, and decided on the guilt or innocence of accused members; but he was always obliged to hold a trial, not in secret, but in the presence of the society to which the accused person belonged, or a select number of them. But the preacher was judge both of law and evidence, and it belonged to him to decide whether he would hold the trial in the presence of the whole society, or of a select number. When the General Conference changed the rule, they took from the preacher nothing but the power to decide on the guilt or innocence of the accused, and placed that power in the hands of the society, or a select number of them. Consequently they left with the preacher all the other powers he had before, and they remain with him still, and no such select number now can be legally appointed but by the preacher in charge; and if in any case he allows the society to elect, that election can be regarded only as a nomination. And if a preacher proceeds to investigate a case, and try an accused member by the decision of such a select number, by that act he appoints those the society has thus nominated, and is responsible for it; and if any mischief is done through the appointment of improper members, the preacher in charge must answer for it. This decision settled the question; "and," says the bishop, "I never afterward heard of a preacher in that conference allowing the society to elect the select number."

The great and afflictive events in the history of the Church this year were the death of two of the bishops. Bishop M'Kendree, the senior in office, was first called away; and then Bishop Emory, the junior in office, about nine months after was stricken down by death. The former was in the seventy-eighth, the latter in the forty-eighth year of his age. Bishop M'Kendree entered the ministry at the age of thirty, laboured some twenty-one years before his election to the episcopal office, and in that office served the Church almost twenty-seven years. He had been tottering on the borders of the grave for several years, and his death was therefore not unexpected. Bishop Emory was born the same year M'Kendree entered the ministry—1788. He entered the ministry in 1810, and was elected to the episcopal office in 1832. In his arduous and successful labours he was suddenly cut short,—being thrown from his carriage on the 16th of December, 1835, and receiving such a severe injury in his head that he was insensible when found, and died on the evening of the same day. Only six days before this fatal catastrophe he wrote a letter to Bishop Hedding, asking his counsel in some difficult matters, and exhibiting some of his plans for personal usefulness, and especially for advancing the great interests of the Church.

The statistics of the Church this year show an aggregate membership of six hundred and fifty-two thousand five hundred and twenty-eight, increase thirteen thousand seven hundred and forty-four;

number of travelling ministers two thousand seven hundred and fifty-eight, increase one hundred and thirty-three.

On account of the death of Bishop Emory, Bishop Hedding was called to preside over the Virginia Conference, which met at Norfolk, February 10th. Some of the incidents of his journey are thus given:—"I took stage from home and went to Providence, Rhode Island; there I expected to find a steamboat for New-York; but Providence harbour being frozen up, I continued on by stage to New-London, Connecticut. There I found a steamboat bound for New-York. We started about sunset, with a violent north-east wind. About dark it began to snow, as powerfully as I ever saw it. In a short time no object was to be seen—neither land nor lights. I went to the pilot, with whom I was acquainted, and said, 'Howard, what are you going to do? you can neither see land nor lights. There are many rocks and islands along the bay, and are you going to keep on toward New-York in this gale?' He said: 'I am going to guess, as nigh as I can, when we are off the mouth of Connecticut River. If we happen to hit the mouth of the river we may get in safe; but if we go one side or the other of the mouth of the river, we shall be likely to be dashed in pieces.' I wrapped myself in my great-coat and tied on my hat, and went upon deck; for I thought if we went to the bottom, or were broken in pieces, I would rather be on the deck than in the cabin. There I continued, the wind howling, and the snow falling, and we could see no object beyond the vessel. We went on. After a while I perceived by the wind that the vessel was turning her course; and also, by the wind appearing to abate, I perceived that we were getting under the land. They began to sound, and proceed more slowly; and the first the captain, or the mate, or myself, knew where we were, the bow of the boat struck something hard, and stopped. They got a light forward, and found that we had struck a pier at Saybrook; but we could see no object beyond the steamboat. In a short time a pilot came on board, puffing and blowing, and said he was awakened a few minutes before, and told that a Providence steamboat had come into the harbour and stove all to pieces, and he had come down to see what the matter was, and, if he could, to afford relief. The captain told him that it was not the Providence, but the New-London boat, and that we had received no damage. Here we lay till morning; and, when daylight appeared, there were vessels, and houses, and stores within a few rods of us. The next morning the snow had ceased, the weather had become warmer, and a dense fog covered the land and water. We proceeded very slowly, sounding and feeling our way along during the whole day, and at night had only reached Cowbay. Here we anchored for the night. The next morning the fog had cleared away, and we went on to New-York. I felt thankful that out of such great danger the hand of my good Father had brought me safely. From New-York I went to Philadelphia, where I learned that I could not go the usual route to Baltimore, the stages having all stopped running, and I went round by York, Pennsylvania. I was yet fifty miles from Baltimore, and there was no stage. Here I fell in with an old friend, going to Baltimore, and we hired a sleigh and two horses to carry us thither, and a cold ride we had. This day's ride gave me such a terrible cold and rheumatism that I was laid up at Baltimore for a week. During that time Baltimore harbour had frozen up, so that no boat had gone for a number of days. They fitted up an ice-boat, that broke through the ice, that was about a foot thick, for seven miles, to the mouth of the river. This took a whole day, and during the night we reached Annapolis, and the next morning by regular steamboat we reached Norfolk. Having been detained so long on my route, the conference had already commenced its session, though little business had been done except attention to some difficult questions and trials."

From Norfolk he returned to Baltimore, and met that Conference on the 9th of March. Thence he went to Philadelphia, and met that conference on the 30th of the same month. This brings us in our narrative down to the General Conference of 1836.

The progress of the Church during the four years exhibited these results, so far as the membership and ministry were concerned:—Increase of members for the four years, one hundred and thirty-nine thousand four hundred and fourteen; of ministers, seven hundred and forty-eight. During the four years, also, two hundred and forty-nine preachers had located. The great number of locations is a striking commentary upon the hardships and privations still endured in the itinerant work. One hundred and fourteen preachers, including two bishops, had ceased from their labours by death. The uniform record of their dying experience is, that the religion they had preached shed its heavenly light upon the closing scene, and they departed in the bright prospect of a glorious immortality.

CHAPTER XV.

FOURTH QUADRENNIAL OF EPISCOPAL LABOURS.

General Conference of 1836 — Representation — Death of M'Kendree and Emory — Address of Bishops Roberts and Hedding — Hedding's Remark upon the Administration of Discipline — Election of three Bishops — Ordination of Messrs. Waugh and Morris — Vote relating to Bishops Roberts and Hedding — Sundry Measures — Adjournment — Bishop Hedding's Labours for the twelve past Years — Conferences met during this Year — Statistical Returns — Causes assigned for declension — True causes — Bishop Hedding removes from Lynn to Lansingburgh, N. Y. — Note made at the close of the Year's Labour — Conferences met in 1837 — An Increase reported this Year — Import of Questions propounded to Candidates for Deacon's and Elder's Orders — Labours of 1838 — Visits the Grave of Benjamin Abbott — Protracted Sessions of the New-York and New-England Conferences — Visits the Northern New-York Conferences — Progress of the Church this Year — Conferences attended in 1839 — Exhaustion — Misses old Friends — Influence upon him — Anti-Slavery Excitement — Course he felt obliged to pursue — Prosperity of the Church — Close of the Fourth Quadrennial of his Labours — Some Reflections — Death of Ministers during the four Years—Mr. Hedding's old Associates — John Brodhead — Martin Ruter — Oliver Beale — Wilbur Fisk — The Dying Testimonies — Substantial Prosperity of the Church — Embarrassment from Locations — Vitality of the Methodist System.

FROM Philadelphia Bishop Hedding proceeded to Cincinnati, by way of Pittsburgh, to attend the General Conference. Bishop Roberts opened the session in the usual manner. This conference was composed of one hundred and fifty-four delegates, distributed among the several annual conferences as follows, namely: New-York, ten; New-England, seven; Maine, eight; New-Hampshire, eight; Troy, seven; Oneida, nine; Genesee, seven; Pittsburgh, eight; Ohio, twelve; Missouri, four; Kentucky, six; Illinois, three; Mississippi, three; Indiana, four; Holston, four; Tennessee, eight; Alabama, four; Georgia, six; South Carolina, six; Virginia, eight; Baltimore, eleven; Philadelphia, eleven. We have already noticed the death of two of the bishops—M'Kendree and Emory—during the preceding year. Their absence produced a profound sensation, not only in the minds of the remaining bishops, but also in the minds of the delegates generally. The first Friday of the session was observed as a day of fasting and prayer. Bangs, in his History, [vol. iv, p. 232,] says that "Bishops Roberts and Hedding addressed the conference very appropriately and feelingly on the general state of the work of God, and on the strict manner in which discipline should be administered, in order to keep the Church pure from immoral members. There was one point especially on which Bishop Hedding insisted with emphasis, as devolving a high duty on those to whom the execution of discipline was intrusted. He remarked in substance that it was the practice of some preachers to wait for a formal complaint, containing charges and specifications, before they proceeded to the trial of a supposed delinquent member. This he considered a defective administration. As the minister was held responsible for the state and character of the Church, it became his imperative duty, whenever a report was in circulation against a member of the Church, to institute an inquiry respecting its truth, and if he found reason to believe there was just cause of complaint, he was bound to proceed to examine and try the case, as the Discipline directs, without waiting for a formal accusation. Nor is it perceived how a minister can otherwise discharge his high trusts so as to give a joyful account to the Judge of all his stewardship."

The conference resolved to elect three additional bishops. This was done on the 23d of May. On the first balloting one hundred and fifty-three votes were cast; and out of these Beverly Waugh received eighty-five, and Wilbur Fisk seventy-eight, and were elected. On the sixth ballot Thomas A. Morris received eighty-six votes, and was also elected. Dr. Fisk was then travelling in Europe. Provision was, however, made for his ordination; but in view of his obligations to the Wesleyan University, and also of his declining health, he finally declined the office, and before another General Conference he had passed away from the Church on earth to the Church in heaven. The other two, after a sermon by Bishop Hedding, were solemnly inducted into the episcopal office, and have continued to serve the Church with unabated zeal and fidelity in this office now nearly twenty years. The conference requested a copy of Bishop Hedding's sermon for publication, but we think it was never furnished.

At this General Conference Bishop Roberts, whose health had become feeble, tendered his resignation of the episcopal office on account of his bodily infirmities. The conference declined accepting his resignation, but passed a resolution that he should be required to do no more service than he might find consistent with his health and bodily strength. Subsequently a similar resolution was passed in relation to Bishop Hedding. The latter had entered the ministry one or two years before the former, and was but two years his junior in age. He had also performed much hard service through many years, and now not only the weight of years, but the increasing infirmities of a broken constitution began to weigh heavily upon him. It was for this reason that the General Conference, unsolicited by him, now proposed to lighten the burden of his labours.

The work at this General Conference was organized into twenty-eight annual conferences, besides the Mission Conference in Liberia. The conference also adopted two measures affecting the administration of discipline, which we must not fail to mention in this place. The first vested in an annual conference the power of locating any one of its members who, in the judgment of the body, had rendered himself "unacceptable as a travelling preacher." He was, however, allowed the privilege of an appeal to the next ensuing General Conference. The other measure provided for the trial of accused superannuated preachers living out of the bounds of the conferences of which they were members. This was to be done by the presiding elder of the district where such person might reside, in the usual form, by the appointment of a committee; the final decision of the case being with the conference of which the accused person was a member.

The educational and benevolent enterprises of the Church received earnest attention at this session of the General Conference, and strong measures were adopted for their promotion.

The great question, however, that excited the most agitation, and occasioned intense interest, grew out of the relation of the Church to the system of slavery that existed in the southern states. As Bishop Hedding's relations to this subject were of the most important charactor, wo shall defer the whole matter to another chapter, in order to present a distinct and connected view of it. This becomes necessary in order to present the administration of Bishop Hedding in its true light, and also to vindicate both his administration and his personal character from those aspersions that were cast upon them.

Having accomplished its work, the General Conference adjourned on the 27th of May. It may not be improper at this point—when we may consider the most laborious, though perhaps not the most trying, period of his labours ended—to glance back over the twelve years of episcopal service already rendered by Bishop Hedding. In doing this, we must bear in mind how vastly the facilities of travel have increased since that period, or we shall obtain very inadequate notions of the great labour, exposure, and weariness incident to the long journeys he was called to take. Now there are few public routes—north, south, east, or west—that do not afford facilities, by railroad or steamboat, for easy and rapid transportation. But even as late as 1836, steamboats were found only on our principal waters; and as to railroads, there were but two or three in the whole country, and they only connecting points not very far removed from each other. Indeed, when he commenced his episcopal labours there was scarcely a steamboat to be found on any of his lines of travel. His journeys—when made by public conveyance—were principally in stages. His long journeys were more frequently in the spring and autumn, at which seasons the roads were in a scarcely passable condition. Those who are acquainted with stage-routes only on beautifully Macadamized turnpikes, can form but little conception of the slow and toilsome work of staging in new countries, and along rough and miry roads. Some of his long journeys had also been performed in his own private conveyance. Thousands of miles had he ridden alone, in storm and in sunshine, in cold and in heat; sometimes belated and lost in the darkness of the night, and often exposed to perils by the way. In this way, during the past twelve years, he had travelled not less than forty thousand miles. He had attended four general, and eighty-one annual conferences—the latter averaging from one to two weeks. He had fixed no less than eight thousand appointments, all of which had cost him care and anxiety, and most of which had been mutually satisfactory to both preachers and people. He had also preached a large number of ordination and dedication sermons, besides almost innumerable sermons on his journeys in almost every part of the country. He had repeatedly travelled into Canada, and had special care of the work in that region for a number of years. He had visited the Indian missions both in the north and the south, and had watched over their progress with intense interest. During all this time his health had been far from being sound, and often he had been brought down to the verge of the grave. More than three-quarters of the time,—or more than nine years out of the twelve,—whether in health or in sickness, he had been absent from home, and deprived of its comforts and joys. To all this must be added the innumerable important and perplexing questions that required almost incessant attention, and also the great and crushing responsibilities of an office which imposed upon him "the care of all the Churches." "Could I have foreseen, in 1824, all I should have been called to pass through in this period of twelve years,—in view of my infirmities, and of my unfitness for so great a labour,—I certainly should have persisted in declining the office; but 'hitherto God hath helped me,'" were his reflections as from this point he looked back over his past labours and sufferings. But humble as were his own views of his fitness for the office, and of the value of his services to the Church, he had already won a name for wisdom and piety, as well as for exalted and useful labours, that secured for him the unbounded confidence of the whole Church, and gave him an influence rarely if ever wielded by any other individual.

At the close of the General Conference Bishop Hedding returned to the East, and met the following conferences, namely:—The New-York Conference at Brooklyn, June 22d; the New-England Conference at Springfield, July 13th; the Maine Conference at Portland, August 3d; and the New-Hampshire Conference at Montpelier, Vermont, August 31. These four conferences were all that had been assigned to him for the year. In three of these conferences there had been a decrease of membership,—in the New-York, of four hundred and fifty-eight; in the Maine, of five hundred and thirty-nine; and in the New-Hampshire, of eighteen; while in the New-England Conference the increase was but nine hundred and eleven: so that the total decrease in the four conferences was one hundred and four. Indeed, this year seemed to be one of general declension in the Church. In the Pittsburgh, Ohio, Missouri, Illinois, South Carolina, New-England, and Alabama Conferences, there was an increase amounting in the aggregate to six thousand seven hundred and fifty-two; while in the Kentucky, Holston, Tennessee, Georgia, Virginia, Baltimore, Philadelphia, New-York, Maine, New-Hampshire, Oneida, Genesee, Mississippi, there was a decrease amounting in the aggregate to ten thousand nine hundred and two,—leaving a decrease in the membership of the Church of four thousand one hundred and fifty. Such are the results we obtain from a careful inspection of the data, though they do not exactly agree with the aggregate results in the published Minutes for that year. This result—so unusual in the history of Methodism—was sought to be accounted for upon various hypotheses. A survey of the results in the several conferences would indicate that, whatever the cause might be, it was *general* rather than *local*. A careful analysis of the returns for the few years immediately preceding, brings to light the fact that those conferences now presenting the most alarming diminution of numbers, had within those few years reported at different times an extraordinary increase. In those times of religious excitement, multitudes undoubtedly had been gathered into the Church who were but poorly instructed in the doctrines and duties of religion, and but poorly prepared to stand the trial of faith and of patience to which they would inevitably be subjected in their religious experience. Accordingly, in "the time of temptation they fell away;" or in the time of "sifting" they were blown away like chaff from the Church. It may be seriously doubted whether the Church was not in even a more healthful condition, and one equally compatible with sound and permanent prosperity, than when she was numbering her converts by tens of thousands. The causes assigned for this declension, in the journals of that day, were weak and flimsy enough. Some asserted that it had been occasioned by the anti-slavery excitement that was then agitating some portions of the Church. Others, that the curse of God was falling upon the Church because of its relations to "the great evil." But both these assigned reasons seemed put to the blush by the fact that the New-England Conference, where the greatest anti-slavery agitation existed, and the South Carolina Conference, which was more deeply complicated in the great evil perhaps than any other—each reported a very respectable increase in their numbers. The other causes suggested were insufficient to solve the difficulty; for they had existed, and were exerting all their force, even in the time of the great and rapid increase of members in the Church. All these considerations lead us to believe that we have presented the true cause of this decline in numbers.

Having completed his conference labours for the year, Bishop Hedding removed his residence from Lynn, Mass., to Lansingburgh, N. Y. Early in October, after he had got settled in his new home, he made the following memorandum:—"On looking over my minutes, I find I have travelled, during the last nine months, about five thousand three hundred and ninety miles. These journeys have been performed in steamboats, canal-boats, stages, wagons, and by rail-roads. When I consider the many dangers through which I have passed, and how mercifully I have been preserved, I cannot but wonder at the goodness of God to me. Truly it becomes me to adore the unseen hand which has protected me from death, and kept me still in the land of the living."

The winter of 1836–7 was spent in visiting the societies in the vicinity of Lansingburgh, and the discharge of such other duties as his office imposed upon him.

The ensuing spring he met the New-York Conference, in company with Bishop Waugh, and at his urgent request, at Brooklyn, May 17th. From Brooklyn he returned to Troy, where he met that conference May 31st. After this he rejoined Bishop Waugh, and met the New-England Conference at Nantucket, June 7th. On the 5th of July he met the New Hampshire Conference at Great Falls; and on the 9th of August the Black River Conference at Potsdam. During the session of this last-named conference a gracious revival of religion took place, and many of the citizens of the place were converted to God. At Courtlandville he met the Oneida Conference, August 30th, and afterward the Genesee Conference at Perry, September 20th. From Perry he returned home, which he reached October 9th, and here he spent the winter in his usual manner; only, his health being very much impaired, he went abroad but little.

The year had not passed away without some prosperity. The total membership of the Church was six hundred and fifty-eight thousand five hundred and seventy-four, being an increase of five thousand five hundred and forty-two, including the Liberia Mission. The number of travelling preachers was now three thousand one hundred and forty-seven, being an increase of two hundred and eighteen. For the first time, the local preachers are reported this year distinct from the members. They numbered four thousand nine hundred and fifty-four.

Early in the present year Bishop Hedding furnished the following communication for the Christian Advocate and Journal:—"At the last session of the New-England Conference, I was requested by a member of that body, and in the presence of the conference, to give an explanation of the promises our preachers make at the time of their ordination, when the following questions are proposed to them, and when they return the subjoined answers:—

"'*Ordination of Deacons.*—Will you reverently obey them to whom the charge and government over you is committed, following with a glad mind and will their godly admonitions?

"'*Answer.* I will endeavour so to do, the Lord being my helper.'

"'*Ordination of Elders.*—Will you reverently obey your chief ministers, unto whom is committed the charge and government over you; following with a glad mind and will their godly admonitions, submitting yourselves to their godly judgments?

"'*Answer.* I will so do, the Lord being my helper.'

"The explanation, as nearly as I can remember, was in the following words:—

"The officers in the Church whom the persons to be ordained promise to obey, are,—

"1. The preachers in charge of circuits and stations. They are to see that the other preachers in their circuits behave well, &c. (Discipline, p. 58.) And the promise is binding on the other preachers in the circuits and stations.

"2. The Presiding Elders. They are to take charge of all the elders and deacons in their districts. (Discipline, p. 43.) And the promise is binding on the ordained preachers in a district.

"3. The Bishops. They are 'to oversee the spiritual business of our Church.'

"But to what class of actions does the term 'obey' refer? Not to keeping or breaking any moral rule, or any special rule laid down in the Discipline, for these rules are enforced by other authorities; nor to actually doing what are acknowledged to be duties, for all we are to do is required in the word of God and in the Discipline, and, therefore, is not a subject of advice. But the term 'obey' refers to abstaining from an act which is deemed by the superior in office to be improper, though it may not be mentioned in the Bible, or in the Discipline, and against which the senior in office admonishes the junior, and from doing which he counsels him to desist. Such, for instance, as preaching or lecturing on party politics—offering, as it is termed in some parts of the country—at elections for *civil office*, or delivering what have been called *Stump Lectures*.

"But it is possible the chief minister may err, and

administer unwise advice, or oppressive admonition; and what is to be done in that case? Is the junior to say, 'I know as much as you,' and disobey? No: for he has promised to 'obey.' He must submit to the directions of his senior in office till the next conference, and if an error has been committed by the preacher in charge, or by the presiding elder, it is the duty of the conference to correct it. And if the error is committed by a bishop, the duty of a preacher who has been aggrieved by it is to bear it as a burden till the next General Conference, to whom the bishop is accountable, then lay the subject before that body, and a suitable correction will doubtless be administered."

The occasion of the publication of these comments was, first, the request of the conference; and, secondly, the fact that they had been misunderstood and misrepresented by persons that heard them, and also the positions taken in them had been gravely questioned. To his communication the bishop adds the following note:—"Every member of the Church is under an obligation as strong as those promises, and he must do as much as those promises engage to do or he will never obey the word of God. 'Likewise, ye younger, submit yourselves unto the elder.' 1 Peter v, 5; 'Obey them that have the rule over you, and submit yourselves.' Heb. xiii, 17. There can be no good government in the Church without as great a degree of submission as this."

The labours of the year 1838 were very similar to

those he had performed during several preceding years. He met the Philadelphia Conference at Wilmington, Delaware, April 4th; the New-Jersey at Bridgeton, April 25th; the New-York at New-York, May 16th; the New-England at Boston, June 6th; and the Maine at Wiscassett, June 27th. The anti-slavery excitement had run high during the preceding year, and had occasioned much trouble in several of the conferences. Referring to the session of the Philadelphia Conference of this year, Bishop Hedding says: "Considering the excitement I had seen in the conferences I had visited the latter part of the preceding year, this was a session of great refreshing on account of the harmony and peace attending it. It had been a year of great revival within the bounds of the conference. Many sinners had been converted, and the work of sanctification had been progressing among both members and ministers. Many of the latter came up to the conference from all parts of the work, baptized with the true spirit of their mission."

On his way from the Philadelphia to the New-Jersey Conference, he visited Salem, New-Jersey. The object of peculiar interest that attracted his attention here was connected with the memory of Benjamin Abbott. Here he lived and laboured as a local preacher, before he began his wonderful career as an itinerant; and to this place he returned when broken health compelled him to desist from travelling. Here also he died, and was buried.

Says Bishop Hedding: "I visited the place 'where they laid him,' and I could not but think, as I stood by his grave, of the wonderful character of the man, of the mighty power with which he preached Jesus and the resurrection, of the great work he accomplished in the Church, and of the time when he laid his hand upon my head and gave me such a tremendous exhortation in the class-meeting on Dutchess Circuit nearly fifty years ago. I shall soon follow him to the grave; but I trust I shall be permitted to see him in the kingdom of his God and my God."

The sessions of the New-York and New-England Conferences this year were exceedingly protracted and exciting. The former lasted fifteen days, and the latter seventeen. As these difficulties originated mainly with the ultraism of individuals connected with the anti-slavery movement as well as the ultraism of their opponents, we shall consider them in that connexion.

After the session of the Maine Conference, Bishop Hedding returned to Lansingburgh. Here he rested a few days and then left home again, and accompanied Bishop Morris to the Black River Conference, held at Fulton, August 1st; to the Oneida, held at Ithaca, August 22d; and to the Genesee, held at Elmira, September 12th. "After passing through the business of this conference," says he, "Bishop Morris and I parted—he for his home in Ohio, I for mine in Lansingburgh. I travelled on, preaching to the people by the way, and reached home the last of September. Glory be to God for his preserving mercy and supporting grace!"

The year had been one of considerable prosperity in the Church. Several of the conferences had reported very large accessions. Among them, the Illinois had reported an increase of three thousand three hundred and sixteen; the Indiana, three thousand one hundred and thirty-eight; the Philadelphia, three thousand and forty-two; the New-York, two thousand six hundred and thirty-six; the Tennessee, two thousand eight hundred and forty-three; the Maine, two thousand five hundred and eighty-nine; the Troy, two thousand one hundred and thirty-two; the Erie, two thousand three hundred and thirty-nine; the Oneida, two thousand four hundred and ninety-two; and the Genesee, two thousand seven hundred and ninety-six. The total increase of members for the year—including local preachers, of which there were five thousand seven hundred and ninety-two—was forty-three thousand two hundred and seventy-five, making an aggregate of six hundred and ninety-six thousand five hundred and forty-nine. The increase of travelling preachers for the year was one hundred and seventy-five, making three thousand three hundred and twenty-six in all.

Early in the spring of 1839, Bishop Hedding left home to resume his episcopal labours. He visited the Philadelphia Conference, over which Bishop Waugh presided, and afterward accompanied the latter to Baltimore on business of the Church. After this he met the New-Jersey Conference at Trenton, April 24th; the New-York, at Brooklyn, May 14th; the Troy, at Schenectady, June 5th; the New-Hampshire, at Sandwich, July 3d; the Black River, at Turin, July 31st; the Oneida, at Norwich, August 21st; and the Genesee, at Rochester, September 11th.

This episcopal tour, in his enfeebled state of health, was exceedingly laborious and trying. At the Black River Conference he became so exhausted that he was obliged to retire from the conference room before the adjournment, leaving the conference to finish its business and the secretary to read the appointments. Yet amid all these infirmities he toiled on,—feeling that his time of labour was growing short,—desiring, above all things, to do the work God had given him to do. "During the past year," said he, "many of my old friends have finished their course and gone to rest in Abraham's bosom. It deeply affects me, in my rounds, to learn that one after another has passed away from earth. These things admonish me to be ready also. Let me be up and doing. I have but little time in which to work. Lord, prepare me to render an account of my stewardship." Impelled by this feeling, he would toil on till exhausted nature compelled him to lie down and rest. Refreshed by rest and by communion with God, he would again rise up and press forward in his toilsome way. These labours were rendered to him more exhausting and trying from the excitement which at this time existed on the subject of slavery.

Ultra and radical ground had been taken, and agitating measures adopted by the leaders in that movement, which, he sincerely believed, threatened the peace and integrity of the Church, while at the same time they could be productive of little good to the enslaved. The measures he had felt it to be his duty to take, in order to guard the sacred interests of the Church committed to his charge, were in conflict with the views and measures of these leaders in the anti-slavery movement. For this he was assailed by them with a shameful virulence; his acts and words were perverted and misrepresented; and his course, to a very great extent, misunderstood. All this was the more trying to him, as several who had once professed great friendship for him were now his most violent enemies and traducers. Excitement was rife everywhere, and he knew not what he might be called to encounter in the midst of the whirlwind that had been raised. The reader will not wonder, then, that the labours of the few past years had been performed under a crushing sense of responsibility, and with incessant and wearing anxiety.

While at the Oneida Conference this year the following beautiful incident occurred, at once illustrative of the general character and of the deep and ardent piety of Bishop Hedding. We give it as we have received it from the Rev. Dr. Paddock, long the intimate personal friend of the bishop. "At this session of the Oneida Conference," says he, "I was quartered at the same house with the venerable bishop. As I was going out to public worship, on Sunday evening, he said to me, 'Brother, I wish you would excuse me from accompanying you, I am so much fatigued; and then you know the exhausting labours of the closing part of the conference are still before me, and I must recruit and prepare for them.' In truth I had no thought of his accompanying me; for I knew he had not only preached a long and fatiguing sermon that day, but had ordained both the elders and the deacons. The circumstance, however, shows what was always an amiable trait in his general character—his tender regard for the feelings of others. He was studiously careful never to say a word or perform an action which would be likely to give pain to any human being, save only when it was clearly apparent that the interests of religion demanded that sort of discipline, and then the infliction was ever accompanied with so much tenderness that even the subject of it was obliged the more to respect him.

"The public service of the evening performed, I returned to our mutual lodgings. Finding the chamber of the good bishop unilluminated, and presuming he had retired to rest, I determined to pass through his room—which I was obliged to do in order to reach my own dormitory—as quietly as possible, so as not to disturb him. As soon as I opened the door, however, I heard his tender voice in the opposite end of the room, saying, 'Brother, please be seated while I light a lamp. You will find a chair to the left of the door.' The venerable old gentleman experienced some little difficulty in igniting his match, but finally succeeded in lighting the lamp, when he said: 'I have been sitting here by this open window, enjoying the cool air, [the evening was excessively warm,] and examining this poor heart of mine, to see whether it loves the blessed Jesus as much as it used to.' After a moment's pause, he added, his voice tremulous with deep emotion, 'And I think it does, full as much—yes, a little more than it ever did before.' These were his precise words—words which I can no more forget than I can forget that I ever saw the man.

"Seating himself, he continued to speak of his own past experience with a freedom and a pathos which were at once most delightful and most edifying. Among other things, he said, 'I do not know whether it is so with others, but I often find great spiritual comfort in reading our hymns. They contain a depth, a concentration of meaning, which comes home to the soul with a kind of divine power. Though I cannot substitute them for the inspired word, I frequently read them with a view to religious edification, as well as from a regard to their unsurpassed poetical beauty.'

"The afternoon sermon that day had turned chiefly on the resurrection of Christ, and the exercises were closed with that incomparable hymn, commencing,

"He dies, the Friend of sinners dies."

To that hymn the bishop particularly referred, and spoke of it as one of the finest in the English language, and as often having been a blessing to his own soul. He repeated the whole of it with the greatest force and propriety, and pointed out its principal beauties with the nicest discrimination."

After returning from the Genesee Conference, Bishop Hedding visited New-York and Brooklyn, but afterward was confined at home through the winter, his physical strength being very much exhausted, and he being greatly afflicted by the return of his old rheumatic complaint.

The year had been very similar to the preceding, so far as the prosperity of the Church was concerned. The total membership was reported at seven hundred and forty thousand four hundred and fifty-nine, being an increase of forty-three thousand nine hundred and ten; the number of travelling preachers three thousand five hundred and fifty-seven, increase two hundred and thirty-five; number of local preachers five thousand eight hundred and fifty-six, increase sixty-four.

In the spring of 1840 he assisted Bishop Waugh at the Philadelphia Conference, which met at Philadelphia, April 1st; and also at the New-Jersey Conference, at Burlington, April 15th. This brought him to the close of the fourth quadrennial of his episcopal labours. "Through God's mercy," said he, "I am yet alive. What toils and trials I have passed through during the past sixteen years! How graciously I have been preserved in my long and wearisome journeys. How mercifully I have been sustained in the midst of trials and cares. My old and early associates have many of them passed away. M'Kendree, George, and Emory, I shall meet no more on earth. My work too will soon be done. The growing infirmities of age admonish me that my time is growing short. O, how my soul longs for greater meetness for heaven! Especially have the last two or three years, on account of the great commotions which distract the peace and threaten to sunder the union of the Church of God, been years of great personal affliction and trial to me. But God is my refuge. God is the refuge and the deliverer of his Church. His will be done. This thing encourages me for the Church: God has delivered her from a thousand dangers, and he is still able to deliver. It also encourages me for myself that our preachers die well."

In looking over the Minutes for the four years, we find that death had been busy along the ranks of Zion's watchmen. No less than one hundred and sixteen had fallen—some of them young men who had just entered the field, others veterans, who had toiled long and hard in the work. Among the latter were some of the early associates of Bishop Hedding. Such was John Brodhead, whose early and paternal regard for the subject of our memoir has already been noticed. Bishop Hedding fully responded to the record of his contemporaries:—"Brother Brodhead was a *good* man; deeply pious, and ardently and sincerely devoted to the interests of the Church and the world. It is known to all who are acquainted with the untarnished excellencies of his character, that a great man and a prince has fallen in Israel." Such was Martin Ruter, D. D., who entered the ministry at the early age of sixteen—the class-mate of Hedding, having with him joined the New-York Conference in 1801. He was no ordinary man. Commencing his career with little more than a common-school education, while performing the duties of an itinerant Methodist preacher he became well versed in languages, science, and history. In 1818 and 1819 he was principal of the New-Market Wesleyan Academy; then he served two terms in the Western book-agency, and was subsequently president, first of Augusta College, then of Alleghany, which latter office he resigned to enter upon the superintendency of the missionary work in Texas, where he died at his post after thirty-seven years of successful labour in the cause of Christ—a fit companion, friend, and co-labourer of the great and good Hedding. Oliver Beale, another associate of Bishop Hedding in his early career, had also passed to his rest. Wilbur Fisk, D. D., also; he was later in the ministry, but his relations to Bishop Hedding for many years, and especially during the few last years of his brilliant career, were such as made his death a personal affliction not soon forgotten. Of his career we need not speak; his character we need not attempt to describe. The Church has been blessed with but few such men; Bishop Hedding had but few such intimate and confidential friends. His letters, found among the bishop's papers, continuing up almost to the close of his life, show the concord of feeling, the harmony of sentiment, and the unbounded mutual confidence that subsisted between them. No wonder that Bishop Hedding was now deeply impressed with the fact that his early associates were passing away.

"Our preachers die well." We were peculiarly struck with the beauty, truth, and fulness of this remark, in glancing over the obituary record for these four years. Of Philip Gatch it is said, "He finished his course with great peace, and with unshaken confidence in Christ;" of Bishop M'Kendree, that "he died as he lived, strong in the faith, and giving glory to God;" of Russell Bigelow, that "in the language of a living faith he was heard to exclaim, 'Glory to God!'" of Thomas Drummond—"his last words were, 'All is well; I die at my post;'" of Richard Henry Lee—"near the closing scene he said, 'If religion is love, I feel it—I know I love God—God is love! All is peace!'" of Benjamin Ogden—"he expired in all the confidence of faith and hope;" of Minor M. Crosby, that "the testimony of his dying hour illustrated the principles of his profession as a minister of Christ;" of William Outten, that "his death was peaceful and triumphant;" of William Adams, that "his death was not only peaceful, but signally triumphant;" of Francis Landrum, that "the same ardour of hope and fervour of faith by which his life had been distinguished, signalized his dying hour, and marked his translation to the heaven he had so long and so faithfully preached to others;" of Parley W. Clenny, that "when asked if he was afraid to die, he said, 'No! if my work is done, I would rather die than live;'" of George W. Huggins, that after exhorting his family to meet him in heaven, he exclaimed, "My work is finished, I am going to heaven;" of Samuel Bozeman, that "he died in full prospect of eternal glory;" of Richard B. F. Gould, that, when he was brought suddenly to the gates of death, "he stood firm and undismayed; death had no terror for him; but with the love of God reigning in his heart, and in the full enjoyment of his mental faculties to the last, he left the world with the note of triumph falling from his lips;" of Christopher Frye, called by sudden accident to stand in the face of death, that, while his crushed and mangled body was racked with pain, he could say, "My soul is calm and stayed upon God—my soul is happy, happy, happy!" of Thomas D. Allen, that just before he departed he said to a friend, "I have always expected to have a reasonable degree of comfort in my dying hour, but I never expected to enjoy such a deep, settled calm as I now feel;" of the venerable Solomon Sharp, when he had preached his last sermon upon the rest that remains for the people of God, [Hebrews iv, 9,] he said, "Now I feel as if my work was done;" of Andrew C. Mills, that his last words were, "'I am now ready to be offered. I have fought a good fight, I have finished my course, I have kept the faith: henceforth there is laid up for me a crown of righteousness, which the Lord, the righteous Judge, shall give me at that day;'" of Samuel Bibbins, that when, after fifty years of faithful labour in the vineyard of his Lord and Master, he came to the close of his career, he exclaimed, "The storm of life has at length blown over! The last tornado has passed by! The victory is gained, and heaven is mine! Sweet heaven of rest *is* mine! Hallelujah! Hallelujah! My life has been spent these fifty years past in the ministry, but I do not regret it. All my sufferings in that laborious employment will render the heaven of eternal rest the sweeter;" of Rufus Stoddard, that his last words were, "My work is done—heaven is mine! Victory, victory, victory through the blood of the Lamb! Death has lost his sting. Come, Lord Jesus—come!" of Josiah Keyes,—the scholar, the theologian, the able preacher,—that when called to die, he could say, "'for me to live is Christ, and to die is gain;'" of Cornelius Jones, that when death approached "he was enabled to give up all;" of Milton Colt, that "his death was completely triumphant;" of Thomas Wiley, that "he enjoyed unshaken confidence in God;" of William Phillips, that "as he lived, so he died, in the possession of abundance of grace, in sure hope of a blessed immortality;" of Nelson R. Bewley, that "he enjoyed a complete triumph over death and the grave;" of John H. Ruble, that "he shouted aloud the praise of God;" of Henry S. Duke, that he closed his career in "the triumphant persuasion that 'to die is gain;'" of John Littlejohn, that "his death was as triumphant as his life had been useful and exemplary;" of Lawrence M'Coombs,—for forty years an able and useful minister of Jesus Christ,—that "his soul was peaceful, willing to suffer still longer, or to depart immediately and be with Christ;" of Alfred Medcalf, that, when informed he was dying, he pleasantly exclaimed, "'All is well—Christ the hope of glory—God is with me!' and fell asleep;" of Ariel Fay, that he was unspeakably happy; and, though he could speak with difficulty, shouted aloud, "Glory! glory! Now I am ready—ready to die or live—to suffer all the will of God;" of Erastus Felton, that "from the first approach of death till its consummation, all was light, and peace, and joy within his soul;" of Charles T. Ramsey, that "he died as he had lived, strong in the faith, giving glory to God;" of Robert L. Kennon, that about an hour before he expired, while contemplating the glorious plan of man's salvation, he said, "Here is true simplicity—here is true grandeur!" of Jesse Richardson, that he said, "I have the best truth of the Bible to die on—the divinity of Christ. I have faith in this. All is consoling to me beyond the tomb;" and again, at another time, "I have nothing to fear. I believe in the Godhead of Christ, have preached it, lived on it, and now I die on it, glad to rest my everlasting all upon my Redeemer;" of James Buckley, that, after his speech had failed, "he raised his hand in token of victory over the fear of death through the blood of Christ;" of James W. Finley, that he exclaimed, "What love and peace I feel. O, how precious the Lord is to my soul! Glory! glory!" of Hiram Loring, that he said, "I die at my post, and in sight of heaven;" of Alexander Talley, that "he expired in perfect peace and triumph," and his last words were, "My work is done;" of Robert C. Jones, that with a smiling countenance he said, "O, the idea of meeting Jesus!" of John Watson, that when sinking by age and disease, he said, "The Lord, who has been my friend so long, surely will not forsake me now;" of James J. Housewheat, that his language was, "All is well, all is well! I feel that Christ is with me! I never had such happy feelings in all my life;" of Thomas Morrell, that "his last moments were those of peace and heavenly triumph;" of Smith Arnold, that his utterances were;—

> "There is my house and portion fair;
> My treasure and my heart are there,
> And my abiding home;
> For me my elder brethren stay,
> And angels beckon me away,
> And Jesus bids me come;"

of Roswell Putnam, that when he could speak only in a suppressed whisper, he replied to one who asked him how the gospel he had preached now appeared, "Never did that gospel appear so valuable as at the present, and never did I see my nothingness, aside from divine grace, as I now do, and never was that grace more sweet;" of Wright Haren, that he said, "That gospel which I have preached to others I find to be my support and comfort in this trying hour;" of Calvin Danforth, that, when expiring far away from home, he said, "My witness is in heaven, my record is on high;" of Ross Clark, that, having bidden farewell to all his earthly friends, he fixed his eyes above, and said, "All is clear! Come, Lord Jesus, come quickly, nor let the chariot-wheels delay;" and of Wilbur Hoag, that his testimony was, "My confidence in God is strong; I have no fears about the future." Many other evidences might we glean, from the record of death's doings during these four years, that "our ministers die well."

During the four years just now closed, the substantial prosperity of the Church, in all the departments of its great work, was highly encouraging. Its missionary collections had greatly increased, and its missionary work, both in the home and the foreign field, greatly enlarged. Churches, more commodious and inviting, had been springing up in every part of the work, and the facilities for carrying forward the great work had been greatly multiplied. The educational system of the Church had continued to develop itself in the increase of colleges and the multiplication of seminaries, and was already producing abundant fruits. The problem that the highest order of mental cultivation was not only compatible with the work of an itinerant Methodist minister, but also highly conducive, when moulded by divine grace and fired by holy zeal, to success in that work, had now received a historical demonstration; and men of the highest educational acquirements were found consecrating them all to the service of God in the itinerant ministry. Methodism had risen up to be a wonder in the land. Even "the ancient men," who had marked the smallness of its origin and had watched the progress of its growth, were astonished at its gigantic development. The increase for the four years, including local preachers, was ninety-three thousand seven hundred and eighty-seven, and that of travelling preachers seven hundred and ninety-nine.

We have already noticed the number of deaths in the ministry. The other great source of loss to the Church in this respect has been the great numbers who have retired from the itinerant ranks by location. The locations during the present quadrennial had reached the astonishing number of five hundred and forty-six, or more than one-fourth of the whole number in the itinerant ranks at its commencement. In Tennessee Conference there had been no less than fifty-two locations; in the Alabama there had been thirty-four: while the whole number in the conference at the commencement of this period was but fifty-six. The general causes of this falling away from the work are patent upon the surface—family necessities, hard labour, and inadequate support. Some of the evils connected with it are equally apparent—the embarrassment of the work, in consequence of being compelled constantly to supply the places of retiring preachers, who were, in many instances, men of cultivated talent as well as of experience, with new and untried men. This added not a little to the difficulties and responsibilities of the episcopal office, and occasioned unquestionably great detriment to the work. This evil, however, had existed from the beginning, and in spite of it the Methodist Church had grown up and spread over all the land. We do not know of a more striking evidence of the inherent vitality of the system, taken as a whole, than that it could produce such vast results, though clogged by obstacles so powerful.

CHAPTER XVI.

BISHOP HEDDING AND THE ABOLITION CONTROVERSY.

The Anti-Slavery Agitation — Movements of Rev. Orange Scott during the Conference Year 1834-5 — Anti-Slavery feeling in New-England and Northern New-York — Stand-point from which Bishop Hedding contemplated the Movement — Anticipation of evil results — Feels it his Duty to oppose Ultra Measures — Gives countenance to the "Counter Appeal" — Anti-Slavery Sentiments expressed in that Appeal — Difficult position of Bishop Hedding — His Pastoral Letter to the New-England and New-Hampshire Conferences — Its effect — Its treatment by the Ultraists — Newspaper Discussions — General Conference of 1836 — The Pastoral Address — Disapprobation of the Measures employed by Abolitionists — Avoid electing a Slaveholding Bishop — Extremists on both sides dissatisfied — Binding force of the General Conference action upon the Bishops — Bishop Hedding at the New-England Conference in 1836 — Declines reappointing O. Scott to the Presiding Eldership — Proposed Action on Slavery — His Administration assailed — New-Hampshire Conference — G. Storrs proposed for Presiding Elder — The Bishop converses with him — Declines to appoint him — Painful feelings — New-England Conference for 1837 — Calls the attention of the body to the misrepresentations of O. Scott — NOTE: Letter from Bishop Hedding to Rev. O. Scott — The Settlement — O. Scott's retractions — NOTE: Previous attempt at Adjustment: written statement of T. Merritt, D. Fillmore, and T. C. Peirce — Events at the New-Hampshire Conference — Bishop Hedding's Vindication of his Administration — His celebrated "Golden-Rule Argument in favour of Slavery," and what it amounts to — An Unpardonable Sin — Ruling of Presiding Elders — Character of some of the Resolutions — Rev. O. Scott in the Field — His offences against Bishop Hedding repeated — A few Extracts from his published Letters — Charges preferred against Rev. O. Scott before the New-England Conference — Decisions of the Conference — Trial of La Roy Sunderland — Mr. Hedding looks to the General Conference for redress — Incident at the close of the New-England Conference — Rev. O. Scott's *ex parte* statement of the Trial — Action in the New-Hampshire Conference — Letter from Bishop Morris — Letter from Bishop Hedding in relation to the Trials of Scott and Sunderland — Subsequent misrepresentation and ill-treatment received by Bishop Hedding — An Apologetic Remark concerning the Ultraists — Light in which Bishop Hedding's Administration is to be interpreted — Subject brought up to the General Conference of 1840.

SOME six or eight years, commencing with about 1834, were years of great excitement in relation to the system of slavery that had gradually grown up and extended in this country. The anti-slavery feeling that had been developing for years, was one of the natural results of the progress of Christian civilization. It comes not within our province to detail the history or to discuss the elements of this great movement. We have rather to do with some of the *incidents* of that movement—especially as they stand in connexion with the subject of our memoir.

During the year 1834, several of the New-England preachers became not only the subjects, but also the active agents of the great excitement then springing up in relation to slavery. Prominent among them was Orange Scott, a popular and influential member of the New-England Conference. Being at that time presiding elder of the Providence District, his position gave him both influence and opportunities to agitate the subject. Accordingly he availed himself of the gatherings of preachers at camp-meetings and on other occasions not only to discuss the subject, but to have resolutions passed in relation to it. By these means the columns of the "Zion's Herald" were opened to such discussions. Mr. Scott also personally subscribed for one hundred copies of the "Liberator," edited by Wm. L. Garrison, to be sent to the members of the New-England Conference. At the session of this conference in 1835, the majority of its members had become abolitionists, and this became a test-question in the election of delegates to the General Conference. A feverish state of excitement pervaded the entire conference; and so high did it rise during the election of delegates that it was not thought best to attempt the election of reserve delegates. Similar measures had been used also in the New-Hampshire Conference, under the leadership of the Rev. George Storrs, with similar results.

In New-England and in Northern New-York a strong anti-slavery feeling had long existed. The exciting lectures, speeches, pamphlets, &c., that were now brought to bear upon the public mind kindled up that anti-slavery feeling into a flame. Looking upon the cause as one embodying true philanthropic and benevolent principles, the apprehensions of the greater part of both ministers and people who were engaged in it, with regard to the ultimate consequences of ultra excitement and ultra measures, were completely lulled to slumber. They looked only at "the great evil;" and, as they supposed, were only rushing forward to its "extirpation." Not so with Bishop Hedding. God had made him an overseer of the whole Church, and he was compelled to view the subject from a different stand-point from that of many of his brethren. From his soul he abhorred the entire system of slavery; but in this movement he foresaw peril to the Church, and could not, consistently with his obligations as a bishop, refrain from endeavouring to counteract the pernicious tendencies of this movement in relation to it, and he conceived it to be the duty of all ministers and members to do the same.

Bishop Hedding witnessed, with painful emotion, the excited state of feeling in the New-England and New-Hampshire Conferences this year. He was distressed beyond measure at the ultra measures that were adopted by many members, the harsh expressions that were used, and the consequent alienation of feeling among those who had long lived and laboured together as brethren, and also at the imperious and arrogant spirit of some of the leaders, which he felt assured, unless timely checked, could end in nothing but the most radical and determined opposition to the government and salutary discipline of the Church. He had also shared largely in the personal abuse that was heaped upon those who, on account of prospective evil, sought to arrest or modify the course of the new and radical movement. The sessions of the New-England and New-Hampshire Conferences for 1835 had been anticipated by an "Appeal" on the subject of slavery, addressed to the members of each by some of the prominent abolitionists, though prepared, we believe, principally by La Roy Sunderland and George Storrs. To counteract the influence of this "Appeal," a "Counter-Appeal," signed by Dr. Fisk, John Lindsay, B. Otheman, Abel Stevens, and others, was issued in the fall of the same year. It was also accompanied by a note from Bishop Hedding, in which he expressed his belief of the correctness of its statements and arguments, especially those relating to the acts of the General Conference. This document was loudly assailed as a pro-slavery affair, and, of course, Bishop Hedding came in for his share of the obloquy. We are not called upon to endorse all that is found in it; some of its positions we think untenable, and some of its arguments fallacious; but to show how little its authors were inclined to justify the system of involuntary bondage, as it then existed, we must be indulged with one or two extracts. They say: "Every diminution of the intensity of suffering, or of the amount of exercisable authority, which could be made, without creating more misery than it subtracts, ought instantly to be made; and the moment the whole can be diminished away, whether immediately or gradually, without causing more suffering than it destroys, then, and not till then, should it be absolutely and entirely annihilated."

In another place they add:—"Christianity, by proclaiming the immortal existence of every human soul, and pronouncing all equally responsible and equally valuable in the eye of God, stamps the stigma of *libelous absurdity* upon the principle that man can, in nature, be a *mere article of property*. What ever may be the temporary state of subjection which Christianity itself may, in prevention of higher evils, rightfully retain in transient existence, it does, at the same time, attest the innate ascendency of his nature, by which he must inevitably rise above this fictitious and unnatural position of *a mere chattel*, into an elevation worthy his true character."

Still further on, it is added:—"The letter of the golden rule and the spirit of the gospel operate with an irresistible tendency to the amelioration, diminution, and destruction of slavery, as a system; holding forth its perpetuation as an abomination, and its continuance, by the authors of legislation, beyond the time of its practicable removal, a *sin*."

Also referring to the course of the abolitionists, the counter-appealants say:—"Did we see prospective emancipation in such a path, we would bid the process of agitation God-speed. We do, indeed, believe that too quickly the course of oppressive legislation cannot be changed; too soon the safe and happy liberation of the oppressed descendants of Africa in this land cannot take place; too rapid cannot be the wing of that angel that bears freedom to the fettered hope of the despairing, and life to the dying. In every feasible hope of philanthropy—in every rational effort to spread just information—to create a healthful tone of public feeling, and to render the free air of our country unrespirable to a spirit of oppression, we rejoice to bear our part."

They also address their brethren in the South, to incite them, if possible, to emulate the noble course of their brethren in the old world in efforts to bring about the emancipation of the negro race. "To our brethren of the South, if our feeble voice may not be wholly unheard by them, in language which we are sure they will recognise as the general tone of Christian brotherly kindness, we would address our most intense entreaty, that, unless it be at the expense of higher and immortal interests, they would NOW, in this day of light, of peace, and of moral power, emulate the memorable stand of our brethren of England, and, with the name of Wesley upon their banners, and his spirit in their hearts, would seize the timely honour of *leading* out the foremost van of the great Christian movements, which, in some of our states, are directing their onward march toward the ultimate achievement of universal emancipation."

A document containing sentiments like the above must have been singularly incongruous to have been pro-slavery in its general character; or, had its authors designed it as a defence of slavery, they certainly shot very wide of their general design in these passages. The pen of so skilful a logician and so sagacious a man as Dr. Fisk, or of Professor Whedon, by whom the main labour of its preparation was performed, could hardly have been guilty of such aberrations; and yet both of these charges were laid against the "counter-appeal" and its authors. The conflict had now fairly commenced. That Church, which had always most strongly protested against the great evil of slavery, was most fiercely denounced. Some of the more ultra and less cautious did not hesitate to declare that they would never faulter till they had "split the great Methodist prop to slavery."

The course of things was exceedingly afflicting to Bishop Hedding. Few men, perhaps, were more sensitive in relation to their personal reputation; and he could not but feel that some brethren—brethren with whom he had long been associated, and in whom he once had great confidence—were doing all they could to place him in a false attitude before the Church, and thus to curtail his influence and injure his reputation. To join them in their peculiar measures against slavery, he conscientiously believed would be to assist in driving the ploughshare of ruin through the Church of God. To stand aloof, would be to subject his character and motives to many misapprehensions and to many rude assaults. Painful as was his position, he seemed shut up to these alternatives. As to which he should choose, he could not hesitate a moment. Self could not be regarded a moment, when placed in competition with the claims and interests of the Church of God.

Actuated by these views, in conjunction with his junior colleague, Bishop Emory, he addressed a pastoral letter to the "ministers and preachers" in the New-England and New-Hampshire Annual Conferences. It is dated at Lansingburgh, September 10th, 1835, and was probably mainly written by Bishop Emory. After stating that they had "marked with deep solicitude the painful excitement which had been producing disturbance" within the bounds of those two conferences, they proceed to say:—"Believing, as we do, that these measures have already been productive of pernicious results, and tend to the production of others yet more disastrous, both in the Church and in the social and political relations of the country, we deem it our duty to address to you a pastoral letter on the subject." The whole letter is couched in the most affectionate, and yet in the most decided and earnest terms. The main scope of the letter is to show that the ultra measures which were then convulsing the community could be productive of but little good, while they were fraught with great evil to themselves, to the Church, and to the whole country. They earnestly entreat their brethren to pause before they are drawn into the vortex which is gathering around them. They earnestly entreat all—and especially the presiding elders and preachers—to discountenance the practice of leaving their regular work and the care of the souls committed to their charge, to travel over the country as lecturers, delivering public harangues and getting up conventions. In this address they endeavour to guard themselves against any imputation of giving countenance to the system of slavery. They say:— "The question of slavery itself it is not our purpose here to discuss; nor is there any occasion for it. The sentiment of the Church on this subject is well known. Our object is rather to confine ourselves to the practical considerations which press upon us in the present crisis, and which, we presume, cannot fail to arrest the attention of the humane, the pious, and the reflecting of all parties." They also add:—"That the New Testament Scriptures, or the preaching or practice of our Lord or his apostles, were ever intended to justify the condition of slavery, we do not believe."

While this letter had but little effect upon the more determined leaders in the ultra movement it was designed to check, it exerted a most salutary influence over hundreds who, from deep sympathy with the great anti-slavery sentiment of the age, were in danger of being precipitated into a maelstrom of excitement and of radical measures, from which little good was to be expected and much evil apprehended. The letter of the bishops was attacked with great virulence. To guard themselves against the imputation of favouring the system of slavery, they, as we have already seen, distinctly avowed their opposition to it. This frank avowal, however, availed them but little with men who were accustomed to stigmatize all who did not approve of *their measures* as pro-slavery, and therefore involved in the guilt and condemnation of those who actually held their fellow-beings in bondage. It is but just to the abolitionists of that day, to remark that they were not alone guilty of using intemperate expressions and of employing extreme measures. The spirit of the law of the "olden time"—"an eye for an eye, and a tooth for a tooth"—was too often manifest in the opposition made to their movements. The newspaper discussions of the time exhibit an amount of rude personalities, and of grave crimination and recrimination, painful to witness among those who were ministers of the Lord Jesus Christ, and, undoubtedly, had the great interests of humanity at heart. We gladly draw a veil over these scenes. They can be accounted for only by the peculiar and unparalleled excitement of the times. Most of these men were unquestionably good men. Many of them have since been gathered to the tomb. Their alienations have been healed, and their discordant views harmonized in that better land where the spiritual vision is unclouded by earthly prejudices, and where all hearts beat in unison under the impulses of a purer and holier love.

While this state of things existed, and these measures were progressing, the General Conference of 1836 commenced its session at Cincinnati. Several memorials on the subject of slavery were presented, and they elicited not a little excitement and discussion in that body. The measures of the ultra-abolitionists were strongly condemned, both in a series of resolutions and in a pastoral address "to the members and friends of the Methodist Episcopal Church." In these documents there is a studious avoidance—perhaps too much so—of any expression that would either condemn or countenance the system of slavery. A simple object was sought to be accomplished, namely, the restraining of measures calculated to convulse and perhaps divide the Church.

In the Pastoral Address, the General Conference, referring to those who had been active in producing the agitations in the Church, says: "We feel it our imperative duty to express our decided disapprobation of the *measures* they have pursued to accomplish their objects." Again they say: "While we cheerfully accord to such all the sincerity they ask for their belief and motives, we cannot but disapprove of their measures as alike destructive to the peace of the Church and to the happiness of the slave himself." They also add: "From every view of the subject which we have been able to take, and from the most calm and dispassionate survey of the whole ground, we have come to the solemn conviction that the only safe, Scriptural, and prudent way for us, both as ministers and people, to take, is wholly to refrain from this agitating subject, which is now convulsing the country, and consequently the Church, from end to end." They beseech brethren who are opposed to slavery, and wish to give utterance to their sentiments, to employ kind and moderate language. They say: "You would do much better to express yourselves in those terms of respect and affection which evince a sincere sympathy for those of your brethren who are necessarily, and, in some instances, reluctantly associated with slavery in the states where it exists, than to indulge in harsh censures and denunciations, and in those fruitless efforts which, instead of lightening the burden of the slave, only tend to make his condition the more irksome and distressing."

In connexion with this point they also say: "The exercise of mutual forbearance in matters of opinion is essential in a community where freedom of speech is guaranteed to the citizens by the Constitution which binds them together, and which defines and secures the rights and liberties of all." Finally, they express themselves in strong terms of reprobation of the violent measures that had often been employed to put down the anti-slavery lectures: "But while we thus express our disapprobation of these measures, we would, with equally strong and decided language, record our abhorrence of all unlawful and unscriptural means to check and to counteract them. All mobs, and violent movements of self-created tribunals, to inflict summary punishment upon those who may differ from them in opinion, are condemned alike by the laws of our land and by every principle of Christianity. We should, therefore, be extremely pained and mortified to learn that any of you should have lent your influence to foment a spirit of insurrection in any manner, or to have given sanction to such violent movements as have, in some instances and places, disturbed the peace of society, and forestalled the operation of the established tribunals of justice to protect the innocent and punish the guilty."

From the preceding extracts, the tone and design of that portion of the Pastoral Address which related to the agitations of the day may be gathered.* At

*The Address in full may be found in Bangs's History, vol. iv, p. 250 *et seq.*; and also in Elliott's Great Secession, Doc. 23, p. 915.

the same time that the General Conference expressed itself so strongly in opposition to what it deemed an unhealthy and pernicious anti-slavery agitation, it showed itself steadfast in its opposition to slavery by refusing, much to the chagrin of the ultraists at the south, to elect a slaveholder to the office of bishop, as well as by its studious avoidance of any endorsement of the system. The result was that the extremists on both sides were dissatisfied; and we think there is reason to believe that from that time forward certain men in the north, and others in the south, contemplated an ultimate rupture in the Church.

The executive officers of the Church, to whom was intrusted the administration of its Discipline, felt themselves bound by this explicit judgment of the General Conference. Especially was this the case with the bishops, who were directly amenable to the General Conference for their acts; and also with the presiding elders, whose responsibilities were in some respects similar to those of a bishop. This is the stand-point from which we are to view the subsequent official conduct of Bishop Hedding in certain specific cases. To form a just estimate of his course, we must bear in mind that *he* cordially and fully approved of, and felt himself ecclesiastically, morally, and religiously bound, as an officer of the Church, to obey the behests of its highest judicatory.

Under these deep convictions of duty and of solemn responsibility, Bishop Hedding came to the

New-England Conference in 1836. Two acts of the bishop here gave great umbrage to the abolitionists. The first was the removal of Orange Scott from the Providence District, where he had laboured but two years. It was currently reported to the bishop—in fact it was a thing notorious—that Mr. Scott had employed much of his time and strength, during the year, in lecturing and in disputations upon the exciting theme of the day. He became satisfied that Mr. Scott had done this to the detriment of his appropriate work. Becoming satisfied of this, he took occasion to have a private and brotherly conversation with him, and earnestly advised him to desist from such a course. The bishop soon found, however, that he was determined to persist in his course, and that no persuasions could avail with him, as he felt conscientiously bound in the matter. He then frankly told him that, in view of the action of the General Conference, and in view of what he conceived to be his obligations to promote the peace and well-being of the Church, he could not continue him in the office of presiding elder. The result was that Mr. Scott was removed from the district; but, that he might not seem to be oppressed, he was sent to Lowell, one of the best appointments within the bounds of the conference. He had even the choice of his own colleague, of whom he says, "Our hearts were united as the hearts of David and Jonathan."* This certainly does not look much like oppression; and

* Scott's Memoir, p. 38.

yet for this act Bishop Hedding's administration was assailed in the most bitter terms. This was done not only in private circles and in lectures, but also in the public press, and by Mr. Scott himself. The bishop himself remarks: "This, I suppose, was the principal cause of Mr. Scott's repeated attacks upon me in a public paper afterward. Up to this time, I never knew one of the members of the New-England Conference to cherish other than the most friendly and fraternal feelings toward me. But the manner I felt it my duty to act in this case, and in one other at this conference, led some—chiefly, if not exclusively, those who afterward left the Church—to manifest often other than kind and fraternal feelings."

The other case to which the bishop refers related to proposed conference action on the subject of slavery. At this conference a committee on slavery had been appointed. From various causes the report of that committee was not presented for conference action till the very last session. This was an evening session, and it was eleven o'clock at night before it was presented. When it was read the bishop found it was a very long and intricate one, referring to facts and maintaining principles which required close examination before the report could properly be adopted. A large minority of the conference too, as he well knew, were not willing the report should be adopted without investigation and an opportunity for debate. When a motion was made, after a single reading of the report to adopt it as a whole, he stated these facts to the conference; and told them there were some things in the report of which he doubted whether they were or were not contrary to Methodism, and he did not feel at liberty to put the question to vote without more time to examine it, and advised them to adjourn, and take the subject up deliberately on the morrow. He further stated that if, on examination, he found it to be consistent with Methodism, he was willing to put it to vote; whereas, if he found it contrary to Methodism, he should violate his duty to the Church in submitting it to vote. A motion was then made to adjourn, but it was not carried. "Then," said the bishop, "we cannot vote on the report;" and, accordingly, he proceeded with the regular business, read out the appointments, and closed the conference.

This act of the bishop was harshly assailed. He was accused of acting "without law and above law," of "depriving the conference of its rights," of "usurping authority not given to him," and the like.

At the New-Hampshire Conference, which succeeded soon after, Bishop Hedding gave additional offence to the ultraists. The same reasons that had induced him to remove Orange Scott from the Providence District, led him to decline the appointment of Rev. George Storrs to a vacant district in the New-Hampshire Conference. The friends of Mr. Storrs strongly urged the appointment, and personally the bishop was not averse to it; but, in view of the previous course of Mr. Storrs on the subject of slavery, and also in view of the action of the General Conference and of his own official obligations, he deemed it his duty to pursue the same course he had pursued with Mr. Scott, and informed Mr. Storrs that he could not appoint him to such an office unless he had some assurance that he would cease to distract the Church by active participation in the ultra measures of the day. Mr. Storrs replied that he could come under no such obligation. Bishop Hedding then said to him,—"My obligations to the Church, then, will not allow me to appoint you presiding elder; for I should only be putting you in a more prominent place that you might do more mischief." This terminated the negotiation. The next morning Mr. Storrs read a paper in conference, stating that he could not take an appointment under an officer of the General Conference in view of the action of that body on the subject of slavery, and he therefore asked a location. So far as we know, Mr. Storrs had been a talented, useful, and influential man in the conference; nor will we call in question the sincerity of his convictions or the purity of his motives. Yet we think his subsequent career fully vindicates the far-seeing wisdom and unflinching integrity of the venerable bishop.

These events, and others connected with them or resulting from the same causes, were, to the last degree, painful to the bishop. He felt himself conscientiously shut up to a course, for the sake of the Church and of the cause of God, which was turning many of his earliest and best friends into bitter opposers. He even felt constrained to change the place of his residence; and, in the fall of this year, removed from Lynn, Massachusetts, to Lansingburgh, New-York.

At the session of the New-England Conference in 1837, Bishop Hedding, believing himself to be misrepresented and injured by the letters of Orange Scott, reflecting upon his course at the preceding session, felt it to be his duty to bring the matter to the attention of the conference. Accordingly he read a paper to the conference, specifying the charges made against him by O. Scott, and showing that some of them were misrepresentations of his action, and that others were absolutely false in fact.* Mr. Scott replied in a

* Some private correspondence on the subject had taken place between them during the year, but without any satisfactory results. The following extract from a letter to Mr. Scott from Bishop Hedding, dated "Lansingburgh, November 26, 1836," relates to this subject, and is worthy of preservation in this connexion. "You certainly labour under a great mistake in supposing that I committed an 'encroachment upon your rights' at the last session of the New-England Conference. The course I took was the same in principle I have always followed in your conference and in all others I have attended. It was the same all the other bishops have followed, so far as I know, from the beginning of my acquaintance with Methodism. We have always practiced putting off questions to such times as we supposed would best contribute to facilitate the business of the conference. We have always practiced setting aside such motions or resolutions as we supposed unconstitutional.

"But the reason you never happened to perceive it before, I suppose, is, the course never before crossed your favourite object. The Discipline gives me a perfect right to do as I did, and I judged the business of the conference required me to do it. The conference, at the close, gave me a vote of thanks by an almost unanimous vote,

speech of considerable length; after which two of the brethren preferred formal charges of slander and misrepresentation against him. Bishop Hedding felt anxious to have an amicable settlement of the matter,

and they cannot *now, as honest men,* complain. You admitted at Lynn that you probably voted for that resolution of thanks, and you cannot now consistently complain. You were either dishonest then, or you are unreasonable now in complaining as you do about my acts in that conference. Why did not you or they oppose the vote of thanks? Why did you not, like honest men, state, in my presence, what you supposed to be wrong in my administration, and give me opportunity to explain or retract, if either were necessary? I believe the truth is, that neither you nor the conference thought '*I encroached*' on your rights at the time; but you, *yourself*, have imagined the idea since, and made others believe it, and now you go about holding me up to public contempt about a supposed evil which is only a creature of your own imagination.

"I was willing to attend to the resolutions on abolition at the proper time, and I told the conference so over and over again. I said the last evening I was willing to stay three days for that purpose, and advised the conference to stay the next day; but the majority were unwilling to stay, and the friends of the resolutions withdrew them, and now you blame me and traduce me before the public because the resolutions were not passed. Dear Orange, where is your reason, where is your conscience, that you can think yourself justified before God or man and do thus? Have I no '*rights*' as well as you? Has the president of a conference, when in the chair, no rights? Must he be under the control of the few or the many in every little question? When would a conference get through its business if the president were obliged to take the course you contend for?

"I admit the General Conference has a right to take that course, and they usually leave a large portion of their business undone. That, probably, was the cause of the loss of the temperance question this year. But with the annual conference it is different. They and the president are a dependent body; they meet to do certain business, and they are not obliged to do anything else unless they choose. The New-England Conference testified that this year in refusing to stay and pass the resolutions on abolition, though a majority doubtless were abolitionists.

"I do not believe there are old preachers in the New-England Con-

believing it would be best for the Church and also for the accused, for whom he really had great respect, and hoped that he might yet be saved to the Church. He therefore proposed a friendly meeting of the parties with a few of the friends of each, which was had. This meeting resulted in the following "retractions," which were satisfactory to the bishop, and were assented to and signed by Orange Scott, as follows:—

Corrections.*—"Whereas I wrote several letters

ference who would say such things as you tell me were said by some 'older and better' than you are, if they understood the matter. You have probably excited them and operated upon them till you have led them to say, imprudently, what they themselves did not understand. I was in hopes that, after our interview at Lynn, you would see the wrongs you had done and take a more prudent course in future; but the statements in your letter impress me with this idea, that if a bishop should happen to do in your conference what a few of you should think improper, you would exert your influence to destroy Methodism in New-England! Surely I thought you loved Methodism better than that! If a bishop does wrong, you ought to take the steps the gospel and the Discipline point out to correct him, and not abuse him in the public newspapers, nor destroy Methodism on his account. Through the whole session of the New-England Conference it never entered my mind that I was taking a course different from what was usual, nor did I suppose that any one else thought so till your printed letter followed me to Vermont in September. I cannot regard your doings in this matter otherwise than what the Scriptures call backbiting; but I still hope you will repent and reform. But I do not suppose you see the evil of your doings any more than slaveholders do theirs; and, believing you do not yet *intend* to be wicked, I still feel toward you as a brother."

* It is due to Bishop Hedding to remark that he had made an effort during the year to adjust this unpleasant matter, so as not to be under the necessity of bringing it to the attention of the conference at all. The result of that effort will be best seen by the subjoined attestation of mutual friends, who were present:—"The undersigned,

to Bishop Hedding, and to the editor of Zion's Watchman, and caused them and several anonymous letters to be published in said paper of August 31, September 21, and December 7, 1836; and

members of the New-England Conference, were present at a conversation which took place between Bishop Hedding and Rev. O. Scott some time in the month of September or October last, in Lynn, relative to certain statements contained in a letter of August 31, 1836, and published in Zion's Watchman, addressed by Rev. O. Scott to Bishop Hedding. In that conversation brother Scott admitted that a number of his statements were incorrect, (we should think seven or eight,) and he promised to correct them in a way which he presumed would give satisfaction. But we are of the opinion he has not done it, but rather made things worse in his second communication.

"1. Brother Scott says, 'Your zeal, however, to put down the abolitionists, and stop the discussion of the slave question, has been to me not only a matter of regret, but of surprise.'

"The bishop showed that he had made no effort to put down *abolitionists*, or stop the discussion of the slave question, but only to restrain certain brethren from what he deemed imprudent and unprofitable proceedings on that subject. Brother Scott admitted he was incorrect in this particular.

"2. The Pastoral Address alluded to in the letter does not 'attempt to silence' the discussion, but only to prevent brethren from performing acts in the discussion which the authors of the Address believe to be improper. Brother Scott could not produce any evidence to the contrary.

"3. The letter attributes to the bishop the manifestation of 'a spirit of disdain' toward two hundred Methodist ministers, and more than three thousand Church-members. This brother Scott admitted was without foundation.

"4. Brother Scott admitted that what he had said respecting the removal of a presiding elder was not strictly correct. Also, that the bishop has a right to remove a presiding elder for '*no cause*,' was a mistake.

"5. The letter states that the bishop said, respecting the report on abolition, that 'there were some parts in it to which he should object.' The bishop said, 'There *might* be some things in it which he could not properly put to vote.' Brother Scott assented to this.

whereas I am now convinced said letters contain a number of statements which are erroneous, and injurious to the reputation of Bishop Hedding, I avail myself of this mode of correcting them.

"6. What was written relating to the sanction of the Counter-Appeal, he admitted was not strictly correct.

"7. There are several passages in the letter which represent the bishop as acting improperly, in allowing the minority to speak and consume time, which ought not to have been written; for members in the minority had a right to speak, as well as those in the majority. Brother Scott could make no very satisfactory reply.

"8. In another letter, published in said Watchman of September 21, he says: 'Our president took, it is believed, an imprudent, if not an illegal course, in order to prevent that report from being acted on.' But the bishop told the conference several times over 'that we would take time at the close to attend to that report, and that the last evening he advised them to adjourn till the next day, and examine the report deliberately—that he was willing to stay three days for it, if necessary.' Brother Scott ought to have published all this, if he published anything. Brother Scott admitted the above to be true.

"9. Brother Scott represents to the public, 'that he presumes a majority of the conference think the bishop oppressed them;' and yet, at the close, the conference gave the bishop a vote of thanks by a unanimous vote; and he said in our presence at Lynn, 'he presumed HE voted for it.'

"On the statements relating to the powers of a bishop, in regulating the business of a conference, Bishop Hedding said he had no controversy with him, as it was with both of them a matter of *opinion.*

"In our opinion, the letter addressed to Bishop Hedding is not only incorrect in point of facts, but is greatly wanting in ministerial courtesy, such as should be manifested between *equals*, and especially be shown by a junior toward a senior—a superintendent and a father in our Israel.

"Finally, of all the men we have ever known, either in civil or ecclesiastical office, Bishop Hedding is the last who ought to be held up to the world as an *oppressor* and a *tyrant.*

(Signed) "TIMOTHY MERRITT,
"DANIEL FILLMORE,
"LYNN, *May* 26, 1837." "T. C. PEIRCE."

"The statements that the bishop exercised 'zeal to put down the abolitionists,' that he showed a spirit of 'disdain' at the last General Conference, that he 'removed a presiding elder from his district for the simple reason that he could not give satisfactory assurance that he would not agitate the question of slavery and abolition in future, by lecturing and writing on those subjects,' and that 'there seemed to be a decided hostility to the anti-slavery brethren,' are mistakes, and they are hereby retracted.

"Also, those statements which represent the bishop as 'oppressing and aggrieving' the New-England Conference at its session in 1836, as denying them their 'rights,' acting with 'partiality' among them, and all similar imputations, are admitted to be errors, and are hereby recalled.

"ORANGE SCOTT."

"NANTUCKET, *June* 13, 1837."

When these retractions had been made, the brethren who had preferred charges against Mr. Scott withdrew them. Here Mr. Hedding hoped the matter would end. Indeed, he hoped further that relations of Christian amity might be preserved between himself and the accused, and also that the latter would return to his regular work.

The New-Hampshire Conference occurred soon after the close of the New-England. Here Bishop Hedding found himself placed in circumstances

22

where official duty compelled him to give further and still greater offence to the ultra-abolitionists. There were two occasions for this offence. First, a motion was made to appoint a committee on slavery. The bishop proposed to put the motion on several conditions, which he specified. The principal of these conditions were, first, "The conference shall not act on the report of said committee till that part of the conference business is finished which is necessary to prepare for fixing the appointments of the preachers;" and, second, "If, in the judgment of the president, the report of the said committee shall contain any article contrary to the Discipline of our Church, or contrary to the advice of the General Conference, as expressed in the Pastoral Address of that body, bearing date May 26, 1836, it is understood and admitted that he, the said president, is under no obligation to put to vote any motion to adopt said report." These conditions were not accepted by the conference, and, consequently, the committee was not appointed.

The second occasion of offence occurred near the close of the conference. One of the members offered a resolution "highly disapproving" of the action of "the Baltimore Annual Conference" in relation to the meaning of the General Rule forbidding *the buying and selling of men, women, and children with an intention to enslave them.* The resolution offered not only introduced the subject acted upon by the Baltimore Annual Conference, but specified the conference and arraigned its action. Bishop Hedding immediately *refused* to put the motion for the adoption of this resolution, assigning as his reason that it would bring the two conferences into collision with each other; that it was not competent in our economy for one annual conference to pass judgment upon the acts of another, each annual conference being amenable to the General Conference only for its individual action; and further, that such a course, if persisted in, would reduce the Church to a state of anarchy and confusion.

As it was claimed by many that in this decision, and in that made at the New-England Conference the preceding year, Bishop Hedding had transcended the limits of his authority, he deemed it to be his duty to give an exposition of his views upon the subject, and vindicate himself from such charges. This he did in an able speech delivered before the conference. This speech, as occasion called for it, was subsequently repeated before several other conferences, and finally published at the request of the Oneida and Genesee Annual Conferences. The following extracts give the arguments of the bishop that specially bear upon the point at issue:—

"Much has been said respecting the duties of the president of an annual conference, and the rights of such a conference. Both the duties of the president and the rights of conference are laid down in the book of Discipline. The president is authorized to appoint the day of the ordinations, (Discipline, pp. 119, 124;) consequently, it is his right so to arrange the business as to prepare for the ordinations.

"The Discipline also gives the president the right to close the conference in a week from the commencement, if he can get through the proper conference business in that time. (See Discipline, p. 23.) 'They shall allow the annual conferences to sit a week at least.' This includes the right so to arrange the business as to close in a week, if practicable and necessary. And it is well the president has that right; for, if he had it not, contentious men might prolong the session to an unreasonable and burdensome length. But, though the bishops have that right, they have always, so far as I know, yielded to the wishes and requests of brethren when they could do so consistently with the general business of the conference, with the responsibility to the General Conference, and their duty to the whole Church.

"It has been contended that the president of an annual conference ought to put to vote every resolution that is offered; but this is too absurd to be believed by any considerate man who understands our plan of Church government. Under constitutional restrictions, this is true of the General Conference, but not of an annual conference. The real question in debate is, Whether a president is under obligation to put to vote any and every resolution an annual conference may wish to adopt?

"An annual conference is not a primary, independent body. Though it was so originally, when there was but one annual conference at the time our Church was organized, in the year 1784, it is not so now. When there was but one annual conference, that was also the General Conference. After our Church was organized, the primary, independent conference met once in four years, under the name of General Conference, consisting of all the travelling preachers in full connexion; then, for a time, of all the travelling elders, and thus it continued till 1808. The General Conference continued to exercise the same powers the original conference did when the Church was organized. During this time, from 1784 to 1808, temporary annual conferences were held, to do particular business, which could not be deferred four years. The bounds of the annual conferences were fixed sometimes by the bishops, and sometimes by the General Conference; yet no one of the annual conferences was the primary body, but only a part of it.

"Since the establishment of the delegated General Conference, which was provided for in 1808, the whole travelling connexion has been supposed to be present once in four years, by representation, in General Conference assembled, and has continued to be the primary body—the same as that which organized the Church. And as the present annual conferences are controlled, divided, and bound by the General Conference, and as any one of them may be scattered into other conferences, and thus annihilated, it is plain they are neither primary nor independent bodies.

"An annual conference is constituted by the General Conference; it is dependent on, and responsible to it. And the General Conference has told the annual conference what to do; its duty and rights are laid down in the Discipline. That is its charter, and it has no other rights as a conference, only those which are granted either by statute or by fair inference in that charter.

"You have other rights as men, and as Christians, and as Methodist preachers, but not as an annual conference. The General Conference appoints your president, and you and he are obliged by law to do just what the Discipline tells you, and no more. I say you are not obliged to do any more. Therefore, the conference cannot compel the president to do any more, and the president cannot compel the conference to do any more. If they do more, they do it by mutual agreement between the conference and the president, and both are responsible for what they do; but the president is so in a higher degree than the conference, for he may be punished for the transaction of improper business in an annual conference to a degree the conference cannot. They may call what they do, over and above their duty, conference business, if they please, and place it on the journals, and if no harm is done no one will complain. But if either party, the conference or the president, refuses to do more than the Discipline requires or authorizes, the other party cannot justly complain.

"The annual conference can do no business without the president. They cannot remove him from the chair, nor appoint another, unless the lawful president be absent, and fail of appointing a president, which, in that case, he has a right to do.

"In conferences where there are slaves and slave-owners, the question of slavery might come up as proper conference business, and often does so. It might there be said, 'I object to this preacher because he has sold a slave;' or, 'I object to that one because he does not emancipate his slaves.' But in this conference, where you have no jurisdiction over slaves or slave owners, it is impossible to make it appear that you have any authority in the case. You might, indeed, recommend to the General Conference new rules, or alterations of the old ones; but that would be a very different thing from the subject of which we have been speaking.

"The Discipline does not require the president to do this kind of business; he has never promised to do it, and the conference has no authority to command him to do it.

"Yet, though I am under no obligation, on the ground of '*right*,' to put any such question to vote; still, on the ground of courtesy, I would do it most cheerfully if I could consistently with other and higher obligations.

"The moment I step beyond the law, and put any

question to vote which that does not require or authorize, I act voluntarily, and I alone am responsible for my own act. What I have claimed on this subject is, a right to judge of my own duty in acts not required by the Discipline. But this '*right*' certain men have attempted to wrest from me, by claiming the right to govern me; and because I was not willing to submit, they have made this terrible outcry you have heard about the loss of 'rights,' which, in my opinion, they never possessed.

"It has been said, 'It is the prerogative of the [annual] conference to decide *what* business they will do, and *when* they will do it.' But I deny it. This is assuming the rights of the General Conference, and usurping the control over the president of an annual conference, which no body of men have a right to exercise but the General Conference. And because I was unwilling to submit to this usurpation I have been severely censured. I have been unjustly and cruelly held up to public view, by certain inconsiderate writers, as one who infringed on the 'rights' of my brethren, merely because I did not consent to do what I was under no obligation to do, what I was bound by no law to do, and what I have never promised to do. And more than this, the acts I was called upon to do were such as I believed it wrong for *me* to do; and this, I believe, was well understood by those who have censured me.

"The men who have written against me, have written against the General Conference also; and hereby have clearly shown that they disregarded the authority of the Church in any department, unless it shall consent to adopt their creed and to follow their measures. There has appeared to be a strong desire in these men to drive me into measures which they knew I believed to be wrong, and which they knew also would be likely to bring me into collision with the General Conference, as well as with some of the annual conferences. *Censures*, *hints* of wrongs where no wrongs were, and even threats, have been employed to accomplish this work of tyranny.

"If an annual conference possessed such rights as these writers have supposed, it might legally censure the very General Conference who gives it existence, and do other things which would scatter our connexion to the four winds. And yet, because I could not consistently acknowledge such 'rights,' I have been indirectly accused of attempting to 'RULE' a conference. I have attempted no such thing: I have only claimed the right to rule myself in my official duties,—to judge for myself, as I must answer for myself, what it is lawful and expedient for me to do; that is, what motion I may or may not properly put to vote in an annual conference. And although I could not with propriety submit a question of this sort to the dictation of a few individuals, or to the decision of an annual conference, yet I have uniformly acknowledged my responsibility to the General Conference, whose agent I am, and to whom I am amenable for acting or not acting in all such cases. Yet individuals have demanded of me, on the ground of 'rights,' services which the General Conference never required, and thereby have attempted to govern me.

"This subject has been connected with the 'rights' of our people to send petitions to the —— annual conference. That the people have a right to petition the general or annual conference, I cheerfully admit; and that an annual conference ought to attend to their petitions on all business which the Discipline requires such conference to do, I admit also; and this is all the business we have covenanted with the people to do in an annual conference. But when they petition us to do such things as are foreign to our duty, I deny their right to *require* us to spend our time and strength in doing those things. If they ask us to do a thing for *them* as a favour, we will cheerfully do it if we can consistently; but if they *demand* such services as a 'right,' they must allow us to judge of our own obligations and duties.

"The great subject on which this demand on our time and services is claimed, is slavery. And I have never refused to attend to it in annual conferences, so far as my time, health, and obligations to the whole Church would admit. But what I have done, I have done on principles of courtesy, not on the ground of obligation or 'right;' for it is proper for me to do many things to oblige my friends, which neither friends nor enemies could demand of me on the ground of 'RIGHTS.' And my respected colleague, who has been represented to the public as taking to himself undue authority at the last session of the New-England Conference, acted, so far as I know, on the same principle I have. He offered to put to vote a motion to appoint a committee to consider and report on petitions and memorials from the people on that subject, on such conditions as he deemed consistent with *his* obligations to the General Conference and to the whole Church. But his conditions were rejected; and the reason why he declined to proceed and act in the case was, claims were made on the part of the friends of modern abolitionism to which the president could not, in his judgment, constitutionally submit. For they claimed the '*right*,' as a conference, to appoint a committee to consider and report on said memorials, as also the '*right*' to act in a conference capacity on any report of such committee. And although, as has been reported, the president did not allow an appeal to that body, as he considered it a question of law, yet he distinctly admitted that the conference had the right to carry the subject up to the General Conference.

"Although I cannot, any more than my colleague, admit what some brethren have claimed as '*rights*' on this subject, yet I am willing now, as I have always been, to do anything I can do constitutionally and safely to oblige brethren. But I cannot act as some have wished, and as I suppose some of you wish me to act, because I not only believe such act would be useless, but *wrong* and *injurious*. It would injure other conferences, and that I cannot do; for I am superintendent—jointly with my colleagues—of the whole Church; I am required to 'oversee the spiritual business' of the whole; I am related alike to all the conferences; therefore, I ought not to do anything in one conference which I know has a tendency to injure another."

Then referring to the specific subject upon which it was proposed to take action, the bishop adds:—"Another reason why I cannot enter into these measures, and act on them as conference business, is, I am advised not to do so, and that by the General Conference. In their 'Pastoral Address' of May 26, 1836, they advise us all to abstain from all such movements. This advice was given by the highest authority in the Church—by the body to which I am responsible—by the collected wisdom of our religious community—by nearly all the delegates of all the annual conferences, which was the same in principle as all the annual conferences in General Conference assembled, and by that body of men who know more on that subject than any other in this nation. A body of Christian ministers, collected from nearly all parts of this nation, who, for piety, benevolence, wisdom, zeal, labours, and sufferings in the cause of Christ, will not suffer by comparison with any other body of the same number, after solemnly deliberating on this subject, have, in their official capacity, given me this advice.

And, whatever others may think of it, I am religiously bound to govern myself by it."

He still further remarks:—"I have been indirectly and repeatedly charged before the public with partiality, because, in some conferences, I have put to vote resolutions relating to this subject, but have objected to doing so in other conferences. But my course has been steady and uniform. In some conferences I have put to vote resolutions which, in my judgment, tended to allay improper excitement, to prevent discord, and to promote peace. In others, I have declined putting resolutions to vote which I believed to be of a contrary tendency, and in these measures I believe I have done my duty.

"On this principle, and on no other, I am willing to act with you in this conference; for the claim on the ground of 'conference right,' to compel me to attend to this business, I think, will now no longer be *assumed;* but if it should, there are two other considerations which *alone*, if nothing had been said, would settle the question in the minds of all men who judge without *prepossession*, and who are *acquainted* with our system of Church government. One of them is, when an annual conference, in conference capacity, has done those articles of business the Discipline *requires*, it has *finished* its DUTY, as a conference, for that session, and any member, or the president, is at perfect liberty to desist, and do no more. If the conference or the president does any more business, it is done on the principle of courtesy: it may be right in itself, but it cannot be demanded on the ground of 'RIGHTS.'

"It ought to be further remembered, that the Discipline gives the president the right of appointing the times of the several annual conferences; and the interests of the Church often require that one conference be appointed at so short a time after another, that there would be no more time than to do the business the Discipline requires in the first, in season for the president to travel to the second. Now, if any number of the preachers, or even a whole conference, had authority, on the ground of the new *doctrine* of 'conference right,' to compel a president to remain at one conference more than a week, to do other business, over and above what the Discipline requires, then that conference might hinder his going to the next one. Also, on this supposition, one conference might *rightfully* prevent the president attending all the others for the season; for if a conference, by '*right*,' could detain a president one hour beyond the time before named, by the same 'right' they might detain him a month, or a year, and altogether hinder his doing his duty in all the other conferences—the supposition of which is absurd.

"I think it must now plainly appear, that the assumed 'rights' claimed by those who have undertaken to rule in this matter, if admitted and carried out into practice, would completely prostrate the government of our Church, and throw all her great plans and interests into utter confusion."

Another item in this very able document, though it has only an incidental relation to the point now before us, we beg leave to introduce, because of the wide celebrity it has attained. It reads as follows:—"But it will be asked, What right has any member of our Church to own a slave? Before I answer this question I will just say, and I wish what I now say to be distinctly remembered, I am ready to disapprove the *slave-trade*, the *system of slavery*, including all the unjust and cruel rights which any laws are supposed to give, and all the injustice and cruelties inflicted on slaves, as decidedly as Mr. Wesley did.

"But all these points are aside of the main question. The main question is, What right have any of our members to hold slaves? Or, What right has the Church to allow them to hold slaves? Lest I be misunderstood, before I proceed I beg you to observe that owning, or holding a slave, does not include exercising all the rights which the laws are supposed to give the master over the servant, but only such as are necessary for the good of the servant and the safety of the master, all the circumstances being taken into the account. Now let us answer the question. The right to hold a slave is founded on this rule: 'Therefore, all things whatsoever ye would that men should do to you, do ye even so to them: for this is the law and the prophets.' Matt. vii, 12. All acts in relation to slavery, as well as to every other subject, which cannot be performed in obedience to this rule, are to be condemned, and ought not to be tolerated in the Church. If no case can be found where a man can own a slave, and in that act obey this rule, then there is no case in which slave-owning can be justified."

Do not be alarmed, gentle reader; this is Bishop Hedding's celebrated "Golden-Rule Argument to justify American Slavery." Analyze it; see what it amounts to. Why, just this. The bishop disapproves of "the *slave-trade* and the *system of slavery*, including all the unjust and cruel rights which any laws are supposed to give, and all the injustice and cruelties inflicted on slaves;" and further, he explicity declares that "if no case can be found where a man can own a slave, and in that act obey the 'golden rule,' then there is no case in which slave-owning can be justified." But he does state that under certain circumstances, which he thus substantially specifies,—"the exercising of such rights as the law is supposed to give the master over the slave only so far as they are necessary for the good of the servant and the safety of the master,"—under these circumstances, "the right to hold a slave is founded on this rule: 'Therefore, all things whatsoever ye would that men should do to you, do ye even so to them: for this is the law and the prophets.'"

Bishop Hedding had now committed "the unpardonable sin." Had he uttered blasphemy on the conference floor, a greater outcry could not have been raised. This passage—"The right to hold a slave is founded on this rule: 'Therefore, all things whatsoever ye would that men should do to you, do ye even so to them: for this is the law and the prophets,'" Matt. vii, 12—was segregated from its connections and explanatory clauses, and heralded over the land as Bishop Hedding's "golden-rule argument in defence of slavery." A more palpable outrage upon all the principles of fair and honest dealing was never perpetrated. Yet so industriously was the libel circulated, and so boldly was it emblazoned before the world, that multitudes, even of our own members and ministers, were deluded into the belief that Bishop Hedding had actually attempted to justify the system of slavery upon this ground. In fact, it was some years before the public mind was disabused upon the subject.

The ruling which was made by Bishop Hedding with regard to the introduction of extraneous matter, or business not prescribed in the Discipline, into the annual conferences, was sustained by all his colleagues. In respect to the quarterly conferences, in some instances presiding elders had felt constrained to take the same position.

The question very naturally arises, Was there any necessity for exercising what seemed to be the full extent of episcopal authority, and what was regarded by many as an unwarrantable stretch of that authority? To ascertain this, we have only to glance at some of the resolutions it was proposed to pass. We have already given an instance in which it was proposed in one annual conference to censure another. About this time, in one of the quarterly conferences on the Meadville District, Erie Conference, it was proposed to pass resolutions condemnatory of the action of the preceding Erie Annual Conference. The presiding elder, Rev. H. Kinsley, arrested what he considered revolutionary action by refusing to put the vote. In Marshfield, Massachusetts, resolutions were offered in the quarterly conference charging the bishops and presiding elders with the assumption of authority "utterly unsupported by either the letter or spirit of our Discipline;" and others, in Duxbury, Massachusetts, reprobating the "system of oppression and persecution set up and prosecuted by the New-York Conference against the abolitionists.." In both these cases the presiding elder, Rev. B. Otheman, stated to the brethren that he could not consent to put resolutions which arraigned the bishops and annual conferences to vote; both the bishops and the annual conferences were amenable to the General Conference, and the proper modes of arresting their action, and reversing it if wrong, were open to them; but for quarterly conferences to take such action as was proposed, was disorderly and revolutionary. In the latter case, the members of the quarterly conference, after the presiding elder had left the house, remained and passed a resolution condemning his course as "contrary to the Discipline and usages of the Church—a violation of their rights as men and Christians." Any one will perceive that had there been no power competent to arrest such proceedings, the whole Church must have been thrown into a state of anarchy, with hostile factions making war upon each other.

But we must now return to trace the course of Bishop Hedding, while providentially thrown into the midst of one of the most exciting popular movements ever witnessed in this country.

We have already observed, that when he had obtained what was considered by all parties a just and honourable retraction of the misstatements that had been made by Mr. Scott, he fondly hoped that his personal as well as official collisions with that brother were at an end. This reasonable hope, however, was doomed to a speedy disappointment. The conference granted Mr. Scott a supernumerary relation, and he wished to be left without an appointment. Bishop Waugh, however, appointed him to Wilbraham, and placed him in charge of the station. From his pastoral charge he was soon released by the presiding elder of the district, and immediately engaged in the work of an anti-slavery lecturer.* Being thus released from his charge, the bishop found him stirring up the elements of discord at every subsequent conference he attended for the season. Though exceedingly afflicted by the perversion of his acts and

* Scott's Memoirs, p. 118.

motives, and the ridicule to which he was constantly subjected in the lectures of Messrs. Scott and Storrs, the bishop carefully avoided an open rupture, and maintained himself in respect to the whole matter as became his position and duty. He felt aggrieved, however, to receive such treatment from those who had been his friends, and with whom he had for so many years maintained Christian fellowship and intercourse.

Notwithstanding Mr. Scott's "retractions" at the session of the New-England Conference in 1836, he repeated the offence by republishing substantially the same letter soon after the session closed, and also by sundry letters published during the year, containing allegations equally offensive and misrepresentations equally unjust.

It is perhaps due to the reader, as well as to the memory of Bishop Hedding, to place some of these allegations upon record, that the provocations he received may be better understood. From "No. 7" of Orange Scott's "Letters to Dr. Fisk," over the signature of "Wesleyan," and published in Zion's Watchman, August 5, 1837, we take the following specimens: "An unprecedented and most painful crisis has arrived in the annals of Methodism! Two of our bishops have *assumed rights* which, if carried out and applied to all parts of our beautiful superstructure, would prove its destruction. In *three several instances* have annual conferences, since the last General Conference, been deprived of their rights—

rights of conscience—rights to express an opinion on a moral question." The italicising is in the original. Again: "Two of them [the bishops] have assumed the astonishing power over annual conferences which prevents them from exercising their rights of conscience and of opinion." And again: "For the unparliamentary and unprecedented course which some of the bishops have taken, as presiding officers, *they alone are responsible!* I doubt whether in the annals of sacred and profane history, among civilized nations, for assumption of power, as presiding officers, *a parallel can be found!*" Still again: "It is to be hoped that the bishop will recede from his *new measures* in his administration on the slavery question. HE MUST DO THIS, or the Church will be rent limb from limb. There are several of our annual conferences that *never can*, and NEVER WILL submit to such oppressive measures!" In the same letter he intimates that the "corrections" already noticed were signed, not from any conviction that "*strict justice*" to Bishop Hedding required them, but as "a peace offering," and from this motive he had consented to "give the bishop *his price*." He also gives it as the opinion of many, that he had committed "an act of injustice to himself in giving the corrections to the bishop" without certain restrictions as to their publication; and also that "the corrections themselves were uncalled for."

In another letter published in Zion's Watchman, (October 14, 1837,) over the signature of "Coke," Mr.

Scott again says: "The bishop may talk of being sent to the conference to do certain business,—*but the Discipline specifies no business which* HE *is to do in the conferences except to 'preside'* in them, (not *rule* them;) and is it presiding in the conference to sit in the chair and refuse to do the duties of president, and thus prevent the whole conference from acting? This, I must say, is a *new way* to 'preside' in a deliberative body." The above will indicate something of the manner in which Bishop Hedding's official acts were reviewed, and also of the little reliance that could be placed on compromises and adjustments. We have no disposition to question Mr. Scott's sincerity and integrity of purpose. We believe that he was willing to, and really did, make great personal sacrifices for the cause of humanity; but he evidently had become so completely absorbed in the one object at which he aimed, and at the same time had become so excited by the opposition he encountered in his mission, that he often took false views of the character and acts of those opposed to him, and gave wrong and injurious versions of them to the public. Palliate his *motives*, however, as we may, no legitimate palliation could excuse the style and manner of his assaults upon Bishop Hedding.

The bishop felt himself to be not only placed in a false light before the public by them, but also to be deeply injured in his reputation and influence. Under these circumstances, he felt that it was due to himself, to the Church, and to the cause of justice and truth, to prefer charges against the Rev. Orange Scott at the ensuing session of the New-England Annual Conference for 1838. The principal charges preferred against him were, in substance:—1. A want of Christian sincerity—in promising to make certain corrections and retractions, and then, subsequently, publishing an edition of the letter in which they were originally contained, with "some of the same injurious matter before retracted." 2. Using Bishop Hedding and other bishops in an unbrotherly and disrespectful manner, unbecoming a Methodist preacher—instancing several communications in Zion's Watchman similar in character to those from which we have taken several extracts. The decision of the conference is somewhat singular. The first charge and specifications were negatived: the specifications as to the fact of publication, under the second charge, were sustained; but the charge itself was decided in the negative by a small majority. At this stage the president, Bishop Soule, stated that "although the conference had, by vote, sustained the specifications of the second charge, which was, 'frequently mentioning our names, or otherwise referring to us in a coarse and disrespectful manner, and that since our settlement at Nantucket;' yet as, by another vote immediately succeeding, the conference declined to sustain the charge which complained of the course as '*unbrotherly*,' and '*unbecoming a Methodist preacher*,' it was his opinion that the conference acquitted brother Scott from blame on the charge and specifications." As no one dissented from this opinion of the chair, and as the character of Mr. Scott passed, we are left to conclude that the conference then adjudged the treatment they admitted by their vote Bishop Hedding had received from Mr. Scott in the publications, of which we have given a few specimens, was neither "unbrotherly" nor "unbecoming a Methodist preacher." This decision we cannot but think has been long since revoked in the sober judgment of the conference, as it unquestionably has in the public mind.

At the same conference, Bishop Hedding also preferred charges against the Rev. La Roy Sunderland, then editor of Zion's Watchman, published in New-York city, but a member of the New-England conference. He charged Mr. Sunderland,—(1,) with treating him in a scurrilous manner; (2,) with publishing against him an injurious falsehood; (3,) with publishing a false conjecture respecting the bishops; (4,) with reporting a falsehood; and (5,) with misrepresentation. It would be a waste of time to go into the details of the specifications and evidence taken in this case. Some curious developments were made during the progress of the trial; but the result was the same as in the case of Mr. Scott—acquittal by the conference. Bishop Hedding felt aggrieved by these decisions; he could not but feel that they were made under the influence of a morbid excitement that had biassed the judgment of the members, and also that they were contrary to reason and truth.

His only redress now was in the General Conference, and he looked forward to its session in full confidence that his course of administration would receive its full vindication.

An incident occurred at the close of this conference somewhat illustrative of the spirit of the times, and which it is more necessary for us to notice, because it has been erroneously stated elsewhere. On the SEVENTEENTH DAY of the session, about noon, Bishop Hedding told the conference that he had done all the business his duty required him to attend to, except the reading of the journal and closing; that he must leave that afternoon, or he would not be able to reach the Maine Conference in time for its session; but if they had other business they wished to attend to, they could adjourn and meet in the afternoon, and Bishop Soule had kindly agreed to remain and preside. If, however, they chose to close then, they could have the journal read, and he would give out the appointments and close. The conference voted to have the journal read and to hear the appointments immediately. After this vote was taken, Mr. Scott rose and offered a number of resolutions on the subject of slavery. The bishop decided they were out of order, as the conference had voted to have the journal read, hear the appointments, and to close immediately. No effort was made, so far as we know, to reconsider that vote. The journal was accordingly read, the appointments announced, and the conference adjourned. Subsequently, this act also was ranked among the usurpations of Bishop Hedding.

Immediately after the close of the New-England Conference, Mr. Scott had a one-sided account of his trial, and of Bishop Hedding's administration during its session, published in a "Zion's Herald extra:" with these he was present at the Maine Conference, scattering them broad-cast among the preachers and people. The object could be no other than to disparage the bishop, and to lessen his influence among the preachers. The bishop, however, took no notice of the matter, and there is reason to believe that the effort was nearly, if not quite, abortive.

As an illustration of the state of feeling that existed at this time in the New-Hampshire Conference, and the singular course of action resorted to, we give the following note concerning its proceedings. It is taken from a letter addressed to Bishop Hedding by Bishop Morris, who had presided there this year. The letter is dated at Burlington, Vt., July 14, 1838. After giving Bishop Hedding a pressing invitation to accompany him in his visit to the conferences in northern and western New-York, he adds:—"The New-Hampshire Conference adjourned last Thursday forenoon. We had a pleasant session, all things considered. In reference to the exciting subject of controversy, we got along full as well as I expected. Four agents of the Anti-Slavery Society were present to aid in their out-door arrangements—Robinson, Buckley, G. Storrs, and O. Scott part of the time. The whole time spent in the conference on the subject, first and last, was perhaps about three hours, and during that time very little warmth of feeling was manifested. The first thing done on the subject was to appoint a committee to prepare a memorial to the General Conference, to which I made no objection. When the examination of character came on, we had a little manœuvering. An abolitionist moved to appoint a committee of five, to whom should be referred the case of every brother who had been to the convention, or lectured against slavery, &c. This was a *farce* played off for effect; and after entertaining us with abolition speeches about two hours, they postponed the resolution indefinitely. We resumed the examination, but objection was made to the passage of every brother's character who had participated in abolition measures. One abolitionist would object; another would move to pass the character under consideration, and, after a few speeches, would vote each other through. This became tiresome, and a resolution was brought in declaring that attendance on *abolition conventions*, *delivering abolition lectures*, or *circulating abolition papers*, did not militate against the character of any member of the conference. This I pronounced out of order, on the ground that it approved what General Conference had condemned. An appeal was taken from my decision, and I agreed to put the question on the appeal, provided the journal should embrace my decision against the resolution, and such list of exceptions as I might choose to write. The appeal was sustained, my decision overruled, and the resolution adopted: whereupon I entered my exception. Another motion was made to publish the resolution in several papers. I agreed to put the motion on condition the mover would so amend it as to embrace my decision and my exception, which was agreed to, and the whole ordered to be published. Here our trouble ended. The committee first appointed brought in nothing but the resolutions which the New-England Conference passed touching the general rule on slavery, which the conference adopted without discussion. The brethren were all courteous and friendly, and we parted in peace. With their abolitionism I am not pleased; but there are many excellencies among them, and, upon the whole, I like the preachers of New-Hampshire Conference much better than I expected. They had a net increase of over eighteen hundred members the past year."

As the spirit with which Bishop Hedding moved and prosecuted the trials of Orange Scott and La Roy Sunderland before the New-England Conference, and also the motives that actuated him, have been impugned, we are happy to have it in our power to place before the reader an extract from a letter bearing upon this very point. The humility and godly sincerity that are so manifest here, were striking characteristics of

Bishop Hedding, and will prove, we doubt not, in the reader's mind, a full vindication from the imputations cast upon him. The letter bears the date of March 24, 1840, and is addressed to Rev. Asa Kent, a member of the New-England Conference. The letter will sufficiently indicate the occasion that called for it.

"MY DEAR BROTHER,—I received yours of the 26th ultimo. I thank you for it most sincerely, and especially for the frank and *kind* manner in which you tell me what you and others believe to have been my fault at the Boston Conference; for I consider him my friend who tells me of my faults—real or supposed—in a Christian manner, as you have done. You say, 'But at Boston I saw you oppressed, and the firmness of patience began to yield, when your *manner* in prosecuting those charges against those brethren was different from anything I had ever seen in you.' Before reading this I had no idea of the thing, either from my own reflections or from the suggestions of others. I have endeavoured to examine myself, and to pray over the subject, but I cannot perceive that I felt impatient. But I may be mistaken; I may not have known myself. After the trial of La Roy Sunderland, I had doubts whether I had not used some words which were too sharp, and I named it to Bishop Soule, saying, 'If I have, tell me, and I will take them back before the conference.' But he said he believed my words were none too sharp. It is very probable that, as you say, my manner was different from anything you had ever seen in me; but, as far as I can now see, it arose from other causes, and not from a failure of patience. However, I will inquire of brethren who were present when I see them, and if they think as you do, I will give up my judgment to yours and theirs, and will make any satisfaction to the New-England Conference, if I live to see them, the nature of the case requires; for it would grieve me more to have indulged in impatience, than to suffer injuries from the tongues, or pens, or hands of men. And I have a desire to see my faults, to repent of them, and to confess and forsake them; and whether you or I have erred in opinion respecting the matter of patience, I hope to profit by the information you have given me in so friendly a manner, and to be more watchful in future.

"The causes of my manner, at the times you name, I think were the following:—1. Excessive fatigue; 2. The heat of the weather; 3. I was oppressed with the business of the conference. That business has affected my nerves for the few past years, so that sometimes I have been unable to speak or stand without trembling; and, in one instance, in a conference, I was supposed by one man to be angry, when I *know* my spirit was as cool as it is now. 4. I think the greatest cause was, my spirit was deeply oppressed with a sense of the wrongs these brethren had done me, and the Church through me; and I felt an ardent desire to convince the conference that they had done wrong,—believing the good of the Church required it, and fearing that many of the preachers had not a proper sense of the sin of evil-speaking, backbiting, and slandering. With all these impressions, and under these circumstances, my feelings were greatly excited—probably too much so; but I cannot yet see that it was impatience. I meant to 'rebuke them sharply' before I commenced, for I believed the cause required it; but probably I allowed myself to feel too much. Wherein I erred I pray the Lord to pardon me, and cover me with that atonement which alone affords me hope."

The state of things indicated in the preceding pages continued to exist till the General Conference of 1840, and, to some extent, a year or two later. Generally a cloud of lecturers hung around the path of Bishop Hedding, perverting and misrepresenting his acts and character. His administration entered largely into their public discourses. It was denounced as "usurpation," "tyranny," "one man attempting to rule the conference," and the like. He became also the butt of their ridicule; and in some of their lectures a mock slave-auction was enacted, and Bishop Hedding and his wife in burlesque sold as slaves. These extravagances reacted against the men who enacted them, and led the way to their final withdrawal from the Church. Even before the General Conference of 1840 the violence of the gale had in a great measure passed; and wise and good men—not abating in the least their determined opposition to slavery, whether in or out of the Church—began to feel that the Church was worth preserving, and that it was not necessary to rend it in pieces in order to resist the monster evil of the times.

It is but just to say that we have felt no disposition to impugn the motives of the men who took the lead in this movement. We cannot doubt the honesty of their convictions and the sincerity of their motives. Could they at the outset—before their minds had become prejudiced by opposition to their measures, and their affections alienated from the Church—have seen the inevitable results to which their course tended, they would undoubtedly have paused, and at least assumed positions and adopted measures less offensive and less perilous. Or while their hearts were yet imbued with the tender sentiments of brotherly love, could they have foreseen the alienation of Christian feeling, the turmoil and strife that would be engendered in the Church, they would have hesitated. And, indeed, it must not be concealed that they were often goaded by the rude personalities with which they were assailed, and also by the opprobrious epithets that were heaped upon them. We confess that at this distance of time, on looking through the files of the current newspapers of that day—those which took the lead in opposition to these radical movements—we are painfully impressed with this fact. Many things were written and said that it would have been well for the fair fame of Christian love if they had never existed.

So also, on the other hand, Bishop Hedding may

have uttered or written some things too palliative in relation to slavery, and may have seemed more anxious to vindicate the south—especially Methodists who were involved in "the great evil,"—than at the present day seems fit or appropriate. But it must be recollected that the evils inseparable from the system have since been more fully developed, and in that day the existence of slavery was generally deplored by good men in the south as an evil; and also that its enshrinement as a "divine institution" is of more recent origin. Taking all these facts into the account, we then have a ready interpretation and vindication of his action in the fact that the Church was placed in great peril, and he was bound by the most sacred obligations to guard its integrity. Rather than compromise the well-being of the Church, he suffered himself for a time to be placed in a false position before the world, and to suffer obloquy such as has rarely fallen to the lot of a good man in this age to suffer. These things he endured—not doubting of the present approval of Heaven, and of the ultimate approval of the Christian world. By his firmness in this hour of trial he performed a great service for the Church and for the cause of God.

These explanatory remarks were necessary, in order to exhibit the true position of both parties. There is forgiveness with God for the errors of good men; and whatever of jar to the concord of Christian men there might have been on earth, it has, with most of the prominent actors in these scenes, been hushed and harmonized long since in that better land, where no cloud of prejudice dims the vision, and no bleak winter chills the genial currents of the soul.

What we have further to say upon this subject will be found in connexion with the General Conference of 1840, and the fifth quadrennial of Bishop Hedding's episcopal labour.

CHAPTER XVII.

THE GENERAL CONFERENCE OF 1840, AND THE FIFTH QUADRENNIAL OF EPISCOPAL LABOUR.

General Conference of 1840—Representation—Bishop's Address—Views of Constitutional Powers—Government of the Church—Appeal of Rev. D. Dorchester—Action in relation to the Prerogatives of Bishops and Presiding Elders as Presiding Officers—Bishop Hedding's Communication in relation to the Trials of O. Scott and La Roy Sunderland—Private Adjustment by the Delegates—Magnanimity of Bishop Hedding—Another instance—Speech upon Striking out the Censure of the New-England Conference—His counsel prevails—The Question on the Testimony of Coloured Persons—Dr. Few's Resolution—Tie Vote upon its consideration—Bishop Hedding declines to give the Casting Vote—Shows that a Bishop has no Constitutional Right to Vote—Pastoral Address—Close of the Conference—Annual Conferences—Michigan—Ohio—Dedicates Bedford-street Church in New-York city—Close of the Year—Dedication of John-street Methodist Episcopal Church—Conferences of 1841—Address on the Administration of Discipline—Address before the New-Jersey Conference on Christian Perfection—Results for the Year—Conferences of 1842—The Resolution proposed about Transfers in the New-Hampshire Conference—Address upon "Man's Natural Ability," &c.—Residence at Saratoga—Great fall of Snow—A hard Sleigh-ride—Conferences of 1843—Death of Bishop Roberts—Condition of the Work in the Eastern Conferences—Letter to his Wife—Missionary Cause—Removes to Poughkeepsie—Unprecedented Increase of Members in the Church—Spring of 1844.

THE General Conference for 1840 commenced its sessions in the city of Baltimore on the 1st of May. There were present one hundred and forty-three delegates, distributed among the annual conferences as follows:—New-York, ten; New-England, seven; Maine, five; New-Hampshire, six; Troy, six; Pittsburgh, five; Erie, five; Black River, four; Oneida, six; Michigan, five; Genesee, six; Ohio, eight; Missouri, three; Illinois, six; Kentucky, five; Indiana, five; Holston, three; Tennessee, five; Arkansas, two; Mississippi, three; Alabama, three; Georgia, six; South Carolina, five; North Carolina, three; Virginia, three; Baltimore, eight; Philadelphia, five; and New-Jersey, five. After the organization had been effected, the body entered upon the usual routine of conference business.

Owing to the detention of Bishop Soule by indisposition, the address of the bishops was delayed several days. It is a document of great length, very diffuse and circumlocutory, especially some portions of it; but it touches upon all the varied general interests of the Church, and especially the agitations that had existed, and the new questions that had been mooted, relating to the prerogatives of bishops, presiding elders, &c. Appropriate reference of those matters that required conference action was made.

As we have already adverted, somewhat largely, to the various episcopal decisions called forth by the peculiar phases of the anti-slavery discussion, and of the proposed measures in some of the annual conferences, it is due that the bishops themselves should be heard upon that subject—the restrictions under which they believe themselves to be acting, and the prerogatives they supposed themselves invested with and responsible for exercising. They say:—"It has been the constant aim and united endeavour of your general superintendents to preserve uniformity and harmony in the administration of discipline, and, as far as practicable, prevent conflicting action in all the official bodies in the Church." . . . "In your Pastoral Address to the ministers and people at your last session, with great unanimity, and, as we believe, in the true spirit of the ministers of the peaceful Gospel of Christ, you solemnly advised the whole body to abstain from all abolition movements, and from agitating the exciting subject in the Church. This advice was in perfect agreement with the individual as well as associated views of your superintendents; but, had we differed from you in opinion, in consideration of the age, wisdom, experience, and official authority of the General Conference, we should have felt ourselves under a solemn obligation to be governed by your counsel."

They also bring to the attention of the body the mooted question of "the constitutional powers of the general superintendents, in their relations to the annual conferences, and in their general executive administration of the government; and the rights of the annual and quarterly conferences, in their official capacities." They say further:—"In the prosecution of our superintending agency, we have been compelled to differ in opinion from many of our brethren composing these official bodies; and this difference of opinion, connected with a conviction of our high responsibility, has, in a few cases, resulted in action which has been judged, by those specially concerned, to be high-handed, unconstitutional, tyrannical, and oppressive." After expressing that, from the beginning, they had assured the parties concerned of their readiness to bring the matter before, and to abide by the decision of the "constitutional tribunal," to which they were responsible, they present the subject in the following manner:—

"When any business comes up for action in our annual or quarterly conferences involving a difficulty on a question of law, so as to produce the inquiry, '*What is the law in the case?*' does the constitutional power to decide the question belong to the president or to the conference? Have the annual conferences a constitutional *right* to do any other business than what is specifically prescribed, or, by fair construction, provided for in the form of Discipline? Has the president of an annual conference, by virtue of his office, a *right* to decline putting a motion or resolution to vote, on business other than that thus prescribed or provided for?

"These questions are proposed with exclusive reference to the principle of *constitutional right.* The principles of courtesy and expediency are very different things."

We have already presented a somewhat extended view of the principle involved in this question. But as the following paragraphs still more distinctly exhibit that principle in contrast with its opposite, and also still further elucidate the arguments bearing upon it, we give them to the reader:—

"As far as we have been able to ascertain," continue the bishops in their address, "the views of those who entertain opinions opposite to our own on these points, they may be summed up as follows:—They maintain that all questions of law arising out of the business of our annual or quarterly conferences are to be, of right, settled by the decision of those bodies, either primarily by resolution, or finally by an appeal from the decision of the president; that it is the prerogative of an annual conference to decide *what* business they will do, and *when* they will do it; that they may have a constitutional right to discuss, in their official capacity, all moral subjects; to investigate the official acts of other annual conferences, of the General Conference, and of the general superintendents, so far as to pass resolutions of disapprobation or approval on those acts. They maintain that the president of an annual conference is to be regarded in the same relation to the conference that a chairman or speaker sustains to a civil legislative assembly; that it is his duty to preserve order in the conference, to determine questions of order, subject to appeal, and put to vote all motions and resolutions when called for according to the resolutions of the body; that these are the settled landmarks of his official prerogatives, as president of the conference, beyond which he has no right to go; that although it belongs to his office, as general superintendent, to appoint the time for holding the several annual conferences, he has no discretionary authority to adjourn them, whatever length of time they may have continued their session, or whatever business they may think proper to transact. From these doctrines we have felt it our solemn duty to dissent; and we will not withhold from you our deliberate and abiding conviction, that if they should be sustained by the General Conference, the *uniform* and *efficient* administration of the government would be rendered impracticable.

"The government of the Methodist Episcopal Church is peculiarly constructed. It is widely different from our civil organization. The General Conference is the only legislative body recognized in our ecclesiastical system, and from it originates the authority of the entire executive administration. The exclusive power to create annual conferences, and to increase or diminish their number, rests with this body. No annual conference has authority or right to make any rule of discipline for the Church, either within its own bounds or elsewhere. No one has the power to elect its own president, except in a special case, pointed out and provided for by the General Conference. Whatever may be the number of the annual conferences, they are all organized on the same plan, are all governed by the same laws, and all have identically the same *rights*, *powers*, and *privileges*. These powers, rights, and privileges are not derived from themselves, but from the body which originated them. And the book of Discipline, containing the rules of the General Conference, is the only charter of their rights and directory of their duties as official bodies. The general superintendents are elected by the General Conference, and responsible to it for the discharge of the duties of their office. They are constituted, by virtue of their office, presidents of the annual conferences, with authority to appoint the time of holding them; with a prudential provision that they shall allow each conference to sit at least one week, that the important business prescribed in the form of Discipline may not be hurried through in such a manner as to affect injuriously the interests of the Church. The primary objects of their official department in the Church were, as we believe, to preserve in the most effectual manner an itinerant ministry; to maintain a uniformity in the administration of the government and discipline in every department, and that the unity of the whole body might be preserved. But how, we would ask, can these important ends be accomplished, if each annual conference possessed the *rights* and *powers* set forth in the foregoing summary? Is it to be supposed that twenty-eight constitutional judges of ecclesiastical law, and these, too, not individuals of age and experience, who have had time and means to thoroughly investigate, and analyze, and collate the system, but official bodies, many members of which are young and inexperienced, and without the opportunity of necessary helps for such researches, and without consultation with each other on the points to be decided, will settle different questions of law with such agreement as to have no material conflict between their legal decisions? Is it not greatly to be feared that, with such a system of ecclesiastical jurisprudence, what might be the law in Georgia might be no law in New-England? that what might be orthodoxy in one conference might be heresy in another? Where, then, would be the identity of the law, the uniformity of its administration, or the unity and peace of the Church."*

The question was also brought to the attention of the General Conference in another form, but involving the same principle. This was upon the appeal of of the Rev. D. Dorchester from the decision of the New-England Conference. As presiding elder, Mr. Dorchester had declined to put a resolution to vote in the Westfield Quarterly Conference. In consequence of this he was charged with maladministration at the next succeeding session of the New-England Annual Conference, and that body found him guilty of "exceeding the powers of his office." From this decision Mr. Dorchester appealed to the General Conference.

The action of the General Conference in relation to these matters was very distinct and decisive:—1. The administration of the superintendents was approved; and it was decided that the president of an annual or quarterly conference had a right to decline putting a resolution to vote if he considered it foreign to the proper business of a conference, or incon-

* The entire Address may be found in Bangs's History, vol. iv, commencing on page 336 and continuing to page 371.

sistent with constitutional provisions, and also to adjourn a conference without a formal vote: 2. The decision of the New-England Conference in the case of Rev. D. Dorchester was reversed by a very strong vote, showing that, in the judgment of the General Conference, he did not transcend the powers of his office: 3. And further, in order to place the matter beyond all doubt as to who should decide questions of law in annual and quarterly conferences, the following enactments were made:—

1. In the answer to the question, "What is the bishop's duty?" the seventh item was added, as follows:—"To decide all questions of law in an annual conference, subject to an appeal to the General Conference; but in all cases the application of law is with the conference."

2. Also in the answer to the question, "What are the duties of the presiding elder?" the seventh item was amended and made to read:—"To take care that every part of our Discipline be enforced in his district, and to decide all questions of law in the quarterly-meeting conference, subject to an appeal to the president of the next annual conference; but in all cases the application of the law shall be with the conference."

It has been charged that "the enactment of these laws prove that the previous action of bishops and presiding elders was without law, if not contrary to law." In the face of all the facts connected with the enactment of this law, such an assertion is not only without foundation, but is absolutely absurd. The prerogatives exercised by the bishops could not be "without law," nor "contrary to law," even if there were no distinct and specific enactment direct to the point, because they formed one of the obvious and indispensable elements of our organic existence. The bishops had so judged, and, from the beginning, their administration had accorded with that judgment, and quadrennially the General Conference approved of that administration. In the judgment of the present General Conference, also, the exercise of such prerogatives was not without law, for they entered their distinct endorsement of this very action, which they could not have done had it been in their judgment unwarranted by law. But then the question comes up, "Why enact a new law if the thing was already legal?" We reply, for the most plain and obvious reasons. The administration of the bishops had been called in question; they had been charged with transcending their powers, and under special pleas put forth upon the subject, many had been led to believe that such was the fact, and in consequence had come to regard them and the office they held with distrust. There was, then, an important reason—though no doubts existed in the minds of the bishops or of the General Conference—why the subject should be placed beyond all question by an explicit enactment.

We have already noticed the trial of Rev. Orange Scott and of Rev. La Roy Sunderland at the session of the New-England Conference in 1838, and the manner of their acquittal. Bishop Hedding brought these two cases to the attention of the General Conference by the following communication:—

"DEAR BRETHREN,—In a session of one of the annual conferences, in the year 1838, two preachers were accused, tried, and acquitted; but, in my judgment, they were acquitted contrary to law and evidence. Of this I informed the said conference at the time, stating that I believed that they had erred in judgment, but not intentionally. I believe so still: nevertheless, that error has done much injury, and in my opinion will do much more, unless it be corrected.

"Those brethren were accused of supposed wrongs done to me, and, by acquitting them, the conference has impliedly censured me, and by that act, as I believe, encouraged the same brethren, and others, to inflict on me still further injuries, which they have done to a great extent.

"I informed that conference that I should lay this matter before the General Conference, *not* by way of appeal, as I supposed I had no right to an appeal in this case, but by way of inviting the General Conference to examine the acts of the annual conference in the premises.

"As the appropriate committee may differ from me in judgment in this matter, I forbear mentioning the name of the conference at this time unless this body shall request me to do so; but by your direction I shall state the case to the committee, and refer them to the journals of the said conference.

"Yours, etc., "ELIJAH HEDDING."

"BALTIMORE, *May* 6, 1840."

This communication was referred to a special committee of five, consisting of N. Bangs, W. H. Raper, George Peck, John Dempster, and John Early. When matters had proceeded thus far, one of the oldest delegates of the New-England Conference waited upon the bishop, and expressed his regret that the communication had been made, for he had hoped a private adjustment of that difficulty might have been made between the delegates and him without bringing the matter before the General Conference. The bishop replied that he had waited several days to give the delegates time to make such a proposition, as it belonged to them to do so if the thing were done at all. He further added that he had no disposition to arraign the action of the New-England Conference before the General Conference, and added that even now he was willing, if they desired it, to have a private settlement of the matter if it could be done on proper principles.

When the committee met, the delegates from the New-England Conference appeared, and presented the following paper as a basis of settlement. It was accepted on the part of the bishop, who had no disposition to prosecute the matter any further than the ends of justice and truth required. The following is the paper referred to:—

"We, the undersigned, acknowledge that there is an inconsistency in some of the votes passed in the cases of brothers Scott and Sunderland in the New-England Conference of 1838, and we believe that the conference may have erred in some of these votes, and will use our influence to prevent the occurrence of the thing complained of in future; and, moreover, we admit that, if any of the votes passed in these cases are liable to be construed injuriously to Bishop Hedding, it was not, in our judgment, so intended by the conference, and was an error; and we respectfully request Bishop Hedding to withdraw his complaint.

(Signed) "Joseph A. Merrill,
Jotham Horton,
Phineas Crandall,
Frederick Upham,
E. W. Stickney,
A. D. Merrill,
O. Scott.

"Baltimore, *May* 17, 1840."

On the presentation of this paper the bishop appended to it the following note:—

"I agree to the above proposition, and hereby withdraw the complaint referred to.

"E. Hedding.

"*May 17th*, 1840."

The committee reported the facts of the settlement to the General Conference, and asked to be dismissed. Their request was granted, and here the matter rested. We, however, cannot dismiss the matter without noticing the magnanimity displayed by Bishop Hedding on this occasion. The course of the conference action complained of had been exceedingly unjust and injurious to himself. He knew that the most of these very delegates had voted with the majority of the conference in the acquittal of Messrs. Scott and Sunderland, and also that the ultra measures of the day had furnished the test-question in the election that had made some of them delegates. Some of these very men, too, had been arraigning him for three or four years before the public as a usurper of authority that did not belong to his office, and the conference to which they belonged had not only failed to call them to account for their course, but had thrown around them the shield of its protection. These facts place the character of Bishop Hedding in a most enviable light: they reflect the highest honour upon him as a Christian man and a minister of the Lord Jesus Christ.

On another occasion during the session of this conference the Christian magnanimity of Bishop Hedding was displayed in an equally striking manner. In the preamble of the report presented by the Committee on Itinerancy, the New-England Conference, Rev. Orange Scott, and Rev. La Roy Sunderland were alluded to in terms of great severity. When this preamble came up for consideration, it was moved that an exception be also taken to the Georgia Conference resolutions, which declared "that slavery, as it exists in the United States, is not a moral evil." Upon this resolution warm speeches were made; but it was finally laid upon the table. Rev. J. Horton then moved that all that part of the preamble of the report relating to the New-England Conference be laid on the table. This motion was lost. The Rev. P. Crandall then moved that so much of the preamble as related to the New-England Conference be stricken from the report. This motion was advocated by powerful speeches, made by the mover and by Rev. E. W. Stickney, of the same conference. The latter especially warned the conference against the fearful consequences that would result to the Church in New-England should such an arraignment of the New-England Conference as that contained in the preamble receive the sanction of that body, and especially as the motion to take exception to the action of the Georgia Conference had failed.*

* The following are portions of the report referred to:—

"The New-England Conference, as has appeared to the committee, have been, during the last four years, disorganizing in their proceedings—indeed, have pursued a course destructive to the peace, harmony, and unity of the Church; in that,

"1. They have gone beyond the proper jurisdiction of an annual conference, and in doing so have pronounced upon the characters of those brethren who were not at all responsible to them; in that,

"2. The journals of that conference exhibit no grounds on which they acquitted Orange Scott, who, by direct implication, had been

At this crisis Bishop Hedding threw himself into the breach. He arose and addressed the conference,* saying, "If the conference would indulge him, he felt it his duty to offer a few observations. He had strong and ardent feelings of friendship for the New-England Conference; and though they had erred in some of their acts, still, as a body, they certainly were good men and fast friends of the Church. If he might be permitted to give his advice upon the subject now occupying their deliberations, he would state immediately what it was, and then offer some reasons which influenced him.

"His advice then was, that the committee amend the report by striking out that part which relates to the New-England Conference. One reason justificatory of this recommendation was, that the brethren

found guilty, by a large majority of the last General Conference, of publishing statements concerning members of that body which were gross misrepresentations, or flagrant and scandalous falsehoods; in that,

"3. The same absence exists of all showing of reasons for acquitting Orange Scott and La Roy Sunderland, on sundry charges of evil doing, growing out of abolition movements in which they were engaged; in that,

"4. The said conference, disregarding the established usages of Methodism, permitted the members of their body to be present during the examination of their own characters; in that,

"5. The conference did, by an official act, advise, or request, that La Roy Sunderland should be left without an appointment; in that,

"6. The conference did sustain Orange Scott in neglecting his appropriate work as a Methodist preacher, while he was prosecuting an agency unknown to, and not recognised by, the Discipline."

* See report of this speech in the Christian Advocate and Journal for 1840, pp. 170, 171.

of that section had been under strong excitement; so powerful, that, to his belief, they had not understood the real nature and bearing of their own official acts. Many causes have been operative in the production and sustaining of that excitement. One which had operated to increase and prolong it was the act of the Georgia Conference. That act, it is true, as explained by the delegates from that conference, has a very different interpretation from that which the words employed in the resolution would signify, and from that which had been attached to them by the northern people. The comments and explanations did not accompany the resolutions. It is understood by those of the north to mean what the phraseology, naked and unqualified, literally imports. Had the resolution *said*, as it seems to have been *intended to do*, that slavery, as it exists in the Methodist Church, is not a moral evil, the great body of the northern membership would unhesitatingly have believed it, and probably but little would have been said about it one way or the other; but the resolution affirms that slavery, as it exists in the United States, is not a moral evil. The northerners say that slavery, as it exists in the United States, confers upon the master unlimited power to dispose of the slave, even to the extent of an involuntary separation of man and wife; that this is frequently done; and *this* they declare to be a moral evil. They contend that slavery, in practice, frequently inflicts great injuries on the subjects of it through the ownership of drunkards, infidels, and other immoral individuals; and they, construing the resolution according to the import of the terms, affirm that it declares that the exercise of all the power allowed to the master, and all the practices incident to the condition of slavery, as existing in this country, are not moral evils. Now, though we are convinced that the Georgia brethren never intended to convey this idea, yet so have they been understood by many of their brethren in the north.

"You have been invited to give an opinion on that resolution: you declined doing so, and, as things now are, you have probably acted wisely; for no opinion could be given which would not be liable to misconstruction either in the north or south, and thus be productive of evil somewhere. As you have not seen fit to express your opinion on that resolution, it seems to be reasonable that you should not pass judgment on the acts of the New-England Conference.

"Another reason is, that the excitement in the north is diminishing, and, if we do nothing to revive it, it is hoped that it may die away. But a declaration of opinion on the acts of one conference, and not on the other, will certainly increase and swell the agitation. It is plain that the brethren of the north and of the south do not understand each other on this subject; but when they shall become calm, and their judgments, unswayed by prejudice, shall allow them mutually to defer to each other's opinions, they will recede from the extremes to which they have pushed themselves, and meet on the true principles of Methodism, become content to treat the subject after the manner of St. Paul, and live together in harmony and brotherly love."

Before the bishop had made his address, the Rev. Mr. Hodges, of the Georgia Conference, had endeavoured to explain the resolutions of that conference, the peculiar circumstances under which they were passed, and also to defend them. But the Rev. Wm. A. Smith, of Virginia, followed him in opposition to the course he suggested, and went largely into the general question of slavery. He in turn was followed by other speakers, and a somewhat extended discussion ensued. But the suggestion of the bishop prevailed, and the offensive references were stricken out.

The general subject of slavery entered into the discussions and measures of this conference in an unusual degree. We have already noticed how the committee on itinerancy found themselves involved in the subject. The committee on slavery reported very stringent resolutions against "Modern Abolitionism;" but their report, so far as we can perceive, was never adopted. The appeal of the Rev. Silas Comfort from the decision of the Missouri Annual Conference, which had charged him with maladministration for receiving the testimony of a coloured person against a white person in a Church trial, brought the question of slavery up in a new form. The appeal was entertained, and the decision of the Missouri Conference reversed. This decision gave umbrage to the southern delegates. They considered it as a virtual sanction of the practice of admitting the testimony of coloured persons against white persons in Church trials; and, by implication at least, a censure of the ordinary administration in the South, where such testimony was rejected. Dr. I. A. Few, therefore, introduced the following resolution, which, after an exciting and protracted debate, was adopted:—

"*Resolved*, That it is inexpedient and unjustifiable for any preacher to permit coloured persons to give testimony against white persons in any state where they are denied that privilege by law."

It comes not within our province to discuss the evil principle imbedded in this resolution, nor the evil practices which it might shield. Suffice it to say, that it gave great dissatisfaction to the northern delegates. So intense was the feeling that a northern delegate, who had at first seconded the resolution of Dr. Few, moved its reconsideration. This occasioned quite a display of parliamentary tactics, and not a little discussion. When the vote was finally reached, it stood sixty-nine to sixty-nine. Bishop Hedding was in the chair, and was called upon to give the casting vote. He knew this had been done in several instances when there was a tie in the General Conference, but it was the first time he had ever been called upon to exercise this function. He now arose and declined giving the casting vote; not, as he said, that he was unwilling to give his opinion in the case pending, but because he did not think he had a constitutional right to do so, and gave the following reasons for this opinion. He said, "In the original General Conference the bishops not only had a right to give the casting vote, but to speak and vote on all subjects if they chose to do so. They had the right, because all travelling preachers who had been in the connexion four years had it, and they had the right as travelling preachers; but when the delegated General Conference was constituted that right was taken away—probably not by design, but inadvertently. Under the arrangement for a delegated General Conference, the Discipline has always said in substance,—The General Conference shall be composed of delegates from the annual conferences. The bishops, not being delegates from any annual conference, have no right to vote, and consequently no right to give a casting vote. The Discipline provides that they shall preside in the General Conferences, but it does not provide that they shall vote. The Speaker of the House of Representatives in Congress can give the casting vote, because he forms a part of the body, and is elected and sent there as others are. The President of the Senate of the United States has a right to give the casting vote, because, though not an elected member, the constitution gives him that right. If our constitution had given the bishops a right to vote, I should be willing now to give the casting vote; but as it does not, I must decline." The bishop went on further to state that this rule applied to presiding elders in a quarterly conference, and to a preacher presiding on a Church trial. Neither of them had a right to give the casting vote.

We have introduced this matter not merely as an item of history connected with Bishop Hedding, but, first, because the mere statement of the facts and his reasons exhibit the folly and injustice of the outcry that was raised against him for declining the vote on this occasion; secondly, the decision, made so clearly and conclusively in a case that was unexpectedly sprung upon him,—and that, too, in opposition to the general usage in such cases,—shows how profoundly he had studied the principles of our ecclesiastical jurisprudence, and how admirably he was adapted to be the presiding officer of a deliberative body. In the third place, this incident shows how careful he was not to trench upon the constitutional powers committed to him, and presents him in a very different light from that in which some had sought to place him, as grasping after authority not legitimately committed to him.

It is perhaps well to add that this offensive resolution was subsequently explained, as to its true intent and purport, by three supplementary resolutions, passed by the General Conference a few days before its adjournment. Thus it continued four years, and was then rescinded by the same body that enacted it.

The incidents we have here spoken of were, in

some sort, episodes in the usual routine of General Conference business. The ordinary business of the conference was transacted with unusual despatch and directness. It embraced a great variety of subjects—Sunday schools, missions, Bible distribution, colonization, temperance, the proper administration of discipline, our fraternal relations to the Wesleyan connexion in England, and also in Canada, and various other interests of a minor character. It is not our purpose to detail them; they belong rather to the general history of the Church, than to the history of the subject of our narrative. The Pastoral Address is brief, but pertinent. It is mild and conciliatory in its character, deeply spiritual in its tone, and was written in a chaste and beautiful style. Considerable harmony and good feeling were evinced at the close of the session. Bishop Soule, who was in the chair at the time, made a brief address, referring to the differences of opinion that had existed, and expressing his gratification at the brotherly kindness and affection that had been so uniformly manifested, and also his firm persuasion that the action of this General Conference would exert a most salutary influence upon the future prosperity, peace, and unity of the Church. "In this," says he, "I do rejoice, and will rejoice."

He exhorted the brethren to go forth resolved to carry out the great measures adopted to promote the interests of the Church, to refrain from unkind expressions toward brethren when differences of opinion existed, and to cherish the spirit of brotherly love and Christian union. Finally he gave out the hymn commencing,—

> "And let our bodies part,
> To different climes repair;
> Inseparably joined in heart
> The friends of Jesus are."

This hymn was sung with great fervour by the conference. A deeply affecting prayer was then offered, and the General Conference of 1840 adjourned *sine die.* The results of this session seemed full of promise for the future peace and unity of the Church.

After the close of the General Conference Bishop Hedding visited the New-York and the New-England Conferences in company with Bishop Soule. The former commenced in the city of New-York, June 10th; the latter in the city of Lowell, July 1st. After this he spent a few days at home in Lansingburgh, answering the letters that had accumulated during his absence. On the 18th of the same month he left home, travelling by land to Buffalo, and thence by steamboat to Erie; he met at that place the Erie Conference on the 5th of August. Then he went by steamboat to Detroit, Michigan, and thence proceeded by land to Marshall, in the interior of the state, where he met the Michigan Conference August 19th. "This," he says, "is a young but promising conference, and the session was one of peculiar interest; but it was a time of great distress on account of sickness, from the bilious diseases of that country which were prevailing. Many of the preachers were sick. Here I ordained one of the preachers in his bed; he was unable even to sit up during the service."

From Marshall he returned to Detroit, and thence by steamboat to Huron, Ohio. He rode from Huron to Norwalk in a wagon, and there met the North Ohio Conference on the 9th of September. "Here," he says, "I found a great many old acquaintances in the membership of the Church that I had formerly known in New-England. Here, too, I found many devoted and consistent influential Methodists." The next and last conference he attended this year was the Ohio, which met at Zanesville, September 30th. Of the members of this conference he says, "They are a talented and devoted body of men, of great influence in that country."

Having completed his conference labours for the season, he turned his face homeward; but as he had a number of engagements by the way, he did not reach home till the last of October. He, however, spent but a few days here before he left again, having an engagement to dedicate the new church that had been erected in Bedford-street, New-York city. His sermon for the occasion was preached from Exodus xx, 24: "An altar of earth thou shalt make unto me, and shalt sacrifice thereon thy burnt-offerings, and thy peace-offerings, thy sheep, and thine oxen: in all places where I record my name I will come unto thee, and I will bless thee." In addition to this he visited the Churches in Williamsburgh and Matteawan, and reached home about the last of November.

The winter was spent mainly at home; though he occasionally visited societies in the vicinity, and preached to them the word of life.

Owing to a change in the time of publishing the Annual Minutes, only nineteen conferences are definitely reported in the issue for this year; but these nineteen reported a general increase of fifty-four thousand nine hundred and eighty-six.

Early in the ensuing spring Bishop Hedding dedicated the John-street Methodist Episcopal Church, a new edifice erected on the site of the old one. The text for the occasion was 1 Thess. i, 8: "For from you sounded out the word of the Lord not only in Macedonia and Achaia, but also in every place your faith to God-ward is spread abroad." The text as well as the discourse was beautifully appropriate to the occasion. Many things contributed to make this dedication exceedingly interesting to the bishop. He says: "It was the third church that had been built on that ground; it was the spot on which was erected the first Methodist church in America. The first church erected upon this spot was the one in which, nearly forty years before, I was admitted into the itinerant connexion. The scene brought many endearing recollections to my mind. The memories of those who were present at the conference of 1801, but have long since been numbered among the venerable dead, came rushing upon me with overwhelming force. Bishop Whatcoat, who presided at that conference, and nearly all the then active members of the body, also all the private members of the Church I then became acquainted with, have passed away."

The occasion, if we may judge from the accounts of it published in the journals of the day, was as deeply interesting to the public as it was to the bishop himself.

The following brief account of this admirable discourse is taken from the report published in the Christian Advocate and Journal at the time:—

"In the introductory part of his discourse the bishop gave a beautiful exposition of his text, in connexion with St. Luke's account, in the Acts of the Apostles, of the labours of St. Paul and his colleagues, and of the introduction of the gospel into Greece, and especially of its success among the Thessalonians, and of their instrumentality in spreading it abroad. Thessalonica was one of the principal seaports of ancient Greece—a great commercial city; and being advantageously situated for trade, had an extensive connexion with other cities in that part of the world. It was one of the first cities in Europe that received the gospel, and on account of its maritime and commercial character was more instrumental in spreading it abroad than any other city.

"In the course of his sermon the bishop showed, in a very lucid manner, that the Word of the Lord was the great instrument employed by the Divine Being in the salvation of souls. After this point had been very ably demonstrated, the bishop took a view of the manner in which the Word had been, and still continues to be, spread abroad in every place. The first apostles were greatly instrumental in this good work, but they were not the only instruments; the merchants and private Christians did much in spreading it. When persons from the distant cities and country places came to Thessalonica to trade, or to make a visit, the Christian merchants would tell them of the work of the Lord among them; they would invite them to hear the apostles, to attend their meetings, and to behold the wonderful works of God among their fellow-citizens. These foreigners and visiters becoming convinced of the truth, would carry the news home with them; would probably invite the apostles to make them a visit also; or when the merchants went abroad to collect their bills, or the citizens went to visit their relations in distant places, they would carry the good word of God with them. It would be in their hearts and upon their tongues; and they would speak of it on every occasion, and in all places whithersoever they went. It was thus that the word of the Lord sounded out from them. Not only in Macedonia and Achaia, but also in every place, their faith to God-ward was spread abroad.

"In many particulars there was a striking similarity between the case of the citizens of Thessalonica and that of the people of New-York. While the apostles were labouring in Asia Minor, a vision appeared to Paul in the night. There stood a man of Macedonia, and prayed him, saying, 'Come over into Macedonia and help us.' This was the introduction of the gospel into Europe; and similar was the introduction of Methodism, by means of itinerant preaching, in this country. A call went over the great waters, saying to Mr. Wesley, 'Come over and help us,' or send us help. The venerable Asbury, 'in labours more like the Apostle Paul than any other man I ever knew,' said the bishop, and others, heard that call, and came to our help. The church was erected on this very spot, Mr. Wesley aiding in its erection by a donation of fifty pounds sterling. Thus the gospel, by means of itinerant ministers, was planted on these shores; and from this place 'sounded out the word of the Lord' to the south, to the north, to the east, and to the west.

"In the progress of this discourse the bishop related many pleasing incidents from his own personal history and observation, and all illustrative of the doctrine contained in the text. A more appropriate text for such an occasion, and a more happy method of illustration, we seldom or never heard. The effect was fine. A spirit in support of that cause which had been so greatly blessed pervaded the assembly. The congregation was not large; but there were present of the first, second, and third generations of Methodists, and some who had worshipped in the first and in the second house, which stood where this now stands, who gave of that in which God had prospered them toward the liquidation of the debt incurred by the present building. We are glad to see a root of primitive Methodism still vigorous and growing, in the very spot where the first scion was planted on these western shores. John-street Church, in a certain sense, is 'the mother of us all,' and we love to pay her the respect which is due to her piety and zeal."

Soon after this he laid the corner-stone, and delivered a discourse, on the foundation of a new church in North Eighth-street, in the city of Philadelphia.

This year Bishop Hedding met the Philadelphia Conference at Philadelphia, April 7th; the New-Jersey, at Newark, April 28th; the New-York, at New-York, May 17th; the Providence, at Providence, June 9th; the New-England, at Worcester, June 30th; and the Maine, at Skowhegan, July 21st.

At the session of four of these conferences he delivered an address on the administration of discipline. Each of them in turn requested its publication, and it was eventually issued in a miniature book form. Like everything else that emanated from the mind of the bishop upon that subject, it is clear, practical, and of great utility. It has become a standard authority upon the subject, and should be the pocket-companion of every one who is called to administer the discipline of the Methodist Episcopal Church.

While at the session of the New-Jersey Conference this spring, Bishop Hedding was requested to address that body upon the subject of Christian perfection; especially to state the nature of justification, regeneration, and entire sanctification, and the difference between them as distinct works of grace. This request was made at the opening of the conference, and having to address the candidates for ordination during the forenoon, he embraced the opportunity to express his views on the subject. The conference requested their publication, and they were subsequently written out and published. As they contain not only the distinct enunciation of Bishop Hedding's views, but also a lucid and satisfactory enunciation of this vital doctrine in the Christian system, we give them entire:—

"BRETHREN,—Among many other important questions, the following have been asked you, and you have answered them in the affirmative:—'Are you going on to perfection? Do you expect to be made perfect in love in this life? Are you groaning after it?'

"It is important for you, as Christians and as ministers, to have a thorough understanding of this great subject. The subject is Christian perfection, or being made perfect in love in this life. It is being delivered from sin, and filled with the love of God. The brethren ask me to state 'the nature of justification, regeneration, and sanctification, and the difference between them as distinct works of grace.' I understand justification to be a pardon of past sins; and regeneration, which takes place at the same time, to be a change of heart, or of our moral nature. Regeneration also, being the same as the new birth, is the beginning of sanctification, though not the completion of it, or not entire sanctification. Regeneration is the beginning of purification; entire sanctification is the finishing of that work.

"The difference between a justified soul who is not fully sanctified, and one fully sanctified, I understand to be this:—

"The first (if he does not backslide) is kept from voluntarily committing known sin, which is what is commonly meant in the New Testament by *committing sin*. But he yet finds in himself the remains of inbred corruption, or original sin; such as pride, anger, envy, a feeling of hatred to an enemy, a rejoicing at a calamity which has fallen upon an enemy, &c.

"Now in all this the regenerate soul does not act voluntarily; his choice is against all these evils. God has given him a new heart, which hates all these evils, and resists and overcomes them as soon as the mind perceives them. The regenerate soul wishes these evils were not in his heart, yet he has in himself no power to destroy them. Though the Christian does not feel guilty for this depravity as he would do if he had voluntarily broken the law of God, yet he is often grieved, and afflicted, and reproved at a sight of this sinfulness of his nature.

"Though the soul in this state enjoys a degree of religion, yet it is conscious it is not what it ought to be, nor what it must be to be fit for heaven.

"It seems that the sinfulness of our nature, or original sin, may remain in the new-born soul independent of choice, and even against choice.

"The second, or the person fully sanctified, is cleansed from all these involuntary sins.

"He may be tempted by Satan, by men, and by his own bodily appetites, to commit sin, but his heart is free from those inward fires which before his full sanctification were ready to fall in with temptation, and lead him into transgression. He may be tempted to be proud, to love the world, to be revengeful or angry, to hate an enemy, to wish him evil, or to rejoice at his calamity, but he feels none of these passions in his heart; the Holy Ghost has cleansed him from all these pollutions of his nature. Thus it is that, being emptied of sin, the perfect Christian is filled with the love of God, even with that perfect love which casteth out fear.

"But is this sanctification instantaneous, or gradual? It is both. In some respects it is one, and in other respects it is the other. In a soul who does not backslide, the work of sanctification goes on gradually till it is finished, and that event is instantaneous. Finishing the work is accomplished in an instant. Mr. Wesley says something like this: 'A man may be some time dying, but there is an instant in which he dies.' So in a Christian, sin may be some time dying, but there is an instant in which it dies, and that event is full sanctification. In some, the fact of its being finished in an instant is more apparent to the subject than it is in others.

"But how is this great work performed? By the Holy Spirit—no other power can effect it; and this work of the Spirit is obtained only through the atonement, and through faith in that atonement. That faith, which is the condition of this entire sanctification, is exercised only by a penitent heart; a heart willing to part with all sin forever, and determined to do the will of God in all things. Believe and pray for it; it is as important that you should experience this holy work, as it is that the sinners to whom you preach should be converted. God is as able, willing, and ready to do this great work for you as he was to pardon your sins. Christ is able to save to the uttermost all that come to God through him. But what would be the fate of a soul born of the Spirit, but not fully sanctified, called to die in that state? If he have not backslidden he would go to heaven; not that he is now fit for heaven, but Christ would fit him should he call him out of the world. Before his departure Christ would either accept his weak faith, or give him a degree of faith equal to his wants, and thus save his soul. This view is supported by the numerous promises in Scripture of eternal salvation to all who die the children of God. Those promises to such as persevere and remain the children of God, include all the work of grace necessary to fit them for heaven. But these views furnish no excuse for us to neglect seeking full sanctification now. If we were sure we should live twenty years, then experience full sanctification and die, there would be many and important reasons for us to seek that great blessing now, and so to believe as to experience it this day. With it we should be more happy, and more useful; and as we are changeable creatures, with this blessing we shall be more safe than we could be without it. But can a person possessing perfect love perfectly keep God's holy law, as angels do in heaven? No; if he could, he would no longer need the atonement any more than holy angels do. Yet, through the atonement, he may acceptably keep the law.

"He loves God with all his heart, and his neighbour as himself; he acts in all things under the influence of that love; and this is the end of the commandment, and the fulfilling of the law. And though this soul is free from what the Bible calls sin, yet he has infirmities and unavoidable failings growing out of the original fall, on account of which he ought to say,—

'Every moment, Lord, I need
The merits of thy death.'

Forgive me my trespasses, &c. Unavoidable mistakes and failings are covered by the atonement, and through it his obedience is accepted."

The returns this year, published immediately after the session of the New-York Annual Conference, are of a most encouraging character. The number of members reported was eight hundred and fifty-two thousand nine hundred and eighteen, being an increase of fifty-seven thousand four hundred and seventy-three; number of travelling preachers three thousand five hundred and eighty-seven, increase one hundred and seventy-eight; number of local preachers six thousand three hundred and ninety-three, increase fifty-four. In the Indiana Conference of this year there was an increase of nine thousand and eighty-one, making that, in point of numbers, the fourth conference in the connexion. It was also a year of remarkable prosperity in the Pittsburgh, Baltimore, and Maine Conferences, their respective net gains in membership being four thousand eight hundred and forty-seven, three thousand seven hundred and thirty-nine, and three thousand five hundred and ninety-six.

In 1842 Bishop Hedding presided over the Troy Conference, which met at Burlington, Vt., June 1st; over the New-Hampshire and Vermont Conferences, which met at Newbury, Vt., June 25th; the Black River Conference, at Watertown, July 21st; the Oneida Conference, at Oxford, August 11th; and the Genesee Conference, at Rochester, September 1st.

During the session of the New-Hampshire Conference, an incident occurred which finely displays the readiness and sagacity of Bishop Hedding as a presiding officer. The ultra excitement on the subject of slavery had, to a great extent, died away since the last General Conference, notwithstanding the great efforts made to keep it alive. We do not mean that the people were less opposed to slavery, but that they had grown wiser by experience, and were determined to exhibit their opposition in a more feasible form. Several, however, who had been foremost in the movement, now, as they saw the public mind becoming quieted, and settling down in the conviction that no good result could be realized from ultra measures, became disappointed, sullen, and alienated from the Church, and prejudiced against its administration. One of this class now offered a resolution to the following import:—

"Whereas Bishop Hedding, in a certain publication, has advanced the opinion that, when the preachers of any conference become disorderly, and will not execute the discipline of the Church, the bishop has a right to transfer them to other conferences, where they may be corrected; and whereas the preachers of the southern conferences do not, and will not execute the discipline—

"*Resolved*, That Bishop Hedding is hereby requested to transfer those preachers to other conferences."

The evident design of the resolution was not only to operate on public sentiment, but also to ensnare the bishop; the mover supposing he would refuse to entertain the subject. He was not so easily entrapped. He at once saw through the design, and determined to meet it. "Very well," said he, "if you pass this resolution to transfer the southern preachers north, we shall have to transfer the northern men south to fill their places. And the first one I shall transfer south will be brother Robinson himself, the mover of the resolution. I will transfer him immediately to New-Orleans, for we want a preacher there now. If you are ready, we will put the question." The trapper found himself entrapped. With not a little haste and tremulousness, a motion was made for the indefinite postponement of the resolution, and was carried by an almost unanimous vote.

This year a brother withdrew from the Genesee Conference, having been led to embrace the doctrine of "man's natural ability," as it is usually termed; that is, that man by his own will has power to change his own heart. This naturally elicited considerable attention, and made the subject a matter of no little conversation and discussion. During the session of the conference, taking advantage of a pause in its business, while the body were waiting for the report of a committee, the bishop arose and addressed them upon the subject. His remarks show how profoundly he had thought, and how closely he had reasoned upon the subject. They made a profound impression upon the conference at the time; and their publication being called for from different quarters, they were finally written out and published in the Christian Advocate and Journal.

"Brethren,—While we are waiting for the report of a committee, let us occupy the time in reflecting on our own religious experience. 'Examine yourselves whether ye be in the faith,' is an admonition necessary for ministers as well as for people. Men are liable to be deceived with regard to their own conversion, and to satisfy themselves with a work of the imagination instead of the work of the Spirit. Let us, therefore, compare our experience with the Word of God, and satisfy ourselves that we are truly born of the Spirit.

"We are in danger of being deceived in another way. Having been really born of God, we may backslide in heart, lose the spirit we then received from heaven, and yet retain the form, the morals, and the profession of Christianity, and still persuade ourselves that we are as pious as when we were warm in our first love! Let us look into this matter, and see whether we are, indeed, as near to Christ as when we were first made partakers of his love. We ought to be nearer; we should be growing in grace, and in the knowledge of our Lord Jesus Christ.

"But what is it to experience religion? It is to have our sins forgiven—to be regenerated, or born again. Two works done at the same time: the one setting us free from the guilt of our past sins; the other changing our hearts, giving us a new spiritual nature. But who is the author of this great work?

God alone. Who can forgive sin, but God only?—who can make the fallen soul 'a new creature,' but the Creator? 'You hath he quickened who were dead in trespasses and sins.' 'Which were born, not of blood, nor of the will of the flesh, nor of the will of man, but of God.' 'That which is born of the flesh is flesh; and that which is born of the Spirit is spirit.' 'For we are his workmanship, created in Christ Jesus unto good works.'

"Yet an opinion has been advanced, that man can change his own heart; and it has been countenanced by a brother who has withdrawn from us during this session. 'Can the Ethiopian change his skin, or the leopard his spots?'

"The school from which this new and strange doctrine proceeds, builds upon the assumption that all sin consists in choice; that there is no sin in man independent of, or prior to, choice. Also, that all holiness consists in choosing to do holy acts; that there is no holiness in the nature of a saint from which holy acts proceed; and consequently, that when a man chooses to turn away from sin, and to perform holy acts, that act of choosing is changing his own heart; it is regeneration; it is the new birth.

"But, if there be no sinfulness in man prior to choice, what becomes of infants who die before they are capable of choice? Upon this theory they could be neither sinful nor holy; consequently they could go neither to hell nor to heaven. Yet the Scriptures teach that 'death passed upon all men, for that all have sinned;' and that 'judgment came upon all men to condemnation.' The same Scriptures teach us that Christ died for all the family of Adam, and that all dying infants go to heaven through his blood. Christ says, 'of such is the kingdom of heaven.' All infants in heaven will join in this song: 'Thou hast redeemed us to God by thy blood.' Christ tasted death for every man—for every human being. 'Neither is there salvation in any other.' Yet he died for none but sinners. Had not infants been in some sense sinful, they could not have been redeemed by Christ. If there is no sinfulness in the human heart independent of choice, why did our Saviour say, 'Neither can a corrupt tree bring forth good fruit?' Why did St. Paul say, 'But the evil which I would not, that I do?' St. Paul spoke this of the depraved nature of an unregenerate man. He teaches, that in a convicted sinner that depravity would sometimes rankle, burn, and rage, not only independent of, but *contrary* to his choice.

"This doctrine is in perfect accordance with our seventh article of religion: 'Original sin is the corruption of the nature of every man that naturally is engendered of the offspring of Adam, whereby man is very far gone from original righteousness, and of his own nature inclined to evil, and that continually.' This is the doctrine taught by our Lord when he said, 'For out of the heart proceed evil thoughts, murders, adulteries, fornications, thefts, false witness, blasphemies,' Matt. xv, 19. 'Never was a stronger and more humbling picture drawn of the corruption of human nature.'—*Watson.* Here our Lord confirms the testimony of Jeremiah on the same subject: 'The heart is deceitful above all things, and desperately wicked. Who can know it?' And that of Solomon: 'The heart of the sons of men is full of evil.'

"This doctrine has been confirmed by experience. Many enlightened Christians have testified, that before their hearts were made new by the Holy Spirit, and while they were under conviction for sin, evil feelings existed in their hearts, which they earnestly tried to remove, but could not. That while, by restraining grace, they could govern their outward conduct, they could not govern their hearts. Pride, anger, covetousness, selfishness, jealousy, envy, malice, hatred to an enemy—wishing him evil, &c., involuntarily moved and troubled their souls. By the help of God, then afforded them, they could restrain those evil feelings so far as to prevent their breaking out into violent outward actions, but they could not eradicate them. The evil was in their hearts, and every one felt it is 'sin that dwelleth in me.' Reason and conscience opposed these evils; the will, the choice, opposed them. The man really wished they were dead, but still they were there; and he cried out, 'O wretched man that I am! who shall deliver me from the body of this death?'

"But when this wretched man believed—that is,

trusted in Christ for salvation—God, his Saviour, gave him a new heart; a heart to love God, and hate sin; a power against sin; a power to govern himself, and to do the will of God, as well in the exercises of his heart as in the practices of his life. This work in his heart was accompanied with a witness of the Spirit that it was indeed the work of God, and that neither himself nor his fellow-man could have done it. He could not see the manner of it; but he knew the work was done, and that God did it. 'The wind bloweth where it listeth, and thou hearest the sound thereof, but canst not tell whence it cometh, and whither it goeth: so is every one that is born of the Spirit.'

"Brethren, we needed this good work to make us Christians; we must walk in the spirit of it if we would continue to be Christians. Without it our ministry will be but a dead letter, and we shall be 'clouds without water, carried about of winds.' But if we live, preach, pray, administer discipline, and visit our flocks in this spirit, it will be 'like the precious ointment upon the head, that ran down upon the beard, even Aaron's beard: that went down to the skirts of his garments; as the dew of Hermon, and as the dew that descended upon the mountains of Zion: for there the Lord commanded the blessing, even life for evermore.'

"If these things be true—if the new birth be the work of God, and not of man—what can we think of that system which teaches the people that they can change their own hearts—that they can convert themselves? What can we think of those operations called revivals, where the people receive this doctrine, and believe and profess that they have changed their own hearts—that they have converted themselves? There is reason to fear that multitudes of them are deceived; that they know nothing of true religion; that they are yet 'in the gall of bitterness, and in the bond of iniquity.'

"Those who teach what we believe to be a false doctrine with regard to the new birth, as above named, have frequently objected to a practice among us of exhorting the people to seek God—to seek religion—to seek salvation—to pray to God to give them new hearts. But this practice, when rightly performed, is in perfect accordance with the teachings of the Holy Scriptures. It is certainly proper for men to seek that they may find 'Him of whom Moses, in the law, and the prophets, did write.' Again; the apostle teaches, 'that they should seek the Lord, if haply they might feel after him, and find him, though he be not far from every one of us.' It is made our duty to seek, and pray, and look to God, that he may do for us what we are unable to do for ourselves. We cannot change our own hearts, but we can pray to God to change them. We cannot pardon our sins, but we can pray to God for pardon. We cannot create the spirit of Christianity in our own hearts, but we can seek for it in the way God directs—by faith—and find it. Hence we are com manded, 'Ask, and it shall be given you; seek, and ye shall find; knock, and it shall be opened unto you.' 'But seek ye first the kingdom of God.' 'Come unto me—and I will give you rest.' 'Look unto me, and be ye saved, all the ends of the earth; for I am God, and there is none else.'"

The returns this year still indicate the wide-spread and growing prosperity of the Church. There was an increase of sixty thousand nine hundred and eighty-three members, making a grand total of nine hundred and thirteen thousand nine hundred and one. The number of travelling preachers was four thousand and forty-four, increase one hundred and seventy nine; number of local preachers seven thousand one hundred and forty-four, increase seven hundred and fifty-one.

For the benefit of his health, Bishop Hedding had removed his residence from Lansingburgh to Saratoga Springs; and in the use of the mineral waters of this place he found for a time sensible advantage.

The latter part of the winter of 1842–3 was remarkable for a great fall of snow, which for a time stopped all travelling. The engines upon the railroad could not make their way through it, and the highways were completely blocked up. Owing to the extreme cold, this state of things continued for several weeks. In the meantime, it became necessary for Bishop Hedding to leave for the Philadelphia Conference Finding there was no immediate prospect of a passage by railroad or by stage, he employed a vigorous and determined man, with two powerful horses and a sleigh, to take him through to Troy. In making this passage of about thirty miles, they were sometimes compelled to plough through snow-banks of great height; sometimes they got around them by crossing the fields or passing through the woods; and sometimes they found the snow packed hard enough to bear up the horses. The driver was often compelled to leave the sleigh, and break away and shovel out the snow from before the horses, and thus work them through places that would otherwise have been impassable. The cold was intense, and the keen north wind whistled and roared over the hills and through the trees, often filling the air with darkening clouds of snow. Bishop Hedding was no man to turn back; and in spite of every obstacle the distance was at length accomplished, to the astonishment of those who knew the difficulties in the way.

He presided this year over the Philadelphia Conference, which met at Philadelphia, April 5th; the New-Jersey, which met at Trenton, April 26th; the New-York, at New-York, May 17th; the Providence, at Warren, June 7th; the New-England, at Boston, June 28th; and the Maine, at Bath, July 19th. Bishop Morris was with him at all these conferences, and shared in the labours and responsibilities of his work.

While at the Philadelphia Conference, the sad intelligence of the death of Bishop Roberts was received. At the request of the conference, he preached a sermon on the occasion from Acts xi, 24: "For he was a good man, and full of the Holy Ghost, and of faith: and much people was added unto the Lord." Subsequently the same discourse was, at their request, delivered before the New-Jersey, New-York, Providence, and Maine Conferences. Each of these conferences passed a vote requesting its publication; but, owing to his other pressing engagements, he did not find time to prepare it for the press.

The death of Bishop Roberts affected him deeply. They were mutually and strongly attached to each other. Bishop Roberts was his senior in age by two years, but his junior in the ministry by one year. He had been elected to the episcopal office in 1816, Bishop Hedding eight years later. For nineteen years had they been associated together in the episcopate. He was a man of great purity of character, of great simplicity of manners, and of unwavering zeal and devotedness in the cause of his Lord and Master. We need not say more, as a well-written memoir of his useful life has been prepared by our venerable friend and associate, Rev. Dr. Elliott, and published by the Western Book Concern in a neat 12mo. volume of four hundred and eight pages. His contemporaries say of him: "He was a faithful and unflinching servant of the Church, who counted not his own life dear so that he might finish his course with joy, and the ministry he had received of the Lord Jesus, to testify the gospel of the grace of God. Bishop Roberts was a man of good natural parts, and he had accumulated a rich store of various knowledge. As a preacher, he was clear and forcible in the presentation of truth, and often truly eloquent. As a superintendent, he was discriminating, affable, kind, and conciliating, yet firm and decided. He visited the Churches, and preached the gospel of Christ in all the states of the Union, and has left behind him much fruit of his abundant labours. He was able to attend to his great work until within a few weeks previous to his death. He died as he had lived, in the faith of Christ, with the certain hope of eternal life, and in love and peace with all mankind. His sanctified spirit has gone home to God, while the earthly tenement awaits in the grave the final resurrection of the just. He was eminently 'a good man, and full of faith and of the Holy Ghost.'"

Bishop Hedding's circuit of the eastern conferences, this year, afforded him great satisfaction. He found both preachers and people gradually recovering from the effects of the agitations and excitements that had existed among them during several previous years. Peaceable sessions were enjoyed at all these conferences, except some few trial cases of preachers involved in Millerism. Several preachers withdrew from the connexion,—among them were Orange Scott, Lucius C. Matlack, Cyrus Prindle, Shipley W. Wilson, and others who had been prominent in the ultra-abolition movement; but these withdrawals occasioned little excitement, having for the most part taken place prior to the sessions of their respective conferences. Indeed the public mind was pretty well prepared for them, as such a result had been regarded as not only probable, but almost inevitable for several years. It is gratifying to notice that, notwithstanding these withdrawals, each of the conferences reported an increase of members, showing that the course of Methodism was yet onward.

As he returned from the Maine Conference, he paid a visit to his old home at Lynn, Massachusetts. From this place, under date of August 4th, he wrote to Mrs. Hedding: "I am tarrying here a few days, visiting among our old friends. I am yet tired, on account of the labours of the conferences. I feel all the time as though I wanted to lie down upon the floor and go to sleep. In other respects my health is good. This poor body must soon fall under the tremendous burdens it has borne for forty-two years; but the unworthy spirit hopes for eternal life through the boundless mercy of God in Jesus Christ the Saviour."

Later in the season he accompanied Bishop Waugh, who was at that time in poor health, to Yates, in Western New-York, where they met the Genesee Conference on the 30th of August.

During this year, also, he had great responsibility and great care with reference to the appointments for the foreign missionary work. This responsibility was frequently put upon him; and the Missionary Board at New-York always found him a wise counsellor and a devoted friend to the cause, giving liberally of his means, and being unsparing in his exertions for its promotion.

During November of this year he removed from Saratoga to Poughkeepsie, being a place more eligibly located, and affording him greater facilities for his work. Here he continued to reside, revered and beloved by all who knew him, till he finished his earthly career.

The year had been one of unprecedented prosperity, so far as the ingathering of members into the Church was concerned. A membership of one million sixty-eight thousand five hundred and twenty-five, being an increase of one hundred and fifty-four thousand six hundred and twenty-four, was reported. The whole number of travelling preachers was four thousand two hundred and eighty-six, increase two hundred and forty-two; whole number of local preachers, seven thousand seven hundred and thirty, increase five hundred and eighty-six.

In the spring of 1844, Bishop Hedding assisted Bishop Morris at the Philadelphia and New-Jersey Conferences, which met respectively on the 3d and the 18th of April. This brings us to the General Conference of 1844.

CHAPTER XVIII.

SIXTH QUADRENNIAL OF EPISCOPAL LABOUR.

General Conference of 1844 — Representation — Slavery Agitation — The Harding Case — Case of Bishop Andrew — Intensity of Feeling excited — Proposition of the Bishops to suspend Action — Objections in the Minds of Northern Delegates — Bishop Hedding withdraws his Name — Assigns his Reasons — Remarks of Bishops Waugh and Morris — The Communication laid on the Table — Passage of Finley's Resolution — Eventual Separation of the Southern Conferences — Resolution relating to Bishop Hedding's Labours — Election and Consecration of Bishops Hamline and Janes — Close of the Session — Conference Labours — Changed Views of Brethren alienated in the Abolition Controversy — Invitation to fix his Residence again in New-England — Conference Labours in 1845 — Death of three Ministers — Action of the Bishops in Relation to giving Bishop Andrew work — Bishop Soule calls Bishop Andrew out — His Allusion to his Colleagues — Southern Organization completed — Bishops Soule and Andrew connected with it — Action of the Bishops remaining in the Methodist Episcopal Church — Conference Labours in 1846 — A Scene in the New-York Conference — Church Difficulties in Relation to John N. Maffitt — Question of Jurisdiction — Bishop Hedding's Decision — Animadversions upon that Decision — General Conference approves it — Church Statistics — Spring of 1847 — New-England Conference — Address on the Occasion of the Death of George Pickering and Joel Steele — Further Labours — Providence Conference in 1848.

The General Conference of 1844 met in the city of New-York on, as usual, the first day of May. It was composed of one hundred and eighty delegates, representing thirty-three annual conferences, as follows:—New-York, eleven; Providence, four; New-England, five; Maine, seven; New-Hampshire, eight; Troy, seven; Black River, four; Oneida, seven; Genesee, eight; Erie, five; Pittsburgh, seven; Ohio, eight; North Ohio, five; Michigan, four; Indiana, eight; Rock River, four; Illinois, five; Missouri, four; Kentucky, six; Holston, three; Tennessee, four; Memphis, four; Arkansas, three; Texas, two; Mississippi, four; Alabama, four; Georgia, six; South Carolina, five; North Carolina, three; Virginia, four; Baltimore, ten; Philadelphia, six, and New-Jersey, five. Bishops Soule, Hedding, Andrew, Waugh, and Morris, were present. The conference was opened by Bishop Soule, who, by the death of Bishop Roberts, had now become senior bishop of the Methodist Episcopal Church.

We shall detail the proceedings of this General Conference only so far as may be necessary to present, in a clear light, any incidents pertaining to the personal history or illustrative of the character of the subject of our narrative. The main topic in the conference at the beginning, middle, and end, was slavery and anti-slavery. The subject came before the conference in a new form, and one that precluded the possibility of evasion or postponement. In the first place, a member of the Baltimore Conference, Rev. F. A. Harding, came before the body with an appeal from his conference, which had suspended him from his ministerial standing for refusing to manumit certain slaves which came into his possession by marriage. The case occupied the attention of the General Conference three or four days; able and eloquent speeches were made on both sides, and an unusual interest excited. The decision was in favour of sustaining the action of the Baltimore Conference, by a vote of one hundred and seventeen to fifty-six. This decision was received with intense gratification throughout all the northern portion of the Church; but it gave great umbrage at the South, where the prevalent theory was that the holding of slaves in the slave states should not constitute any bar or impediment to any grade of ministerial office in the Church.

The second and more serious aspect in which the subject came before the body, resulted from the connexion of one of the bishops—the Rev. James O. Andrew—with slavery, he having become connected with it first by inheritance, and afterward by marriage. The revelation of these facts produced a profound and painful sensation. In other instances, where the subject of slavery or anti-slavery came before this or preceding General Conferences, there had always been some mode by which the matter could be adjusted to the satisfaction of the great body of the conference and of the Church, and yet so as to avoid sectional differences. But now a distinct issue was made between the North and the South. For the North to yield, and to give up the principle which had always been preserved inviolate from the organization of the Church, namely, that the episcopacy should be kept free from any taint of slavery, would have been not only disastrous to the Church in all the free states, but also, in their judgment, an unwarrantable sacrifice of moral principle. On the other hand, the

South, though they had yielded in former years when only the election of men to the episcopal office was concerned, were now equally strong in their convictions that for them to yield to the deposition of a bishop, because he had become a slaveholder, would be disastrous to the Church in the slaveholding states. In fact, they had come to a point where they must either boldly assert, or forever surrender, the principle long maintained by most of them, that the mere fact of slaveholding should constitute no impediment to any official station in the Church.

It would be scarcely possible to depict the intensity of feeling that existed. The wisest men saw the dark cloud gathering over the prospects of a united Church, but they saw no way to avert the coming storm. Prayer and fasting, deep and earnest consultation were had, and yet no lighting up of the dark horizon was seen. The subject had occupied the attention of the General Conference, more or less, for thirteen sessions, and a motion was pending, expressive of the sense of that body, that Bishop Andrew should desist from the duties of his office so long as the impediment of his connexion with slavery remained. The previous question had been moved, but failed from not obtaining a two-thirds vote. At this crisis Bishop Hedding, who was in the chair, suggested that the conference intermit its usual afternoon session, and thus allow the bishops time to consult together, with the hope that they might be able to present a plan for adjusting the difficulties with which they were environed. "The suggestion," says the journal of the day, "was received with general and great cordiality; and, on motion, the discussion of the pending resolution was postponed until the next morning."

The day following Bishop Waugh presented a communication from the bishops, stating that it was their most deliberate conviction that a decision of the pending question, whether affirmatively or negatively, under existing circumstances, would most extensively disturb the peace and harmony of the Church; they therefore unanimously recommended the postponement of further action in the case of Bishop Andrew until the ensuing General Conference. They stated that such a disposition of the episcopal work could be made as to employ Bishop Andrew in those portions of the work only where his connexion with slavery would be no detriment to his personal acceptability to the preachers and people. They further stated, that should the embarrassments in the case of Bishop Andrew not be removed before the next General Conference, that body, constituted as it would be of delegates fresh from the annual conferences, and elected after all the facts were known, would be better qualified to adjudicate the case wisely and discreetly. And it is but just to add, that the bishops, in making this proposition, felt assured—perhaps had been assured—that all impediments in the way of Bishop Andrew, growing out of his relation to slavery, would be speedily removed if the case at the present stage of proceedings could be dropped.

But in the minds of the northern delegates there were insuperable difficulties opposed to the suspension of the matter. To drop their proceedings at the present stage, and without any pledge from Bishop Andrew that he would relieve himself from his disability, would be a surrender of the great principle to which they felt conscience-bound, namely, that which excluded slaveholding from the episcopacy. They further knew that the question could not be left open, and become a subject of exciting discussion and controversy among the people and in the annual conferences for the next four years, without immense injury to the Church. The question was laid over from Friday morning to Saturday morning; but the more it was canvassed among the members, the more strongly did the above views prevail.

Bishop Hedding, as well as some of the other bishops, had signed the paper as a dernier resort, and with a faint hope that it might be instrumental in averting the impending calamity from the Church; but when he learned the feelings and views of the northern delegates with reference to it, and the opposition that would be made to its passage, he became convinced that it would be a source of discord rather than a minister of peace in the Church. Under this conviction, when the subject came up the next morning—having first privately consulted his colleagues, and finding they were not willing to withdraw the paper—he arose and addressed the conference, withdrawing his name from the document. He said, "he had not been argued or persuaded into signing it, but had attached his name of his own free will and accord, because he thought it would be a peace-measure; but facts had come to his knowledge since which led him to believe that such would not be the case. Again: he thought it would be adopted without debate; but he was convinced now that it would give rise to much discussion, and therefore he wished to withdraw his name from the paper on the table."

Bishops Waugh, Morris, and Soule followed with a few remarks. Bishop Waugh stated that he considered the proposed measure as a last resort to promote the future peace of the Church; but he had not been very sanguine upon the subject, and if it failed he should not be disappointed. Bishop Morris said he wished his name to stand on that paper, as a testimony that he had done what he could to preserve the unity and peace of the Church. The communication of the bishops was subsequently laid upon the table, by a vote of ninety-five to eighty-four. The pending resolution was then passed, by a vote of one hundred and ten to sixty-eight. Against this action the southern delegates presented their solemn Protest, which was entered upon the journals of the conference. Subsequently, on the representations of some of the southern delegates, a committee of nine was appointed, who reported a Plan of Separation, to take effect on receiving the sanction of the annual conferences, if the southern brethren found it impossible to retain their ecclesiastical connection with us. The final result was the dismemberment of the Methodist Episcopal Church,—after the lapse of sixty years from its organization,—and the organization of the Methodist Episcopal Church, South.

Bishop Soule eventually separated himself from the Methodist Episcopal Church, and became connected with the southern organization. By this means Bishop Hedding became senior bishop of the Methodist Episcopal Church. Before the adjournment of the General Conference, a resolution was passed, in view of his infirm health, releasing him from the performance of any more labour than in his own judgment he should be able to perform.

The General Conference resolved on the election of two additional bishops. On the third ballot, Rev. L. L. Hamline and Rev. E. S. Janes were elected bishops—the former having received one hundred and two, and the latter ninety-nine votes out of one hundred and seventy-seven, the whole number cast. They were solemnly inducted into the episcopal office by the usual services, and by the imposition of the hands of Bishops Soule, Hedding, Waugh, and Morris, on the 10th of June.

This session of the General Conference will ever be regarded as one of the most memorable in the history of the Church. It was protracted through the unprecedented period of forty days,—much of the time holding two sessions each day,—and finally adjourned a little after midnight on the eleventh of June.

After the close of the General Conference, Bishop Hedding resumed his labours in the annual conferences. He met the New-York, at Brooklyn, June 13th; the Providence, at Newport, Rhode Island, July 3d; the New-England, in company with Bishop Janes, at Westfield, July 24th; and the Maine, at Bangor, August 14th. During this year he also visited many of the Churches in different sections, especially in his old field of labour; and these visits were very refreshing to his own soul. On this episcopal tour, also, he was greatly rejoiced to witness the gradual healing of party feeling, and the restoration of brotherly affection among many who had become alienated in the ultra-abolition excitement. He was also greatly cheered at finding the Church recovering from the shock occasioned by the Millerite delusion which had swept over the land.

Many brethren in New-England had become estranged in their feelings from himself, because they thought he leaned too much toward pro-slaveryism in his efforts to save the Church from distraction and dismemberment. But most of them had now become convinced of the wisdom and propriety of his course; and many of them had the magnanimity to express to him the change which had been wrought in their views and feelings.

We have already noticed his removal from New-

England, and the causes of it. During the present year, the preachers stationed in Boston and vicinity united in a formal request for him to return and make New-England his future home. They say that, in this urgent request, they but "express the sentiments of all New-England Methodists—both preachers and people." These manifestations were peculiarly grateful to the feelings of Bishop Hedding; but he felt that it was too late in life for him to think of another removal.

In the spring of 1845 he assisted Bishop Waugh at the session of the Baltimore Conference, which commenced on the twelfth of March. He also met the Troy Conference, at Schenectady, May 7th; assisted Bishop Waugh at the New-York, immediately after; the Black River, at Mexicoville, July 9th; the Oneida, at Utica, July 30th; and the Genesee, at Buffalo, August 20th.

During the spring of this year he was deeply affected by the death of three ministers—with two of whom he had been long and intimately acquainted. The first of these was the Rev. James Covel, who died while the Troy Conference was in session. He had been pastor of the State-street Church, in Albany, and in that church Bishop Hedding preached his funeral sermon, to an immense audience, from 2 Tim. iv, 6–8. The second was the Rev. Samuel Cochran, at whose funeral he was called to preach, in Poughkeepsie, a few days after the occasion just mentioned. He had known Mr. Cochran from his youth, even before he was a preacher, and had been intimately acquainted with him during the whole period of his ministry, which commenced only three years later than his own. The very day Mr. Cochran's funeral had been attended, he received intelligence of the death of the Rev. Timothy Merritt—an aged and excellent minister, and a long and well-tried friend of the bishop. His language, on the reception of this news, was: "These three brethren have just gone to heaven. Their warfare is over. I must fight a little longer. Lord, help me to conquer!"

Growing out of the relation of Bishop Andrew to the system of slavery, and the consequent action of the General Conference in his case, a new controversy had sprung up in the Church. Into the merits of that controversy—the principles involved, or its final results—we are not called to enter. But as one of its incidents has occasioned some animadversion upon the action of the bishops, and especially upon the action of Bishop Hedding, it demands of us a passing notice.

Immediately after the action of the General Conference in this case, Bishop Andrew returned to his home in the south. After he had left New-York, he addressed a note to Bishop Soule, assigning the reasons for his departure—stating that he did not know whether the bishops would feel authorized, in view of the action of the General Conference, to assign him a place among them for the next four years. This letter contained neither a request nor a refusal to take his regular appointments. In this state of affairs, when the bishops came to meet for the arrangement of their episcopal labour for the four years, a difference of opinion was found to exist as to the propriety of assigning to Bishop Andrew his appropriate share of episcopal service. The majority of them believed that it was the design of the General Conference to devolve on him the responsibility of determining whether, in view of their action, he would "desist" from the exercise of the episcopal office, or whether he would not; and therefore they did not feel themselves warranted in calling him out. Under this view, Bishops Hedding, Waugh, Morris, and Hamline appended their names to the following document: "It is our opinion, in regard to the action of the late General Conference in the case of Bishop Andrew, that it was designed by that body to devolve the responsibility of the exercise of the functions of his office exclusively on himself. In the absence of Bishop Andrew at the time of arranging the Plan of Episcopal Visitation for the ensuing four years, and he not having notified us of his desire or purpose with respect to it, we should regard ourselves as acting in contravention of the expressed will of the General Conference if we apportioned to Bishop Andrew any definite portion thereof. But if he shall hereafter make a written application for a portion of the general oversight, we should feel ourselves justified in assigning it to him."

In consequence of this, the name of Bishop Andrew was left out of the regular Plan of Episcopal

Visitation for the ensuing four years. The bishops, however, took the precaution to prepare a second plan, including his name, which was to take effect upon Bishop Andrew's making a "written application" for his portion of the episcopal oversight. The object of this was to leave the responsibility of determining the question precisely where the General Conference had placed it. They also provided that should such "written application" be made, the senior bishop might cause the second plan to be published in connexion with such application, that the reason for the substitution of the second plan might accompany its publication. This action was eminently wise and prudential.

Thus matters stood, when Bishop Soule, in the fall of 1844, on his individual responsibility, called out Bishop Andrew, by inviting him to accompany him in his tour of the southern conferences, and assist him in his episcopal work. In his letter to Bishop Andrew, Bishop Soule holds forth the following language: "It has often been asked, through the public journals and otherwise, why Bishop Andrew was not assigned his regular portion of the episcopal work for the ensuing four years, on the Plan of Visitation formed by the bishops, and published in the official papers. *It devolves on the majority of my colleagues in the episcopacy*, (if, indeed, we have any episcopacy,) *rather than on me, to answer this question.*"

This statement elicited inquiries through the public journals, "Will the bishops explain?" It also provoked not a little animadversion. These inquiries, as well as a subsequent communication from Bishop Soule, elicited from Bishops Hedding, Waugh, Morris, and Hamline a plain statement of the case as we have given it. At first a few extremists demurred at this action; but it was so manifestly in accordance with the design and action of the General Conference, that the sober judgment of all intelligent men soon came to approve of it; and, at the present day, a plain statement of the facts is all the vindication their action demands.

During the year 1845, the Convention of Delegates from the conferences in the slaveholding states was held in Louisville, Ky. That convention organized the annual conferences in the slaveholding states "into a distinct ecclesiastical connexion, separate from the jurisdiction of the Methodist Episcopal Church," and solemnly declared that such jurisdiction was now "*entirely dissolved.*" They also decreed that the "separate ecclesiastical organization" should "be known by the style and title of the *Methodist Episcopal Church, South.*" Under these circumstances, the five bishops remaining in the Methodist Episcopal Church, at a regular meeting, came to the unanimous conclusion that they would not be justified in presiding in any of the conferences thus separated from the jurisdiction of the Methodist Episcopal Church. Thenceforward their action was conformable to this resolution.

It may be well, in this connection, to place upon

record the judgment of Bishop Hedding in the matter of dividing the capital of the Book Concern with the Southern organization. In a letter addressed to Bishop Hamline, under date of December 8th, 1847, he says: "I am decidedly of the opinion that the General Conference has no constitutional authority to yield to the claims of the South, and set off to them a portion of our book interest. The General Conference, without the concurrent act of the annual conferences, cannot set off part of the 'produce,' much less part of the stock of the Book Concern. To do either the one or the other would be a direct violation of the constitution, and would forfeit all confidence of the Church in the wisdom of that body. If anything is done in future, in relation to a division of the Book Concern, it must be by a vote of two-thirds of the General Conference, and of three-fourths of all the votes in the annual conferences, taken in the aggregate. Whether such a vote of the General Conference and of the annual conferences, directly on the question of the division of the Book Concern, would be constitutional or not, is a matter of difference of opinion. On that question I am not prepared to give an opinion. I can see but one constitutional way in which anything can be done on that subject; that is, for the next General Conference to pass a two-third vote recommending to the annual conferences to concur in suspending the sixth restriction, for one object and only one; that is, to give the General Conference authority to give the Church

South a given portion of the Book Concern; then, if the constitutional votes can be obtained in the annual conferences, the succeeding General Conference may set off a portion."

In 1846 Bishop Hedding attended the following conferences, namely: Baltimore, at Baltimore, March 11th; Philadelphia, at Philadelphia, April 1st; New-Jersey, at Newark, April 22d; New-York, at New-York, May 13th; and also the Oneida and Genesee, in company with Bishop Janes, the former at Auburn, July 22d, and the latter at Lyons, September 2d.

The session of the New-York Conference, this year, was one of extraordinary labour, as well as of extraordinary length—being continued fifteen days. A very unusual number of trials occurred; and there was also unusual difficulty in fixing the stations of the preachers. There were so many special applications, so many committees, so many petitions, and so many remonstrances—that the bishop began to fear that it was impossible to give general satisfaction in the appointments. When he came to the close of the conference, when the church was crowded with the members of the conference and of the Churches in the city, the bishop stated to them the difficulties he had experienced in making the appointments; he also expressed his apprehension that they would not all be satisfactory to either preachers or people; but he had done the best he could. He then expatiated upon the importance of the itinerancy, the honour

God had put upon it in making it instrumental in building up and extending the Church, and in saving the souls of men: "in saving our souls," exclaimed he. "Shall this itinerancy be sustained?" he then inquired. An earnest affirmative response came up from both preachers and people. He then briefly alluded to the indispensable elements of an effective itinerancy, and the spirit that must animate both preachers and people where it is maintained. "And now, brethren," said he, addressing himself to the members of the conference, "you who want to preserve our itinerancy, and will receive your appointments and go to them as true itinerant Methodist preachers, and labour for the salvation of the souls of men—*rise up*." Instantly the whole conference were on their feet. Then, turning to the great body of laymen who were present, he said: "You who want to keep up this itinerancy in the Church and will receive your preachers and try to labour in love and fellowship with them, say, *Amen*." One hearty and prolonged "*Amen*" arose from every part of the vast assembly. "Now," continued the bishop, "I hope the preachers will be a great blessing to you and to sinners in your congregations; and that you will love and pray for them, and coöperate with them with all your hearts." The appointments were then announced, and the assembly dismissed. As we retired from the house we heard a gentleman, who had been drawn into the assembly from curiosity, say to his friend: "Was n't that a grand stroke of generalship?" The moral influence of that scene, we are certain, will not soon be lost from the minds of many —both preachers and people—who witnessed it.

During the fall of this year, and the winter of 1846–7, Bishop Hedding was called to give an official decision in the celebrated trial case, or rather attempted trial case, of the Rev. John Newland Maffitt. For some years there had been reports prejudicial to the Christian and ministerial character of Mr. Maffitt, in the city of New-York and vicinity; but as he was in a distant part of the country, and was travelling from place to place, no opportunity for investigation had occurred. In the fall of 1846 Mr. Maffitt came to the city, bearing a regular certificate of his relation to the Church as a local elder, and on the strength of that became connected with one of the city charges. Learning these facts, the preachers' meeting appointed three of their number as a committee to have the reports investigated. The committee found occasion to prefer charges of immoral and unchristian conduct against Mr. Maffitt, and notified his pastor of the existence of such charges. Subsequently Mr. Maffitt obtained certain papers from his pastor, and continued to evade the trial of the complaint against him, on the ground that jurisdiction where he first joined had ceased. This state of things continued till the 17th of December, when he was received, on the strength of the papers in his possession, as a local elder in the Centenary Methodist Episcopal Church, Brooklyn, by the Rev.

John C. Green, pastor of the Church. Mr. Green proposed to have an investigation of the reports against Mr. Maffitt in his charge, and so notified the committee who had been appointed to prefer charges against him, and others interested in the case. The committee, believing that Mr. Green had received Mr. Maffitt on insufficient authority, and therefore had no jurisdiction in the case; and also fearing that a fair, full, and impartial trial before a proper committee would not be had under such circumstances, declined appearing in the proposed trial, but appealed to Bishop Hedding to stay proceedings in the case, and to determine the question of jurisdiction.

Bishop Hedding first wrote an advisory letter to Mr. Green, but was soon authentically apprized that he still persisted in trying the case. Whereupon he wrote a mandatory letter, as follows: "I request you to stay all proceedings in his [Maffitt's] case, until the question of jurisdiction is legally settled." At his earliest convenience, Bishop Hedding had an interview with the parties, and investigated the facts in the case. After describing the certificate upon which Mr. Maffitt was received into the Asbury Church by Rev. S. Martindale, the pastor, and showing its sufficiency, he proceeds to discuss the question of present jurisdiction, as follows:—

"On the application of the Rev. Mr. Maffitt, by a friend, Rev. Mr. Martindale returned to him the before-described certificate, having written upon it the following words:—'Correct. S. Martindale.'

This was one of the papers on which Mr. Green admitted Mr. Maffitt to membership in the Centenary Methodist Episcopal Church, Brooklyn.

"This certificate, when it had procured Mr. Maffitt's membership as a local elder in the Asbury Methodist Episcopal Church, N. Y., was of no further authority or use. What Mr. Martindale has written upon the certificate does not renew its authority, for it is without date, and is not signed as preacher in charge, and does not assert any of the facts necessary to show that Mr. Maffitt was a local elder in the church of which Mr. Martindale had charge, consequently was still of no authority after he had written those words upon it, and could not dismiss Mr. Maffitt from the Asbury Methodist Episcopal Church, New-York, or give him membership elsewhere.

"The next paper upon which Mr. Green received Mr. Maffitt was the following:—

"'This is to certify that the Rev. John N. Maffitt, a local elder in the Methodist Episcopal Church, has spent several weeks with me in my station in the city of New-York, having placed in my hands a regular certificate of his good standing in Auburn, in this state, as a local elder in the Methodist Episcopal Church. During his stay with me he has laboured with great acceptance and usefulness.

(Signed) "'S. Martindale, Pastor.'

"This paper asserts that Mr. Maffitt was a local elder in the Methodist Episcopal Church, that he was in good standing in Auburn, as proved by his certificate, and had laboured several weeks in the Asbury Methodist Episcopal Church, New-York, with great acceptance and usefulness; but does not assert his membership as a local elder in the Asbury Methodist Episcopal Church, or his official standing in that Church at the time it was given, and is without date, and therefore was incompetent to dismiss him from the Asbury Methodist Episcopal Church, or give him membership elsewhere.

"Another paper, presented by Mr. Green, as part of the authority upon which he received Mr. Maffitt, is the following:—

"'I certify that I have taken the name of Rev. John N. Maffitt from the church books of the Norfolk-street Methodist Episcopal Church, of which I am pastor, and claim no jurisdiction over him.

(Signed) "'S. MARTINDALE.'

"'*December* 16, 1846.'

"This paper has none of the properties of a disciplinary certificate: it only proves that Mr. Martindale had once received Mr. Maffitt, and that his name had once been upon the church books of the Asbury Methodist Episcopal Church. Another paper, on which Mr. Green relied for authority in the case, was the following:—

"'This is to certify that I called on Rev. S. Martindale with a certificate of membership of the Rev. J. N. Maffitt, signed by the presiding elder, by order of the Auburn Quarterly-Meeting Conference, on the —— day of November, 1846, in order that brother Maffitt should unite himself with the Asbury Methodist Episcopal Church in Norfolk-street, and that brother Martindale received said certificate, and said that would do, and directed me to keep it, and put brother Maffitt's name on my class-book. About two weeks after, I called on brother Martindale, by request of brother Maffitt, to ask for his certificate of membership, as he wished to change his relation from Norfolk-street to some other charge. He, 'said Martindale,' asked me for the Auburn certificate. I gave it him, and he wrote on it 'correct,' and signed his name, then gave it to me for brother Maffitt, saying he was now at liberty to go where he pleased, as he was no member there, and could join anywhere.

(Signed) "'HENRY R. PIERCY.'

"This paper, also, in the first place, goes to prove that Mr. Maffitt joined the Asbury Methodist Episcopal Church in New-York. It does not show that Mr. Maffitt was dismissed with a disciplinary certificate. Besides, such testimony is of no authority, except when great distance, or some uncontrollable circumstance renders it impracticable to obtain a disciplinary certificate from the proper authority of the Church.

"Further, all these papers upon which Mr. Maffitt's transfer from Asbury Methodist Episcopal Church to Centenary Methodist Episcopal Church, Brooklyn, is claimed, were given after the preacher furnishing them was informed that cha. ²es existed against Mr. Maffitt.

"After being requested, as above stated, 'to interfere in the case with' my 'official authority,' it being inconvenient for me at the time to attend to the business, I transferred it to Bishops Hamline and Janes, as they were then in this city; but they referred it back to me—the business thus devolving on me. Now, therefore, it becomes my duty to say, it is my judgment that, according to the rules and usages of the Methodist Episcopal Church, the Rev. John N. Maffitt is a local elder in the Asbury Methodist Episcopal Church, Norfolk-street, New-York, and, consequently, that he cannot now be a local elder in the Centenary Church, Brooklyn.

"ELIJAH HEDDING."

"NEW-YORK, *February 4th*, 1847."

To this decision Bishop Janes appended the following note:—

"I concur in the opinions of Bishop Hedding, as expressed in the foregoing document.

"EDMUND S. JANES."

"NEW-YORK, *February 4th*, 1847."

The finale of the matter, if our recollection serves us, was, that by episcopal authority Mr. Maffitt was left under the jurisdiction of the Rev. S. Martindale, and amenable to that quarterly conference as a local elder; but as he persisted in repudiating said jurisdiction and amenability, the presiding elder of the New-York District declared him withdrawn from the Methodist Episcopal Church.

The decision of Bishop Hedding in this case was commented upon with great severity by the friends of Mr. Maffitt. They regarded it as a usurpation of episcopal authority. The case was discussed in such a form in one of the public journals of the day, that, at the ensuing General Conference, Bishops Hedding and Janes expressed the wish that it might be referred to the Committee on Episcopacy. Accordingly the reference was made. The committee, after investigating the case, reported,—

"1. That in the judgment of the committee, in the decision of Bishops Hedding and Janes, in the case of J. N. Maffitt, in determining the place of his membership, they acted entirely within the limits of their episcopal jurisdiction, and in perfect accordance with the discipline and usages of the Methodist Episcopal Church.

"2. That the circumstances in that case were such as fully to justify and require their authoritative interference."

The report in the case was adopted with great unanimity.

The reaction after the Millerite excitement was unfavourable to the growth of the Church as to any increase of members. At the close of 1845, while yet the southern conferences were included in the returns, it was found that there was a decrease of thirty-one thousand seven hundred and sixty-nine in the membership. The membership of the Church then was one million one hundred and thirty-nine thousand five hundred and eighty-seven; ministers, four thousand eight hundred and twenty-eight; local preachers, eight thousand one hundred and one. At the close of the present year there was a further decrease of twelve thousand three hundred and forty-three reported. The southern conferences having now withdrawn, the statistics for the year were—members, six hundred and forty-four thousand two hundred and ninety-nine; ministers, three thousand five hundred and eighty-two; and local preachers, four thousand nine hundred and thirty-five.

About the last of February, in 1847, Bishop Hedding left home to attend a meeting of the Board of Bishops in Philadelphia. It had been his intention afterward to be present at the session of the Baltimore Conference; but his health was so very feeble that he relinquished the idea, and, after resting a few weeks in Philadelphia, he returned home. He, however, met the Providence Conference at Fall River, April 1st; and the New-England, at Lynn, April 28th. His visit to the latter conference was made solemn to him by the death of two of the old veterans of the cross—George Pickering and Joel Steele. The former, at the time of his death, was the oldest effective minister in the connexion. Bishop Hedding improved the occasion by an address to the conference, at its special request. While speaking of the high Christian and ministerial character of the dead, his sensibilities were intensely aroused. At one time his thoughts turned upon himself and his approaching change; then he said, with much feeling, and with powerful effect: "Brethren, I know I may be the next to go. At all events I *must* go soon; and in view of it I turn to my own heart and life, and discover so much frailty, and so many infirmities, that I repeat the words of the poet with deep feeling:—

'And can it be, thou heavenly King,
That thou should'st me to glory bring?
Make me the partner of thy throne,
Deck'd with a never-fading crown?'"

And then placing his hands upon his hoary head, he exclaimed, "O that crown! Shall *I* ever wear it? But I remember again it is written, 'This is a faithful saying, and worthy of all acceptation, that Christ Jesus came into the world to save sinners, of whom I am chief,' then I cling to the atonement, and count all my sufferings and privations as but drops; and could there be such a thing as commencing life again, with present experience, I would be an *itinerant* preacher. I have no fears of being lost. Once I was in bondage unto fear. Before my conversion I suffered profound agony in anticipating the wrath of God against my sins; but I have been saved. Brethren, I do not believe I shall go to hell—Christ has rescued me!" The address throughout was exceedingly affecting, and made a profound impression.*

* Report in Zion's Herald.

He also attended the New-Hampshire Conference, which met at Northfield, May 19th; the Vermont, at Irasburg, June 9th; and the Maine, at Saco, June 30th. After making this tour of the New-England Conferences, he says: "I find but here and there an old preacher, who was here when I travelled in this country. Most of them have ceased from their labours. And why am I spared? I feel that I am under deep obligations to Providence and grace for the numerous mercies that have crowned my poor life. O that I may be thankful, and improve the privileges of my few remaining days to the salvation of my soul and to God's glory."

In the spring of 1848 Bishop Hedding met the Providence Conference at New-London, April 5th; and soon after left for the General Conference, which was to assemble on the 1st of May, in the city of Pittsburgh.

CHAPTER XIX.

SEVENTH QUADRENNIAL OF EPISCOPAL LABOURS.

General Conference of 1848—Bishop Hedding requested to prepare some Biographical Sketch of himself—His Views on the Pastorship of the Methodist Episcopal Church—Appointed Delegate to the British Wesleyan Conference—Feeble Health—Rev. Manning Force accompanies him—Revives an Acquaintance with an old Friend—Sermon before the New-Hampshire Conference—Visit on part of an old Circuit—Vermont Conference at Barre—Maine and East Maine Conferences—Conferences in 1849—The old Cambridge Circuit—The Bishop's Notes of Travel, &c. —A strong Christian—His singular Death—Sunday Labours—Attends the Funeral of Rev. J. A. Merrill—Sick—First failure in Twenty-five Years to meet his Conferences—Travels in 1850—Remarks upon his Notes of Travel—Views about Preaching—Comparison of Methodism with the Former Time—Zeal of the Early Methodists—Class-meetings —Novel case of proving the Mind—Compliment to a Sermon—Success of Methodist Agencies.

The General Conference of 1848 assembled in the city of Pittsburgh, on the first day of May. Bishops Hedding, Waugh, Morris, Hamline, and Janes were present. The conference was composed of one hundred and fifty-one delegates, representing twenty-three annual conferences. Among these conferences the representation was as follows:—Baltimore, eleven; Philadelphia, seven; New-Jersey, seven; Providence, five; New-England, six; New-York, thirteen; New-Hampshire, four; Troy, eight; Vermont, three; Black River, five; Pittsburgh, 8; Oneida, eight; Maine, eight; Erie, six; Rock River, five; North Ohio, six; Genesee, nine; Ohio, ten; Iowa, two;

North Indiana, five; Michigan, five; Illinois, five; and Indiana, five.

Bishop Hedding opened the conference by reading a lesson from the Scriptures. An appropriate hymn was then sung; after which, Bishops Waugh and Morris led in prayer. The bishops presented no formal address at the opening of the conference, but at different stages of its progress brought to the attention of the body such matters as the interests of the Church seemed specially to require. The course of action in the conference was harmonious and cordial almost beyond precedent.

In relation to Bishop Hedding, it was resolved, in view of his age and bodily infirmities, that "he consider himself at liberty to use his own discretion as to the amount of episcopal or other pastoral labour" he will perform during the coming four years. He was also requested "to prepare his biography for publication, including especially his observations and opinions in relation to Methodism." He was further "requested to prepare and publish, or cause to be published at our Book Concern, his views on the Pastorship of the Methodist Episcopal Church in its various grades of class-leaders, preachers in charge, presiding elders and bishops, with the concurrence of his colleagues." The failing health of the bishop, and finally his decease, prevented his compliance with these requests. Had he been able to prepare the work proposed in the last request, it would have embodied an exposition of our economy of inestimable value to the Church. Such a work, emanating from a mind so clear and discriminating, and after such profound study of our economy, and such large and varied observation and experience of its practical workings, would, no doubt, have left its lasting impress upon every department of the administration of the Church. But it was too late in life, and too little physical energy and endurance were left for him to accomplish it.

The conference also resolved unanimously to request Bishop Hedding to visit the British Conference at some time within the ensuing four years, to reciprocate for himself and in behalf of that body, and of the Methodist Episcopal Church in the United States of America, the fraternal salutations received from that body. With this request also, it was impossible for him to comply. He was now verging toward the close of his long earthly career.

This General Conference was regarded with very general and deep interest; and it assumed an importance from its being the first succeeding the organization of the Methodist Episcopal Church South. Its deliberations were conducted with universal care and discretion, and the results attained have tended powerfully to harmonize and strengthen the Church. Its details belong to another department of history.

During the latter part of the conference Bishop Hedding was too feeble to be present at its sessions; and at its close he found himself unable to endure journeying with the delegates returning home, and yet he was in such an enfeebled condition that it was not safe for him to journey alone. "While in this condition," he says, "the Rev. Manning Force—an old friend, and one who had many times shown me kindness—remained to accompany me, and brought me safe through as far as Philadelphia. We came through by canal and railroad by the Juniata route."

The bishop also gives the following incident connected with his return:—"Unexpectedly on this journey I fell in with another old and dear friend, whose company and conversation were of great interest to me—it was the Rev. Mr. Avery. He had been for many years a local elder in the Methodist Episcopal Church, and resided at Pittsburgh. He was a man of great wealth, and of benevolence and liberality equal to his wealth. Prior to the General Conference of 1828, and during that conference I had made his house my home when I was in Pittsburgh, and had received many tokens of brotherly love at his hand; but after that he had withdrawn from the Church, and connected himself with the Methodist Protestant Society. At the General Conference of 1848, I had not seen him for twenty years, and supposed, from his having left the old Church, he had became alienated from his old friends. He now resided at Alleghany city, and was living in princely style. He entertained a number of delegates during the session of the General

Conference. One day he sent his carriage for me to go over and dine with him. I rejoiced at the opportunity of renewing my former acquaintance with him. I found him the same brother Avery he had been twenty years before—differing in opinion, to be sure, on some points of Church government, but the same in doctrine, in spirit, in zeal for Christ, in brotherly love, and in friendship to his former brethren from whom he had separated. He and brother Force and myself had a delightful journey across the Alleghany Mountains. Our Christian intercourse was mutually edifying, and our souls were knit together in love."

At Philadelphia, Bishop Hedding parted with his kind travelling companion, and continued his course homeward alone. After recruiting his strength a little, he went to Manchester, N. H., where he met the New-Hampshire Conference on the 21st of June. He says of the session, "We had a pleasant, interesting and profitable time. The Sabbath was a day of special interest and of the manifestation of God's power. The Methodists have a large church and a flourishing society in the place. By the arrangement I was designated to preach Sabbath morning. The great size of the building, and the vastness of the congregation, excited the apprehensions of many, that I would not be able to make myself heard by the multitude. I apprehended this myself; but through the abundant mercy and grace of the Redeemer, I was enabled to preach so that all could hear, being, as it then seemed to me, and as it has since appeared, miraculously strengthened and blessed in both soul and body." In this discourse the bishop seemed to have renewed his age and his strength. Many of the congregation gave evidence that God was in his word; and many of the preachers were deeply affected. It was probably the last great effort of Bishop Hedding.

The Sabbath after the close of this conference he spent in Lebanon, on the western border of the state. "Here," said he, "I had been circuit preacher forty-four years ago, and presiding elder forty-one. In those days the only place in which we could worship in Lebanon was a small school-house, and that on week days, with but few members and few hearers. Such were the prejudices against the Methodists then, that few would countenance them in any way. But, "behold, what has God wrought!" We have now a large, flourishing, and prosperous society; a good house of worship, and a good station. Most of the members I had formerly known were dead; but I found two or three who wept at the remembrance of former times. Here, in company with two or three other preachers, I spent a delightful Sabbath."

From Lebanon he was carried by one of the preachers in his carriage across the country to Barre, Vt., where the Vermont conference commenced on the 5th of July. The session of the conference passed off delightfully. Bishop Hedding seemed to feel that he was visiting his brethren for the last time. Of this place, he also says,—"Here I had been circuit preacher in 1805—forty-three years ago. Most of my old friends had gone to 'Abraham's bosom.' But a few remained; many of them, who were young men when I was on the circuit, I knew now because they looked as their departed fathers did forty-three years before." The preaching on the Sabbath at this conference was in the open air, and Bishop Hedding found it impossible, in his enfeebled state of health, to preach loud enough to make the vast multitude hear. "But," said he, "my failure was made up by another preacher of strong voice and powerful spirit, who preached in the afternoon, so that the *whole people* could hear: so that, on the whole, we had a profitable Sabbath."

After this conference closed, he went, by the way of Boston, to Portland, Me., where he met the Maine Conference on the 19th of July; then to Bangor, on the Penobscot River, where he met the East Maine Conference on the 2d of August. This closed his episcopal labour in the conferences for the year. He returned home by easy stages, and was pretty much confined there, on account of his feeble health, through the ensuing winter.

In the spring of 1849 Bishop Hedding met his colleagues at Newark, New-Jersey, on the 9th of April. Afterward he assisted Bishop Hamline at the New-England Conference, which met at Springfield, April 25th; also Bishop Morris at the New-

York Conference, at Poughkeepsie, May 9th; and Bishop Hamline again, at the Troy Conference, which met at Sandy Hill, New-York, May 30th.

Of this latter place he says: "The village where we held the conference formed a part of the circuit which I travelled part of the year 1801, under the presiding elder, Shadrach Bostwick, long since dead. It was then called Cambridge Circuit, and embraced an extent of territory larger than any district now in the Troy Conference." Great, however, as the circuit then was in extent, there were but two churches within its bounds, and those were small. The bishop adds the following reminiscences of his early experience on this circuit: "We preached usually every day through the week as well as on the Sabbath, through a journey of six weeks to get around the circuit. Our temples of worship were private houses and school-houses; and we established preaching wherever we could get a few hearers. In this circuit was one appointment where I used to ride twenty miles out, over a bad road, to preach to about twenty or thirty people on a week-day, where we had about a dozen members; and then back again twenty miles. Sometimes we used to make this journey through storms of rain, or sleet, or snow." What a lesson is this for young preachers of the present day! Verily, this was going unto "the lost sheep of the house of Israel." "In the extreme north part of this circuit," he continues, "was a brother at whose house I used to preach, who was converted in Ireland under the ministry of the Rev. John Wesley. He brought with him to this new settlement the true spirit of Christianity, and most of his family were partakers of like precious faith. I have heard from his own lips his testimony in regard to the power of saving grace; and heard him say that for forty years there had not been a moment that he doubted if he should die at any time he should go straight home to heaven. This experience was fully corroborated in his life, his daily walk, and conversation. A few years after his settlement in this country he was licensed as a local preacher, and continued such to the end of his life. The last sermon he preached was at one of the two meeting-houses mentioned. I have been credibly informed that at this time, while preaching this sermon, he told the congregation he was preaching for the last time—his work was done! God was about to give him a release, and call him home. His sermon was preached with unction; he and the people shouting aloud the praises of the Redeemer. After he had finished his discourse he left the pulpit, seated himself in a chair in the altar, and calmly resigned his spirit to God.

"If we were wanting proof that Methodism was the child of God, and that it has received the fostering care of the great Head of the Church, we need look no further for a confirmation of these facts than to its rise and progress within the bounds of what was formerly Cambridge Circuit. The state of the Church in all this region in 1801, with its two meeting-houses, scattered population, and scanty membership, forms a striking contrast with the state of the Methodist Church here in 1849. Thriving villages have sprung up in the place of the lonely farm house; stately houses of worship have succeeded the school-houses and lowly dwellings where we used to congregate; the "tens" of God's true worshippers have been multiplied into "thousands;" so that we can but exclaim of a truth, "The wilderness and solitary place has been made glad, the desert has rejoiced and blossomed as the rose!"

We cannot do better here than to favour the reader with the bishop's own account of his travels and labours, which we find in the handwriting of the Rev. L. M. Vincent: "After the close of the Troy Conference, at Sandy Hill, I returned home, where I arrived the 8th of June. June 15th, left home again for the Black River Conference. Preached the following Sabbath at Rome, New-York. June 18th, preached at Syracuse, at a meeting held for the Indians of the Oneida mission, and admitted an Indian to deacon's orders.

"From Syracuse I proceeded to Fulton, New-York, where I met the Black River Conference. Conference commenced its session the 20th of June, and continued about a week. It was one of great interest to preachers and people. June 27th, left Fulton; and returned by way of Syracuse, Utica, and Schenectady to Saratoga Springs. Thence I went north to Lake Champlain, chiefly to visit relations in New-York and Vermont; but employed part of the time in visiting the Churches and ordaining local deacons who had before been elected by the conference. Returned home the 13th of July.

"On the 18th of July left home again, and went by the way of New-York to Middletown, Connecticut, where I preached Sabbath, July 22d.

On Monday, July 23d, I was called to Wilbraham, Massachusetts, to attend the funeral of the Rev. Joseph A. Merrill, of the New-England Conference. I had before been informed by letter, that it was the request of brother Merrill, while living, that I should preach his funeral sermon. On Tuesday the 24th I performed this solemn duty, taking for my text 2 Tim. iv, 7, 8. Brother Merrill had been a travelling preacher forty-three years. My acquaintance with him had commenced when he was about seventeen years old. I had frequently seen him, and been intimate with him through the whole course of his ministry.

"He had left a fair character as a Christian and as a minister. He died in peace, and in full hope of eternal life. He had left a widow with six sons and four daughters, all members of the Methodist Episcopal Church. Three of the sons and a husband of one of the daughters were travelling preachers, and members of the New-England Conference. Two of the sons were lawyers, and one a farmer. 'He, being dead, yet speaketh.'

"About thirty travelling preachers were present at the funeral; and though we had met on a mournful occasion, we were comforted with the belief that our departed brother had gone to rest. Another circumstance was interesting to me. I had been presiding elder there forty years before, and well acquainted through all the country. Many of my old friends, whom I had not expected to see again in this world, assembled on this occasion, and we mingled our joys, and sorrows, and tears.

"After the funeral of brother Merrill, I returned to Middletown, attended the commencement of the Wesleyan University the 1st of August, passed a few days at Middletown, and returned home, where I arrived the 11th of August.

"On my way home from Connecticut I was taken sick, and was obliged to remain at home under the care of a physician about two months, consequently I was not able to attend the East Genesee and Genesee Conferences, at both of which I should have presided had health permitted. Bishop Hamline attended the former, and Bishop Morris the latter, in my stead.

"This is the first time I have failed in getting to a conference where it was my duty to preside since I have held the office—*twenty-five* years. At several of the conferences during that time, I was so sick I could do but little; a number of times I have travelled when I was sick, in order to reach the conferences.

"The state of my health and my age required me to remain at home through the winter; but through

God's mercy I was enabled most of the time to preach once every Sabbath, and have enjoyed many seasons of religious comfort with the people of God in the house of prayer. Yet, though at home, I have had plenty of care of the churches, and plenty of letters on Church business to answer from different parts of the country. But God has kept my soul in peace. Glory be to His holy name!

"March the 14th, 1850, I left home and went to New-York, where I passed a few days, and preached the following Sabbath. March 19th, I went to Philadelphia. March 20th, met my colleagues (all but Bishop Hamline, who was detained at home sick,) on important Church business, in which we laboured a week.

"March 27th, the Philadelphia Conference commenced. Bishop Waugh presided, and I assisted. At the preceding session of that conference a request had been made, by vote, that the president of the present session should preach the opening sermon, which is a custom of that conference; and though Bishop Waugh was president, and this duty naturally devolved on him, he requested and urged me to perform it, which I attempted, on 1 Tim. iv, 10. The conference requested that the sermon might be published, which was afterwards done.

"April 13. Went to Burlington, New-Jersey, to see an old friend who was sick, and passed the Sabbath there, though having taken a severe cold I was unable to preach.

"April 16. Returned to Philadelphia again, and met my colleagues, by previous arrangement, on the business we had not been able to finish.

"April 17. I opened the New-Jersey Conference at Camdem, New-Jersey, at which I presided, and Bishop Waugh assisted. At this conference we had a delightfully pleasant and agreeable session, with the exception that we had a great amount of trouble in making the appointments.

"After the conference I returned home, where I arrived April 26th. During most of the time of my absence I have been very much affected by severe cold and pain in my head, so that I was able to preach but twice during my absence.

"May 2. Went to New-York to meet the General Mission Committee. After the business of that committee was over, returned home, May 4th.

May 7. Went to New-York again to Conference. May 8th, opened the New-York Conference in Eighteenth-street Church, which continued its session till May 18th. A long session of great labour and burdensome business; more than I could have endured had not Bishop Janes been there to assist me.

"May 19. Rested the Sabbath-day.

"Monday, May 20th, proceeded to New-Haven, Conn., to attend the New-York East Conference. Met the presiding elders, Monday afternoon and Tuesday, to make preparatory arrangements for the business of the conference. May 22d, opened the

New-York East Conference, which continued till the 30th. Great difficulties in the stationing part of the business called for labour and patience. Bishop Janes was also present here, and rendered me great assistance.

"Cold and cough, and sore lungs, have kept me from preaching from March 27 till this time; but I am now getting better, and hope I shall soon be able to speak for my Master. After the conference at New-Haven I returned home, where I arrived the 1st of June. From the 14th of March to the 1st of June my labours have been excessive—far too heavy for one of my age; but the Lord has mercifully preserved me. Glory be to His holy name!

"On the 20th of June I left home and went to New-York, where, by previous appointment, I ordained a coloured brother from Liberia both deacon and elder.

"At 5 P. M. the same day I went on board the steamboat, and during the night sailed to Fall River, Mass.; thence by railroad to Boston, thence by steamboat to Frankfort, Maine, on the Penobscot River, where I assisted Bishop Morris in the business of the East Maine Conference. This conference commenced June 26th. A pleasant and profitable session.

"Then returned to Portland, where I passed the following Sabbath, and visited my old friends with whom I formerly officiated as pastor, a few of whom are yet alive.

"Then came to Kennebunk Port, where the Maine Conference commenced the 10th of July. There also I assisted Bishop Morris in the labours of the conference. I found peculiarities connected with this place, where we held our session of conference, such as I scarce ever found in a village or town before. I was credibly informed by ministers and others that there was not a drunkard in the place, nor a pauper in the town; that every person or family were in circumstances to provide comfortably for themselves, and no place where ardent spirits were sold.

"After this conference, returned to Lynn, Massachusetts; paid a visit among my old friends there. Then to Boston; then to Concord, New-Hampshire. Here I was called suddenly and unexpectedly, the next day after my arrival, to go and deliver a lecture to the students of the Biblical Institute at this place. After this visit at Concord, I returned by the way of Wooster and Norwich to New-York; thence home, where I arrived on the 25th.

"Great mercies have been my protection and comfort during these journeys and labours. O that I may be thankful and obedient!

"After resting a season at home I was called to visit Newark, New-Jersey, and attend the laying of the corner stone of a new Methodist Episcopal Church in that place. The service was of course out of doors; the weather rainy, the air damp; took cold, and was sick through the night, and was barely able to reach home the following day.

"After this, passed the time comfortably, at and about home, until the 28th of December."

This brings us down to the close of the active service of Bishop Hedding in the Church of God. The account of his last sickness and death—the interviews had with him, the remarkable sayings he uttered, and the trial and triumph of his faith—we have reserved for a distinct chapter.

Referring to the simple record of his travels, which extended through the period of fifty years' labour, he says: "I might have mentioned a great many difficulties I have met with in travelling from year to year,—being thrown off of horses, turned over in carriages, losing and laming horses on journeys, crowded in stages, sometimes riding all night in dark and miry roads, at the rate of two miles an hour, sometimes crowded in canal boats so full of people that in hot nights we were well-nigh suffocated; sometimes performing hazardous voyages in sloops, on the coast from New-York to Maine, before there were any steamboats. I have been in perils at sea, on steamboats, in dark and stormy nights; I have been in perils in the wilderness, in perils among the heathen, perils among false brethren—worst of all! but out of them all the Lord has delivered me.

"When I commenced preaching I verily believed God called me, and that I could not serve him acceptably in any other way. Without this belief I should not have undertaken to be a preacher, nor continued in the work after I commenced. I knew my own weakness, my want of learning, and of suitable qualifications for a minister of Christ.

"I had no expectation, and I may say no desire, of ever being a preacher capable of giving satisfaction in polished and enlightened congregations; but, as I believed God called me, I thought I might be able to speak so as to be understood and acceptable among the unpolished people of the wilderness, the new countries, and the poor circuits; and this was the height of my expectations and of my desire. I cared not where I went, nor to what field of labour I was assigned, only so that I might preach Christ, and be the means of saving some of the souls he had redeemed.

"I have gone through a life of toil, and in many respects of privation and suffering; I have been a great many times sick—severely so; and a great many times sick among strangers, but especially so with that dreadful sickness which has before been named, when I was broken down with the rheumatism in New-Hampshire, in the year 1803. I think I suffered more there in six weeks than I ever have in all my sufferings, put them all together, from my infancy to the present day; but God has mingled mercies with my sufferings all through, so that on the whole I have had a life of great comforts,—great comfort in the fellowship of Christ, great comfort in the friendship and fellowship of his ministers and people.

"I am now beyond three score and ten, my strength to labour in the vineyard is gone, I am daily looking forward to the hour when I must give an account of my stewardship; but through the merit of Christ I look into eternity with hope and comfort.

"Many people have asked me whether I think Methodism is in as good a state now as it was fifty years ago. The condition of the Methodist Church is now far different from what it was then; great improvements and enlargements have been made, great prosperity has attended the Church. In many respects the Church is now far better than it was then; in other respects, perhaps, not as good: but whether as to real Christianity it is now better or worse than it was then, I do not consider myself a competent judge. It would be difficult to make up an opinion on that point.

"There was a great amount of real religion among the preachers and people then, and there is also now; but this one thing I would say, both preachers and people bore heavier burdens fifty years ago than they do now. I would say still further, that fifty years ago the Methodist preachers and people were a holy people, they were so as a body; and they made great sacrifices and performed great labours for the cause of Christ."

During his latter days, Bishop Hedding took peculiar pleasure in calling up the reminiscences of the past; especially the incidents of an early itinerant life.

Speaking of the zeal of some early Methodist preachers, he remarked that he once visited a place where the Rev. Billy Hibbard and a young colleague had formerly held meeting in a private house. Once each of the young ministers kneeled to pray, and in their earnest pleadings they so far forgot themselves as to lift the chairs at which they were kneeling, and dash them violently down against the floor. This they continued to do till they had each made a complete wreck of their seats, and all with entire unconsciousness. The propriety of such vehement and absorbing zeal may be called in question; but it is certainly preferable to a precise and frigid uniformity, which cramps the energies of the soul and robs religion of its aggressive power. Those were times of great spiritual darkness and of fearful apathy on the subject of religion, and it required extraordinary means to break that apathy; and if those means sometimes came rather harshly across some of the nicer rules of propriety, they, nevertheless, were effective in bringing about great and good results.

On another occasion, speaking of class-meetings and the want of a more uniform and general attendance, he remarked, "There are two difficulties in the way. The first, and most general one, is this: Many are cold in religion, and they do not wish to go to class and tell a dull story. The second is: Some good people are disgusted by hearing the flaming testimonies which are sometimes made by persons whose lives are at wide variance from their professions—who talk one thing and practise another.

Honest, conscientious people see this discrepancy, and forsake the class-room to avoid the annoyance. "To illustrate this," said he, "I saw a case when travelling in the north part of New-England in my younger days. My circuit was large, and I preached mostly in private dwellings. In that region there were many Free-Will Baptists. Their doctrines differing but little from ours, they freely admitted me to their churches where they had them, and in other places to their habitations, to preach. It was their custom after preaching to exhort, or, as they called it, '*free their minds.*' After I had preached in one of their houses, (where I had a regular appointment, but no Methodist society,) one of the Baptist brethren arose in front of me to '*free his mind.*' He was warm, earnest, and vehement in his warning to the people. But during his exhortation my attention was arrested by the movements of a well-dressed, gentlemanly man, who arose at the back part of the room, and crowded over the tops of the seats until he pressed his way to a position in front of the speaker. His look was earnest and determined. He evidently intended to 'free *his* mind.' Soon as the first speaker had finished, this second one arose, and fixing a scorching look upon the man who had just taken his seat, he said, 'You preach very well, but I should like to have you *practise* what you preach. *I wish you would call and settle for the stove timber you* STOLE *from my woods.*' The exhorter, without pleading to the charge, arose in a storm of excitement, clenched his fist, elevated his arm, and vociferated, 'Depart from me, ye cursed, into everlasting fire prepared for the devil and his angels!' Here I closed the meeting. The neighbours said that the charge of theft against the exhorter was true. The family where this occurred afterward became Methodists, and a good society was raised up in that place.

"At another time, when I had finished a sermon among the Free-Will Baptists, several arose to confirm the truth of what had been said in the sermon. One brother, wishing to 'free his mind,' and pay the sermon a high compliment, said, 'You have heard the truth, the whole truth, and *more than the truth.*'"

At another time, not long before his death, speaking of Methodism, he said, "For more than fifty years I have been permitted to be a witness of the wonderful works of God in this land. I have witnessed the glorious effects of the Methodist doctrine, proclaiming a free salvation to all men on the easy condition the gospel prescribes, making the way to heaven plain to all who try to walk therein, opening to every soul of man a precious privilege of escape in being saved from sin and hell.

"I have seen also the wonderful effects of the Methodist itinerant system in carrying the gospel to the poor, to the wicked, to the people that dwelt in the wilderness, to many thousands who never would have sought for it, or asked for it, or heard it, had not the '*itinerant system*' brought it to their doors and urged it upon them. I have seen these, I say, sufficiently to make me love and cherish that system, and to pray and hope that it shall be kept pure and in efficient operation, until the whole world shall be converted to God. But I am obliged to lament that I see among some of our preachers, and among some of our laymen, signs of a departure from the purity of that system, bringing it under limitations and restraints, which, if permitted to prevail, will ultimately weaken or destroy it."

CHAPTER XX.

LAST HOURS OF BISHOP HEDDING.

Bishop Hedding viewed in a New Scene—First Attack of Acute Disease—Second Attack—Hopes—Their Disappointment—State of his Mind—Assailed by Satan—Record of God's Mercy—Notes taken of his Experience and Remarks—Gradual Decline—Conversations during the Last Months of his Life—Expression of his Feelings to Rev. Mr. Ferris—Last Public Exercise—Infirmities Increased—Draws up his Will—Unabated Interest in the Church—Prospect of Seeing and Knowing Friends in Heaven—Interest in Prayer—Views on leaving the Church on Earth—Last Sacrament—His Trust in the Midst of Distress—A Day of Suffering and of Triumph—Terrible bodily Condition—Wonderful Grace—Visited by Bishop Janes and Dr. Peck—The Closing Scene—Funeral Services—Epitaph upon his Monument.

WE have traced the history of this eminent servant of Christ through the long and eventful course of his active ministry. We come now to contemplate him in another and widely different sphere—one of disease, suffering, and death. We wish to know how he passed through his final conflict, and how he met his last, great enemy. We have seen the hero warring nobly on the great battle-field of the cross; we come now to inquire whether the faith and hope of that cross sustained him when called to put off his armour, and lie down to die.

The first attack of acute disease was experienced on the 28th day of December, 1850. The attack was as sudden as it was fearful. He had been taking his accustomed walk, though the day was severely cold, and was returning home, when he was suddenly seized with difficulty of breathing. The difficulty was so great that he seemed nearly suffocated, and his strength entirely exhausted. With difficulty he reached the parsonage of the First Methodist Church, then occupied by the Rev. L. M. Vincent, the pastor, and was barely able to say: "Carry me home—I am suffocating." He was immediately conveyed home, apparently in a dying state. Physicians were soon in attendance, but it was more than an hour before the severity of his suffering abated. About a week after this he had a second attack, of still greater violence than the first; and for more than two hours of intense and unremitted suffering it seemed as though nature was sinking in its last conflict. These attacks, from which he only partially recovered, were succeeded by others of less violence and shorter continuance. The complication of diseases under which he had laboured for many years, and also the growing infirmities of age, rendered his recovery hopeless. It was painfully evident that his system had received a shock from which it could not recover. Yet, through the skill and care of his medical adviser, he was made comfortable; and it was hoped that with the return of spring his health might be still further improved, and that he might be relieved, at least to some extent, from the great weakness and exhaustion that had succeeded his violent attacks. But these hopes were disappointed. Summer brought but little relief. Yet, as he seemed to revive somewhat in the early part of the winter, his friends began to hope that his life might be spared, and his health permit him once more to mingle, as the patriarch of the Church, in her councils at the ensuing General Conference; or at least, that he would be able to make his appearance in that body, and bestow upon it his final counsel and dying blessing. In the latter part of the succeeding winter, however, he suffered successive attacks, which completely blasted that hope, and made it apparent that "the time of his departure was at hand."

It will be well to pause in the current of our narrative, and notice the state of his mind in the midst of these sudden, unexpected, and terrible attacks. In the afternoon of the first attack, after the severity of his distress had subsided so that he could speak, he said to the Rev. Mr. Vincent: "I expected to die this afternoon. I fully believed the hour of my departure had come; but, O, how mercifully I was sustained! I had no fear of death or eternity. I felt that through the merits of Jesus, my Saviour, alone, it would be well with me; and knew that if my work was done, and God ordered my discharge, it was right, all right." After his second attack, he said: "In all this the enemy was not permitted to come nigh me." And subsequently, speaking of these attacks, and the development of what he believed would be a fatal disease, he said that God had so mercifully dealt with him, that for three months after his severe attack he had not suffered a single temptation from Satan, but had enjoyed wonderful grace and support. At the end of this period, Satan attacked him violently, and tempted him to disbelieve God's word. It was a terrible conflict. Objections more subtle than any he had read or heard from infidels were thrust sorely upon him. But he was enabled to answer them all; and came out of the conflict with a faith radiant with heaven's own glory, to be dimmed and obscured no more. "I *have conquered*," he exclaimed, "and believe I shall *overcome* at last, through the mercy of God and the merit of Jesus Christ my Saviour, my only hope."

On the 7th of May, 1851, he made the following record, by the assistance of an amanuensis: "I have now been confined by affliction more than four months. I have not been able to attend public worship, nor to go from my house more than about one hundred rods; and that distance but once. But I have realized the truth of that wonderful word, 'My grace is sufficient for thee.' When the storm first burst upon me, and the wind howled, the waves roared, the surges beat upon my head, and the deep yawned, nature said, A shattered, ruined wreck you are, the proud waters will soon come over you! But by faith I saw Jesus walking on the water, and heard him say, 'It is I, be not afraid;' and my soul replied, 'Behold God is my salvation, I will trust, and not be afraid.' About the middle of April, in a night when I could not sleep, being on my knees in prayer, I was led to see more clearly than I had ever seen before the goodness of God in afflicting his children, and I was enabled to 'sing of mercy and of judgment.'

> 'Good is Jehovah in the rain and sunshine,
> Nor less his goodness in the storm and thunder;
> Mercy and judgment both proceed from kindness,
> Infinite kindness.'

"Jehovah-jireh! O, what a name! O, how he provides, and at what a price!

> 'His dying crimson, like a robe,
>   Spreads o'er his body on the tree;
> Then I am dead to all the globe,
>   And all the globe is dead to me.'

"More than fifty years since, God led me to give up the world, in the common acceptation of that phrase; long ago I gave up earthly friends and earthly interests and hopes, to go and preach Christ's gospel; but now I am called to give up the Church on earth. To think of seeing the thousands of God's children, whom I have known and loved, no more on earth, grieves me; but my heavenly Father has been saying to my heart, ever since this trouble came upon me, 'Be still and know that I am God;' and I am quiet. A poor unworthy sinner I am, but Christ is my friend!

> 'In age and feebleness extreme,
> Who shall a helpless worm redeem?
> Jesus, my only hope thou art,
> Strength of my failing flesh and heart.'

I have long believed the promises, but I realize them now more than I ever did before. My Saviour has said, 'Him that cometh unto me I will in no wise cast out.' I know my will and my heart come to him; and I believe his promise, and feel safe.

'His word of grace is sure and strong,
As that which built the skies;
The voice which rolls the stars along,
Speaks all the promises.'

From the first attack I have felt no anxiety—no disturbance from within or from without, except when Satan made his fierce assault; all is calm, and joy, and peace. But how is it so? Nature could not have done this. Nearly sixty years ago, a little before I found Christ, I was placed in a condition of imminent danger; to human judgment it seemed certain that I should be dead in five minutes. I had no hope of escaping; and I expected to drop at once into hell. I had no more expectation of being out of hell five minutes, than I now have of going back to the time of that event, and of again becoming a youth. But O, the horrors! No one can imagine, unless he has seen and felt them.

"But in the danger of this sickness I felt that hell had no claim upon me; for Christ had redeemed me.

'When I survey the wondrous cross
On which the Prince of glory died,
My richest gain I count but loss,
And pour contempt on all my pride.'

God has wrought this change, no one else in the universe could have done it.

'Close by thy side still may I keep,
Howe'er life's various currents flow;
With steadfast eye mark every step,
And follow where my Lord doth go.'"

In the spring of 1851 the Rev. William H. Ferris and the writer were stationed in Poughkeepsie, and for nearly a year—till the close of Bishop Hedding's life—were in almost constant communion with him. We immediately commenced taking notes of many of his most remarkable and striking expressions. From these notes the subsequent account of his last hours is mainly drawn.

From the time of his first attack, his decline was gradual, sometimes relieved by favourable indications, and at other times accelerated by sudden and alarming steps. His intellectual powers remained vigorous: his memory, perception and judgment continued, with but few intermissions, clear and distinct to the last. In the midst of intense and protracted bodily suffering, he retained that calmness and serenity of spirit, and that supreme confidence of faith, so eminently characteristic of the mature Christian. His conversations during the last months and weeks of his life were heavenly and edifying in a high degree. In intercourse with his Christian brethren he often gave full vent to his feelings in the most graphic and touching expressions. At one time he broke out in the exclamation: "O what a wonder it is that such a poor, worthless, hell-deserving wretch as I am should ever be saved! What a mercy! what wondrous love! It is all of Christ. What could we do, or what could we hope for without him? How could we preach, how could we pray, how could we live, or how could we DIE, without the Saviour?" The record conveys but a feeble impression of the force with which those words were uttered. This could not be realized without the presence, the appearance, the heavenly countenance, the deep pathos, the quivering voice, and the holy energy of the venerable man now numbered with the dead.

About the same time, he said one morning to the Rev. Mr. Ferris: "I have been singing. In my earlier days I was quite a singer; and I have been singing one of our excellent hymns, (one that is all glory,) and while singing I received a wonderful blessing." The hymn is this:—

"He dies, the Friend of sinners dies."

He continued repeating the hymn till he came to the third verse, when, catching the inspiration of the mighty theme, he commenced singing with a feeble voice, rendered more indistinct by his deep emotion:—

"Break off your tears, ye saints, and tell
How high your great Deliv'rer reigns;
Sing how he spoil'd the hosts of hell,
And led the monster death in chains!"

Here his feelings overcame him, and he wept like a child, exulting in the certain prospect of a final and complete victory over the "monster," so terrible to the natural man. A few days after, he said to the same friend: "I do not depend so much upon past experience, nor upon present states of feeling, as upon a clear inward witness, like the shining light, that Jesus died for me; that he *loves me*, and *owns me* for his child. I am going down to the dust; but I expect to go to a better world. This supports me. Sometimes the state of my body presses down the mind so that I do not feel much joy; but there is a settled peace, and *an assurance* that the Saviour is mine."

During the autumn of 1851, and also during December of that year, he was able to attend Church quite regularly once a day. On the first Sabbath in November, he closed the morning service by prayer, or rather, *by praise.* With feeble steps he ascended from the altar into the pulpit; and at the close of the singing, he fell down upon his knees, and with laboured and broken utterance —his voice only the shattered remnant of what it had been—he poured out such warm and heartfelt expressions of praise to Christ, as indicated the depth of his own feelings, and produced a powerful effect upon the audience. The theme of the sermon had been—Christ precious to the believer. His heart seemed to glow with the subject. The entire audience were bathed in tears. He arose from his knees; an expression of holy joy was upon his countenance; the suppressed sigh was heaving almost every bosom, and tears were falling like drops of rain. The minister of half a century, who had so often and so usefully occupied the sacred desk, slowly and silently descended from the pulpit for the last time. As the echo of that prayer died away upon the ears of the people, the sanctuary labours of the sainted man of God ended for ever.

In the early part of the winter his infirmities increased upon him to such a degree that he could no longer visit the house of God. The dropsy, added to his old afflictions, and attended with a distressing cough, made it evident that his stay on earth was short. Of this no one was more sensible than himself, and he calmly occupied himself with setting his house in order. The writer was often with him and acted as his amanuensis, and also assisted him in drawing up his will, by which he made a final disposition of all his earthly goods, after making provision for his wife, to the cause of Christian benevolence. All these items of business were transacted with his accustomed clearness and precision. He was truly setting his house in order that he might die.

He talked freely and with deep feeling upon the great interests of the Church; showing that, though in daily expectation of leaving it, he suffered no abatement of interest in whatever concerned its weal. He also discussed the deep questions of Christian theology with his accustomed interest and perspecuity. At one time, referring to some discussions on the subject of Christian holiness, he said: "Some brethren seem to think that Mr. Wesley could not properly say of himself,—

'I the chief of sinners am,
But Jesus died for me.'

But I can truly and properly say it, for I feel it in my heart." At another time he said: "I have laboured fifty years in the cause of Christ, and have had, especially in my earlier ministry, many hard appointments; I have had many privations to endure, and have suffered a good deal, and am now so worn out with labours, sufferings, and age, that I shall soon go to my long home. But, after all, I can say:—

'This all my hope, and all my plea—
For me the Saviour died.'

And that is all the plea we need. O what a mercy it is that God has given his Son to redeem us, so that we, vile wretches, can get to heaven!"

While dictating a letter to an old friend, who had invited him to the hospitalities of his house, he paused in the midst of his letter, overcome with emotion, and while the tears were rolling down over his cheeks, said: "I am going to the dust; I shall probably never go out again till I am borne to my long home. I shall never see brother —— again on earth; but I feel certain I shall meet, yea, and KNOW him too, in heaven —both him and his dear wife. I have been entertained at their house; it has been a home to me; they have ministered to my wants. I shall see them on earth no more; but I SHALL SEE and KNOW them in heaven!" While watching with him one night, after he had somewhat recovered from a distressing turn, he beckoned the writer to him from the opposite side of the room, and said: "Brother Clark, I want you to pray for me every day—every night and every morning—so long as I shall need to have prayers offered for me." Upon my remarking that I had, and would still pray for him, and also that our brethren remembered him in the prayer-meeting, he replied, with a look of satisfaction, "I thank you. I have many praying friends, I know. It has often encouraged me to think so. It has helped me to preach and to bear my burdens when I was well, and now it helps me in the midst of my afflictions."

When asked how he felt about leaving the Church, for which he had toiled and laboured so long, he said: "When I was first taken sick, more than a year ago, the thought that I was cut off from labouring for the Church, and that I should see the dear brethren with whom I had become acquainted no more on earth, hung like a millstone upon me, until one night in the winter of 1851, as I was kneeling in my bedroom praying, about midnight, God so impressed upon my mind that the Church was not mine, did not belong to me, or depend upon me, that I have felt all that burden removed from that hour. I love the Church and the brethren still; but I leave them in the hands of God, and I can say, 'Thy will be done.'" Then fastening upon me an intense and expressive look, he said, with great emphasis: "*The Church is not mine—it is God's. God has taken care of the Church; God will take care of the Church; and he can do it as well without me as with me.*"

A few weeks before his departure several brethren, by special invitation, met to partake with him of the holy eucharist. There were present Revs. William Thacher, William Jewett, M. Richardson, William H. Ferris, and the writer, besides his own family circle. The bishop was seated at the head of the table, being unable to kneel on account of his limbs and body being so swollen with the dropsy. While the elements were being distributed, he was deeply affected; and when the service was concluded, he began to sing, with a tone of voice tremulous with age and emotion:—

"Praise God, from whom all blessings flow;
Praise him all creatures here below;
Praise him above, ye heavenly host;
Praise Father, Son, and Holy Ghost."

It was an affecting scene, that touched every heart, and drew tears from every eye. But we were still more affected with what followed. With his voice often choked and stifled with emotion, he said:—

"'Whither should a sinner go?
His wounds for me stand open wide;
Only Jesus will I know,
And Jesus crucified.'

Brethren, my work is now done on earth; I am about to go hence. My body is going to the dust; but I have a good hope that my soul will go to God in heaven. I am a poor, weak, wretched creature; have many imperfections and many sins; but I hope for, and expect to receive, salvation through our Lord Jesus Christ:—

'Other refuge have I none;
Hangs my helpless soul on thee.'

I had laboured fifty years and one month in the itinerancy before I was broken down. I have come short in many things; but I have laboured sincerely and earnestly. I have suffered many privations, and endured many trials; but, after all, if I had a hundred lives, I would be willing to spend them all in the same way—believing, as I do, that God called me to the work. Blessed be God! I have seen many a wanderer reclaimed and brought back to him; I have seen many a sinner awakened and led to Christ for salvation; and many, many men and women have I attended upon dying beds, who, with their last breath, shouted 'Glory to God! I am washed and made clean in the atoning blood of the Lamb.' The recollection of these things comforts me now. I look back upon them with more pleasure than crowns and kingdoms, or than all the riches and honours of the world could ever have given.

"Brethren, while you have life and strength, preach; preach Christ; call poor lost sinners to repentance. Bring them to the Saviour! He is a blessed Saviour! How could we preach, or pray, or labour; how could we come to God, or hope for heaven, were it not for him?

"My time of labour is now past, and I am going to

my rest. A few years since, my oldest sister died. She was converted to God at the same time I was, and had been a faithful Christian more than fifty years. Her last words were:—

'Forever here my rest shall be,
  Close to thy bleeding side;
This all my hope, and all my plea,—
  For me the Saviour died.'

This, too, is my dying testimony. I don't know how long God will spare me, nor how soon he will call me away. But, brethren, whether you are present or not, or whether I can speak or not, that is now, and I trust will be, my dying testimony."

Here the little remnant of his strength failed him, and his wife, overwhelmed with emotion, besought him to desist from an exertion for which his strength was so inadequate. We soon after retired. The above was a scene not to be forgotten. It seemed as though heaven itself was near. No forms of language and no powers of description can do it justice. We mourned that a father in Israel was so soon to depart from our midst; that the Church was so soon to be bereft of a faithful and time-honoured guide; and that the cause of Christ would so soon lose one of its noblest champions. But, on the other hand, our tears of sorrow were mingled with sacred joy; for we felt that for one so mature in Christian virtues to depart and be with Christ would be far better; we felt, indeed, that it was fitting that the old veteran, who had battled for more than half a century in the front ranks of Zion, one who had fought many a hard battle and now wore many a scar received in his Master's cause, should be released from toils and sufferings, and enter into his glorious rest. Never did we so fully feel before, that

> "The chamber where the good man meets his fate
> Is privileged beyond the common walks
> Of virtuous life—quite on the verge of heaven."

Humility was a striking trait in the character of Bishop Hedding; and his piety, ever at the furthest remove from ostentation, was strongly marked by that predominant trait in the closing scene. He felt that it was an awful thing to die; but, through grace, death was shorn of all its terrors. "All my dependence," says he, "is in the atonement. If I had to depend on the covenant of works, or on my own faithfulness, I should come short; but I depend alone on Christ, and I feel that he accepts me. I have no doubt of it. *I am as conscious of it as I can possibly be of anything.* I do not believe that he will cast me off. I expect it will be well with me when I go. While I remain here, I expect to suffer more and more. There is no more rest for my body in this life; but this is the will of my Father, and I know it is best. I pray that the cup may pass from me, if it is the will of God; but he knows best, and I submit all to him. I trust it will work for me a far more exceeding and eternal weight of glory."

A few days after, he said: "Christ is all my hope.

I can say nothing about my own faithfulness; I might have prayed better, preached better, and done more good. But I have been honest and sincere, and my good God accepts me. *I have no doubt of it;* and here I rest!"

The 26th of March was a day of great suffering; but with great calmness he said to the Rev. Mr. Ferris: "I am very sick; I suffer much. But why should a living man complain? I dare not pray or wish to die. I desire to lie in the hands of God. I know not what I should do, if I had not the assurance that God is with me. I need help from heaven every moment, and I have it; I *feel that I have it*, and this is my support. I sometimes wonder how such a poor wretch, taken out of the dust and mire of pollution and sin, can ever be made pure and fitted for a holy place—to dwell with God and Christ, and all the holy beings of heaven forever! *I could not believe it* if the glorious truths of the gospel were not so wonderfully supported by astonishing evidence!"

From this time his difficulty of breathing continued to increase, and his dropsy became more distressing. He could not lie down without experiencing a sense of suffocation that required immediate change; and thus, whole days and nights were passed in the most excruciating distress, and almost without sleep.

March the 30th, I made my usual call upon him, and found him in a most wretched bodily condition. The throbbing of the arteries in his neck, occasioned by the affection of his heart, had become intense.

He was so bloated that his clothes could no longer be put upon him; his skin was so distended and inflamed that every motion was attended with excruciating pain. In the hollow of his limbs, at the knee joint, the skin had burst, and water was freely running from the aperture. His difficulty of breathing was very great, from the collection of water upon his chest and lungs. And in addition to all this, he had been unable to get any sleep for several days; and for want of this, he could neither keep his eyes open, nor hold up his head. He presented the most pitiable spectacle of bodily suffering; it haunted me for days, and disturbed my slumbers in the night. When I approached him he raised his head, seized me by the hand, which he held for some time, and then feebly gasped:—"Brother Clark, I am in a most miserable condition; but, through the mercy of my blessed Redeemer, I trust I shall overcome at last."

The very next day, (March 31,) after referring to the sudden and terrible attack he suffered fifteen months before, he said to the Rev. Mr. Ferris: "With the stroke, God gave me wonderful grace; and it has been with me ever since. My prospect has been clear ever since. Not a day, not an hour, not a moment, have I had any doubt or tormenting fear of death. I have been at times so that it was doubtful whether I would live five minutes; but all was bright and glorious. I have not had joy all the time; but great support and comfort. But to-day

I have been *wonderfully blessed.* I was reflecting upon the wonder of God's mercy—how a just, and infinite, and holy God could take such vile creatures to dwell with him in so holy a place—so unworthy, so sinful, so polluted; and I thought of his great mercy to me—how much he had done for me; and I had such glorious views of the atonement by Christ—his sufferings and the glory that should follow—that my soul was filled in a wonderful manner. I have served God more than fifty years; I have generally had peace; but *I never saw such glory before—such light, such clearness, such beauty!* O, I want to tell it to all the world! O, had I a trumpet voice,

'Then would I tell to sinners round
What a DEAR SAVIOUR I have found.'"

Here his emotion overcame him, and choked his utterance for a moment. . . . "But I cannot. I never shall preach again—never shall go over the mountains and through the valleys, the woods, and the swamps, to tell of Jesus any more. But, O what glory I feel! it shines and burns all through me; it came upon me like the rushing of a mighty wind, as on the day of Pentecost." "Alas!" says the narrator, "the *pen* can never represent this scene—the broken accent, the laboured effort, the deep feeling, the holy fervour, the uplifted and radiant countenance, the eye that gleamed with unearthly lustre, the tears choking the utterance, and the whole frame shaking with emotion; these cannot be represented, but will never be forgotten. I retired, resolved to be a better Christian and a more faithful minister."

About this time the Rev. Dr. Peck, in company with Bishop Janes, visited Poughkeepsie for the purpose of holding a final earthly interview with Bishop Hedding. The account of the visit can be best given in the doctor's own words:—

"On Sabbath morning we entered his room, and were happy to find him much relieved by the discharge of a large quantity of water, which had forced an opening through the skin of his legs. He had rested tolerably well, and was able to converse for ten or fifteen minutes at a time. He was feeble in body, but strong in spirit. When animated, his eye resumed its natural expressiveness, and he seemed to have lost nothing of his great intellectual strength.

"Upon entering the room he reached out his hand, giving two fingers to Bishop Janes, and indicating that the other two were reserved for us. When he had in this manner taken our hands, he said, 'I am more glad to see you than I can possibly express. I am full of disease—old diseases and new ones are upon me, and I am prostrated. I am so feeble that I cannot talk much. I would be glad to ask you many questions about the conferences and the preachers, but my strength will not admit.' Pausing a little, he then resumed his remarks and said: 'One thing I wish to say now, lest I should not be able to say it at any future time, for I may drop away at any moment—and that is, that God has been wonderfully good to me; his goodness has been overwhelming—overwhelming.' Here his utterance was stifled by emotion, and he wept freely. When he recovered himself he resumed: 'To think that such a poor miserable sinner as I am should be so favoured, so filled with the goodness of God, so completely saved from the fear of death, so filled with the hope of a glorious immortality!' Here again his utterance failed, and the whole frame of the once strong man seemed on the point of falling to pieces with emotion. 'Don't weep so, husband,' said his excellent lady, 'you will become exhausted.' 'I am not weeping for sorrow,' added he, 'but for joy and thankfulness.'

"We now took leave of this truly sublime scene until evening, when we had the favour of another interview. He was now seated in an easy chair, and consecutively uttered a series of sentences which seemed almost as weighty as though they had come from the land of spirits. 'I suffer severely,' said he; 'and although I have no fear of death, I have some dread of pain. The flesh repines; the flesh of our Saviour repined. He said, "O, my Father, if it be possible, let this cup pass from me; nevertheless, not my will, but thine be done." Could I live, I should desire to do so, only that I might preach Christ and him crucified. O, to preach Christ! I would rather preach Christ anywhere—on the hardest circuit—than to have all the wealth and the honours of the kingdoms of this world.

> "O for a trumpet voice,
> On all the world to call,
> And bid their hearts rejoice
> In Him who died for all."'

"Here he paused, and for some time gave vent to his feelings in tears. Recovering the power of utterance, he proceeded: 'When I think of the dear preachers with whom I have become acquainted all over the length and breadth of the land, it seems hard not to be able to visit them again. But the will of the Lord be done; my will is lost in his will. I have no will of my own.' After a short pause, he said: 'Fifty-two years ago, last December, I gave up my all to God, and I have never taken back the gift. I have been a most fallible creature, and have committed many involuntary offences, but have never wilfully departed from God. I have always needed the atonement of Christ, and have trusted in that alone for the forgiveness of all my short-comings. I feel that I can sing with Mr. Wesley—

> "I the chief of sinners am,
> But Jesus died for me."

I used to wonder how it could be that Christ could have mercy upon such a poor miserable sinner as I am, and save me. There was a kind of mist over the subject; but within a few days all this has been cleared away. I now see such goodness, such glory, such power—such *power*'—repeating the word with great emphasis—'in the Redeemer, that there is now no difficulty in it!' We remarked, 'Your spiritual vision is now clear.' 'Yes,' responded he, 'it is all plain now.' During the conversation he remarked: 'Since this dreadful disease struck me, more than a year ago, I have not had one really dark hour, or one pang of guilt.'

"We retired from the room with the strongest feelings of admiration of the humility, the deep and unaffected piety, and the gigantic intellectual strength of our venerable senior bishop. We have known and admired his real greatness from the period of our first acquaintance with him. But if he was great in the field of action, he is still greater in the hour of suffering, and in the prospect of death.

"We must pause—our heart is full. God be praised for this fresh illustration of the majesty and power of true religion."

The suffering days of the revered man of God were now drawing to a close. His sufferings gradually abated; his breathing became less difficult, and he was able to lie down and rest with some degree of comfort. His quietude, however, was not that from which the system rallies to victory, and triumphs over disease; but that in which its exhausted powers, fully spent in the conflict, sink to rally no more. He was not merely calm, but cheerful; and often exhibited flashes of that genial sprightliness, humour and wit, so characteristic of him in earlier days. Yet a heavenly atmosphere reigned around him. His work was done; he was tarrying for a moment on the bank of Jordan, waiting permission from his Master to pass over.

That permission was not long delayed. About three o'clock on the morning of the 9th of April a change took place, betokening the near approach of death. Early in the morning his sufferings were great; his extremities were cold, and his death-agony was upon him; but his intellectual powers—consciousness, perception, memory, reason—were unaffected. Several Christian friends witnessed his dying struggles and the glorious triumph of his abiding faith. The Rev. M. Richardson came in, and inquired whether his prospect was clear; he replied with great emphasis: "O, yes, *yes*, YES! I have been wonderfully sustained of late, beyond the usual degree." After a pause he continued:—

> "'My suff'ring time will soon be o'er;
> Then I shall sigh and weep no more;
> My ransom'd soul shall soar away,
> To sing thy praise in endless day.'

I trust in Christ, and he does not disappoint me. I feel him, I enjoy him, and I look forward to an inheritance in his kingdom."

He looked at his hands, and calmly marked the progress death was making. Feeling that death was fast approaching, he made repeated efforts to straighten himself and to adjust his limbs in the bed. Then, after remaining quiet a few moments, summoning all his strength and elevating his voice, he said: "I trust in God and feel safe!"

The Rev. Mr. Ferris said to him,—"Bishop, you are almost over Jordan." He looked calmly up, and answered, "Yes;" then raising both hands, he said, scarcely above a whisper, "Glory, glory! Glory to God! Glory to God! Glory to God! Glory!" Awhile after, he was asked if death had any terrors; he replied: "No, none whatever; my peace is made with God. I do not expect to live till sunset; but I have no choice; I leave it all with God." Then, placing his hand upon his breast, he said: "I am happy—filled."

After shifting his position several times without finding relief from his sufferings, he broke out:—

"'When pain o'er my weak flesh prevails,
With lamb-like patience arm my breast;
When grief my wounded soul assails,
In lowly meekness may I rest.'"

Subsequently, he said: "My God is my best friend, and I trust in him with all my heart. I have trusted in him for more than fifty years." Then, after pausing for breath, he added: "'Because I live, ye shall live also.' What a promise!" Soon after this his powers of speech failed; his breathing grew tremulous and short; life ebbed gradually away, and at last its weary wheels stood still.

Thus passed away one of the purest and noblest spirits of our earth. He died as might have been augured from his character and life; he died as the Christian only can die. Up to the last moment of earthly communion, he was calm and serene. Eternity was breaking upon his view, but he knew in whom he had believed. To see the Christian, who, with the intellect of a philosopher and the wisdom of a sage, had scanned the evidences and the doctrines of the gospel to their very depths; to see such a one maturing for the skies, going forth to the last conflict with no misgivings of spirit—calmly, firmly, constantly trusting in the atonement of his Saviour; to mark his trembling humility, the low estimate he placed upon his services in the Church of Christ, and upon his Christian piety—these were privileges of no ordinary moment, and afforded lessons of indescribable value. We have often visited the dying couch of the saint of God, and there witnessed the triumph of the Christian faith; but never before did sickness and feebleness seem to enshrine such loveliness, or death such beauty. The full significance of that couplet of Coleridge seemed to be realized:—

> "Is that his death-bed, where the Christian lies?
> No! 't is not his; 't is death itself there dies!"

The funeral services took place on the 14th, in the Washington-street Methodist Episcopal Church. Bishops Waugh and Morris were present, and also a large number of preachers—amounting to nearly a hundred. An appropriate and affecting discourse was preached by Bishop Waugh. The whole scene was one of deep and solemn interest. The speaker was often overcome with deep, unutterable emotion; and we doubt whether there was a heart in that vast assembly that did not beat in sympathy with him. Indeed, the congregation often seemed completely overwhelmed with emotion; and tears were poured out like water. We were constantly reminded of the burial of the first Christian martyr —"And devout men carried Stephen to his burial, and made great lamentation over him."

The body was at first deposited in the family vault of Henry Storms, Esq., but has since been removed to the beautiful cemetery on the eastern banks of the Hudson, just below the city of Poughkeepsie, where a noble monument has been erected to his memory. At the request of the executors—the Rev. L. M. Vincent and the Rev. William Jewett—the epitaph which appears on the following page was prepared by the writer, and has been inscribed upon the monument. A view of this monument, engraved upon steel, together with the inscriptions, appeared in the November number of the Ladies' Repository for 1854. Here all that was mortal of our venerated bishop now slumbers, waiting the resurrection of the just.

HEDDING'S MONUMENT.

On the side fronting to the west and toward the river, is the simple inscription within a circular wreath:—

ELIJAH HEDDING, D. D.
Born June 7, 1780.
Died April 9, 1852.

On the side of the monument fronting to the east is the following:—

This Monument
has been erected as a memorial of one whose name is
honoured in the Church of Christ.
He was for fifty-one years an Itinerant Minister, and for twenty-
eight a Bishop, in the Methodist Episcopal Church.
In his earlier ministry he performed an astonishing amount
of labour, and endured many hardships.
He was a man of unaffected simplicity and dignity of manners,
of deep and consistent piety, of sound and discriminating
judgment; a well-read Theologian, an able Divine;
a pattern of Christian propriety and integrity,
and a model Bishop.
As an expounder of Ecclesiastical Law and Discipline, he has had
no superiors; and his judicial decisions are regarded
with profound veneration in the Church.
His last sickness was protracted and painful, but was
endured with a constant resignation.
His last hours were peaceful and triumphant; future generations
will rise up to bless his memory.

CHAPTER XXI.

ESTIMATE OF THE CHARACTER AND SERVICES OF BISHOP HEDDING.

Concluding our Work — Bodily Appearance of Bishop Hedding — Habits and Manner of Life — Social Qualities — Care of the Feelings and Reputation of Others — A Keen Observer of Human Character — Cast of his Intellect — His Literary and Scientific Attainments — Character as a Divine — Character as a Preacher — Character as a Presiding Officer and an Expounder of Ecclesiastical Law — Tone and Character of his Piety — General Excellence and Harmony of Character — Results witnessed in his Life and Labours — His Memory.

Our labour thus far has been one of absorbing interest: our feelings have become so deeply interested in it, and the pleasure attendant upon it has been so unalloyed, that we almost instinctively shrink back when we find ourselves so near its conclusion. Yet have we only one more duty to complete, and then our delineation of the life of Bishop Hedding must be left to the scrutiny and judgment of the Church and the world. That duty is to attempt, in our concluding chapter, a sketch of his personal appearance, and a brief estimate of his character and services.

1. In Bishop Hedding there was a noble development of the physical man. When in his prime he measured six feet in height, and his frame was of fine proportionate development. In later years he inclined to corpulency, and probably from the time he was a young man he weighed considerably over two

hundred pounds; his usual weight, in later years, being about two hundred and twenty-five pounds. His features were too coarse to be beautiful, but there was a fine manly expression, a noble, commanding mien, that would instantly excite admiration and respect. His head was one of those massive Websterian conformations, that are ever reminding one of the antique models we have seen. His complexion was naturally light, but had been rendered swarthy by exposure and disease; and in his temperament the sanguine and nervous predominated. His eyebrows were heavy; and his eyes, which were of light blue, bordering upon gray, were neither very large nor very prominent. The expression of his countenance would indicate him to be a man of great evenness of temper, of calm and clear deliberation, not easily ruffled or thrown from his equipoise; of keen perception, and of solid good sense. You might not have caught the fancy that he was an amateur of the fine arts, or that he would be easily fascinated with the beautiful imaginings of the poets, or captivated with the flowers of rhetoric; but you would have been impressed with the conviction that he would be a somewhat severe, though a very reliable critic in them all. You would, also, unhesitatingly have assigned to him a prominent position in any of the ordinary avocations of life. As an agriculturist, you would expect that his operations would be upon a more philosophical basis than those of his neighbours; that there would be a wiser expenditure of labour, and that he would realize more ample returns. Thus, whatever he undertook, you would expect to see him prosecuting, slowly, it might be, but always surely, to its legitimate results. His countenance usually wore a quiet, benignant expression; and it was only when it was irradiated by the workings of the giant mind within, as that mind was roused up to grapple with some subject worthy of its powers, that its power of expression was fully realized. His motions were naturally deliberate, and rather slow—but never so slow as to indicate lethargy; for though his frame was massive, it was formed for activity and endurance.

2. Bishop Hedding's habits of life were exceedingly plain and simple. Everything about him—his dress, his travelling equipage, his house, his furniture, his garden—exhibited a pattern of neatness and studied propriety. If anything about his person attracted your attention at all, it would be because of its fitness or utility; the thought of display or show seemed never to have once entered his mind. His manners—exceedingly courteous—partook of the same simplicity. They were frank, cordial, open—never constrained. It was, however, a simplicity that was never wanting in dignity,—a simplicity that never "let him down" when in the presence of the noble, nor gave license to undue familiarity when among those of a different character. It was natural, and so well established in all his thoughts and habits, so completely harmonious with all his feelings, that he could never be surprised out of it. It had no kinship

to that boorishness which some deem "primitive simplicity;" for its grace commanded respect even in the most refined circles. Nor had it any kinship to that want of character which divests a man of authority, and which is so pervious to the sly, but designing shafts of wit and ridicule; for though never laid aside, it never divested him of the highest dignity while presiding over conferences and popular assemblies; nor did any one—unless his perceptions were exceedingly obtuse—ever dream that there was to be found in it anything with which it would be safe to trifle.

3. The social qualities of Bishop Hedding were of a high order. Few men enjoyed society more than he did. His conversational powers were superior. He had read much, and his observation and experience had been extensive and varied. From the rich storehouse that had been thus filled, he could draw forth incident and anecdote, fact and philosophy, criticism and even poetry, in such a manner that it would at once interest and benefit the intelligent listener. He often plied his brethren with whom he was on familiar terms with knotty questions in philology, theology, &c., and thus not only exercised their powers at the moment, but gave them something to think of afterward. Indeed, it was not unfrequently the case, that in this way solid and useful information was imparted. This habit of questioning was first formed when he was labouring in New-Hampshire in the early part

of his ministry, and was then employed as a means of solving the obstacles he encountered in the prosecution of his studies. It proved then of incalculable advantage to him, and he never wholly relinquished it. He told a story usually with fine effect in social intercourse, and relished a joke as highly, and could laugh as heartily, as most men; but never indulged in or gave license to that which was low or debasing in its character. Connected with these other qualities, there was a genial wit and humour about him, and an open-heartedness of sympathy, that made him a most companionable man. He had a keen perception of the ludicrous, and would often, on fitting occasions, give utterance to most amusing fancies. This genial and innocent play of the imagination gleamed out even amid the triumphs of his faith in his last sickness, and continued almost to the last day of his life. In illustration of this, we give the following anecdote, furnished by the Rev. W. H. Ferris:—"About ten days before his death I called to see him. He was sitting in his rotary-chair—a great sufferer, and unable to lie down. Weary with watchfulness and worn out with pain he would occasionally fall asleep, and as he did so, his head and the weight of his body would fall a little on one side, when the chair would swing round and wake him up. This occurred several times. At last he aroused, and looking up with a smile, he said, 'Brother, can't you fix this chair so that it won't turn round?' I got a cord and lashed it fast. He responded, 'Thank you, that is it;' and in a moment his head sank down, and he was fast asleep. I quietly withdrew. About five days after, and about the same number before his triumphant death, while in his room, I observed that his efforts to sleep were defeated by the same rotary motion of his favourite and familiar chair, and said to him, 'Bishop, allow me to fasten your chair so that it will not move. He gave his head that peculiar toss so often observed when anything quaint or amusing struck him, and a smile lit up his coun tenance as he hastily replied, 'No, no, brother; you fixed it the other day, and I thought I should like it, but I had to have it unfastened again. The fact is, *I never could endure to ride a hobbled horse.*' In two minutes that manly head sunk in sleep again, and the *unhobbled* horse turned, perhaps for the hundredth time, and awoke him."

These social qualities made him the genial companion of children. Though not blessed with any of his own, yet was he unusually fond of them; and every little boy and girl in his neighbourhood knew and loved "the bishop," as they called him. Only let one of a group of school children exclaim, "There comes the bishop!" and it was a signal that wreathed sunny faces in smiles, and called forth rival efforts to be foremost in the friendly salutation that was sure to follow. The writer will not soon forget the scene that greeted his eyes when, the morning after the bishop's death, he took his little children around to have them look upon that countenance, then calm in death, but which had so often beamed upon them in life, in order that they might learn at once the lessons of our mortality and of our holy faith. Not less than a dozen children were hanging around the gate in front of the house, and earnestly besought the privilege of once more seeing "the bishop." Their wish was gratified, and they gazed upon his lifeless form with an expression of sorrow which told that they felt they had lost a friend. Among the sincere mourners that lamented the death of this godly man were very many little children.

Bishop Hedding was also firm and abiding in his friendships. No one who had honourably gained his friendship, and had done nothing to forfeit it, ever had reason to question the continuance of his sentiments of brotherly confidence and affection. Friendship was with him too sacred a thing to be employed in any commerce for selfish ends, either in its origin or continuance.

He was also exceedingly courteous, careful to make proper recognition of a friend, careful to make proper acknowledgment of the courtesies shown him, careful to treat no one with neglect, while at the same time his courtesy was too sincere and unaffected to permit him to burden any one with officious attentions. These elements of the true gentleman shone conspicuously in his social character.

4. While Bishop Hedding, in social intercourse,

was exceedingly careful of the feelings of those present, he was equally careful of the reputation of those who were absent. Of the reputation of Christian ministers he was particularly careful. In a letter to the author, Dr. Paddock, referring to this point, says of him, "If others indulged in injurious reflections, the bishop would be sure to throw in some kind word with a view to shield the interested party. He, doubtless, sometimes spoke approvingly of a pulpit performance, rather to forestall criticism than to hold it up as a model. Indeed, I do not remember to have heard him speak disparagingly of a brother's public performance; and, to avoid doing it, he sometimes displayed the most amusing dexterity.

"At one of our conferences it was announced, at the close of a day's session, that a venerable and honoured brother would preach in the evening. Fatigued as the bishop was, he deemed it his duty, in view of the age and position of the brother, to attend the service. The discourse was hortatory and impassioned in a very high degree, but was far enough from being a *sermon*, as that word is ordinarily used. Of this fact no one could be more sensible than the bishop; but he was evidently determined that no one should hear him speak of it disparagingly. Stepping into his lodgings, which were near the church, he was followed by some half a dozen or more of the preachers; some of them quartered at the same house, and others coming in, as the bishop evidently apprehended, to hear what he would say about the sermon. He waited for no queries, not even indeed to be seated, but standing out in the midst of the floor, he lifted his right arm with his hand slightly clenched, and looking round upon the company, said, 'Now, brethren, was not that *real!*' Of course no one ventured to ask an explanation, while each was left to conjecture for himself what the bishop might mean by the unassociated adjective."

5. He was also a keen observer of human character. He read men as easily as most men read books. He was rarely imposed upon by the designing; he was rarely deceived as to the true character of a man. Not only was this penetration striking on the conference floor, and in relation to ministers with whom he had more constant intercourse, but in relation to any one of the multitude encountered in public places, or on the great thoroughfares of travel. "In this respect," says Dr. Paddock, in the letter just referred to, "I have seldom, perhaps never, known his superior. After becoming somewhat intimately acquainted with him, as I did at an early period of my public life, it really seemed to me that he was 'a discerner of spirits.' Whenever he turned his eye upon me, however mild and benignant his aspect, I could hardly resist the impression that he knew all that was passing in my heart. He was almost constantly scanning the character and measuring the intellectual height and depth of those about him.

"A striking instance, illustrative of this, now occurs to me. Some twenty years since, the Oneida Conference held its annual session at Owego. The bishop spent the previous Sabbath at Utica, where the writer was then stationed. A canal packet-boat was then our medium of conveyance from Utica to the seat of the conference. Among the crowd of passengers on the boat was a venerable old gentleman, apparently about seventy, attired in the costume of the former generation—single-breasted coat, ruffle in his bosom, cue hanging down between his shoulders, &c., &c., and along with him was a young gentleman and lady, seemingly about twenty-eight or thirty years of age. The latter were richly and neatly clad, but as far from mere display as can well be imagined. The whole bearing of the trio was at once so calm and so dignified, so easy and so graceful, that it was impossible to avoid noticing them a good deal. It was quite evident they belonged to the better class, wherever their home might be. Being seated near the bishop, he tapped me on the knee, and beckoning my ear to himself, smiled and said, 'Do you want to know who those persons are?' I replied, 'Yes; are you acquainted with them?' 'No,' said he; 'I never saw them before, and yet I *guess* I can tell you who they are.' 'Do, then,' said I. 'Well,' responded the bishop, 'the old man is a Connecticut judge; the lady is his youngest daughter, and the young gentleman is his son-in-law, and a lawyer.' Of course I was a little curious to ascertain how far the bishop was correct. The young gentleman had previously made some advances in the way of sociality, and I soon found an opportunity to draw him out, even without the necessity of resorting to any inquiries that could be offensive to a Yankee, and found that the bishop's almost instinctive sagacity had not misled him, but that his conjecture was right."

6. In this connexion it is proper we should make some note upon the general character of his intellect. We would not claim for him the highest order of the philosophical intellect, but in the philosophical element his mind was by no means deficient. The logical powers of his mind were, unquestionably, of the highest order. His abstractive and analytic power was very great. It was most interesting to see him grapple with a complicated and knotty proposition; first, with what cool, clear deliberation he would divest the terms of those ambiguities and obscurities that infest language, so that the point or points in the questions would stand out with unmistakable distinctness. Then, through the verbal proposition, how would he penetrate to the very heart and substance of the thing itself! With him reasoning was not a mere display of technical expertness—not a mere exercise of skill in logical terms and distinctions—but a sober and earnest inquiry after truth. Old Socrates himself could hardly hold a thought with a firmer grasp, or turn and examine it with greater deliberation or

with more unblenching scrutiny. He often struck into a subject where, to others, it seemed least of all pervious, and surprised you by the exposure of hidden fallacies where, to less penetrating intellects, all would seem to be legitimate and sound. He both thought and reasoned. He not only went behind the logical form, but he also mastered the logical form. His dialectics were of the acutest kind. He could prick out the gas that inflated a sophism with the same ease and dexterity with which he often pricked out the conceit of a self-sufficient ignoramus.

In all this, however, his mind was of too practical a character for him to have much affinity with that transcendentalism, Germanism—or whatever else you choose to call it—which, by many at the present day, is considered an inseparable adjunct and sign of a great mind. He had no affinity, no patience with it. The robustness of his intellectual structure was brought out and established, not amid scholastic influences, but in the stern warfare of opinion in practical life. Hence it partook of that character. Thought, with him, was not day-dreaming, but an earnest grasping after truth: reasoning not a mere intellectual gladiatorship, but an earnest effort to discover the practical ends of truth, and the means of obtaining those ends.

7. Of his literary and scientific attainments we may speak with great respect and admiration; and the more so from the early embarrassments under which he la-

boured, and the comparatively few helps he had during that portion of life when intellectual acquisitions are usually made. We have already noticed that he never attempted the study of the ancient languages; but he did what many who are called classical scholars have failed to do,—he acquired a thorough mastery of the English language. It is rarely the case that a scholar of any grade could be found who had so critical a knowledge of its intricacies, and so genuine an appreciation of its beauties.

He was a great reader—not in the sense of running over a great deal of surface, but of reading much in choice books, and of continuing to read, and to read well. Of those books which he found rich in matter, he was not merely a reader, but a *student;* he mastered their contents, analyzed and thoroughly digested their principles. His discrimination was nice, and his memory tenacious and exact.

His acquirements in natural science and philosophy in general were quite respectable for a general reader; but in rhetoric, logic, mental and moral philosophy, and the elements of taste and criticism, his attainments were very great, and his views generally profound and critical as well as correct.

He was regarded worthy of literary honours. In 1829, the Trustees and Faculty of Augusta College unanimously conferred upon him the honorary degree of *Doctor of Divinity.* In 1837 the same degree was conferred upon him by the Corporation of Union College; and in 1840 he was again doctorated by the

University of Vermont. In 1843 he was elected a member of the Board of Trustees of Union College. He was also, for several years prior to his death, President of the Methodist Biblical Institute at Concord, New-Hampshire.

8. As a sound, able, and critical divine, our Church or our country has produced but few superiors. He commenced his career as a student in theology, with the determination to thoroughly overcome every difficulty, to thoroughly trace out every obscure or doubtful point, and to store up in his memory every leading principle and every important fact. By these means, though his progress at first was slow, he laid the foundation of his profound, extensive, and ready theological knowledge. His views were comprehensive, logical, and well matured. Not only had they been elaborated with great care, but the analysis was very distinct; and the successive steps were not only clearly defined in the original analysis, but distinct even in the minutiæ of their detail. It was difficult to surprise him by the introduction of any topic in the whole range of theology or of ecclesiastical polity, on which he had not read carefully and thought profoundly. One who had considered himself carefully posted in these matters, would often be surprised with new and unexpected views, which the bishop would suddenly bring up, showing how profoundly he had studied those subjects, and how retentive and ready was his memory.

9. His discourses were an example of neatness,

order, perspicuity, and completeness. There was no effort at any unnecessary verbal criticism, but when called for by the subject, it was not wanting. There was no effort at logical skill or acuteness; but when clear and delicate discrimination was required, no man could execute it with greater fidelity and success. He would not be regarded as a *popular* preacher. The ability and skill to charm the multitude with the flowers of fancy, with the figures of rhetoric, with beautiful quotations, with flippant or dramatic speech, were evidently neither coveted nor cultivated by him. He was a plain preacher of the gospel of Christ. Of figurative illustrations and anecdotes he was sparing,—perhaps too much so, in view of their effect upon popular audiences; but his discourses abounded in those illustrations which are best of all—apposite quotations from the Sacred Word. His delivery was slow and his action deliberate. He never stormed or ranted in the pulpit or in exhortation; but spoke with the dignity, earnestness, and feeling of one who was called to deliver a message of life or of death from the August and the Eternal to frail, sinful, dying men. He excelled as an exegetical preacher; he could draw out the meaning of an intricate text or paragraph in the Bible, and make its import perfectly transparent in the view of his hearers. His ministry was such as would feast the soul and the intellect of the intelligent and pious; and when they had received the good things handed out to them from the pulpit, the confidence would be begotten in their minds that the rich banquet that had been spread before them was only a small draught from an overflowing storehouse. We should add that he went not into the pulpit without the most careful, thorough, and prayerful preparation. His motto was, "Beaten oil for the sanctuary." And to his careful preparation for the pulpit—both in his earlier and later years—more than to any fitful or accidental impulse, is the success of his pulpit efforts owing. In this, as well as in other traits of character, he may be commended as an example worthy to be imitated by his sons in the ministry.

10. Few have ever excelled him as a presiding officer. In the exercise of the episcopal functions, he developed those rare qualifications that have distinguished him as a presiding officer, and especially as an expounder of ecclesiastical law. He was rarely, if ever, thrown from his balance, whatever sudden excitement, tumult or opposition might arise in a conference; nor could he be perplexed by the most complex questions of law or of order, however suddenly they might be propounded. He was shrewd, quick, intrepid; and, surely, the man who thought by any strategy or dexterity to outmanage him, counted without his host. If he had license for the moment, it was only that the galvanic battery, which would soon bring him to his senses, might be more heavily charged.

When he entered the episcopal office, our ecclesiastical jurisprudence was in its inchoate condition.

No one has done more to develop and mature it than Bishop Hedding. The soundness of his views upon the doctrines and discipline of the Church was so fully and so universally conceded, that in the end he became almost an oracle in these respects; and his opinions are regarded with profound veneration.

Playful as Bishop Hedding often was in his private and social intercourse, in public he was ever remarkable for his gravity. His complete control of himself—which, by the way, did not seem in the least otherwise than natural—was one of the secret causes of that great control he had over others. Dr. Paddock, in the letter before noticed, says, "Sallies of wit that sometimes made sad havoc with the dignity of the conference over which he was presiding, would move him little more than if he were a statue. A clergyman of another denomination was once sitting near me at the session of the Oneida Conference, when these sallies were interchanged with great effect, materially disturbing the risibilities of more than one reverend brother, notwithstanding all his efforts at resistance. But Bishop Hedding was not of the number. A pillar of granite could scarcely have been more immovable. My companion turned to me, and said, 'I wonder whether your bishop ever smiles? I have watched him closely, and cannot see even a muscle of his face move.'

"In this regard I never saw the bishop thrown

from his balance, save only in a single instance. At a certain conference a brother was recommended for admission on trial. But his reception was strenuously opposed by an excellent and influential member of the body, chiefly on the ground of alleged inadequate mental training. This, however, was denied by those who claimed to be much better acquainted with the candidate than the brother who opposed his admission. But the latter was by no means willing to yield the point; and in his rejoinder gave instances of false syntax in a discourse which the candidate had delivered in his presence. In the midst of his remarks, a son of the Emerald Isle, and a member of the conference, whose ready wit was a striking mental characteristic, hastily sprung from his seat, and advancing a step toward the speaker, said, with an air and earnestness which it would be difficult to describe,—'*Broother! broother!* don't you think he was *embarrassed* because you were there?' The stroke—coming as it did suddenly and unexpectedly—was irresistible. The conference was convulsed. Even the bishop could not stand before it; giving himself up to his emotions, his whole frame shook as if receiving successive shocks from a galvanic battery."

11. Bishop Hedding was a man of deep and unaffected piety. His piety was not devoid of feeling, but it rested rather upon the basis of religious principle than of religious emotion; it was at the furthest remove from asceticism, or that repulsive

austerity which so often makes religion itself seem unamiable. In him trifling and levity found no place; but cheerfulness—the genial sunshine of the heart—diffused its loveliness all around him. There was no self-reliance, no confident nor high professions; but there was what was far better—piety, silent but incessant, consistent, deep, all-pervading; working out practical results, producing genuine fruits, forming the character, regulating the life. No one can doubt his deep experience of the things of God and of the sanctifying of the blood of Jesus. But of this he studiously avoided any public profession; and even when importuned during his last sickness, by one zealously devoted to the promotion of the doctrine in its special aspects, to make a profession of entire sanctification, he kindly but firmly declined. He seemed much more inclined to make that other confession:—

> "I the chief of sinners am,
> But Jesus died for me."

Yet in the trying hour he did not lack the confidence of faith, nor the presence of the divine Comforter; and in heaven, we confidently believe, the divine plaudit—"Well done, good and faithful servant"—awaited him. This unwillingness to make any profession or acknowledgment of high attainments in religion, may have resulted as much from the extreme modesty of his nature, the poor estimate he always formed of himself and of his performances, and his painful consciousness of his errors and imperfections, as from his profound sense of the high responsibility attached to such professions. He may, too, have thought that the profession that he was a sinner seeking salvation through the blood of Jesus, was more fitting to his condition, and more congenial to his feelings, than any other. He evidently sought to encourage experience and practice rather than profession.

13. We cannot further particularize. The great excellence of Bishop Hedding's character consisted in the harmonious development of all its parts, and not in an undue development of some particular feature. Many of his contemporaries surpassed him in particular acquirements, or in specific talents. Some were more learned as scholars; some were more eloquent in public discourse; and some were more attractive in personal form and address. But in Bishop Hedding there was a combination of noble qualities, which gave him completeness of character.

So of his services in the Church. They consist not of sudden and striking acts of heroic daring; but of a long life of patient labour in the highest sphere of usefulness. The striking characteristic of him was not that he was a fast worker—a brilliant performer; but that he was a judicious, faithful, earnest labourer in the cause of God and the Church. He was faithful and patient in small as well as in great matters. No duty was so insignificant as not to receive earnest and faithful attention. The greatness of his service to the Church consisted in the devotion of half a century, in this manner, to the promotion of her interests and of the Redeemer's glory.

Few men have left behind them a more spotless reputation, or have been more widely or more sincerely mourned than Bishop Hedding. The journals of the day—both secular and religious—made mention of his death, and bore honourable testimony to his virtue, piety, and usefulness. Funeral discourses, almost without number, were preached, and in every part of the country. The preachers' meetings in various cities, the annual conferences, and the General Conference, that occurred soon after his death, passed resolutions expressive of their high estimate of his talents, services, and character.

14. The life and labours of Bishop Hedding extended through an important epoch in the history of Methodism in this country. When he first entered the ministry, the work, then extending over the whole United States and Canada, comprised but eight annual conferences, three hundred and seven preachers, and seventy-two thousand eight hundred and seventy-four members. Now we have on the same territory (1853):—

	Conferences.	Tr. pr's.	Lo. pr's.	Members.
In the M. E. Church,........................	31	4,450	5,700	721,804
In the M. E. Church, South,............	20	1,700	3,955	514,601
In Canada, (including N. B. & N. S.)	3	116	198	19,013
Making a grand total of................	54	6,266	9,853	1,255,418

A man who had participated in labours and witnessed results like these, might well feel that he had not lived in vain.

But this was not all. Within the period of his labours the character and genius of Methodism have been largely developed; the capabilities of our general Church organization have been closely tested; our vast educational systems operating upon the public mind through the press, the Sunday school, the seminary, and the college—have all received character and direction, if not their very existence. The Church has been increasing in resources and intelligence, and a higher tone of educational influence has been brought to bear upon the ministry. In all this substantial progress he had a deep sympathy, and contributed his full measure of influence.

In his life and in his death, Bishop Hedding has left to the Church of Christ one of the richest legacies, his life was a triumph of goodness, his death a triumph of faith. The benedictions of the Church rest upon him, and future generations shall rise up to bless his memory. Devout men, with great lamentation, bore him to his burial. He rests from his labours; his works do follow him. "The memorial of virtue is immortal, because it is known with God and men. When it is present, men take example at it; and when it is gone they desire it; it weareth a crown and triumpheth forever."

THE END.

Wesley, (Charles,) Life of.

Life of Charles Wesley; comprising a Review of his Poetry, Sketches of the Rise and Progress of Methodism, with Notices of Contemporary Events and Characters. By Rev. THOMAS JACKSON. With a Portrait.

8vo., pp. 800.	**Plain sheep**	**$1 75**
————	**Plain calf**	**2 25**
————	**Calf gilt**	**2 50**
————	**Calf extra**	**3 00**

The name of Charles Wesley will ever be in honourable remembrance as the coadjutor of his brother in that extensive revival of true religion which distinguished the last century, and as the author of the greater portion of those incomparable hymns, the use of which has, for nearly one hundred years, formed so prominent a part of the devotions of "the people called Methodists." Although more than fifty years have passed away since he rested from his labours, there has been no separate memoir of his life until the appearance of the present volume, which is, in many respects, one of the most interesting and important works on religious biography that has issued from the press for many years. It is chiefly prepared from the journals and private papers of Mr. Wesley, which were kept in his family till the death of his daughter in 1828, when they became the property of the Wesleyan Conference. No Methodist preacher should be without it

Wesleyan Preachers, Memoirs of Several.

Memoirs of several Wesleyan Preachers, principally selected from Rev. T. Jackson's Lives of Early Methodist Preachers, and the Arminian and Wesleyan Magazines.

12mo., pp. 346. Muslin **$0 65**

It will not be easy to read their histories, so evidently truthful, without being profited. Dr. Clarke, in a letter to a young preacher, says, "Make yourself familiar with the works of Mr. Wesley and Mr. Fletcher, and read the lives of the early Methodist preachers."

An important addition to our means of acquainting ourselves with the early history of Methodism. A work to be read by all lovers of eminent examples of piety and zeal.—*Methodist Quarterly Review.*

Harris on Covetousness.

Mammon; or, Covetousness the Sin of the Christian Church. By Rev. JOHN HARRIS.

18mo., pp. 249. Muslin **$0 23**

A work which, almost beyond any other of the present day, has secured the approbation of the public. A more-pointed and searching exposure of the secret workings of covetousness can scarcely be found. The late Andrew Fuller says:—"The love of money will, in all probability, prove the eternal overthrow of more characters among professing people than any other sin, because it is almost the only crime which can be indulged, and a profession of religion at the same time supported."

Golden Maxims.

Golden Maxims; or, a Thought, Devotional and Practical, for every Day in the Year. With an Index to Authors' Names. Selected by Rev. ROBERT BOND.

32mo., pp. 112. Muslin, gilt edges **$0 25**

BOOKS PUBLISHED BY CARLTON & PHILLIPS,
200 Mulberry-street, New-York.

Ruter's Gregory's Ecclesiastical History.

A Concise History of the Christian Church, from its first Establishment to the Present Time: containing a general View of Missions, and exhibiting the State of Religion in various Parts of the World. Compiled from the Works of Dr. Gregory, with various Additions and Improvements. By MARTIN RUTER, D.D.

8vo., pp. 446.	**Plain sheep**	**$1 50**
——	**Plain calf**	**1 75**
——	**Calf gilt**	**2 00**
——	**Calf extra**	**2 25**

This work forms part of the course of study adopted by the last General Conference.

This work, as prepared by Dr. Gregory, was intended to furnish a comprehensive abridgment of Ecclesiastical History. The author's labours do not, however, extend to the close of the eighteenth century. Dr. Ruter has ably carried on the work to the year 1830, making numerous additions and improvements, and enriching the whole with a comprehensive view of missions, &c. It is, therefore, one of the very few Church Histories which bring the subject down to the nineteenth century.

M'Owan on the Sabbath.

Practical Considerations on the Christian Sabbath. By Rev. PETER M'OWAN. Treating on the Design and Moral Obligation of the Sabbath; its change from the Seventh to the First Day of the Week; and the Spirit and Manner in which it ought to be sanctified.

18mo., pp. 200. Muslin **$0 30**

The desecration of the holy day is so common, that no effort should be spared to bring about a better state of things. This manual is recommended as a timely and thorough exposition of the subject. It treats of the original and general design of the Sabbath; moral obligation of the day; its change from the seventh to the first day of the week; and the spirit and manner in which it ought to be sanctified.

Curiosities of Animal Life.

Curiosities of Animal Life, as developed by the Recent Discoveries of the Microscope. With Illustrations and Index. Revised by Rev. D. P. KIDDER.

16mo., pp. 184. Muslin **$0 50**

One of the most novel and interesting books of the times.

Wesleyan Student.

Wesleyan Student; or, Memoirs of Aaron H. Hurd. By Rev. JOSEPH HOLDICH.

18mo., pp. 288. Muslin **$0 35**

An excellent memoir of a most promising young man. We commend it to the young, and especially to students in our Seminaries and Colleges.—*Methodist Quarterly Review*

Father Reeves.

Father Reeves, the Methodist Class-leader: a Brief Account of Mr. William Reeves, thirty-four Years a Class-leader in the Wesleyan Methodist Society, Lambeth, England.

18mo., pp. 160. Muslin **$0 18**

We sincerely thank Mr. Corderoy for this little volume, which cannot fail of being perused with great advantage as an incentive to strict punctuality, never-failing diligence, eminent devotedness, and fervent Christian zeal.—*(London) S. S. Teachers' Magazine.*

The narrative presents one of the most interesting developments of the honest man, fearing God and working righteousness, that for a long time has come before us: a fine specimen of the best order of Methodism in its best period.—*Christian Witness.*

Let "Father Reeves" pass along through all our congregations; he will leave a blessing wherever he goes. It is just the book to stir up the Church. A hundred thousand volumes should be scattered at once.—*Rev. A. Stevens.*

The Philosophy of Faith.

Philosophy and Practice of Faith. By Lewis P. Olds.

12mo., pp. 353. Muslin **$0 65**

Part I. A General View of Faith—Pure, Simple, or Intellectual Faith—Practical, Relying, or Saving Faith—The Unity of Faith—A Living Faith and a Dead Faith—Unbelief the Native Condition of the Mind—Walk by Faith—The Three Antagonisms of Faith—Faith and Works—Increase and Diminution of Faith.

Part II. Ancient and Modern Faith compared—Faith of Nations—Congregational Faith—Faith of the Christian Ministry—Prayer and Faith—Faith of the Cloister—Faith of Active Life—Faith of the Ignorant—Faith of the Young—Faith in Prosperity—Faith in Adversity—Faith in Life and in Death.

This book belongs to a class that has been rare of late years. It is a calm, thoughtful, yet uncontroversial survey of a great Christian doctrine in its bearings upon theology in general, and upon the Christian life in practice. We hope it may find many readers.—*Methodist Quarterly Review.*

Bible in Many Tongues.

The Bible in Many Tongues. Revised by Daniel P. Kidder.

18mo., pp. 216. Muslin **$0 24**

A biography, so to speak, of the Bible; and a history of its translations and versions in ancient and modern times. It gives, in brief, a large amount of religious and historical information. It is divided into four chapters, treating respectively of the biography of books in general, and of the Bible in particular—the Bible in the ancient East and at Rome—the Bible at the Reformation—the Bible and Christian missions.

The Converted Infidel.

Life and Experience of a Converted Infidel. By John Scarlet, of the New-Jersey Conference.

18mo., pp. 274. Price **$0 40**

We commend this autobiography as worthy of a place among the multitude of sketches of a similar sort which Methodism has produced. It is specially adapted, from its simple narrative, its pleasant vein of anecdotes and its sound moral and doctrinal spirit, to attract and benefit young readers.

Smith's Sacred Annals.

Sacred Annals: or, Researches into the History and Religion of Mankind. By George Smith, F. S. A., M. R. S. L., etc. In three large volumes. Each volume is complete in itself, and may be had separately.

8vo. Price $7 00

Vol. I. The Patriarchal Age: or, the History and Religion of Mankind, from the Creation to the Death of Isaac: deduced from the Writings of Moses, and other Inspired Authors.; and illustrated by copious References to the Ancient Records, Traditions, and Mythology of the Heathen World.

Vol. II. The Hebrew People: or, the History and Religion of the Israelites, from the Origin of the Nation to the Time of Christ: deduced from the Writings of Moses, and other Inspired Authors; and illustrated by copious References to the Ancient Records, Traditions, and Mythology of the Heathen World.

Vol. III. The Gentile Nations: or, the History and Religion of the Egyptians, Assyrians, Babylonians, Medes, Persians, Greeks, and Romans; collected from Ancient Authors and Holy Scripture, and including the recent Discoveries in Egyptian, Persian, and Assyrian Inscriptions: forming a complete Connexion of Sacred and Profane History, and showing the Fulfilment of Sacred Prophecy.

Mr. Smith has, in his Sacred Annals, made a valuable contribution to the literature of the Christian evidences, as well as of ancient history. . . . The third volume presents as complete and clear a view of the religious systems of the great Gentile nations of antiquity as can be prepared from existing records.—*(London) Literary Gazette.*

Mr. Smith has achieved a great work. . . . We praise the book as an exceedingly important addition to the class of literature to which it belongs. It supplies a great want, and supplies it fully.—*(London) Christian Witness.*

Strickland's Biblical Literature.

A Manual of Biblical Literature. By William P. Strickland, D. D.

12mo., pp. 404. Muslin $0 80

The work is divided into nine parts, treating severally of Biblical Philology, Biblical Criticism, Biblical Exegesis, Biblical Analysis, Biblical Archæology, Biblical Ethnography, Biblical History, Biblical Chronology, and Biblical Geography. This enumeration will suffice to show the extent of the range of topics embraced in this volume. Of course they are treated summarily: but the very design of the author was to prepare a compendious *manual*, and he has succeeded excellently.—*Methodist Quarterly Review.*

Memoir of Rev. S. B. Bangs.

The Young Minister: or, Memoirs and Remains of Stephen Beekman Bangs, of the New-York East Conference. By W. H. N. Magruder, M. A. With a Portrait.

12mo., pp. 388. Muslin $0 70

There are some classes who may derive peculiar profit from a study of this book. Young ministers of the gospel may deduce from it the elements of a happy and prosperous professional career. Students may be led to inquire closely into their duty, and may be prepared conscientiously to decide whether or not God is calling them to the responsible work of the Christian ministry. Parents may see the effect of a careful and rigid and truly kind training of their children. And finally, all may be stimulated to a holy life by the energetic and eloquent discourses that follow.—*Rev. E. O. Haven.*

Friendships of the Bible.

THE FRIENDSHIPS OF THE BIBLE. By AMICUS. Embellished with Engravings.

12mo., pp. 140. Muslin **$0 55**

The subjects of this attractive volume are, David and Jonathan; Abraham and Eliezer; Elisha and the Shunammite; Paul, Joseph, and Ruth; Fortuitous Acts of Friendship; Rulers; Bethany; Jesus and John.

Home Truths.

HOME TRUTHS. By Rev. J. C. RYLE, B. A., Rector of Helmingham, England.

16mo., pp. 292. Muslin **$0 33**

Seldom has a book been issued from the English press more vigorous with mental and moral vitality. It pretends to nothing recondite, though it treats often of subtle subjects; but it is pregnant with pithy thought, and there is a naturalness, an aptness, a freshness and fulness in its thoughts that render it, altogether, a most sterling and effective volume. Its fervid earnestness, though without pretentious rhetoric, becomes an infectious eloquence that sways the reader's mind and heart irresistibly, and bears him along from page to page as by a sort of fascination. Its subjects are not only illustrated, and often in the happiest manner, but they are urged and enforced, and reiterated, and pressed irresistibly home, with a manner so simple, so full of persuasion and entreaty, so tenderly sincere and solicitous, so increasingly emphatic as you pass from paragraph to paragraph, that the reader can hardly fail to feel the moral spell of the book.—*Editor's Preface.*

Asbury's Journal.

JOURNAL OF REV. FRANCIS ASBURY, Bishop of the Methodist Episcopal Church. 3 vols.

12mo., pp. 524, 492, 502. Price **$3 00**

Mr. Asbury's Journals extend from the meeting of the Conference held in Bristol, England, August 7, 1771, when he received his appointment from Mr. Wesley as a missionary to America, to December 7, 1815, within a few months of his death, a period of forty-four years.

The Journals have long been out of print. The edition now offered is far better than the old one: the dates have been carefully collated and rectified, and a careful index to the three volumes is given at the end. In these volumes will be found the beginnings (almost) of the history of Methodism in America; and, as such, their value is incalculable to the Church. But as a record of apostolic zeal and fidelity, of a spirit of self-sacrifice rivalling that of the saints and martyrs of the early Church, of an industry which no toils could weary, of a patience which no privations could exhaust, it is full of interest to every minister of the gospel, and to every Christian. —*Methodist Quarterly Review.*

History of the Inquisition.

THE BRAND OF DOMINIC: or, Inquisition at Rome "Supreme and Universal." By Rev. WILLIAM H. RULE. With five Engravings.

12mo., pp. 392. Muslin **$0 75**

This small volume should be in the hands of every one who takes an interest in the Papal question.—*Church of England Quarterly Review.*

We cannot know too much of that horrible and Satanic institution, of which this valuable little work treats, and treats so ably.—*Evangelical Christendom.*

www.ingramcontent.com/pod-product-compliance
Lightning Source LLC
LaVergne TN
LVHW021047110826
845150LV00001B/6

* 9 7 8 1 4 2 5 5 6 8 6 5 8 *